SOUTHWEST PACIFIC

Southwest Pacific

A GEOGRAPHY OF AUSTRALIA, NEW ZEALAND,
AND THEIR PACIFIC ISLAND NEIGHBORS

by

KENNETH B. CUMBERLAND

FREDERICK A. PRAEGER, *Publishers*
New York · Washington

BOOKS THAT MATTER

Published in the United States of America in 1968
by Frederick A. Praeger, Inc., Publishers
111 Fourth Avenue, New York, N.Y. 10003

*This book was first published in New Zealand by Whitcombe and
Tombs, Ltd., in 1954 and was revised in 1958 and in 1960. An
American edition was issued in 1956. The present edition has been
extensively revised and brought up to date.*

Printed in New Zealand

Preface

AUSTRALIANS and New Zealanders long neglected each other. This was the outcome largely of their preoccupation in the first century of settlement with their own internal problems and development. In the initial stages of development, young nations like Australia and New Zealand—however enlightened and progressive—have enough to occupy their time and energy in subduing and taming their own land and converting their virgin landscapes and untouched resources to productive uses.

Both countries also long neglected their other neighbours in the Pacific. These were people of different culture and of a different world and were dispersed sparsely throughout the immensity of the ocean. Their economies had little significance, and their minute and insular homelands had little commercial or political attraction at a time when the vast Australian and New Zealand wildernesses were still to be tamed. Moreover, last century the indigenous populations of the Pacific were rapidly declining in numbers and it appeared as though they might well disappear.

This neglect and ignorance of each other and of their scattered indigenous neighbours was reflected in the newspapers and in the schools of Australia and New Zealand. As a result New Zealand was to Australians no more than a group of islands known for little other than its earthquakes, floods, volcanoes and strange and warlike Polynesian natives. To New Zealanders, Australia was an immense continent of drought, desert, bush fires and faunal oddities. To both countries the island territories were imaginary south sea paradises which might be of potential significance only if Britain allowed them to fall into the hands of foreign powers. To the north the eastern rim of Asia slept and slumbered, its monotony of famine and poverty disturbed only by the early attempts of Japan to shake off its traditional way of life and to imitate the great nations of Europe. Such was the impression so long provided by contemporary colonial newspapers and bone-dry classroom textbooks.

Not until after World War I had the fast-growing Commonwealth and the increasingly prosperous Dominion the opportunity and the time to appreciate the significance of their Pacific settings, or to cast a surprised and apprehensive eye over their Pacific neighbourhoods. They had scarcely begun to do so when World War II and the hurtling speed of Japan's southward surge forcibly imprinted on the minds of both Australians and New Zealanders the significance to them of the island territories within their immediate Pacific neighbourhoods. It also emphasized the importance of those populous lands that are either part of Asia or part of the Indonesian Mediterranean and which no longer separated Asia and Australia but rather linked them together.

Awareness of the significance to the two dominions of their broad Pacific setting and of their Pacific island neighbourhoods is reflected in a number of postwar developments. The Anzac Pact, the South Pacific Commission, the ANZUS Defence Agreement with the United States, the SEATO agreement, the participation of both countries in the work of the Economic Commission for Asia and the Far East (ECAFE) and the Colombo Plan by which Australia and New Zealand seek to assist in bringing technical aid to the southeastern perimeter of Asia—all these formal arrangements show an increasing official cognizance of the geographical setting and geopolitical status of Australia and New Zealand in the Pacific.

The increasing recognition of the importance of the southwest Pacific makes more urgent the dissemination of information about it. The region is still not well known. In the absence of knowledge its problems cannot be understood, much less can they successfully be solved. The physical and human geography, the history of the peoples and of the economies of the region, and the prospects and problems of all the many territories must be better known. It is the prime aim of *Southwest Pacific* to contribute to the spread of basic information about the multifarious territories of the region from which it takes its title.

This book is designed to make available to the people of
Australia and New Zealand especially, and to the younger
generation of future politicians, administrators and businessmen
in particular, an objective geographic account of the territories
of the southwest Pacific. It draws attention for the first time
to the geography of an area in which the two countries have
special responsibilities—responsibilities which have often been
neglected or overlooked. Both Australia and New Zealand
have their own distinct and separate neighbourhoods; and
together these neighbourhoods and circles of interest and
responsibility comprise most of the insular, oceanic world of
the Pacific. All Australians and New Zealanders should be
aware of their position in the Pacific and of the people, lands
and problems of their neighbourhoods.

It is much to the credit of the educational authorities in New
Zealand that they have seen fit to insist that most young New
Zealanders will have been required to make a study of the history
and geography of the southwest Pacific before they assume their
share of responsibility for its administration on leaving the
post-primary school. In Australian schools, geography has not
yet had the recognition so rightly accorded it in almost all
other advanced western nations. It is hoped, however, that this
book may also be of some service there now that, with the
wide development of the science in the universities, its prospects
of extension in the schools is a real possibility.

But *Southwest Pacific* is not only designed for schools. There
has long been no other objective geographical study—certainly
none so richly illustrated with maps and photographs—of this
particular area. It should be of value not only to the people
of the southwest Pacific but also to others in many different
parts of the world if only because it is the only geographic
survey of this area written more particularly from the New
Zealand point of view.

The material used in the book has been drawn from innumerable sources. It would be a major task and would take too much
space to acknowledge them all. This account relies also on
personal contact over some twenty years with much of the area
from Perth to Papeete and from Manokwari to the Marquesas.
An attempt has been made to keep the story as simple as

possible and suitable for classroom use without making the book obviously and exclusively a school text.

For the assistance I have had in preparing the book for publication I should like to thank in particular the Australian High Commissioner in Wellington; the illustrations editor of the *New Zealand Herald;* Mr Rob Wright and the Public Relations Office, Suva; the South Pacific Commission; the British Phosphate Commissioners; and the New Zealand Tourist and Publicity Department—for photographs; Mrs Margaret Sexton for typing and clerical assistance; and Messrs Don Branch and Hugh Stewart-Killick for assistance with the preparation of the maps.

KENNETH B. CUMBERLAND

Contents

Maps in the Text

AUSTRALIA'S ISLAND NEIGHBOURHOOD

NEW ZEALAND

NEW ZEALAND'S ISLAND NEIGHBOURHOOD

List of Plates

CHAPTER ONE

The Setting

F EW 'NEIGHBOURS' live as far apart as do Australians and New Zealanders. From Auckland to Perth is farther than from London to Mecca, Kabul or Novo Sibirsk. And no nations of European origin or of western culture are as remote from the centres of European civilization around the margins of the North Atlantic as are the two British Dominions in the southwest Pacific. Just as the British Isles, whence the peoples of both Australia and New Zealand have sprung, lie near the centre of the land hemisphere, so the two younger nations lie near the centre of what is sometimes known as the water hemisphere—that half of the world which contains most ocean and least land. With the Pacific Ocean to the north and east, the Indian Ocean stretching away to the west and the chilly waters of the Antarctic seas to the south, there are few parts of the world which are more cut off and isolated by the sea.

THE ISOLATION OF AUSTRALIA AND NEW ZEALAND

New Zealand lies well within the Pacific Ocean. The island continent of Australia borders the ocean and opens its front door to the often stormy expanse of the Tasman Sea. (Its back door provides access to the Indian Ocean.) Both nations are by location Pacific nations and Pacific neighbours. In the past distance by sea made physical isolation a fundamental characteristic of their geography. But isolation is a relative thing. It is not what it was when Tasman, Cook and their successors probed the great unknown. Today, in an era of eager 707s and giant DC8s, isolation is not what it was in the period of sturdy sailing vessels a hundred years ago, when Australia and New

Zealand were busy growing up. Nor is isolation the protection it used to be. Distances themselves have not changed, only man's ability to conquer them.

Figure 1 illustrates very effectively the distances that separate the two British dominions from the rest of the world. It shows

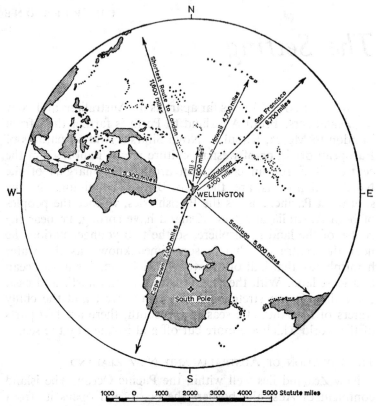

NOTE: This scale applies only to distances along straight lines through Wellington

Figure 1   THE ISOLATION OF AUSTRALIA AND NEW ZEALAND

distances from Wellington true to scale, and the outer edge of the map defines the half of the globe which is centred on New Zealand. All places at the margin of the map are more than 6000 miles from Wellington. Apart from Antarctica's frozen wastes, only the 'empty' continent of Australia, a small fringe of Asia, the southernmost tip of South America and the minute and scattered islands of the Pacific world fall within the New Zealand half of the globe. To the northwest, north, northeast and east stretches the vast expanse of the Pacific Ocean. To the south are the cold and wind-driven waters of the Southern Ocean. Separating Australia and New Zealand is the stormy Tasman. New Zealand's is indeed a watery, oceanic, isolating environment.

THE IMMENSITY OF THE PACIFIC

Today, as in 1520-1521 when Magellan took four months to sail across it, the Pacific is still 'a sea so vast that the human mind can scarcely grasp it'. It is the vastest expanse of water on earth. It occupies a third of the earth's surface and is itself larger than all the land masses put together. There is room in the Pacific for twenty continents each the size of Australia, and for the appropriate number of Tasman Seas separating them. From Singapore to Panama is half the distance round the earth—more than 12,500 miles. From Bering Strait, separating the remote extensions of the Asiatic and North American continents, to the Ross Territory in Antarctica is a journey (which none ever makes) through 150 degrees of latitude, or 10,500 land miles.

The blue waters of the Pacific occupy the greatest structural feature on the earth's surface. But the term Pacific 'Basin', so often applied to this structural unit, is misleading. The Pacific is not only the largest but also the deepest of the world's oceans. Its average depth is over 14,000 feet: it is almost everywhere at least half as deep again as Mount Cook is high; its floor is on the average two and a half times as far below sea level as the highest part of the Australian continent (Mount Kosciusko) stands above it. There are a series of deep trenches near the western margin of the ocean reaching down more than 30,000 feet beneath the surface. In the Philippine Trench, east of Mindanao Island, a depth of 35,410 feet has been recorded —the greatest known in any ocean. Yet the difference in elevation between the summit of Mount Everest and the abyss of the Mindanao Deep is so slight in relation to the size of the earth that, if you were to draw the earth's circumference in pencil on this page, the thickness of the pencil line would mask all irregularities in the shape of the earth on that scale. Even the deep waters of the Pacific, then, occupy no 'basin' but only the shallowest of 'saucers'. The saucer has a regular, upturned rim to the east and a chipped and broken edge to the west, with occasional, deep, elongated gashes towards its western margin that are much deeper than the average level of its floor.

THE STRUCTURAL PROVINCES OF THE PACIFIC

Structurally we may look upon the Pacific saucer as having three parts: (1) the narrow *eastern rim*; (2) the *central Pacific proper*; and (3) the broad *western margin*. If we examine briefly the structural and geological differences between these three distinctive parts of the Pacific we shall better understand the geography of the Pacific area, the distribution of the island groups within the ocean, and the striking differences between the Asiatic-Australian and American continental margins. See *Figure 2*.

The narrow *eastern* (American) *rim* of the Pacific extends without break as a series of lofty, elongated chains of young fold

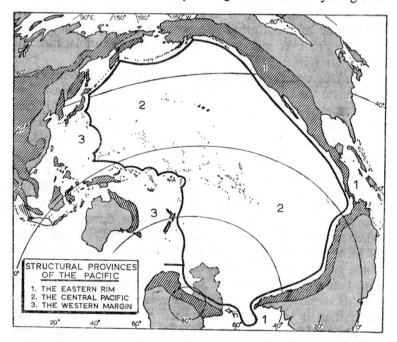

Figure 2

mountains. These *cordilleras* include the Rocky Mountains, the Sierra Nevada, the towering Andean chains and the series of parallel, coastal fold mountains extending from Alaska to Tierra del Fuego. Although their geological structure is complicated enough, they make a pattern which is simple and clear-cut compared with that of the opposite margin of the ocean. The mountain chains rise continuously and quite abruptly from the ocean floor; in Alaska, Peru and Chile they reach altitudes of more than 20,000 feet within a few miles of the shore. This up-folded Tertiary rim of the saucer is steep, regular and continuous.

Of the structural provinces, the *central Pacific* province is by far the largest. This is the floor of the saucer, and it accommodates the Pacific Ocean proper as distinct from the marginal and continental seas around it. It is the most stable and uniform structural unit of the earth's surface. It is also the largest. Wide stretches of its floor have a depth of from 10,000 to 15,000 feet. These are free from earthquakes, whereas the ocean's margins are regularly shaken. Here and there—more particularly in the western half of the province—volcanic piles, singly and in groups, rise from the ocean floor and sometimes break the water's surface to form volcanic islands. So immense is the extent of ocean that the hundreds of volcanic islands, and the thousands of coral islets perched atop submerged volcanic cones, are lost over its blue expanse like a handful of confetti scattered on a lake.

The structure of the *western margin*, of which Australia and New Zealand are part, is more complicated. The western margin of the Pacific involves not only portions of the adjacent continents, but also a wide series of island arcs with partially enclosed, deep basins behind them, and especially deep ocean trenches immediately in front of them. Great festoons of mountain chains, each shaped like a giant's bow (and therefore called *arcuate*) bound the ocean proper. Each rises sheer from ocean abysses to the east, and together they stretch from the Aleutians to New Zealand. Kamchatka, Japan, the Philippines, and New Guinea, as well as the Aleutians and New Zealand, are all examples of such arcuate, mountainous island groups. Others, like the Ryukyus or the Marianas, break the ocean only as a series of minute island specks. The mountainous arcs sometimes tower more than 40,000 feet above the depth of adjacent ocean trenches and rise to peaks—usually volcanic—12,000 feet above sea level. All belong structurally to the continents to the west rather than to the ocean basin. The structural boundary between the continents and the ocean floor is not, as in the case of the Americas, immediately off the mainland shore, but some hundreds of miles out to sea. It is marked by the outermost broken line of ocean deeps. On *Figure 2* these are linked up by the line which separates structural provinces 2 and 3. This boundary is sometimes called the Marshall Line, after the New Zealand geologist who mapped it and emphasized its significance.

On the broad western margin of the Pacific, islands are both larger and more frequent than out in the Pacific Ocean proper. In some places the structural margin reaches a third of the way out into the ocean, and whilst there are few islands off the American shores, they are strewn thickly and widely off the coasts of Asia and Australia, and in the Indonesian 'Mediterranean'.*

ARCUATE ISLANDS OF THE WESTERN PACIFIC

Geologically the festoons of islands in the western Pacific and the scattered small islands out in the central Pacific province are quite different from each other. The *arcuate* islands are geologically and structurally akin to the continental margins to the west rather than to the ocean floor to the east. The island arcs are in fact partially submerged chains of unstable fold mountains. They consist in part of sedimentary rocks and of acid, andesitic volcanic materials. Their rocks and general structure, though geologically much younger, are not unlike those of the fold mountains of the eastern rim of the continents —the mountains of the Kamchatka Peninsula, of Korea, of Indo-China and eastern Australia. The outer arcuate island groups, and the deep ocean trenches which they overlook, represent the easternmost edge of the continents. They are the frontal ranges of great belts of fold mountains in the making; they are the outer edge of what is the most unstable portion of the earth's surface, an immense region of frequent earthquake disturbance and continued volcanic activity. We shall study

*For an explanation of the term 'Indonesian Mediterranean' see pp. 128-9.

some of these arcuate island groups in more detail later. New Zealand itself is one of them (*Fig. 3*).

STREWN ISLANDS OF THE CENTRAL PACIFIC

Over the central Pacific thousands of small islands and tiny islets are scattered without pattern or apparent discrimination. They are more frequent in the western portion of the central province than in its eastern half. There are immense stretches of the eastern Pacific, opposite both the North American and

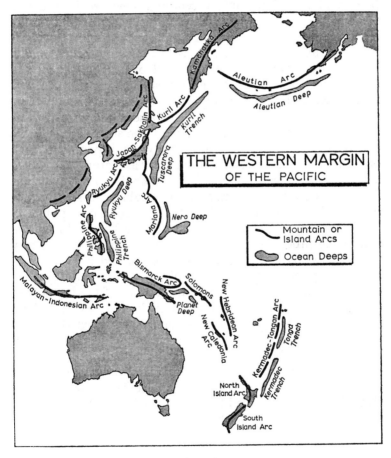

Figure 3

the South American continents, completely devoid of islands to break the monotonous and endless expanse of ocean. In general there are many more islands in the lower latitudes (i.e. nearer the equator) than there are in middle and higher latitudes. Together they may be conveniently referred to as the *strewn* islands. These islands are in general sometimes referred to as coral islands, but this is not the best term to describe them because, although many appear above the ocean surface only as coral islets, some in higher latitudes and in colder water where coral does not grow are made up entirely of dark volcanic rocks. In fact all the islands in the central Pacific province have a volcanic basis, even if the dark volcanic rocks do not always break the blue surface of the ocean.

Structurally the strewn islands are all of volcanic origin. Without exception their cores consist of a dense hard black rock called basalt, poured out in great piled-up flows of lava from fractures in the deep floor of the Pacific. Here there are no sedimentary rocks and no light, acidic volcanics such as are found in the arcuate islands and on the adjacent continents enclosing the Pacific saucer. When the volcanic pile stands high out of the water as one isolated island, or as a group of elevated islands, these are called simply *high islands* (*Fig. 4*). Such are the Hawaiian Islands, the Samoan group, Tahiti and some of the scattered islands in the Southern (or 'Lower') Cook group.

Some volcanic islands, especially near the Marshall Line, are still in the process of formation. You will have read of new volcanic islands in the Pacific being born, and no doubt will have seen photographs of some of these. The belching cone of ash sometimes appears above the surface of the ocean only to be washed away by pounding waves. In such cases an island is reported by one vessel, but by the time the next ship visits the locality the island earlier reported can no longer be found. There have been such islands in the Tongan group. Niuafo'ou, or Tin Can Island, as it is more often called, also in the Tongan group, is an active volcano. It was so active a few years ago that all its inhabitants had to be evacuated and taken for safety to Tongatapu and 'Eua, other islands in the group.

But most of the strewn islands of the Pacific are coral islands, in which case no volcanic materials appear above the surface of the water, although all coral islands out in the Pacific proper

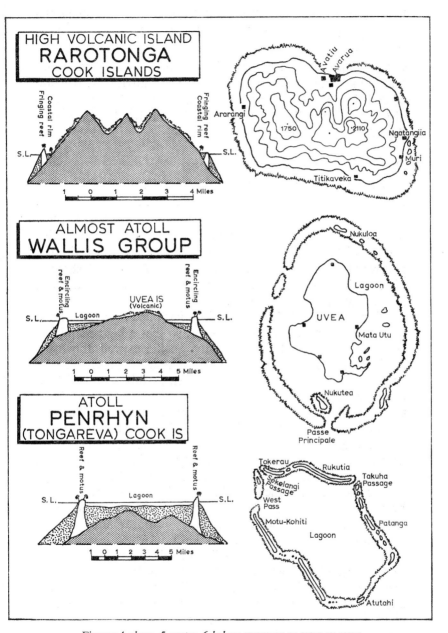

Figures 4 *above,* 5 *centre,* 6 *below:* TYPES OF PACIFIC ISLANDS

have a volcanic core. The coral islands, and especially the typical atolls, are referred to as *low islands*. Many of them rise no more than ten or twenty feet above sea level—not high enough to prevent them from being swamped by the great waves that are sometimes whipped up by violent hurricanes. Because of their low elevation and because they cannot be sighted at a distance sailors called them *low islands* to distinguish them from the lofty volcanic piles of the *high islands*.

Different Kinds of Coral Islands

A coral reef is a mass of limestone built up slowly over a long period of time by small, marine, lime-secreting animals, most important of which is the minute coral polyp. Such animals live only in warm, shallow, salt water, which explains why coral formation takes place only in the lower latitudes, and why islands are more numerous there. *Figures 4-9* show in plan and in cross-section the different kinds of islands found out in the central Pacific province.

After a series of volcanic eruptions has piled layer after layer of basalt lava on top of one another, so that a high island has been built up from the floor of the Pacific to well above sea level, lime-secreting plants and animals attach themselves to the flanks of the island just below sea level. In this way the island is slowly furnished with a *fringing reef* of coral (*Fig. 4*). If the ocean floor should sink, or if water released by the melting of polar ice caps should raise the level of the ocean, so that only the eroded and dissected peaks of the volcano remain above sea level, the busy polyps may be able to build up a reef as fast as the ocean level changes. In this case we have one or more small volcanic islands within a lagoon, enclosed by an *encircling* or *barrier reef* of coral (*Fig. 5*). This is an *almost-atoll*. The volcanic rocks may disappear altogether as a result of a further change in sea level, in which case an *atoll* is created. This is a reef, usually roughly oval in shape, enclosing a shallow lagoon. The lagoon may be anything from one mile to more than one hundred miles across. The reef is usually broken by a number of shallow rocky passages. It is thus divided into parts, each a small island of coral rock, or *motu*. On such *motus* there is usually an accumulation of coral sand

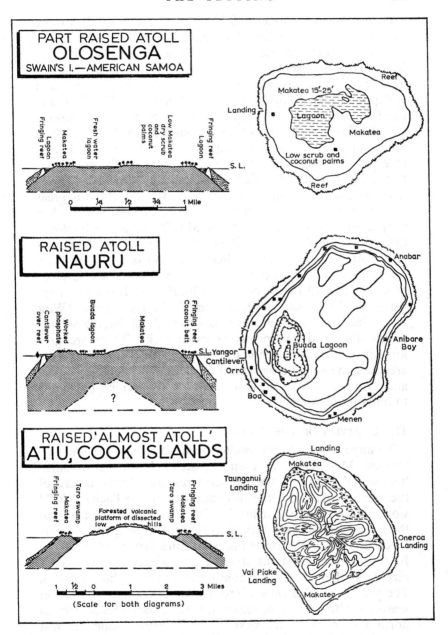

Figures 7 *above*, 8 *centre*, 9 *below:* TYPES OF PACIFIC ISLANDS

on top of the limestone reef. No part of the *motu* rises more than fifteen or twenty feet above sea level (*Fig. 6*).

If, on the other hand, the ocean floor should rise, or if the level of the sea should be lowered, then the mass of coral growth might be raised clear of the ocean water. *Figures 8* and *9* depict a *raised atoll* and a *raised almost-atoll*. What was the floor of the shallow lagoon now becomes a plateau-like stretch of rough, dry, rocky, cavernous limestone, or *makatea*. Raised atolls of this kind are often the source of rich and valuable phosphate deposits, such as are found on Ocean Island, Nauru, Makatea (in the Taumotus) and Christmas Island.

In size, shape, position, structure and origin there is great variety amongst the myriad islands of the Pacific World. They vary in size from New Guinea's 314,000 square miles (over three times the size of New Zealand) to the innumerable coral islets, often with an area of but a fraction of a square mile. They range in elevation from a few feet above sea level to Moana Kea's 13,784 ft. cone on Hawaii, and Karstensz Toppen's 16,400 ft. snow-capped summit in Irian Barat (West New Guinea). There are islands of coral, of basalt, and of sedimentary and continental volcanic rocks. There are geologically ancient islands and others new-born. These differences are strengthened by a variety of climates, by differences in soil and by a vegetation that is so often largely peculiar (endemic) to one island group.

THE CLIMATES OF THE PACIFIC

To anyone used to the sweltering summer heat of cities like Sydney, Melbourne, or even Christchurch, in the so-called 'temperate' latitudes, the temperatures and steady breeze of the smaller islands in the low latitudes of the Pacific World would often seem a delightful relief. Temperatures on all but the largest islands vary little throughout the year, rising rarely much above 80° F. and falling still more rarely below 70° F. In such insular locations summer and winter are not recognizable as they are on the continents and in higher latitudes. The year is divided rather into 'the dry season' and 'the wet season' (or 'the hurricane season'). Between latitudes 30 degrees north and south, as far west as the Solomons—and the vast majority of the strewn islands of the Pacific World are found here—climates are controlled by the trade winds. On the equatorial side of the great anticyclones that move eastwards across the central portions of both the north and south Pacific, winds blow steadily and persistently towards the Equator and the west. These are the trades. To the windward side of high islands the trade winds bring heavy rain most of the year; but there is a marked difference in the amount of rainfall occurring on the 'wet side' and the 'dry side' of such islands. Many a low coral atoll, however, derives little precipitation at all from the persistent trades, and rainfall is often surprisingly low and unreliable. Drought occurs frequently; and on many atolls, in the Gilberts for example, even drinking water is often short.

The northeast and southeast trades often come together near the Equator and blow parallel to each other, or gently merge and blend. When they come together at an angle, however, and when they vary appreciably in temperature, density, and humidity, the warmer and lighter mass of air over-rides the other, giving rise to weak cyclones and usually to heavy precipitation. When such low pressure centres develop, winds often become variable and frequently westerly, and rain falls even on parched atolls and the 'dry side' of high islands. Meteorologists refer to the line of contact of the northeast and southeast trades as the *intertropical front*. This front is best developed in the western part of the ocean, and it moves north and south with the seasons (*cf Figs 10* and *11*). Rain associated with the intertropical front is restricted to a relatively narrow equatorial belt. This lies a little to the north of the Equator in July and south of it in January.

A few Pacific islands lie near the poleward limit of the trades, and in mid-winter have variable westerly winds. Apart, however, from the Aleutians and the Kuril Islands in the foggy far north of the Pacific and the 'subantarctic' islands of Australia and New Zealand in the stormy high latitudes of the southern ocean, no Pacific islands lie wholly in the belts of variable westerly winds.

The climates of the islands north and northeast of Australia and of the island groups throughout the Indonesian 'Mediterranean' and off the Asiatic mainland are determined not by the free circulation of air over the open ocean but by the marked seasonal variations in pressure, temperature and wind direction

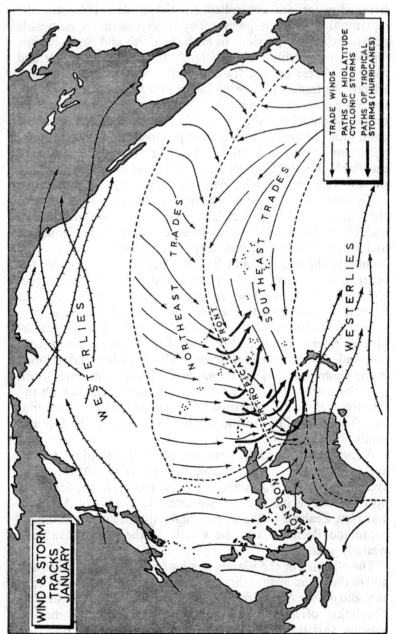

Figure 10

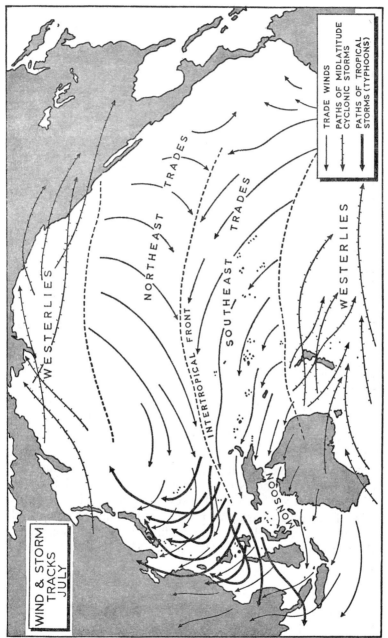

WIND & STORM
TRACKS
JULY

WESTERLIES

NORTHEAST TRADES

SOUTHEAST TRADES

INTERTROPICAL FRONT

WESTERLIES

MONSOON

TRADE WINDS
PATHS OF MIDLATITUDE
CYCLONIC STORMS
PATHS OF TROPICAL
STORMS (TYPHOONS)

Figure 11

B

over the adjacent continents. Summer heating over the continent gives rise to seasonal low pressure centres. Under the influence of the Asiatic low pressure centre in the northern-hemisphere summer, the intertropical front in the westernmost Pacific weakens or disappears, and the air masses of the southeast trades are drawn across the Equator to form the Asiatic summer monsoon (*Fig. 11*). This flows north over Indonesia, Borneo, the Philippines and Japan and on to the continent. In northern Australia winds are mainly dry, they blow offshore, and desert conditions extend to the coast. But this is the rainy season in monsoon Asia and in off-shore island groups from the Equator north to beyond Japan. In January the prevailing flow of air is reversed. Winds are generally from the north, blowing off Asia, southwards over the islands between the continents, and they carry rain and damp air for an all-too-brief season deep into the northern half of Australia (*Fig. 10*).

HURRICANES

The tropical western Pacific is one of the regions in which tropical cyclones have their origin, where they occur frequently, if erratically, and where at times they do a great deal of damage and take many human lives (*Figs 10* and *11*). Off the coasts of China, Japan and the Philippines such confined, whirling, fast-travelling cyclonic storms are known as *typhoons*. In the southwest Pacific the tropical cyclones, in which winds reach gale force and cause damage in the islands in their paths, are referred to as *hurricanes*. Fortunately the most violent hurricanes in this part of the world are confined to the oceanic area between the Solomons and the Society Islands, but occasionally in autumn they sweep south along the line of the Queensland coast and even reach the North Island of New Zealand from the direction of New Caledonia. However they usually lose intensity, wind force and destructive power as they invade the middle latitudes. Fortunately they are confined to the late summer of the respective hemispheres (January to March in the southwest Pacific).

ISLAND FLORA AND FAUNA

Between the Asiatic (or Oriental) World and the Pacific World there is a sharp contrast in the plants and animals present, apart, of course, from what man has carried from Asia out into the Pacific in the last 25,000 years. There is, however, a narrow zone of transition where both Australian (or Pacific) and Malayan (or Asiatic) species of plants and animals are found. This zone cuts the Indonesian 'Mediterranean' from southwest to northeast. It includes the islands of Lombok, Flores, Timor and Celebes. Java, Bali, Borneo and the Philippines are in the Asiatic life zone, and Halmahera, New Guinea and Australia lie east of the transition belt within the Australian-Pacific life zone. In the islands of the western Indonesian 'Mediterranean' there were Asiatic mammals such as tigers, rhinoceros, deer, wild pigs and wild buffalo: in New Guinea the only large indigenous land animals were marsupials, or pouched mammals, and animals which both lay eggs and suckle their young, like the platypus.

Although much of the vegetation of the oceanic islands of the Pacific World must have come originally from continental sources, most islands have derived their plants by way of New Guinea and the Indonesian 'Mediterranean'. Australia and New Zealand both have a natural vegetation that is largely endemic. But New Guinea was a rich source of plants. Its natural vegetation is a compound of species imported at widely different times from both Asia and Australia. Some of this variety of flora was carried to the oceanic islands of the Pacific World by wind, birds and ocean currents long before man passed the same way. The number of genera declines noticeably as one goes eastwards from island to island across the Pacific. In many instances, however, it is difficult to separate with certainty (1) those plants which were carried out into the Pacific by natural agencies (migrating birds, or natural rafts and logs of wood driven by hurricane winds) from (2) those which, on the other hand, had to await the oceanward migration of man. The coconut and the fruit of the pandanus can both survive for a long time partially immersed in salt water, and it seems likely that they drifted to the coral strand of many a small oceanic island and became established in coastal, sandy situations which both prefer as habitats. Other islands and whole groups in the central and eastern Pacific, however, may have received the coconut and pandanus only at the hands of the first Polynesian navigators. But animals were less easily spread either by natural agencies or by man. In the Pacific sea birds are universally present, but land birds were few, if any, in the isolated oceanic groups. Bats were the only mammals to reach some islands. Other islands had also rats, snakes and lizards.

At a later date man added to the list of plants and animals. In the restricted space of his canoes, the early islanders carried only essential items and did so intentionally. Later comers brought plants and animals almost as often by accident as by design. Today, therefore, the Pacific islands, like Australia with its rabbits and prickly pears, and like New Zealand with its deer, gorse and ragwort, also have introduced plants and animals which are not always desirable and useful.

ISLAND SOILS

The soils of the larger islands of the western Pacific vary very considerably, and will be discussed when these areas are dealt with in more detail later in this book. But at the risk of over-simplifying the picture, the soils (and mineral resources) of the islands of the Pacific may be most conveniently referred to in general terms in the summary of the physical geography of the islands of the Pacific World which follows.

The insular habitats may perhaps be reviewed most usefully under four broad headings: (1) the low, coral islands; (2) the raised, coral islands; (3) the high, volcanic islands; and (4) the large, 'continental' islands. These different classes of Pacific islands each have their characteristic associations of soils, flora and fauna. Each offers man quite different possibilities.

CORAL ISLAND HABITATS

The smallest and driest of the *motus* of coral sand comprise treeless atolls. Such islands have little soil—only accumulations of raw sand; they had no solid rock from which man could fashion tools and weapons; their lack of drinking water also made them unsuited to native settlement, even though coconuts occasionally find root-space and moisture enough. These islands were thus left uninhabited until Europeans found specialized uses for some of them. The *motus* around the lagoon at Canton —like those on a number of other similar islets—have been used for the construction of civil and military airstrips and now form stepping stones or emergency landing places for aircraft on trans-Pacific flights. Although soil resources are limited, fish nevertheless abound in the lagoons, and their presence has always attracted immense numbers of sea-birds, whose droppings over the years have resulted in the accumulation of guano fertilizer which was early exploited by Europeans.

Larger, low coral islands have a dry-forest vegetation, restricted to a few species able to survive in coastal, sandy situations and on water supplies which are unreliable and often brackish. The strand flora usually includes pandanus (screw pine), coconut palms (sometimes introduced by man), casuarina (ironwood), hibiscus, woody vines and grasses and sedges. The first two are the basis of native food supply, although damp patches may be excavated in the coral sand to provide artificial pits in which sufficient humus and moisture can be maintained to make possible the cultivation of special varieties of coarse taro. A rich supply of fish foods in the lagoon supplements a limited range of vegetable foods. In addition to the large deep-water fish off the reef, and the fish on the reef and in the lagoon, there are edible snails, octopus, eels, crabs, crayfish, turtles, clams, trochus shell and pearl shell. New Zealand's Tokelau Islands and the islands of the Northern Cook group are coral atolls with habitats of this sort. There is a tendency here, but more particularly in similar insular environments in the Gilbert, Ellice and Marshall Islands, for population to outrun resources. Many islands have 300 or 400 persons per square mile of sandy limestone *motu*, a density of population fifteen to twenty times greater than that of New Zealand, and over a hundred times that of Australia. Here mass migration and infanticide were not unknown.

Raised atolls and raised almost-atolls are usually larger than the low coral atolls. In these cases what was once the expansive shallow lagoon is now the raised plateau-like surface of the island. It is a jagged, pitted surface, its coral limestone often riddled with caves. Only here and there have the more level parts of the coral limestone weathered into red clay soil. In the case of raised almost-atolls, like Mangaia or Mauke in the Southern Cook group, deeper more fertile volcanic soils fringe the inner edge of the limestone plateau. Here drainage from the slopes (of what was formerly a volcanic island in the lagoon) makes possible the cultivation of taro in deep, damp swamp beds. The occasional thin clay soils of the *makatea* support a low, dense cover of dry-land plants—low trees, shrubs, vines, ferns and grasses. But the economic importance of raised coral islands, like Nauru, Ocean, Makatea and Anguar (Palaus) lies in their rich phosphate deposits rather than in their limited soil and vegetational resources.

VOLCANIC ISLAND HABITATS

The Pacific's upstanding piles of basalt—the high volcanic islands—have hard rocks for tools and weapons, abundant water and streams, and a variety of soils and vegetation, the character of which depends most on their age and the extent to which the dark volcanic rocks have been weathered. But even the occasional thin pockets of dark soil on the unweathered lava flows of the younger islands are very fertile, and support a dense natural vegetation or a rich array of cultivated crops. The people of Niuafo'ou claim that before they were transferred to 'Eua they grew, on the coastal rim of the active volcano which was formerly their home, the largest coconuts and the heaviest taros produced in the Tongan group. But on youthful volcanic islands lush vegetation and cultivable soil are restricted to a coastal rim and to some of the lower valleys. Even on rich volcanic islands, like Savai'i and Upolu in Samoa, the younger lava flows can be picked out by their scantier vegetation and lack of population and cultivation. One extensive flow on Savai'i is now barely fifty years old, but even on Upolu the surface of the coastal lowland, for all the density of its vegetation and population, is frequently without soil and is littered with fragmented pieces of black basalt, large and small. It is amazing that vegetation of any sort will grow, let alone the lush natural increment of tropical forest, the productive commercial plantations of coconut, cacao and banana, and the exotic, decorative wealth of colourful hibiscus and heavily-scented frangipani.

But the Hawaiian islands, the Society Islands, and Rarotonga in the Southern Cook group have deeper soils, except only on the steepest slopes. They are usually rich and productive, except where the processes of soil formation under tropical climates have gone too far. The dark red-brown volcanic soils of Rarotonga are naturally of high fertility. But in all cases where temperature and rainfall are so favourable to plant growth the virgin forests of the high islands were tall, dense and varied, and characterized by massively-buttressed trees, with palms, rattan vines and tree ferns. Only at higher elevations on the loftier volcanic cones did the density of the forest gradually give way to grassy heights and rocky peaks. Today, however, much of the vegetation is secondary forest or even man-induced grassland or fern scrub. Periodic burning and intermittent shifting cultivation, both on the high volcanic and the 'continental' islands, has destroyed the primary forest, and replaced it with a cover of smaller trees, bamboo, scrub, fern and even —in drier leeward situations—with open savanna.

'CONTINENTAL' ISLAND HABITATS

The still larger 'continental' islands of the Pacific World, including New Guinea, the Solomons, New Caledonia, New Zealand, and Viti Levu and Vanua Levu (Fiji), together with such groups in the Oriental World as the Philippines and Japan, have much greater variety of human habitats. Only the new-born volcanoes and the associated low atolls of the Marianas, the Bonin Islands and the Tongan group, although they belong structurally to the western continental margin of the Pacific, have the more restricted environments of the high and low islands of the central structural province of the Pacific. The larger islands have a range of sedimentary, metamorphic and volcanic rocks. Occasionally they also have extensive lowlands built of alluvial or diluvial materials. Soils vary from the thin skeletal soils of high mountains and the podsols of the rainy middle latitudes to the deep residual clays of the tropical red and yellow soils and the laterites of the warm tropics. Plant life ranges from the dry tussock grassland of the rain-shadow areas of the South Island of New Zealand to the broad mangrove swamps of Indonesia, from the man-made forests of Japan and the tropical jungle of the Philippines to the *lalang* savanna and alpine vegetation of the drier uplands and mountain heights of New Guinea. To the biotic resources must also be added mineral resources: between them the 'continental' islands have coal, petroleum, gold, nickel, chrome, bauxite and other valuable minerals.

If to all this we add the continent of Australia itself, we get some impression of the diversity of terrain and of physical habitat available to the black-skinned men who first stepped off the mainland of Asia and to their lighter-skinned successors who slowly and unsteadily populated the immense watery environment of the Pacific World from Australia to Easter Island and from Hawaii to the Chathams.

CHAPTER TWO

The People

THE DISTINCTIVE character of the many Pacific island groups and of the Pacific coast areas of the Australian and Asiatic continents derives as much, if not more, from the people living there as from the diversity of physical conditions described in Chapter One. And the people are as varied as the natural environments in which they live. The many different ethnic groups have equally different cultures, languages and histories. The once-distinctive racial stocks from which the 'indigenous' (or 'native') peoples of the Pacific are derived are so many, and the inter-breeding during the thousands of years since man first stepped off the continent of Asia and made his way out into the Pacific has been so complex, that it is almost impossible today to disentangle the early history of the peopling of the Pacific. It is also almost impossible to set out this history in simple terms.

THE COMING OF THE ISLANDERS

As evidence slowly accumulates, the date of first human penetration of the Pacific is set further and further back in time. The peopling of the Pacific World, as here defined (see *Figure 13*), may well have started more than 30,000 years ago. At that time much of the water of the oceans was frozen and was piled in giant sheets of ice on parts of the continents and in all high-mountain areas. In an Ice Age like this the sea level stood lower than it does today. It was probably possible to walk from Malaya to Java and Borneo and on to the Philippines, and crude rafts of logs would be enough to get even the most primitive men across the narrow seas to New Guinea and Australia. This was a time of general human migration as a result of increasing cold and ice accumulation and developing technologies. Under such conditions small bands of primitive hunters and collectors—Old Stone Age men—stepped out from Asia into the westernmost Pacific. They probably included both dark-skinned, short Negritoid people and taller, heavy-browed Australoids (*Fig. 12*). Despite a thousand generations of interbreeding similar people still form the basis of the native population of parts of New Guinea and Australia.

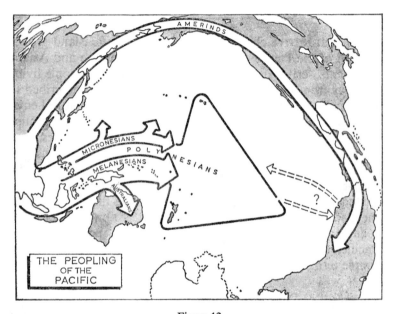

Figure 12

More than 15,000 years later there appears to have been a further major migration from Asia again by way of the Malayan Peninsula, which points like a finger to the island stepping-stones in the Indonesian 'Mediterranean'. About 8000 years ago tall, brown-skinned people, with many racial characteristics like those of the Caucasoid peoples of Europe, moved into the islands in small groups but did not reach Australia. They were a sea-voyaging people and had a New Stone Age culture which they carried to most of the islands between Australia and Asia. They were fishermen and primitive agriculturalists. With their arrival the earlier people of inferior culture were often obliged to retreat to isolated inland and mountainous areas.

MELANESIANS, POLYNESIANS AND MICRONESIANS

In the thousand years immediately before the birth of Christ the western Pacific was increasingly penetrated by Asian-type folk of dominant Mongoloid character. Through inter-breeding with the people already in the areas they came to occupy, they developed the ethnic characteristics which are today dominant in Malaya, Indonesia and the Philippines. These later arrivals had a still better developed culture, and a more intensive garden agriculture, including the cultivation of rice, and industries which included the working of metal. The pressure exerted through the expansion in the numbers of these more advanced people and in the areas they occupied tended to push the earlier folk not only into the forested mountain fastnesses of the Philippines and New Guinea but also eastwards out into the vast ocean spaces of the Pacific World. It is as a result of this relatively recent peopling of the arcuate and strewn islands of the Pacific that the Melanesians, Polynesians and Micronesians first become distinguished—primarily in language and culture and in insular localization but also broadly in ethnic characteristics (*Fig. 14*).

With intensified archaeological and anthropological research the problems that occur in sorting out the origins of the indigenous human elements in the islands of the Pacific are not becoming easier of solution, but it is increasingly clear that the human occupancy of this remote area is more ancient than has sometimes been suspected.

Melanesia—the island region of dark-skinned people—was probably occupied first. In New Guinea, the Solomons, the New Hebrides and Fiji, Europeans found a variety of dark-skinned folk, tall and short, wavy-haired and frizzy. But almost everywhere either Negritoid or Australoid characteristics were dominant and Caucasoid and Mongoloid tendencies were few.

The Polynesians came later. They probably left the Indonesian 'Mediterranean' by way of the Philippines two or three thousand years ago. By prodigious feats of seamanship and

Figure 13

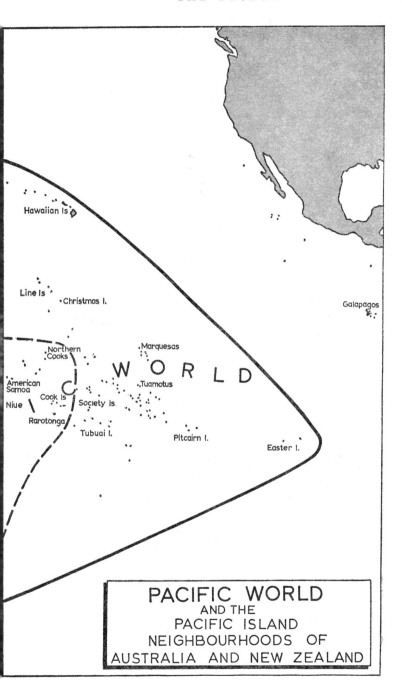

PACIFIC WORLD
AND THE
PACIFIC ISLAND
NEIGHBOURHOODS OF
AUSTRALIA AND NEW ZEALAND

navigation they earned the appellation of 'the supreme navigators of history'. They spread out over the greater part of the ocean's vastness to occupy the triangle of 'many islands' between New Zealand, Hawaii and Easter Island. Their ethnic character suggests that they left the western Pacific before Mongoloid traits came to be dominant there. The Polynesians

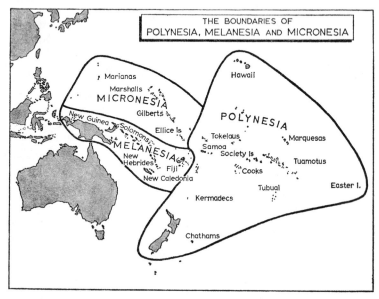

Figure 14

thus have major Caucasoid and minor Negritoid and Australoid features, and are of a stock not strikingly different from that of the Europeans who arrived in the central Pacific many centuries later. The achievement of the Polynesians lies principally in the fact that, before the epic voyages of the Phœnecians and those of the Vikings, they mastered the largest body of water on earth, and found and colonized diminutive island specks sometimes 7500 miles apart. They probably steered their outrigger and double canoes by way of the Carolines, out into the ocean voids and on towards the rising sun, until they reached the high volcanic island groups of the south-central Pacific. From 'Hawaiiki' (their more recent 'homeland' in the Society Islands) they dispersed in the following centuries north to Hawaii, east to the Tuamotus and Easter Island, south to the Austral Islands, the Cooks and New Zealand, and west to Samoa, Tonga and the Lau group in Fiji. New Zealand's earliest Polynesian inhabitants—the Moahunters—were established in the South Island well over a thousand years ago.

The Micronesians—so-called because they occupy minute low coral islands—were probably the last of the three distinctive racial and culture groups to penetrate the Pacific World. In their make-up the later Mongoloid tendency is apparent. They are generally shorter and have a lighter or more yellowy skin than the Polynesians. They occupy the myriad scattered atolls and occasional small volcanic islands of the Marianas, the Carolines, the Marshalls and the Gilberts. But even here (and in northern Melanesia) there are isolated islands with peoples of different appearance, language and custom from their Micronesian (or Melanesian) neighbours—peoples whose presence shows that in their oceanic migrations the Polynesians once passed this way.

THE EUROPEANS ARRIVE IN THE PACIFIC

Such was the pattern of distribution of people and culture in the Pacific when in 1513 Balboa looked upon the ocean, the first European to do so, and when, eight years later, Magellan made his four months' voyage across it. In the next four and a half centuries the already complicated picture was to be disturbed as never before, with Europeans of many nationalities coming to the Pacific for many different reasons, some as passing visitors, some as permanent settlers. As a result of this the numbers of native peoples have been violently and seriously reduced, although recent decades have revealed a renewed growth. Everywhere their way of life has been disrupted. And more recently, with the introduction of Chinese, Japanese and Filipinos to Hawaii, of Indians to Fiji, of Javanese and Tonkinese to New Caledonia, and with the penetration of Chinese into Malaya and the islands of the Indonesian 'Mediterranean', the ancient, age-long migration from Asia to the Pacific has been resumed.

The coming of Europeans into the Pacific falls into three periods. The first—the sixteenth century—was that of the Spanish. Their voyages of discovery had the joint objectives of discovering sources of gold and of finding converts to the Catholic faith. Their zeal led them across Central America and through the Straits of Magellan to explore the eastern rim of the Pacific, to discover the Moluccas, the Carolines, Papua, Hawaii, the Ellice Islands and the Solomons, and to plant in the Philippines the Pacific's first European colony as early as 1564. Before Drake brought the first British ship into the Pacific in 1577, there had been as many as a dozen large-scale Spanish expeditions.

The expedition of van Noort in 1598 marked the beginnings of Dutch Pacific exploration, and introduced the second period of European discovery—the seventeenth century. This was dominated by Holland's determined and matter-of-fact efforts to expand trade. The dour Dutch navigators came mainly to the Pacific via the Cape and from the west. In proceeding to the Spice Islands of the East Indies they incidentally investigated the repelling desert coast of western and northwestern Australia. In 1642-1643 Tasman not only demonstrated that Australia was an island continent and thus not part of a Great South Land, but he also revealed to Europe for the first time the existence of Tasmania, New Zealand, Tonga, Fiji, New Britain and New Ireland (*Fig. 15*). However, Tasman did not bring back to Batavia much evidence of potential trade that could be tapped and opened-up to Holland's profit. His remarkable discoveries did not therefore appear especially successful to his employers —the Dutch East India Company—and no attempt was made to extend them.

After Tasman the southwest Pacific remained unvisited for 127 years, when the third period of exploration began with the first of Cook's great voyages (bringing him in October 1769 to Young Nick's Head on the eastern coast of New Zealand, and in April 1770 to Botany Bay), and with the contemporary expedition of Bougainville. This was a period in which many nations took part in extending knowledge of the ocean and of the islands and people within it. English, Dutch, French, German, Danish, Russian and American expeditions all took part, and many had as their primary aim the extension of the bounds of knowledge and the expansion or correction of the available volumes of scientific information about the geology, geography,

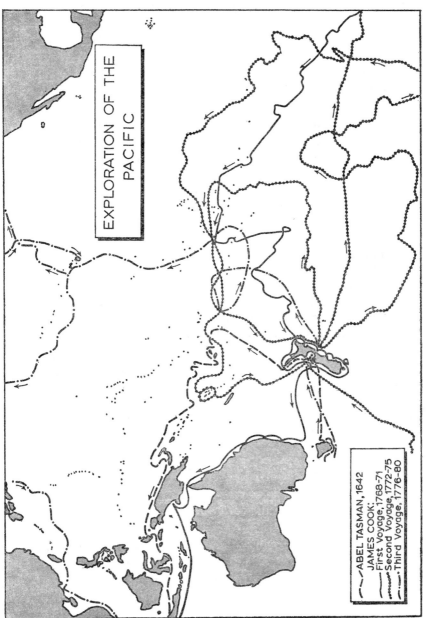

EXPLORATION OF THE PACIFIC

ABEL TASMAN, 1642
JAMES COOK:
First Voyage, 1768-71
Second Voyage, 1772-75
Third Voyage, 1776-80

Figure 15

botany, zoology, oceanography and ethnology of the Pacific. Cook on his second voyage, for example, had been charged with the task of proving or disproving the existence of the Great South Land, the Terra Australis, which had so long occupied the minds of geographers, and which was thought to lie between South America and Tasman's shadowy western New Zealand coast.

To this third period—and especially the last 150 years of it—belongs also European colonization of Pacific island groups like New Zealand and Hawaii and of the marginal continental areas of Australia and western North America. It is in addition a period in which European, and later American, commercial enterprise has been responsible not only for developing many of the resources of the region—the soil, the minerals, the timber—but also for destroying others—like seals and whales and sandalwood. In the process commercial interests have not only developed international and local trade in the Pacific but have almost everywhere disrupted native economies, replacing a subsistence on traditional, age-old skills and local resources by dependence upon imports and exports and the vagaries of distant, overseas markets and prices.

The period since 1800 has been one of expanding missionary enterprise in the Pacific. Religious zeal, animated by humanitarian motives, though often misguided in its actions, has taken missionaries into all the island groups. Its effect has been to replace traditional beliefs by imported ones, thus further disturbing the ancient way of life of native populations. And since the middle of last century the Pacific World has been the scene of political and territorial ambitions and strife. At first it was a struggle for colonies and a scramble for coaling stations. It was a struggle that brought European administration and administrators, law and order, to the Pacific World. But it was also a struggle that was later to culminate in the land, sea and air combat of World War II, when the nations of Europe, Asia and North America were to carry the weapons of modern warfare, including the atom bomb, from island to island in giant strides, and further to disrupt and confuse the native peoples. Its effects are to be seen in many parts of the Pacific World today; and, as is made evident in later chapters, they are of considerable importance in the geography of many of the island territories under review.

THE ORIGINAL NATIVE ECONOMY

Before the arrival in force of Europeans the Pacific islanders were fisherfolk and cultivators of the soil. Their simple methods of fishing and still simpler agricultural techniques enabled them to make their village communities self-sufficient in food and drink and clothing. On the larger islands of the western Pacific, rice-growing communities often lived some distance inland, and relied entirely on what they grew or on what they collected in the tropical forest. They lived in considerable numbers without the help of the resources of the sea. In other western islands taro, brought from Asia, was the staple food and the central item in the agricultural economy. In New Guinea, lowland village communities often relied largely on the sago palm growing in fresh-water swamps; and at higher and cooler elevations, in valleys in the interior of this large island, the kumara— brought first to the Pacific from South America by unknown voyagers—furnished the bulkiest food. The rich volcanic soils of the high islands out in the central Pacific provided a variety of foodstuffs and fibres. Here kumara, there taro and elsewhere yams figured prominently in the untidy garden patches which the villagers burnt in the forest, but everywhere the coconut was supreme. Throughout the tropical Pacific the coconut palm is still the most important plant, but its importance today lies mainly in the fact that it is the source of copra (dried coconut meat), the Pacific's front-rank commercial product. But to Pacific folk four centuries ago, the milk of the coconut was a principal beverage. On isolated coral atolls it was sometimes the only drink available. Its meat, grated and served with fish or fruit, was a staple food. Oil from the meat was used for cooking and for rubbing on the skin. The empty shell was a cooking vessel and a cup, and a material for carving. The trunk of the palm was used for building; and cord made from the fibres of the husk was used to lash house timbers together. Leaves were used to make food baskets, hats and clothes, and for the roofing of dwellings. There was no more indispensable plant in the Pacific.

Almost all the island folk of the Pacific World lived in an

oceanic environment and close to the sea. They had been canoe-paddling and ocean-going people for centuries before. Tropical shores, coral reefs and the waters of the multi-coloured lagoons and of inland streams were rich in plant and animal life, and to skilled fishermen they were a source of plenteous variety of sea-foods. On most islands the resources of shallow waters were an essential part of the diet. On the smaller coral atolls, with their restricted and erratic rainfall, with little soil other than coarse coral sand, and with only the fruit of pandanus, a few coconut palms and small, laboriously-made, saline taro pits, fishing was more important than gardening, the sea more rewarding than the land.

The islander's techniques and his wants were both very simple. But, apart from the most barren atolls and the islands of the cold higher latitudes, many thousands of fragments of land in the Pacific had resources enough to satisfy these wants once the techniques had been adapted to meet the natural conditions. Food for health and comfort; a little clothing mainly for festive occasions; rude shelter from rain and hurricane; shell and fishbone for making ornaments; timber, fibre and stone to provide the raw materials of simple arts and crafts—this was about all the Pacific peoples demanded. A simple digging stick was the standard agricultural implement, and often the only one available. Gardening generally involved the shifting of crops from place to place. Each year irregular patches of new ground were cleared in the forest by burning; and after one or two years of cropping these were abandoned to secondary forest growth. Such shifting cultivation has been termed 'fire-farming'. It involves the rotating of land rather than of crops. To Europeans it appeared wasteful and haphazard, but is as good a system as is available—even today—for utilizing tropical soils without exhausting their fertility and causing serious erosion of the soil.

THE IMPACT OF EUROPE

But in the 450 years between Magellan's voyage and the introduction of one-day trans-Pacific crossings by giant jet-aircraft, Europeans and Asians have wrought greater change throughout the Pacific World than did their neolithic predecessors in a thousand generations. In general the newcomers have in the past taken more than they have given. In succession they came to take, and sometimes to exterminate, seals, whales, sandalwood trees and guano deposits. Most took land, too, and colonies and foreign administrations were set up. Some territories were used as homes for settlers—especially Australia, New Zealand and Hawaii—some as strategic outposts of empire. Many islands were exploited by traders, and the production of many villages was channelled through a trading post. Other newcomers used land and soil and climate to produce commodities required by the rapidly and recently industrialized communities of western Europe and North America. If local people were not adapted for conversion into profitable labour on the plantations, Asian manpower was introduced without thought of the social problems this was to make for future generations. The ground was searched and penetrated and disfigured in the exploitation of its minerals. Finally, the last and most remote islets were taken over to make airstrips. All these and many other activities were pursued with energy and without rest, and as a result the white and yellow men responsible for them became the dominant element in Pacific affairs. The indigenous folk suffered; their traditional modes of life were disrupted and sometimes destroyed or forgotten. Some people, like the Tasmanians, were exterminated; others, like the Hawaiians, were left to adopt wholly western ways and almost die out; still others, like the Fijians, whilst preserving much of the native land and life, became the minority alongside an immigrant Asian majority.

DECLINE OF NATIVE POPULATION

Although by now no island in the Pacific's vastness has not been washed by a wave of western or oriental civilization, the storm of change raged most violently in the last century and a half, and its fury culminated with the impact of World War II between 1941 and 1945. In Magellan's time there were probably almost four million people in Melanesia, Micronesia and Polynesia, including New Guinea and Australia. At the time of the beginnings of European colonization and the appearance of whaling vessels in the Pacific, one hundred and fifty years ago, the number of indigenous people was probably little changed, although in Micronesia a decline set in early in the period of Spanish contact. But after 1800 a general and rapid decline in numbers began. The Polynesians declined from possibly a million to no more than 200,000; Melanesians, including the people of New Guinea, decreased in number from nearly three millions to about one million; the number of Australian aborigines fell from 300,000 to 50,000; and Micronesia's native population was reduced from 270,000 to almost 100,000. The factors producing this decline by two-thirds were much the same as those which operated in New Zealand, where the Maori population fell so rapidly (from possibly 400,000 to less than 50,000) that there were many experts at the end of the nineteenth century who predicted the total disappearance of the Maori. One-sided wars with the newcomers, native feuds made more destructive of life by the use of new weapons, catastrophic new diseases against which the islanders had no resistance, and lower birth rates due to disease, enforced labour, later marriages and loss of faith in life and the future—all these were operative, and until quite recently native populations were declining rapidly.

Today, fortunately, there are increasing signs that the decline of native populations has been arrested, excepting only in Australia, Hawaii and some of the smaller islands in the Solomons and New Hebrides. Elsewhere the rate of natural increase is high again, and is rising; indeed in some groups—in high volcanic islands, like Samoa, as well as in the poorer atolls of the mid-Pacific—the day appears to be approaching when the growing native population will outstrip both the food supply available and the environmental resources still to be developed. In 1966 there were probably 3.8 million *native* people in the Pacific World. Of these, two-thirds live in British territories. They include a million and three-quarters in the Australian portion of New Guinea, 47,000 Australian aborigines and more than 200,000 Maoris. They are, however, greatly outnumbered by the 16,000,000 Europeans and Asians who today live in the same area, though mainly, of course, in Australia, New Zealand, Hawaii, Fiji and New Caledonia.

THE POLITICAL MAP OF THE PACIFIC

In the four centuries since Spain began the process of acquiring territory in the Pacific by establishing a colony in the

Marianas in 1564, the complex history of international rivalries and annexations has produced a complicated and ever-changing political map of the ocean. The boundaries of the political units are artificial, and islands under the one administration may be scattered in different parts of the region. These units often overlap and interpenetrate, and they vary in size from territories larger than some European countries or American states down to individual island specks, which may, like Nauru, be the joint administrative responsibility of as many as three different powers. Apart from the independent sovereign nations on the continental margins of the Pacific, the islands within it today constitute upwards of a score of separately administered dependent or independent territories. Some of them are held directly, or by virtue of trusteeship agreements with the United Nations, by the United Kingdom, the United States, France, Chile, Mexico, Australia and New Zealand. In addition China and the U.S.S.R. lay claim to Pacific island areas. Until 1899 Spain was also involved; before the First World War Germany had large territorial holdings; and between the wars Japan administered and exploited Micronesian island territories formerly within the sphere of Germany and Spain.

To complicate the matter further the political status of the Pacific's non-selfgoverning territories varies widely and many have recently won, or are now in the throes of winning and sampling, their independence. There are Crown colonies, protectorates, territories, trusteeships, condominiums, an independent (but protected) kingdom, and possessions with different types and degrees of political organization. Among those which have recently acquired independent status are Western Samoa and the Cook Islands. An attempt should be made to sort out this confused and complicated situation with the help of the accompanying map (*Fig. 16*) and the list of jurisdictions in the Appendices.

BRITISH AND AMERICAN INTERESTS

Today the United States is the dominant power in the Pacific. Apart from the cloudy, stormy but strategically important Aleutians, which became United States territory with the purchase of Alaska in 1867, the United States did not acquire territories in the Pacific until the turn of the century. The Philippines, Guam and Hawaii became American territory as late as 1898, over a century after the planting of the first British settlement at Port Jackson in 1788. Tutuila, American Samoa, was acquired the following year; and after World War II, the United States accepted responsibility under the United Nations for the former Japanese islands of Micronesia, now termed the United States Trust Territory of the Pacific Islands. The Pacific north of the Equator is today exclusively within the American sphere; it is virtually an American 'lake'. From the continental mainland of North America, by way of Hawaii and the outliers of Micronesia to Formosa and the Ryukyu Islands, and by way of Alaska and the Aleutians to Japan, there are chains of strategic bases, strongly fortified, and all in American hands.

The Pacific south of the Equator is largely a British sphere of influence. Australia largely controls the islands off its northern shores. New Zealand's territories and the independent islands for which it still accepts some responsibility are scattered in the southwest Pacific, and extend in fact almost to the equator and most of the way from Wellington to San Francisco. The Solomons, Fiji, the Gilbert and Ellice Islands, Pitcairn and various atolls in the Line Islands and the Phœnix group are colonies or possessions of the United Kingdom. The Kingdom of Tonga is under Britain's protection. Other groups within this area are French, or are under joint Anglo-French jurisdiction, and western New Guinea, formerly Netherlands territory, was in 1963 taken over by Indonesia and is now known as Irian Barat. Many of the island groups of the southwest Pacific —that is, within Australia's and New Zealand's Pacific Island Neighbourhoods—are the responsibility of those two British countries. These groups conduct an increasing proportion of their trade with the Commonwealth and the Dominion, are today tied directly with them by rapid and improving communications, and look to them for technical help in many fields—medical, educational, administrative, commercial and agricultural.

THE PRODUCTION AND TRADE OF THE ISLANDS

If for the moment we overlook Australia and New Zealand, then the Pacific World under consideration, including New

Guinea and extending east from it, does not count for very much in a world of power politics, scientific exploitation of large-scale resources and advanced industrial technology. Its four million people form but an insignificant fraction of the world's 3500 millions. Its land area is small, fragmented and scattered. Communications within the Pacific, if not across it, are inadequate. Its people still lack the skills, experience and 'know-how' to compete openly in modern commerce. Resources that count for so much in the modern world—coal and iron, uranium and petroleum—are virtually non-existent. There is no extensive area of subdued relief, deep, fertile soils and suitable climate for the large-scale, mechanized production of foodstuffs, animal products, fibre or industrial raw materials. The dependent and newly independent island territories of the Pacific World contribute relatively little to world trade, and take only an insignificant part in the international exchange of commodities by which profit is made and by which the standards of living and material progress of those practising it are raised.

But to the administering powers concerned and to the islanders themselves, most of whom have come to rely to some extent on monetary income and the now indispensable store goods which money can buy, the exploitation of the islands' limited resources is of increasing significance. It is especially significant to Australia and New Zealand, because they have more immediate commercial and other ties with the Pacific's island territories. Amongst the changes which in the last century have caught up the island folk, none is more important to them than the introduction of commodities formerly unknown, but which have come to be prized as highly as most of the material objects of their native culture. Amongst these are manufactured goods like colourful cotton materials, simple iron tools, matches, oil lamps, corrugated iron and trucks, transistors and toiletries; also soap, canned foodstuffs like bully beef and Norwegian sardines, and processed commodities like flour and kerosene. In order to be able to purchase these at the trading store, the islander must produce in his own tribal gardens, or by working for wages on European plantations or in foreign-operated mines, goods for which there is a ready market in the world outside. In this way there comes from the scattered islands of the Pacific a flow of assorted produce which is only

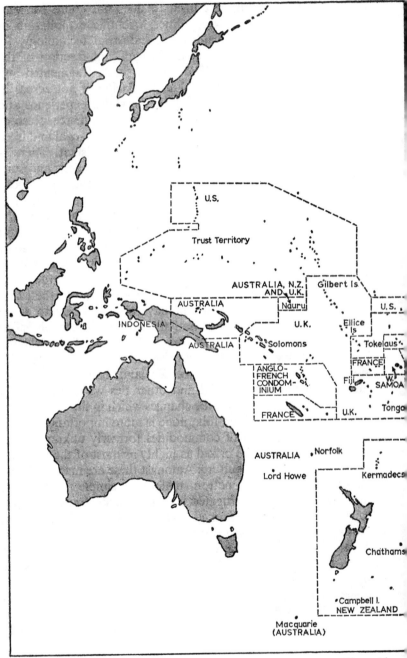

Figure 16

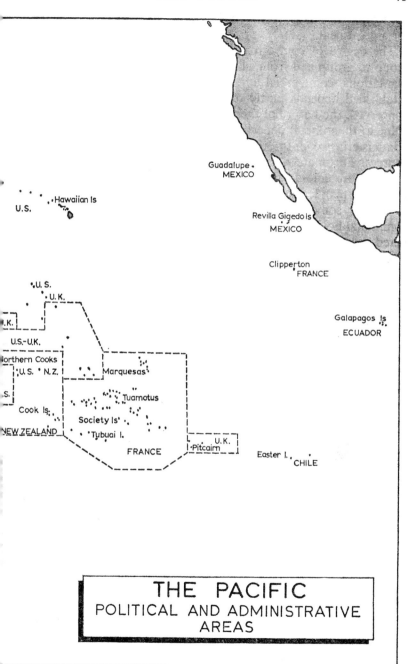

Guadalupe •
MEXICO

Hawaiian Is
U.S.

Revilla Gigedo Is
MEXICO

Clipperton
FRANCE

•U. S.
• U. K.

.K.

U.S.-U.K.

Galapagos Is
ECUADOR

lorthern Cooks
U. S.   N. Z.   Marquesas

S.
                     Tuamotus
Cook Is
            Society Is
NEW ZEALAND   • Tubuai I.
            FRANCE   U. K.
                        Pitcairn   Easter I.
                                              CHILE

THE PACIFIC
POLITICAL AND ADMINISTRATIVE AREAS

by world standards relatively insignificant—locally it counts for a great deal.

The degree of commercialization of native life varies from group to group and from island to island. The extent to which plantations, commercial agriculture and mining have become established depends partly on the accessibility of the islands concerned, the nature of their land resources, and the size and value of the mineral deposits, and partly on the attitude of the administering country towards the exploitation of such resources. Fortunately, apart from early land sales which took place before colonial government was established, the land of the native peoples has in all cases been adequately safeguarded. In fact, in some groups the rigidity with which the tribal and communal holding of native land has been preserved has hampered economic development, and has worked out to the disadvantage of the natives themselves. This is well exemplified by the situation in the southern volcanic islands of New Zealand's Cook group. And in Fiji land remains unused because it is reserved for the Fijians and is not available for the use of the majority Indian population.

Some more isolated, forested interior areas in larger islands and some poorer and smaller territories have little, if any, alien commercial development. The islanders continue to practise a little-modified subsistence economy, but in addition, cut, dry and sell copra, collect shells and weave baskets for sale. Even the least disturbed communities require a little money for trade goods, church collections and occasional fines. But in other cases, and especially in the coastal villages of the richer and larger islands, there has been an almost complete adoption of the commercial economy of the outside world. Towns have grown up at the nearest ports, native agriculture has been reorganized to produce for export, there are European and native-operated plantations, small industries, roads and sometimes small-gauge railways, modern schools, taxi-stands, supermarkets, libraries, electric power, and picture theatres and radio and television stations and studios.

PLANTATIONS, MINES AND NATIVE GARDEN PLOTS

Plantation agriculture and other introduced commercial enterprises, including sometimes large-scale mining operations, have developed more particularly in the larger 'continental' islands of Melanesia and in Hawaii. The European planter is perhaps most successful and at home today in New Guinea, the Solomons and Fiji. Mining is best established in New Caledonia, Fiji and both Australian New Guinea and the former Netherlands New Guinea. Agriculture in Hawaii and in the two largest islands in the Fiji group is dominated by immense, highly-capitalized corporations which buy the product from immigrant tenant producers, supervise methods of production, insist on scientific practices, process the sugar or pineapples in giant refineries and canneries, and market the products all over the world. But in some Polynesian and Micronesian islands— Western Samoa, the Society Islands and the Carolines—the plantations tend to be small and are owned, not so much by immigrants, as by natives and part-native descendants of early settlers who in many cases were German, French or Spanish. Such commercial holdings contribute to the Pacific's marketable surplus of bananas, cocoa, coffee, sugar, copra and vanilla. The 'native' crops—those produced in small quantities on thousands of village gardens, and prepared for market spasmodically as the spirit of the native cultivator is moved—are copra and other coconut products and, less frequently, bananas. Copra, coconut oil, coconut meal and desiccated coconut are together the Pacific islands' principal contribution to world commerce. Copra is all-important, and the value of copra exports is almost as great as that of all other agricultural products together. Apart from Hawaii, Guam and those territories in the higher latitudes where the coconut does not grow, all island groups contribute significantly to the copra trade. Copra apart, only sugar (from Hawaii, Fiji and the former Japanese mandate), tropical fruit (especially pineapples from Hawaii and bananas from Fiji, Samoa and Tonga), cocoa (from Samoa, Australian New Guinea and the New Hebrides) and coffee (from New Caledonia and Papua) are of importance in the commercial agriculture, as distinct from the local subsistence agriculture of the islands.

Mining is similarly restricted to a few items. The gold of New Guinea and Fiji, the nickel and chrome of New Caledonia, and the petroleum mined until recently in the Vogelkop of former Netherlands New Guinea are associated with the essentially 'continental' rocks of the islands of the Pacific's broad western margin, as are the gold and coal of New Zealand, or the coal, iron and copper of Japan. In the central Pacific province the only mining is that of phosphate, and there are today large-scale workings at Nauru, Ocean Island, Makatea in the Tuamotus, and Angaur in the Palaus. To Australia and New Zealand, however, phosphate rock, the basis of indispensable artificial fertilizers, will in the long-run be as valuable as all the gold the Pacific has produced, or is likely to produce.

The Flow of Trade

The direction in which the trade of the Pacific World flows is largely determined by the political affiliations of the different territories (*Fig. 17*). Hawaii, for example, ships its export products largely to the west coast of North America, and derives its imports of manufactured goods and processed foodstuffs and its tourists almost entirely from the United States. The tropical produce of the United Kingdom's scattered colonies and of the French possessions in the Pacific go to furnish the factories of the home countries with raw materials or to dollar markets in the United States and Canada. But the commercial interests of Australia and New Zealand in the Pacific are gradually expanding. They conduct the bulk of the foreign trade of their respective territories. Australia takes, for example, the rubber, cocoa and coffee of New Guinea; New Zealand imports the bananas of Samoa and the oranges and tomatoes of the Cook Islands. They enjoy also an increasing share of the export and import trade of the other island groups within their Pacific island neighbourhoods—the Solomons, Fiji, Tonga and the French possessions. Australian capital plays a big part in the economy of Fiji—in the goldmining and sugar-producing industries. The Commonwealth's connections with the mining and metal-refining industries of New Caledonia are being strengthened. New Zealand, with Australia, supplies the many different groups in the southwest Pacific with more and more of the store goods which continue to swell their import lists—soap, tinned meat, bottled sauces, tobacco and cigarettes, packing cases for island produce, flour, sharps, plastic ware and cheap cosmetics.

The most important mercantile firms and shipping concerns within this part of the Pacific are Australian, their capital raised

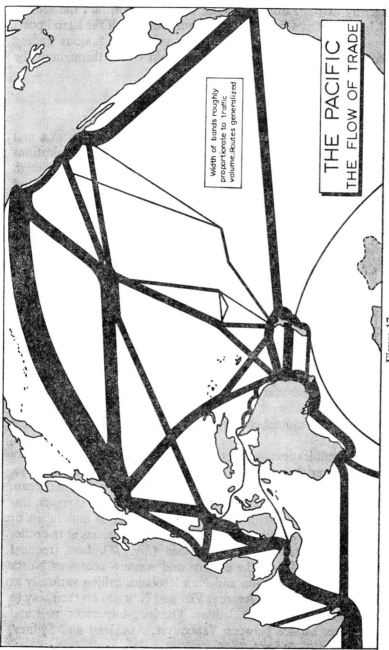

Width of bands roughly proportionate to traffic volume. Routes generalized

THE PACIFIC
THE FLOW OF TRADE

Figure 17

largely in the Commonwealth, the Dominion and the United Kingdom. On a hundred island outposts, in all the island ports and larger towns, there are firmly established famous trading companies whose names are household words throughout the southwest Pacific.

COMMUNICATIONS IN AND ACROSS THE PACIFIC

As one would expect on realizing its size and distances, and the scattered nature of its diminutive territories, communications in the Pacific World are few, far between and inadequate though fast improving. The island capitals are linked with cable and wireless facilities, and many of the outlying islands have their native-operated radio transmitters. But the movement of people and goods from group to group, and even from island to island within a group, is often infrequent. Ocean-going vessels pick up bulk cargoes from the principal port in each group with fair regularity, and one or two of these ports are on regular mail and passenger shipping lines. But many an outlying island, and some whole groups of coral atolls, may see no vessel in a whole year, and supplies of store goods are exhausted before a small copra cutter arrives to renew them and to empty the island storage sheds of copra. The only other occasional visitor to such far-flung outposts has been an RNZAF flying boat on a mercy mission, the missionary schooner, or perhaps a New Zealand frigate, or the small naval vessel of some other power, on an annual or bi-annual cruise to preach the gospel or to show the flag.

Communications across the Pacific, especially by air, are very much better than those within it. But these touch at, and serve, very few of the island groups strewn so widely within the ocean. Regular shipping services, for both freight and passengers, traverse the north Pacific between North America and Japan or the Philippines, calling at Honolulu and sometimes at the other American territories in Micronesia (*Fig. 18*). Less frequent freight services link the eastern and western coasts of North America with Australia and New Zealand, calling variously at Papeete, Apia, Suva, Avarua, Vila and Noumea on their way to Auckland, Brisbane or Sydney. The long-important mail and passenger service between Vancouver, Auckland and Sydney, withdrawn during and after the war, is now operated by English or American liners. The United Kingdom-New Zealand passenger services via Panama sometimes call at isolated Pitcairn, but little shipping traverses the empty southeastern part of the ocean. Large civil (and military) aircraft daily span the north Pacific, some following a northerly great circle route and putting down at Anchorage and skirting the Aleutians on their way from, say, Stockholm, Frankfurt or London to Japan, others using Hawaii and Midway, Wake and Guam as staging posts from the American west coast to Tokyo or Manila. Other daily air services traverse the ocean from northeast to southwest. They originate in Europe or Canada and the United States and terminate in both Australia and New Zealand. In this case the staging posts are Honolulu, American Samoa, Fa'a'a (Tahiti) and Nandi (Fiji). But all these services carry civilian passengers or military personnel, mails and some freight (of high value and small bulk) *across* the Pacific, rather than from place to place *within* it. They have little significance for the islands themselves or their people, except perhaps for the tourist traffic they bring to Hawaii and, to a less extent, to Fiji and Tahiti.

Since the war, however, services have been designed to meet the needs of the islands themselves. New Zealand National Airways Corporation Dakotas for some years linked Norfolk, Fiji, Tonga, Samoa, Aitutaki and Rarotonga, facilitating the movement of administrators, businessmen, islanders and mail not only between the different groups but also between each of them and Auckland. A similar run, now operated by Air New Zealand, is called the Coral Route. Its extension to Tahiti brings the French Society Islands much nearer to New Zealand, and it should encourage the growth of tourist traffic in all the island territories at which the service calls. (Temporarily, however, Air New Zealand's authority to fly into Tahiti has been suspended.) Australian airlines link together the territories off Australia's northern and northeastern coastlines from New Guinea to New Caledonia, and each of them with Sydney, whilst QANTAS not only reinforces the B.O.A.C. link between Australia and Singapore, India and Europe beyond, but, like Air New Zealand, skirts the western margin of the Pacific

c

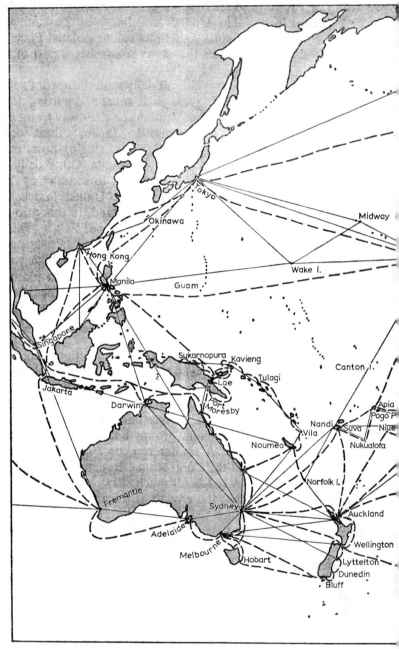

Figure 1

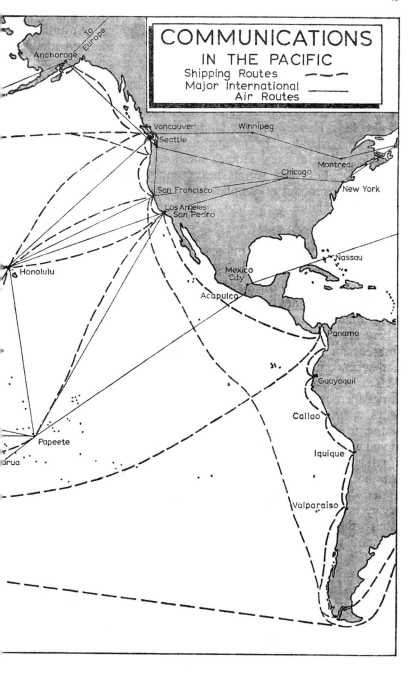

COMMUNICATIONS
IN THE PACIFIC
Shipping Routes ———
Major International _____
Air Routes

in traversing the Indonesian 'Mediterranean' between Sydney and Hong Kong and Sydney and Tokyo and flies from Australia to both North and Central America. Air New Zealand now flies DC8s across the Pacific to Los Angeles, as also does the French overseas airline U.T.A. And both B.O.A.C. and Air India have extended their Europe-Australia services to Fiji—the former via Auckland. Fiji now has its own internal services, as also have Hawaii and the United States Trust Territory of the Pacific Islands. The mining industry of otherwise inaccessible valleys of New Guinea has long depended on commercial aviation, first for its heavy equipment and later for its constant renewal of supplies and the replacement of both men and machines.

OTHER EFFECTS OF THE EUROPEAN IMPACT

In the last one hundred and fifty years European civilization has brought profound changes to the Pacific, not only to the island territories, but to Australia and New Zealand, where new occidental nations have been founded; to Japan and China where age-old, hitherto-unchanging cultures have been transformed; and to the Philippines and Indonesia, where backward and dependent colonial territories have emerged to independent, but as yet unstable, nationhood. In the smaller island territories there is today a confusing assortment of native and alien ways of life. In the last few generations some of the peoples native to the Pacific World have been swept from their traditional ways of life, in which they could locally produce sufficient for their needs. In some areas the change has been slow and has not gone far. In others it has been rapid and has penetrated deeply. In places it has been so rapid that side by side today are found the university-trained native medical practitioner, the native government officer and Cambridge graduate, the, until recently, head-hunting tribal warrior, and the gardener who has never been beyond the next village or wielded as an agricultural tool anything other than a digging stick of his own making. In the same scene might appear a Boeing 707 jet and a cluster of fern and grass-walled hutments under wind-lashed palms. Scattered groups of Stone Age people have been brought abruptly into contact with the European World.

With the prayer book, canned foods, new crops like corn, cassava, coffee and citrus fruit, with aircraft, bulldozers and the atom bomb have also come booms and depressions, new diseases, insect pests, weeds, formal education, western medicine, new and little-understood forms of government. The change has not been brought about without difficulties or without giving rise to complex problems.

Throughout the many islands and archipelagos the administrator faces formidable difficulties. The islander's old and expert agricultural methods are being lost or forgotten. He has turned with little skill and less experience to commercial production of crops, usually those requiring the minimum of labour and attention. But he has neither the capital, the technology nor the tradition of persistent effort for successful commercial agriculture. Boom times, like those following World War II, put money in his hands and, without effort, bring him luxuries he does not need. A depression or a fall in the market price of copra or cocoa beans leave him stranded and confused, for he has meanwhile forgotten the procedures which formerly gave him his self-sufficiency. Diet has deteriorated, and with it physique, teeth and general health. Sugar, flour, biscuits and canned foods have replaced the traditional balanced diet of green vegetables, bulky root crops, fresh fruit and seafoods. Employment for wages has taken young people from the villages and the family gardens to the ports and larger towns. In the ports there are spreading slums and shanty towns. House-building skills have deteriorated. Inferior dwellings of rusty and unpainted corrugated iron, packing cases and even cardboard, are replacing the *mbure* or *fale*. These were built communally with care and skill. Local timbers were used for the frame while other materials like pandanus, reedgrass or coconut leaves, carefully bound together, were used for walls and roofing thatch. Cotton goods from Lancashire or Bombay have taken the place of the local materials that went into traditional dress, especially of *tapa* obtained by pounding the bark of paper mulberry.

But these things have come to stay. There is no turning back the clock. The Pacific islanders themselves would be the last to want to revert to the ways of earlier times.

Fortunately the impact of an upheaval such as the people of the Pacific World have experienced can be cushioned and its worst effects largely avoided. The powers which administer the territories of the Pacific World or watch over the struggles of the newly independent territories to manage their own affairs realize this today and, as we shall see later, have established the South Pacific Commission, whose object it is to study and improve the physical, economic, social and political well-being of their wards.

CHAPTER THREE

Australia

FOR MANY centuries, almost from the time when the western-most part of the Pacific World was first peopled, the Australian aborigines had the continent's three million square miles to themselves. There were probably never more than 300,000 of them. That is the estimate of their total number on the arrival of Europeans, and it gives a population density of one to ten square miles, or one to each 6400 acres. This sparse and largely nomadic population had one of the simplest and most primitive technologies found amongst native people.

The limited numbers and the uniformly simple way of life of the aborigines were both largely the product of physical conditions, which included immense distances, marked aridity, a restricted and monotonous plant life, and few animals. These same conditions in Australia have confronted even the modern skills and technology of Europeans with formidable problems, and have hitherto noticeably restricted the spread of immigrants to a relatively narrow coastal rim of the continent. It is of interest to note that, like the aborigines, Europeans have not found in the indigenous flora and fauna of the continent one animal worthy or capable of domestication. The aborigines on the other hand did find in the insects and animals of the island continent species suitable for use as food. But the primitive state of the aborigines was also due to the few and simple tools they had, to their prolonged isolation, and to their lack of contact with the later invaders of the Pacific World. While elsewhere the Old Stone Age developed into the New Stone Age, while the arts of plant and animal domestication were acquired and the working of clay and metals provided others with pottery and iron tools, the Australians lived for millennia in almost complete isolation from the rest of the world, and out of touch with even the simplest technological and cultural advances made elsewhere.

The aborigine was a hunter and gatherer. He took what nature provided. He collected seeds, but he did not sow them. He hunted animals with wooden spears, boomerangs and stone clubs, but he did not breed them. But so restricted was the edible, seed-bearing flora, and so sparse was the number of wild animals, that a sedentary life was out of the question. Only land was abundant, so that related family groups of aborigines were nomadic parties that could wander over enormous areas in search of food without conflicting with the interests of other groups. A group's possessions were few. It had little to carry from water hole to water hole. Hunting tools of wood or stone, sticks for digging out insects or edible plant roots, a few wooden bowls and string bags, next to no clothing: this was all they had to carry. Shelter was temporary—no more than a crude windbreak of clay, leaves or brushwood. Most slept in the open with, at best, a small fire on frosty nights to comfort the naked body.

EXPLORATION

But from 1788 onwards, after thousands of years of deep isolation, the aborigines were brought into contact with a strange and alien culture. As a result they lost much of their land and their numbers dwindled. Today there are less than 47,000 fullblooded native Australians—nearly half of them in western Australia—and forty per cent of them still follow a miserable nomadic existence.

From the beginning of the seventeenth century the Dutch frequently touched the continent's arid western shore and later investigated much of the inhospitable coast of the Great Australian Bight. In 1642 Tasman's voyage took him to the south of New Holland and Van Diemen's Land, and showed that Australia was an island continent and not the Great South Land so long imagined. But, by his wide sweep into the Pacific, by way of New Zealand, Tonga, Fiji, and the Bismarck Archipelago, Tasman missed the eastern coast of the continent. It was left to Cook, nearly 130 years later, to investigate what proved to be the most attractive part of Australia, the eastern coastlands, which were subsequently to contain the vast bulk of the Commonwealth's population. The results of Cook's voyages in the Pacific were little less important than those of Columbus in the Atlantic. One of the first direct results of Cook's reports was the planting of a British penal colony in 1788 at Botany Bay, soon removed, however, to a new site at Sydney Cove in Port Jackson. Appreciation of the remoteness of the New South Wales coast was thus one of the factors that led to the first settlement of Australia, and to the founding in time of a string of scattered, isolated and for long almost-forgotten British colonies around the narrow, moist, southern and eastern fringe of a hot, arid continent that might otherwise have remained New Holland or become a domain of Napoleonic France.

EARLY SETTLEMENT

What was the wilderness like to which the convicts and free settlers came at the close of the eighteenth century? In 1788 it was still a vast *terra incognita;* its plants, animals, climate, weather, soils and native people were all strange and forbidding to the newcomers. But they were slowly to discover and get to know its characteristics as at first they consolidated a succession of beach-heads at Sydney, Hobart, Brisbane, Perth, Portland, Melbourne and Adelaide, and later penetrated on foot and by bullock wagon inland towards the desert heart. This was no inland surge of many immigrants, but a slow and fumbling exploration of the inland wilderness by intrepid adventurers, squatters and sheepmen. There was no surplus of folk in the tiny, nuclear coastal beach-heads ready to leave for the interior and face isolation and difficulties still greater than those of the infant ports. Only individuals and small parties penetrated the mountain gorges and passes of the east. Pioneers were few, and progress was slow and uncertain. Not until 1810 were sheep taken through to the inland plains of New South Wales; not until 1840 were interior settlements established on the downs and tablelands across the uplands from Brisbane.

From Portland in the south to Brisbane in the north the early coastal settlements of Victoria, New South Wales and Queensland were shut in by what became known as the Eastern

Highlands, part of which, in terms especially appropriate to the early pioneering days, was referred to as the Great Dividing Range.

THE NATURE OF THE LAND

This most elevated part of the continent of Australia, extending from Cape York to the Grampians near the Victoria-South Australia border, and including the mountainous island of Tasmania, constitutes one of the three great structural and landform regions into which Australia might conveniently be divided (*Fig. 19*). But it is no chain of lofty alpine mountains.

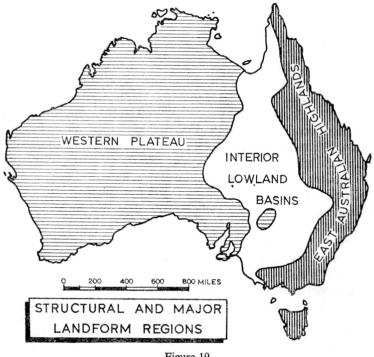

Figure 19

Indeed, as a continent, Australia is structurally incomplete, for it lacks young fold mountains of Tertiary age. Australia's equivalent of Asia's Himalayas or Europe's Alps lie to the east and north of the present continental block, far out in New Zealand and New Guinea.

THE EAST AUSTRALIAN HIGHLANDS

It was not the elevation of the East Australian Highlands that shut in and hampered the coastal settlements so much as their broken surface, the lack of obvious breaks in them, and the absence of passes across them. The first to penetrate the eastern valleys of the coastal highland found the going hard. About Port Jackson and Botany Bay the valleys led back into deep sandstone gorges which terminated abruptly in vertical walls. Others turned and ran parallel to the coast without providing access to the interior. Still others ran back to high forested plateaus or steep-sided, hazy, blue ranges. It is only south of Brisbane, however, that the highland averages more than 3000 feet in elevation. It is a region of ancient mountains and of old and hard rocks, long since reduced to low elevations, only to be elevated in recent geological times as a series of plateaus and low mountain blocks. These are now being actively dissected by rivers which have already eaten deep valleys into the highland. South of Sydney itself is a sterile, inhospitable plateau of massive Triassic sandstones cut by deep gorges. Its valleys are walled by sheer rocky bluffs and terminate in giant cliffs. And the whole is still largely covered with a grey forest of eucalyptus. Elsewhere along the 1200 mile stretch of the eastern structural province of the continent local descriptive names indicate the variety of terrain present and suggest that the highland is rarely one of elevated mountain ranges. In Queensland are the Atherton 'Plateau' and the so-called Dividing 'Ranges', the latter often under 2000 feet in elevation. In New South Wales is the New England 'Tableland' and the dissected block of the Blue 'Mountains'. Only in southern New South Wales, where the Australian Alps culminate in Mount Kosciusko's 7328-foot peak, and in Tasmania, are there mountains comparable even with the foothill approaches to New Zealand's alpine ranges.

But amongst the variety of rocks of many different ages which make up Australia's eastern highland, including Tasmania, are many that bear minerals. Gold, copper, tin, silver, zinc, lead, tungsten, molybdenum and others are, or have been, mined. It was the gold of Bathurst, Ballarat, Bendigo and Castlemaine

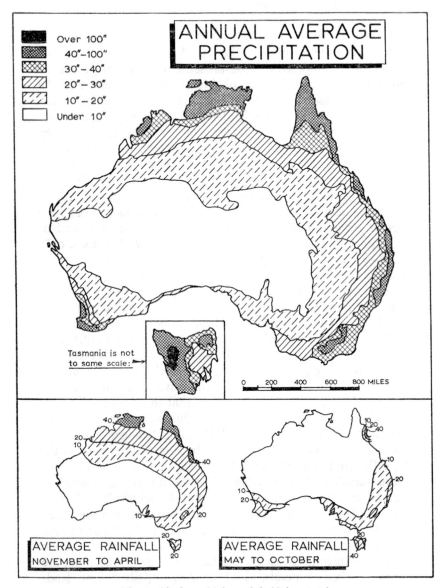

Figures 20 *above*, 21 *lower left*, 22 *lower right*

that in the middle of last century made possible the more rapid development of the Australian colonies. And most of the coal in Australia is found in, or on the flanks of, the eastern highlands, especially in coastal New South Wales and in southern and central Queensland.

With the exception of the southwestern tip of the continent and the Arnhem Land Peninsula, eastern Australia is the only part of this vast land area that enjoys a rainfall of twenty-five inches or more. The precipitation in much of the landform region is quite exceptional also in that it is relatively reliable and fairly evenly distributed through the year. (See *Figs 20, 21* and *22.*) The coastal valleys and plateau ranges which confronted the first settlers were heavily forested or wooded (*Fig. 26*). It was a forest of trees such as they had never seen before. From the Queensland border round to Portland, the coastal plateaus of New South Wales and the hills and valleys of Victoria were covered everywhere by sclerophyll forest dominated by some of the many hundreds of species of eucalyptus which are so characteristic of both humid and sub-humid regions in Australia. Although the average annual precipitation is one normally adequate for rainforest, its unreliability, the frequency of sharp droughts, the high summer temperatures and great evaporation gave rise to a tree cover of eucalyptus (stringybarks, bloodwoods, ironbarks, mountain and alpine ash and blue gums) and a dense community of shrubs all alike adapted to withstand occasional drought and dry winds. Only here and there in small patches along the coast, and especially in Queensland, was the heavy dark foliage of rainforest found. In New South Wales and Tasmania, there were also beeches and 'pines' (Huon pine) and other trees not unlike those of the New Zealand forest, and on the coasts of Queensland there were trees related to those of the tropical islands to the north, including species of kauri, cedar and araucaria (hoop 'pine' and bunyan 'pine').

Coastal soils were almost everywhere leached and difficult to work. The best of them, the pockets of meadow soils on the small alluvial flats, had to be drained and cleared of their forest. For thirty years the progress of the penal settlement at Port Jackson and of the increasing numbers of free settlers in the Nineteen Counties of New South Wales was very slow. With primitive methods—sickle and scythe—poor seed and little experience, they attempted a mixed self-sufficient agriculture relying largely on maize, wheat and vegetables. They met with little success. The settlement of Hobart made faster progress in its first decade after 1803. By 1810 it was supplying Sydney with some of its wheat.

THE INTERIOR LOWLAND BASINS

But neither nature nor government decree could contain the settlers. A retired army captain, MacArthur, early envisaged the future of the wool industry. He saw its urgent necessity if New South Wales was to have an export product and the cash with which to buy the food it could not grow and all the capital goods which the development of new settlements demanded. He set about breeding a strain of fine-woolled merinos for the job, using stock from South Africa and later from the Royal Stud at Kew.

Meanwhile hardy pioneers were exploring to the west. Hard on the heels of the explorers of new country came the sheep-men, driving their Shorthorn cattle and their flocks of small merinos over virgin tracks through forest and savanna, seeking especially the better grazing land and the reliable water supplies. They were the 'splendid infantry of Australian settlement', the pioneers who in the thirty years before the discovery of gold in 1851 laid the foundations upon which rests Australia's establishment as the world's greatest supplier of wool and as one of its great primary producers; and upon which the woollen textile industry of Yorkshire was so largely built.

First on the Bathurst plains within the highland, then out on to its western slopes via Lake George and the Monaro Table-land, and south to the upper reaches of the Murrumbidgee and the Murray, the squatters moved and took up land in great blocks. Later the flow of pioneer graziers and sore-footed flocks turned north, and by 1840 the first run had been taken up on the Darling Downs. The Murray had been explored and sheep driven into what later was to become Victoria; and after the founding of South Australia in 1836, flocks were 'overlanded' from New South Wales to Adelaide.

By now the settlers had come into contact with the extensive Interior Lowland Basins (*Fig. 19*). These are a series of basins of sedimentary rocks which occupy a third of the continent between the western slope of the Eastern Highlands and the inner eastern margin of the ancient shield which forms the Western Plateau. Between the shallow waters of the Gulf of Carpentaria and Spencer Gulf there is little land more than 500 feet above sea level; about Lake Eyre land is, indeed, below sea level. Low rises separate the drainage to the Gulf of Carpentaria from the inland drainage basin of Lake Eyre, and the latter from the Murray-Darling Basin. Spencer Gulf and Lake Torrens occupy a rift valley between the iron-rich southeastern extension of the Western Plateau in the Eyre Peninsula and the block of mountains north and east of Adelaide. (These include the Mount Lofty Ranges and the Flinders Range. The offshoots to the northeast and the mineral-rich Barrier Ranges north of Broken Hill are detached portions of the ancient ore-bearing rocks of the Western Plateau.)

Except where the lowland is broken sharply by the high ridges of South Australia, the early explorers (and the sheepmen who followed them) found the inland a dry, drab and monotonous expanse of territory, crossed more often by broad, incised, bone-dry riverbeds with occasional billabongs and waterholes than by rivers of running water. South Australia's lakes, so blue and prominent on many a map, are in fact more often dry expanses of encrusted white salt rather than of water. Only occasionally, and temporarily, are they occupied by a sheet of shallow water dirty with silt and clay. The eastern and elevated rim of the basins has a rainfall of from ten to twenty inches, nowhere as effective as it sounds because of high temperatures and evaporation. But most of the Lake Eyre basin has less than ten inches of very erratic rainfall. Many of the rivers from the western slope of the Eastern Highlands in Queensland dry up and become lost in their braided beds on the journey southwest to Lake Eyre. Crossing the inland basins by air between Sydney and Darwin the traveller sees a succession of riverbeds running from northeast to southwest—broad, incised, braided—but he is rarely able to pick out signs of running water, although dark lines of straggling eucalypts follow the rivers and relieve the parched yellow-brown colour of the sparsely covered soil.

The western slopes of the Eastern Highland and the adjacent easternmost rim of the inland basins proved to be easier going for the immigrant flockmasters coming from the thickly-forested plateau ranges to the east. Here forest gave way to *savanna woodland and savanna* (*Fig. 26*). This was ideal country for the merino sheep. There were many native grasses to provide forage for them. In Queensland there were species of Mitchell grass; on the Darling Downs there were wallaby grass (related to New Zealand's native danthonias), kangaroo grass and several species of *Stipa*. The unimposing brigalow scrub (acacia) also occurred widely. Elsewhere there were scattered trees and shrubs, mainly eucalypts, apple gum, stringy bark and red box in Queensland, red gum in New South Wales and peppermints, blue gum and ironwood in South Australia. They provided shade and shelter and, in the driest of years, many trees and shrubs furnished a reserve supply of fodder. But westwards, beyond the fifteen-inch rainfall line, the vegetation was rapidly reduced in density and grazing value as the rainfall decreased in amount, reliability and effectiveness. Much of South Australia and northwestern Victoria (see *Fig. 26*) was occupied by *mallee*. The mallee provided little grazing, for grassy ground growth was excluded and in the thicket livestock easily got lost. The mallee was thus often avoided by the graziers, and had to await the development of mechanical techniques and the demand for wheat land before much of it was cleared and occupied.

Inland from the dry margin of the mallee in the south, and of the savanna in New South Wales and Queensland, is a 200 mile-wide crescent of low scrub and shrub steppe. The former is an open shrubland—grey and parched—dominated by acacias, the chief of which is *mulga*. Between the low-growing shrubs is a wealth of ephemeral flowering plants and grasses which spring into life after the occasional rains. The shrub steppe on the other hand is a close formation of three foot-high *saltbush and bluebush*, drought-resistant shrubs with deep tap-roots, with the ability to absorb moisture from nightly dew through succulent, hairy leaves which have a high protein content and are valuable for grazing. These shrubs provide the bulk of the feed available to the merino and make grazing possible in areas with only five inches to eight inches of very irregular precipitation. But this was as far as even the most adventuresome of the early sheepmen could go, for beyond Lake Eyre and to the north was the dead heart of Australia—the desert wasteland.

In most parts of the Interior Lowland there is often water available beneath the ground when it is not available at the surface from rainfall. The coastlands of the Gulf of Carpentaria, practically all the Lake Eyre watershed and the northern part of the Murray-Darling drainage basin are within the largest of Australia's artesian basins. The Great Australian Artesian

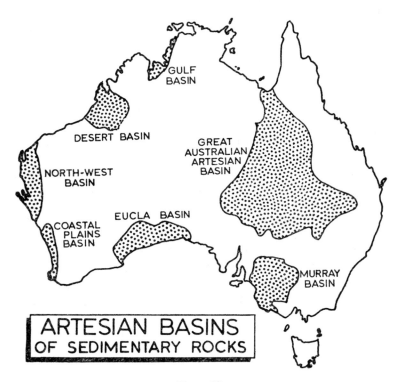

GULF BASIN

DESERT BASIN

GREAT AUSTRALIAN ARTESIAN BASIN

NORTH-WEST BASIN

EUCLA BASIN

COASTAL PLAINS BASIN

MURRAY BASIN

ARTESIAN BASINS
OF SEDIMENTARY ROCKS

Figure 23

Basin (*Fig. 23*) is a structural and geological saucer. Porous strata outcropping on its eastern rim in Queensland are the gathering ground from which water flows inland beneath the surface. It can be tapped by putting down wells in the drier savanna and saltbush country many hundreds of miles to the west. Normally the underground water supplies are used to augment the sporadic rains, but in years of prolonged drought artesian water may be the only source of supply. Most wells are sunk from 1000 to 2000 feet. The water is too strongly mineralized for use in irrigation, although station gardens might sometimes be made possible by using it, and occasionally it is used for domestic purposes. The importance of the underground water resources of the Great Australian Artesian Basin can be appreciated when it is realized that the arid and semiarid area it serves is five times the size of New Zealand, that there are 5000 artesian and sub-artesian bores and that the *daily* flow of water—though slowly diminishing—is over 300 million gallons.

THE WESTERN PLATEAU

The Western Plateau (*Fig. 19*), Australia's largest structural unit and major landform region, occupying almost three-fifths of the continent, or not less than 1,750,000 square miles, was not approached from the east. Its western coastlands had been the first part of the continent to be sighted by Europeans, but it was not until the late eighteen-twenties that its only attractive part—the southwestern tip—was occupied with the planting of an outpost at Albany and the annexation of the Swan River Settlement. In the century and a half since then settlement has been confined until the last year or two to the southwestern corner of this enormous plateau, with the exception only of sparse coastal and semi-coastal pastoral occupancy and mineral exploitation in the tropical north and short-lived mining camps in the desert interior.

The Western Plateau is a great shield of ancient rocks, the geological nucleus of the continent. Its surface of granites, metamorphic rocks and hardened sedimentaries stands largely between 750 and 1500 feet high. Much of it is also buried in desert sand. Occasionally, as in the Macdonnell and Musgrave Ranges, ancient mountains have withstood the ravages of æons of erosion, and stand high above the monotonous desert plateau, buried largely in the rock and gravel debris of age-long destruction. Most of the plateau has only local ephemeral streams, and a net of inland drainage to scattered salt lake basins which are more often dry than not. The limestone Nullarbor Plains are both treeless and riverless. Much of the desert surface of the plateau, and of the adjacent portions of the interior lowland north of Lake Eyre, is occupied by great sand plains and sand ridges. The sand of the interior of the Western Plateau is arranged in ridges up to fifty or sixty feet high—quite unlike the dunes of other deserts. They run remarkably parallel for great distances from northwest to southeast. They are much more fixed and permanent features of the arid landscape than are the migratory dunes of other deserts.

Only north of the latitude of Broome, and in the southwest, does rainfall reach twenty inches. Over most of the interior it is as little as five inches or less. But in both the more humid areas rainfall is markedly seasonal. The southwestern corner of the continent, like Tasmania and the southeast, projects in winter into the belt to which rain is brought by mid-latitude cyclones moving east. In summer the southwest corner is but a projection of the desert, with only very sparse and erratic rains.

The rains of the northern part of Western Australia, of the Northern Territory and of the adjacent parts of Queensland, are condensed from moist, tropical air masses which invade the northern half of the continent in summer under the monsoonal influence of the high temperatures and low pressures over the desert interior. These rains practically all fall in the five hot months from November to April, when they are least effective. During the rest of the year, desert conditions spread north almost to the sea (*Figs 21* and *22*).

Many of Australia's concentric belts of vegetation are largely absent in the area of the Western Plateau, for desert and steppe extend to the coast between Broome and Carnarvon and close to it again on the coast of the Great Australian Bight. The southwestern corner has a succession of vegetation not unlike that of the east, except that the belts are narrower. Sclerophyll forest occupies the land inward to the line joining Perth and Albany and gives way soon to savanna woodland. Here are some of Australia's most valuable eucalypts—karri, jarrah and marri. From Geraldton to Esperance runs the line close to which savanna gives way to mallee, and mallee is soon replaced by mulga, and later by steppe and desert. In the north, desert grasses and shrubs like the tussocky porcupine grass (*Triodia*) with occasional coolibahs and baobabs extend north almost to the latitude of Broome. Beyond this a belt of savanna and Mitchell grass stretches away to the east. North again towards the coast the grasses are taller and less palatable and trees occur more frequently in the tall savanna grassland until, near the coast itself, where the summer rains may total over fifty inches, is found a richer monsoon woodland with tall bamboo, pandanus and mangrove swamps on the coast and eucalypts along the rivers.

The poverty of the agricultural resources of the Western Plateau is in part compensated for by the mineral wealth which its ancient rocks have yielded, and in places are still yielding (*Figs 42* and *43*). The wealth from the desert gold-mining settlements of Wiluna, Kalgoorlie and Coolgardie, and from the smaller temporary encampments further north, aided and hastened the economic development of Perth and Western Australia at the end of the century. There are other auriferous rocks and gold workings, past and present, in many parts of the plateau. After 1888 the Pilbara goldfield and the mining centre of Marble Bar were the principal focus of attention in the arid northwest of the plateau. In the Barkly Tableland the plateau extends over the Queensland border and here at Mount Isa are deposits of lead, zinc and silver second in importance only to those in the separate extension of the plateau at Broken Hill in western New South Wales. The ancient rocks of the plateau also provide the ore for Australia's expanding heavy iron and steel industries. Iron ore deposits are found in the Middleback Ranges (Iron Knob) in the Eyre Peninsula west of Spencer Gulf. Others, on Koolan and other small islands in Yampi Sound, north of Derby, furnish a valuable reserve supply. The plateau also has supplies of uranium of sufficient size and importance to attract the attention and interest of the Unites States Government. Rum Jungle, south of Darwin, has since World War II become an important producer. All these, however, were unknown to the pioneers. The graziers found little to attract them on the Western Plateau; its landscapes were monotonous, its climate repelling, its vegetation and soils rarely sufficiently productive to warrant attention. Indeed, even today, with the exploitation of its mineral resources and in an atomic age in which uranium is a great attraction, the plateau and its adjacent coastline, together comprising threefifths of the area of the continent, have only one-twelfth of the Commonwealth's population, only one person to every three square miles. And most of these people live in the southwestern extremity of the continent.

Yet new discoveries of minerals and improved, mechanized methods of exploiting them are bringing renewed interest to the Western Plateau, and unaccustomed activity today characterizes especially the northwest margin of the ancient shield. Indeed the arid coast of Australia from Carnarvon round to Darwin is today in the throes of an iron boom that will doubtlessly prove as exciting and more economically significant than the gold booms of the past century. Since 1960 the Federal Government ban on the export of iron ore has been lifted. This has encouraged exploration and development with the result that there have been discovered in Western Australia what are probably among the three or four largest deposits of iron ore in the world. Today there is feverish activity, not only in prospecting and mining, but in building roads, towns and airstrips and in altering the shape of the coastline to build new ports from which to export the ore. This activity centres especially on Cockatoo and Koolan Islands, Mount Tom Price in the Hamersley Range (south of Roebourne), Mount Goldsworthy (east of Port Hedland) and at Koolyanobbing, 250 miles east-northeast of Perth.

EXPANSION AND CONSOLIDATION OF SETTLEMENT

After 1851 Australia's economic development was rapid. Gold provided the stimulus required. It brought people and it provided the wealth with which to replace bullock tracks by roads and railways, and with which to secure overseas the capital equipment needed for the fuller development of the continent's resources. In ten years population expanded threefold; in thirty years it jumped from less than half a million to two and a half millions. The railways inland from the ports made possible the cultivation of wheat on the better grassland and savanna soils across the divide. Machinery was introduced, or devised locally, for dealing with virgin land, tree roots and mallee scrub. Artificial fertilizers were used, and new varieties of wheat, adapted to the local climatic conditions, were bred. Land was subdivided and closer settlement followed. Sheep runs were fenced. Graziers pushed inland almost to the desert margin. In some

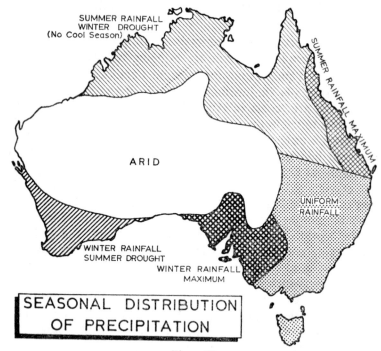

Figure 24

areas they went too far; the mulga, saltbush and bluebush were overgrazed and sometimes destroyed. Soil erosion followed.

But refrigeration made possible the export of meat and dairy produce and the diversification of the livestock-rearing industries. The coastal valleys and hills were deforested mainly by ring-barking of trees, and in Victoria and New South Wales the scrub and forest cover was removed by fire. Exotic pastures were thus established and on them increasing numbers of beef and dairy cows were reared and lambs fattened. Irrigation can be traced back to the experience and skills of immigrants who came to Australia in search of gold, and on the land irrigated —largely in the Murray-Darling Basin—rests the large-scale cultivation of the vine, citrus and temperate fruit, as well as the later-developed production of rice. The tropical rainy climate of the Queensland coast was used, with the aid of indentured Melanesian and other Pacific island labour after 1870, to establish the cane-sugar industry. After the federation of the Australian states into the Commonwealth in 1901 and the subsequent repatriation of kanaka labourers, the sugar industry was made permanent only by the use of artificial protection and the introduction of Italian field workers.

The physical resources which Australia possessed, and which the culture of the aborigines enabled them to use, were very restricted. Until after 1788 the whole continent supported no more than 300,000 people. Physically Australia is virtually the same now as it was then. Today, however, the continent supports almost twelve million people at a standard of living and of comfort rarely exceeded in the world. The difference is entirely a cultural one. It is due to the introduction of European skills and technology, to the importation of domesticated plants and animals from many parts of the world, and to the development in Australia of new techniques and practices peculiarly suited to the needs of the land. Australia still has its physical limitations; although with the continued introduction of new techniques resources have had to be repeatedly reassessed. As technology is advanced, resources must be reappraised upwards.

But for all the irrigation and dry-farming skills which have been brought in or developed locally, Australia remains the most arid of all the continents (*Figs 24* and *25*). One-third of it is so lacking in rain that under present conditions no people on earth could make out of it a living which Australians would consider reasonable. Another third has deficient precipitation and, in the light of predictable scientific developments, must, it appears, remain the habitat of a sparse pastoral population. The remaining third has adequate rainfall, but it is the most elevated and broken part of the country. Its soils are often difficult and infertile. On the other hand Australia has mineral and power resources which, in relation to the size of its present population, are more than adequate for the Commonwealth's needs, although still dwarfed by those of other continents. Yet, despite these handicaps, Australia has been developed, in a little over a century and a half, from the expansive domain of a handful of Stone Age aborigines into a modern industrial and agricultural nation of twelve million people whose voice already counts for something in the world. The Commonwealth is today one of the most advanced and important nations on the rim of the Pacific Ocean.

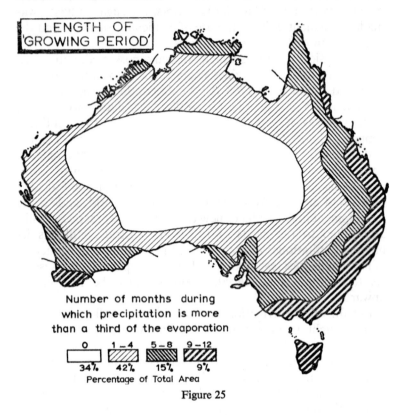

LENGTH OF 'GROWING PERIOD'

Number of months during which precipitation is more than a third of the evaporation

0	1—4	5—8	9—12
34%	42%	15%	9%

Percentage of Total Area

Figure 25

SHEEP AND WOOL

The Australian economy is still dominated by the pastoral industries. Fine wool, its first source of income, is still by far the country's principal product and export commodity. Since 1831, when 2,500,000 lb. of wool were exported, production has expanded until in the 1960s as much as 1,780,000,000 lb. of greasy wool have been produced each year. Meanwhile refrigeration has also made possible the production and export of a whole list of perishable pastoral products. The pastoral industry today, as in the 'squatting age', rests to a large extent upon the natural grazing lands of indigenous grasses and shrubs. They still carry between one-half and one-third of Australia's livestock. Unfortunately the marked seasonal incidence of precipitation makes for a limited seasonal growth of the natural pastures, and stock subsist in many areas almost entirely on dry feed—a natural hay—for part of the year. The tall tropical savanna grasses of the north, and the shorter bunched grasses of the east thus provide unsatisfactory feed, deficient in protein content, in winter and summer respectively. At such times the edible saltbush, bluebush and low-growing acacias provide valuable supplementary grazing.

Figure 27 presents a generalized picture of the distribution of the major categories of pasture in Australia. Grazing and burning of these natural pastures has often reduced the variety of species, and grasses adapted to withstand grazing and fire—like danthonia and the spear grasses—have become more prominent. Over-grazing has often reduced the density of shrubs and grasses, and has thus exposed large areas towards the desert margin to erosion, especially by wind. The fall in sheep numbers from 106 millions in 1891 to less than fifty-three millions twelve years later was due in the main to a succession of droughts, but soil erosion, the depredations of rabbits, and the occupation by prickly pear of over ten million acres of grazing land all contributed to the disastrous decline.

Even with improved contemporary methods of stock and pasture management, with deep wells and irrigation, droughts can be disastrous. The 1965-66 drought—one in an 11 to 14-year cycle—affected especially western New South Wales, and in that state alone more than 2,600,000 sheep perished. The value of total rural production in the Commonwealth as a whole fell by $300 million and this had a depressive effect throughout the Australian economy.

PASTURES AND STOCK

Most stock today is carried on pastures of exotic grasses— permanent pastures in the moister coastal areas of the south-east (including Tasmania); irrigated pastures in the Murray Valley; and rotation pastures in the wheat-growing areas of Victoria and New South Wales, and between the twelve-inch and twenty-inch rainfall lines in Western Australia. As the forest was gradually cleared in the coastal valleys of the Eastern Highlands, ryegrass, cocksfoot and white clover were the pasture species most often sown. On these, sheep and Shorthorn beef cattle were first grazed. Later such pastures in the valley bottoms

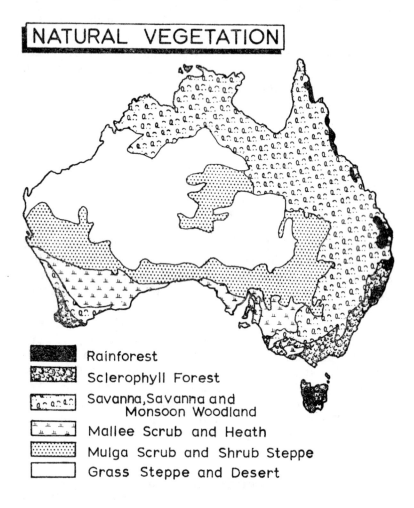

NATURAL VEGETATION

- ◼ Rainforest
- ▨ Sclerophyll Forest
- ⬚ Savanna, Savanna and Monsoon Woodland
- ⬚ Mallee Scrub and Heath
- ⬚ Mulga Scrub and Shrub Steppe
- ☐ Grass Steppe and Desert

Figure 26

and on the hillsides were used to found the dairy industry and to support herds of Jersey, Illawarra Shorthorn and Ayrshire cows. In more recent times, however, the improved pastures

of the cooler, heavy rainfall areas and of adjacent lighter winter
rainfall areas in Victoria and South Australia have been
improved and extended. This has been achieved by increasing

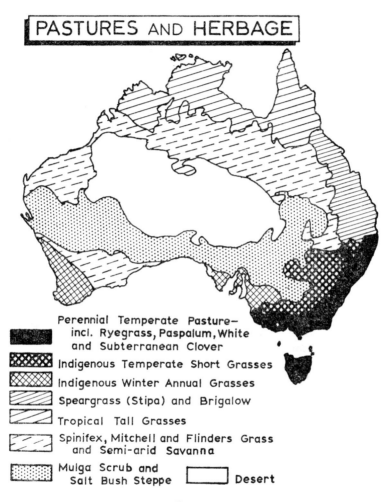

PASTURES AND HERBAGE

Perennial Temperate Pasture—
incl. Ryegrass, Paspalum, White
and Subterranean Clover

Indigenous Temperate Short Grasses

Indigenous Winter Annual Grasses

Speargrass (Stipa) and Brigalow

Tropical Tall Grasses

Spinifex, Mitchell and Flinders Grass
and Semi-arid Savanna

Mulga Scrub and
Salt Bush Steppe   Desert

Figure 27

the use of artificial fertilizers, by correcting the mineral deficiencies of the soils by the addition of trace elements and by
sowing new grasses, especially *Phalaris* and paspalum, and

subterranean clover. This clover is now the most important sown species in Australia. In the coastal areas of Queensland attention has been given to the improvement of dairy pastures by the extended use of Rhodes grass and varieties of paspalum, and by the introduction of Guinea grass and molasses grass to the pastures of the wet tropics. With all these improvements in the herbage available, and with parallel refinement of stock-grazing practices, with closer subdivision of farms, and with the improvement of livestock breeds, sheep and cattle numbers have in recent years reached record numbers. This growth in the number of livestock has taken place despite the reduction in the area available for grazing, both as a result of the retreat of the stockmen from the arid fringe of the steppe land, and of the expansion of the arable crop area in the districts suited to crop production. In 1966 Australia's sheep numbered almost 171 millions despite drought losses; and its beef and dairy herds total more than 18.7 million cattle. Yet the density of livestock in Australia is only one-tenth of that in New Zealand or the United Kingdom.

One well known example of recent large-scale land and pasture development projects in Australia is that financed and undertaken by the Commonwealth's largest life insurance company in the Ninety Mile Desert near the townships of Keith and Bordertown in South Australia, 150 miles southeast of Adelaide and near the Victoria border. In the 1940s officers of the Commonwealth Scientific and Industrial Research Organization had demonstrated that this so-called 'desert' area had remained sterile and unproductive, despite its 17-22 inches of precipitation, because of copper and zinc micro-nutrient (trace element) deficiencies of its leached, mildly podsolized soils.

In 1949 the insurance company secured leases from the two state governments of 750,000 acres of undeveloped rolling land clothed in mallee (a eucalypt) and broombush (*Melaleuca* spp.). It was largely unsurveyed and roadless and fenceless. Operating from three base camps, linked by radio-telephones, it was decided to attempt the development of 30,000 acres a year. Recruiting labour and building accommodation came first. Then the scrub was 'knocked over' using ships' anchor chain hauled by 140 h.p. caterpillar tractors. The dried-out scrub was then burned by drawing a lighted, oil-fuelled wick behind a Landrover. The mallee stumps remained and had to be ploughed out to prevent their sprouting. After 'scrub bashing' came seeding and fertilizers. Heavy applications of superphosphate with small amounts of copper and zinc sulphate and a seed mixture including *Phalaris tuberosa* and ryegrass and clovers (subterranean and strawberry) were the basis of successful pasture establishment. The developed land was provided with necessary buildings and fences and then allotted to farm settlers, often to men who had worked on the project.

In ten years more than 150 farms on 300,000 acres had been occupied. On them were 700 miles of fences and 300 watering points, largely sub-artesian wells. By 1960 the new farms, each carrying from 1500 to 2000 ewes and other stock, were producing wool and lambs each with an annual value of more than $2,000,000. The success of the insurance company's project has given impetus to further private land development in the region. As a result, Keith and Bordertown had become thriving country towns and the Ninety Mile Desert was known now more appropriately as Coonalpyn Downs.

THE WOOL CLIP

Wool was the 'cash crop' on which the Australian nation was founded. Since 1850 its place in the economy has declined relative to that of other agricultural products, but since World War II it has again become the 'golden fleece', and its place in the economy has been re-established as a result of the high prices which persisted until the mid-1960s. In the 1950-1951 season Australia's wool clip was worth eighteen times as much as the pre-war clip. Its value was indeed equal to the entire national income from all sources in 1939, and greater than the value of all the gold ever mined in the continent. The importance of the wool production of Australia can be gauged from the fact that it amounts to one-quarter of the world's total output. Australia furnishes half the wool that enters international trade, including two-thirds of the fine merino wools. The total replacement of wool by synthetic fibres would not only be disastrous to the Australian economy, but would result in a considerable modification in the pattern of international exchange of commodities.

The vast majority of Australia's sheep are reared in the broad crescent between the Eyre Peninsula and central Queensland (*Fig. 28*). The sheep crescent is broadest in New South Wales. New South Wales has, indeed, 44 per cent of the Commonwealth's total of 171 million sheep. Victoria has nearly one-fifth, Queensland one-sixth and South Australia a little less than one-tenth. Outside the crescent, Western Australia has about twenty million sheep (12½ per cent) and Tasmania three and a

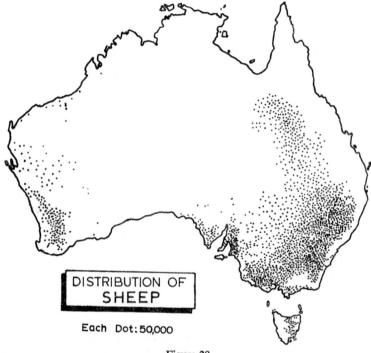

DISTRIBUTION OF
SHEEP

Each Dot: 50,000

Figure 28

half million. There is a close relationship between climate (rainfall especially) and the distribution of flocks, but climate is not the only determinant of distribution. Sheep densities are greatest between the 15-inch and 25-inch isohyets in both the southwest and southeast of the country. Inland, with lower and less reliable rainfall, sheep decrease in number: on the other hand they do not increase in density towards the coastal areas of heavier and more reliable precipitation. Few merinos are found in areas with more than 25 inches, although dense sheep populations of crossbreds and British breeds, reared for lamb and mutton production, are found locally in cooler areas with as much as thirty inches of rain. In the sheep regions temperature varies between wide extremes, but it is noticeable that sheep occur only occasionally in districts with high temperatures *and* heavy rainfall, or in those with high temperatures and a mo-

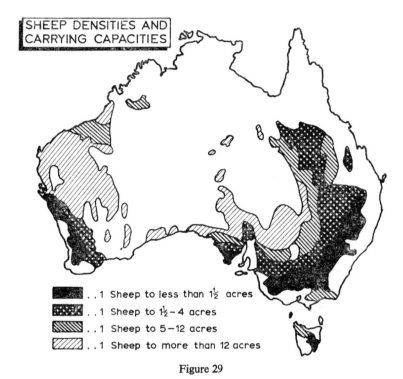

SHEEP DENSITIES AND CARRYING CAPACITIES

■ . . 1 Sheep to less than 1½ acres

▩ . . 1 Sheep to 1½ – 4 acres

▨ . . 1 Sheep to 5 – 12 acres

▨ . . 1 Sheep to more than 12 acres

Figure 29

derate to small rainfall concentrated in the season of high temperatures. The sheep crescent thus terminates in a wide, blunt end in central Queensland, between Cloncurry and Hughenden; and flocks are very rare across the continent north of latitude 20 south.

Between a quarter and one-third of the sheep are reared on wheat farms, and as many again on farm properties of more broken land in the wheat belt on which arable farming is not practised (*Fig. 30*). It is a mistake, then, to think of the Australian sheep industry as occurring only in the arid 'outback' towards the desert margin with a deficient rainfall. In fact such areas make but a relatively small contribution to the output of wool. Even in the wheat belt, however, the sheep-rearing industry remains an example of extensive commercial grazing, dependent largely upon native grasses for herbage, and with carrying capacities which, by New Zealand standards, are low. The lower rainfall areas of the inland today carry fewer sheep than in the past. While the number of sheep in New South Wales remains as great as it has ever been, the number carried on the mulga scrub and saltbush steppe pastures of the Western Division of the state is less than half what it was in the early eighteen-nineties. Over-grazing (especially during periodic droughts), wind erosion and the rabbit pest have led to degeneration of the herbage—a degeneration which some consider to be permanent. If that is so, then the very extensive phase of pastoralism has been but a passing feature in the history of Australian agriculture; and in the future, as in the last thirty years, increases in production and in sheep numbers must be expected only as a result of increasing efficiency, higher carrying capacity and intensification of land use in the better grazing areas and in the districts of more reliable rainfall.

SHEEP-REARING SYSTEMS

Three major sheep-rearing economies may usefully be recognized. First from the point of view of the area it occupies, though not first in terms of sheep numbers or value of production, is the extensive rearing of merino flocks for wool production on the semi-arid natural herbage of the Australian inland (*Figs 30* and *31*). Leasehold properties of as much as 200,000 acres are characteristic. Homesteads are often distant scores of miles by dry earth tracks from one to the other. They are found in the eastern part of the Interior Basin east of the inland state boundaries of Queensland and New South Wales, and again on the western part of the Western Plateau between the widely-scattered mining townships. On these expansive sheep stations, herbage ranges from semi-desert steppe (of occasional bunched porcupine grass) and shrub steppe (of annual grasses growing only after periodic rain with mulga, myall and gidgee scrub, which provide invaluable grazing in drought years) to central Queensland's grassy downs of Mitchell and Flinders grass and brigalow savanna. In inland New South Wales and South Australia there are dusty, treeless, eroded and deteriorated stands of saltbush and bluebush. In Western Australia the outback grazing lands have mainly pastures of mulga scrub and open sand-heaths with stunted eucalypts. Lack of potable water,

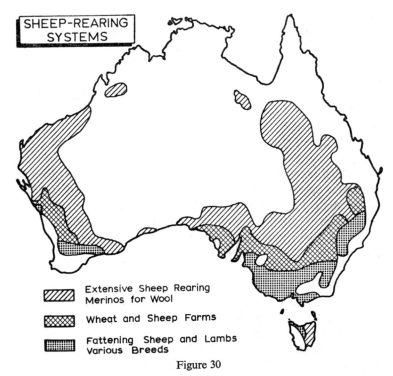

SHEEP-REARING SYSTEMS

Extensive Sheep Rearing Merinos for Wool

Wheat and Sheep Farms

Fattening Sheep and Lambs Various Breeds

Figure 30

saline soils and others which are lateritic and deficient in trace elements, and wide areas of rocky or stony desert, as well as lack of fodder, restrict sheep numbers in Western Australia.

The provision of water is everywhere a major problem. Streams carry water only after rain, and even the wide river-beds of southwestern Queensland rarely have a continuous ribbon of discoloured water in them. But fortunately most of

D

the inland sheep country of the east is in the Great Artesian Basin, and underground sources of water can usually be tapped for stock-watering purposes. Stock-carrying capacity depends upon the quality and availability of herbage in the driest part of the year. Storage of hay or other fodder is rare, cultivation still rarer. In periods of prolonged drought, annual grasses are not available, bunched perennial grasses are grazed to their roots, saltbush is eaten back and mulga and kurrajong cut down for herbage. Lack of transport makes it difficult to bring fodder in from other areas. Some sheep are sent away to moister districts, but millions may perish (as they did as recently as 1965-1966 when drought affected the New South Wales and Queensland inlands) and so contribute to the marked fluctuations in the number of Australia's sheep.

Even on the drier fringe of the wheat belt, where merino sheep are reared for wool under the best of extensive grazing conditions, pastures carry only one sheep to five acres. The better Mitchell grass herbage of Queensland supports one sheep to from six to ten acres. The deteriorated bluebush country in western New South Wales and outside the counties of South Australia carries only one sheep to 20-40 acres, and stocking of the steppelands of Western Australia varies from one sheep to forty acres to one sheep to 500 acres in the spinifex semi-desert of the Hamersley Range inland from Carnarvon and Roebourne.

SHEEP IN THE INLAND

A flock of 5000 sheep is in such country the usual minimum economic unit: many flocks range from 10,000-50,000 sheep. The sheep are medium fine-woolled merinos of the Peppin and South Australian strains evolved in Australia, and are capable of producing a bulky and profitable fleece under conditions of parsimonious feeding. A large proportion of the flock is made up of wethers. Enough ewes are run merely to maintain the size of the flock. On sheep stations of this kind there is a minimum of fencing, and three or four immense 'paddocks' are characteristic (*Fig. 31*). The homestead, squat, spacious and with a wide shady veranda on all sides; an enormous wool and storage shed; accommodation for aboriginal and half-caste musterers and for itinerant shearing gangs; the superstructure of the artesian well; and occasionally an isolated tree or two; all surrounded by miles and miles of rather featureless, often brown, bare and barren-looking country traversed by the dried out and braided channels of ephemeral rivers, in which

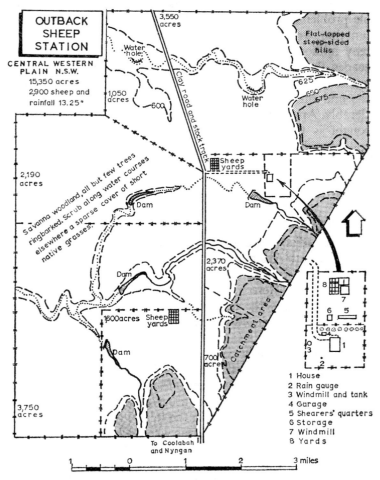

Figure 31 (Sheep yards, dams and buildings not drawn to scale)

sheep are few and far between and difficult to spot—such is the typical outback sheep station. Its isolation has been reduced in recent years by the introduction of radio-telephone facilities, by the flying doctor service and by the graziers' increasing use of small aircraft and homestead landing strips. High prices and good rains compensate for the isolation, but reliance cannot be placed on either.

On such outback stations the deterioration of the herbage, the blowing of soil, erratic rains and prices all present formidable problems. Two others appear to be much less significant than they were: since 1925 the insect *Cactoblastis* has freed many millions of acres of prickly pear, and in the last two decades the introduction of an extraordinarily virulent virus disease (*Myxomatosis cuniculi*) of rabbits carried by stickfast fleas and other agents has reduced their numbers very considerably. Apart from the physical difficulties of which recurrent drought is the chief—in the years between 1943 and 1946 drought reduced the number of sheep by thirty millions— the maintenance of overseas markets for wool, in face of the growing threats of the increasingly varied synthetic fibres, is the most important problem.

SHEEP ON WHEAT FARMS

In and adjacent to the wheat belt in New South Wales, Victoria, South Australia and Western Australia are found from twenty-six per cent to forty-seven per cent of the sheep of the different states. Here in two regions—one in the southeast of the continent and the other in the extreme southwest—sheep and wheat are produced in areas of from 13 inches to 25 inches of rain where low plateaus, undulating downs and broad river valleys were originally covered with savanna woodland, open savanna grassland or a thicket of mallee scrub. Here sheep are raised under a variety of systems of land use, and for a number of different purposes. Practices are everywhere more intensive, and properties smaller, than in the inland (cf. *Figs 31* and 36).

Most of the sheep are on farms where wheat is grown, often as the principal source of income. More than a quarter of all farms growing wheat carry a flock of sheep. On wheat farms two kinds of flocks are evident. On some the flock is one of bought-in cast merino or crossbred ewes which are mated with rams of English breeds to produce lambs for sale either fat or in store condition. Fattening of lambs is often completed on the irrigated pastures of farms along the Murrumbidgee, Murray and Lachlan rivers. Other wheat farms have flocks of wethers and dry ewes mainly from the drier merino country. They produce wool and fat mutton sheep. In both cases the flocks find grazing: (1) on the stubble which, with light rain in December or January, provides abundant fodder; (2) on the weed growth of fallow land between arable crops; (3) in paddocks on the rougher parts of farms where Wimmera ryegrass and clovers have often been sown; (4) on run-down cropland allowed to revert to volunteer pasture species; and (5) occasionally (but not often) on forage crops of oats, peas and, in Western Australia, lupins. A farmer with a small farm of, say, 400 acres, and with most of it in crop, will sell the grazing of his stubble and fallow to a neighbour with a flock. Others with as much as 3000 acres of rather broken land may crop only a tenth of it, and keep a large, permanent flock for lamb and wool production.

Finally, within the wheat belt there is a large number of sheep stations on which wheat is not grown, and only rarely is any supplementary fodder produced. These have merino flocks, often stud flocks, from which sheep are drawn to maintain the quality of those on the great outback stations. Much of the herbage is of indigenous species amongst which danthonia is prominent, but introduced grasses have spread widely into the pastures together with clovers and medicks. Such merino stations are dispersed amongst the wheat farms, and especially in areas where subdivision of properties has not yet enforced more intensive systems of land use.

In all cases the livestock economy is more intensive and the investment and labour supply greater in relation to the area involved than in the drier regions inland. The number of sheep is rising and the size of farms is getting smaller. Increasing areas are being ploughed and sown to Wimmera ryegrass, subterranean clover and other exotic species. Phosphatic fertilizers are being used in increasing quantities, not only with the wheat crop and in sowing down of pastures, but also on the fallows. Irrigation is extending and better use is being made of the already available water supplies for irrigation and for livestock and domestic consumption. With the use of trace elements, the more sterile soils and the last domains of mallee scrub in Victoria and South Australia are coming into production. The carrying capacity of the wheat belt ranges from one sheep to four acres up to one sheep to less than one acre; it is rising and can still be lifted very considerably. It is to this area rather than to the sparsely-occupied, drier pasturelands that Australia must look for an expansion in the output of its grazing industries.

SHEEP FOR MUTTON AND LAMB

The third general category of sheep farming in Australia is the production of meat—lamb and mutton. The fattening farms are found in coastal and semi-coastal districts of the southeast, between western Victoria and Brisbane, including Tasmania (*Fig. 30*). Here, with thirty inches of rain and more, permanent pastures of introduced grasses can be maintained. Close to markets and freezing works, in areas of reliable rains and good communications, these intensive grassland farms use Southdown and other English rams on merino and crossbred ewes, whose teeth are no longer capable of maintaining them on the hard and scanty grazing of the big stations, to produce a quick-maturing and shapely lamb. On some farms wethers from the inland are topped off for market, and although on this fattening country the object is to use the feed of improved pastures, supplementary arable crops are sometimes grown to provide extra feed in periods of deficient rain. The fodder crops vary from place to place: oats, rape and turnips in Victoria and Tasmania; barley, sudan grass, lucerne and millets further north. In these coastal flats and adjacent valleys sheep are often associated with either beef or dairy cattle.

After a century and a half Australia's sheep and wool industry is large-scale, highly-organized and efficient, particularly in its small use of manpower. On the outback stations one permanent employee cares for 3000 sheep. The itinerant shearing gangs move through the country with the season and, using machines, shear each year more than 100,000,000 sheep at very low cost, despite the high wages they are paid. Breeds ideally adapted to the variety of dry climates and unusual pasturage have been evolved. The average weight of fleeces has risen from 3½ lb. to over 10½ lb. The average fleece weight of South Australia's 16,300,000 sheep shorn in 1963-1964 was 13 lb. Some flocks average as much as 18 lb., and with the higher level of nutrition that improved pastures can provide, a Commonwealth-wide average fleece of 12-15 lb. is not out of the question.

After the enormous annual task of shearing is over, 5,300,000 bales of wool, each weighing more than 300 lb., flow by train or lorry hundreds of miles over the dusty, brown plains towards the ports where the wool sales are held. A million bales are sold each year at the Sydney sales alone. Then almost ninety per cent of the clip has to be shipped to foreign buyers. Wool is indeed woven firmly into the economic and social fabric of Australia. No wonder all daily papers carry in great detail reports of the points (hundredths of an inch) of rain that have fallen in all districts in the previous twenty-four hours, and long accounts of the prices of wool at auction sales, not only at the markets held in Australia, but also in London and in other wool-producing countries, like New Zealand, South Africa, Argentina and the United States.

CATTLE

Cattle are second in importance only to sheep. Excluding years of phenomenal prices, wool normally represents more than thirty per cent of the total value of farm and station production, meat (mostly beef, but some of it lamb and mutton) another ten per cent, and dairy produce (all but a small fraction of it now consumed within Australia) thirteen per cent. Together, all livestock products account for almost two-thirds of the gross value of agricultural production.

Australia's first cattle played no small part in the development of the infant colonies. Cattle pioneered the damp coastal clearings, and provided the penal settlement and free settlers with milk, butter, cheese and a change of meat. Above all they dragged the timber for building; they hauled the squatters' supplies and chattels inland over virgin bush tracks, and his wool back to the ports. Not until after 1880 and the advent of refrigeration did cattle provide marketable export produce. Then they were used to pioneer the tropical savanna lands and to establish an extensive grazing economy on the flush of tall summer growth in those hot northern grasslands, too remote and isolated for sheep, which could not walk out to the coast or travel far enough on the stations to find water and forage in the winter half-year of drought. Dairying came later and more slowly.

BEEF CATTLE

There are today over 18,777,000 cattle in Australia, 4,940,000 of them dairy cattle of all ages. Of the beef cattle half are in Queensland, and a fifth in New South Wales. Northern Territory

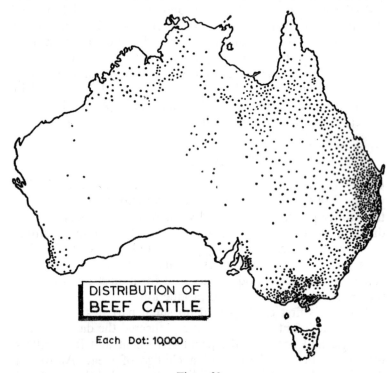

DISTRIBUTION OF
BEEF CATTLE

Each Dot: 10,000

Figure 32

has a tenth and Victoria and Western Australia each have about seven per cent (*Fig. 32*). Some sixty per cent of the beef cattle are found in the tropical savanna inland of the north —from the Ord and Fitzroy valleys about the Kimberleys to northern Queensland—and, more densely, in eastern Queensland in savanna woodland country of bunched speargrass and brigalow. These represent the largest single herd of cattle of

European origin within the tropics, and they produce beef for domestic markets in the southeast as well as all Australia's dwindling exportable surplus. They are mixed-bred cattle with Shorthorn, Hereford, Aberdeen-Angus and Devon blood in that order of frequency. Big, strong, muscular cattle of a roving type, slow to fatten, are the rule. The herds are not of tremendous size; there are only 800 herds of more than 1000 head. But the stations are often over a million acres in extent, and may be as big as Belgium or New Zealand's Canterbury Plains. They are frequently operated by companies.

The fodder on these enormous stations has a short season of growth. The effective growing season—the period during which evaporation is not more than three times the precipitation—rapidly decreases from five months to less than two months as you go inland from the northern coast (*Fig. 25*). In the long dry season the tall tropical savanna grasses die, and the Mitchell and speargrasses of Queensland produce much less feed. The pasture grasses thus vary in both quantity and nutritive value not only each year with the season, but also from year to year with the variable rains. Cattle rapidly lose condition during the 'dry', and there is little good-quality country on the coast or elsewhere to which they can be trekked. Most of the cattle also lose condition on their long trip to the meat works on the coast, for usually they have to be trucked or driven more than 250 miles. Some are 'overlanded' from Northern Territory to the Darling Downs or to South Australia. As it is, the meat works are able to operate for only a few months, so that the building of more works is out of the question until the carrying capacity of the tropical pastures is raised.

On the stations fences are few and far between. The cattle are little-cared-for between annual musters. The headquarters of neighbouring properties may be hundreds of miles apart. With the bombing of Darwin during the war and the threat of Japanese invasion many cattle were driven overland to the east coast. But the war brought some new roads to the tropical north, and since then efforts have been made to furnish the overland stock routes with new wells. More cattle can now be trucked to the works. But buffalo fly and the cattle tick—the former spreading south in Queensland—are serious pests.

In addition to the isolated cattle stations, lost in the expanse of northern monsoonal savanna, tropical Australia also has its remote mining camps, occasional coastal settlements near the meat works, and small ports at which pearl shell, beche-de-mer and trochus shell are landed. But, in all, the territory furnishes a livelihood for only a minute fraction of the country's population. In this enormous area north of the tropic both the cattle population and the human population have remained stationary for over forty years, excepting only in the more favoured parts of Queensland and at Darwin. This vast tropical territory presents the Australian Commonwealth with one of its greatest problems.

It is a problem land of limited promise but not without possibilities. There is the possibility of providing some irrigation facilities, particularly on the Ord River, of developing in a limited way the production of tropical crops, of improving savanna grazing land, especially by introducing new grasses and legumes, and there are undoubtedly potentially valuable minerals still to be discovered. The postwar development of the Rum Jungle uranium deposits south of Darwin is an indication of this. The attention which is now being paid to the north by both the Queensland and Commonwealth governments suggests that there may well be greater changes in tropical Australia in the next half century than there have been in the last.

The remaining forty per cent of Australia's beef cattle are reared in the more humid coastal areas of the east and the south. Here beef is produced from store cattle overlanded in stages from the north, from rejects from the dairy industry, and from cattle bred in hilly, forested country in coastal Queensland, New South Wales, Tasmania and Victoria where beef cattle are kept—sometimes on sheep properties—to keep down rough grass and second-growth forest vegetation. They are usually fattened on ill-drained valley flats, where the growth of paspalum, cocksfoot and swamp grasses is too rank for dairy herds, and may sometimes be turned on to arable crops, especially in southern Queensland and northern New South Wales, where maize, sorghums and other fodder crops are available. The chief advantage of these beef-fattening farms, other than their usually sufficient rain and abundant feed, is their nearness to the market for fresh beef provided by Australia's largest cities and industrial and urban population.

DAIRY COWS

About 3,078,000 dairy cows 'dry or in milk' were responsible for almost a seventh of the value of Australian farm production in 1964-1965. Since 1900, when dairying emerged from being a local subsistence activity, its products have figured prominently in the export trade. It expanded rapidly during the depression of the nineteen-thirties which hit the wool and sheep-rearing industries especially hard. Regular monthly cheques for butter fat were then more attractive than much-reduced annual wool

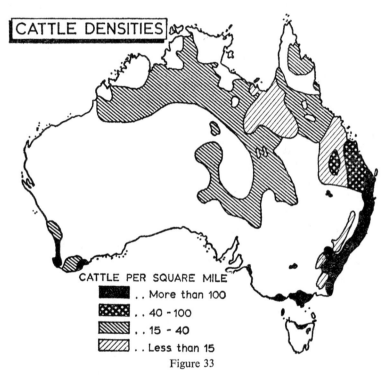

CATTLE DENSITIES

CATTLE PER SQUARE MILE
■ .. More than 100
▨ .. 40 - 100
▨ .. 15 - 40
▨ .. Less than 15

Figure 33

cheques. But during the mid-1950s, with the growth of domestic requirements as a result of immigration, internal population growth and increasing *per capita* consumption, exports have dwindled, and it has been forecast that Australia might one day become an importer of New Zealand dairy products.

Dairying is sharply confined to a coastal fringe of the continent (*Fig. 33*). With four exceptions, it is concentrated in coastal valleys. The exceptions are the small inland irrigated pockets in Western Australia, the irrigated permanent pastures in the Murray Valley, the mixed-farming areas on the Darling Downs in Queensland (where one-third of the state's dairy cows are found), and the pioneer dairying in a damp forested tropical environment on the Atherton Tableland. Queensland, New South Wales and Victoria have each between one-quarter and one-third of the country's dairy cows. Victoria, however, with fewer cows in milk than the other two states, has a considerably higher production per cow—though it is considerably less than the New Zealand average—and is thus easily Australia's foremost producer of dairy products. South Australia, Western Australia and Tasmania have each about one-twentieth of the dairy cow population.

The cows are of various breeds, most of the herds being of crossbred grade cows. Jerseys, Illawarra Shorthorns, Ayrshires, Red Polls, Friesians and Guernseys are all frequent, but the first two breeds are favoured in northern New South Wales and Queensland because there, with mean maximum temperatures over 70° F. throughout the year, they maintain their production better than other breeds. The herds are reared under two different systems. Those dairy farms adjacent to the cities, or linked with urban markets by fast road transport, produce whole milk for immediate domestic consumption. On the Darling Downs and in coastal Queensland and northern New South Wales, the cattle are largely stall fed with supplementary rations of maize, millets, sudan grass, sorghums and oats; and in Western Australia, South Australia and Victoria they are fed on hay, bran and crushed wheat during the summer dry season. The second system of dairying is more like that practised in New Zealand, and cattle under it are almost wholly grass fed, either on irrigated permanent pastures or on much-improved pastures of exotic grasses on former forest land. In these cases whole milk is sold mainly for manufacturing purposes, or is separated on the farm, and the cream sold to the butter factory.

It is significant that of all the major livestock industries only dairying is not primarily dependent upon native pastures; but, even so, auxiliary fodder crops are often necessary, especially during short periods of deficient rainfall, and there is rarely a surplus of grass for hay and silage. In the 1800-miles long but narrow coastal extent of the dairy lands between Cairns and Hobart dairy-farm economy varies very much more widely than it does in New Zealand. On the Atherton Plateau it is a specialized pioneering activity practised in high humidity and frequent heavy rain amongst the stumps of a tropical forest recently cleared. On the Darling Downs dairy cows share the farm with sheep or beef cattle, and wheat, sorghums and lucerne are amongst the variety of cash and fodder crops grown on the same property. On the river and coastal flats of northern New South Wales pastures of paspalum and Rhodes grass are found alongside sugar cane, and income is derived from both cane and butterfat. In Victoria, Gippsland is Australia's single most important dairying region, and improved pastures of top-dressed ryegrass and white clover, not unlike those of the Waikato, are characteristic. Whole milk for Melbourne's large urban market is the principal product. On the Loddon, Goulburn, Mitta Mitta and Murray rivers cheap irrigation water is utilized on permanent pastures of ryegrass, *Phalaris*, and white clover. Here paddocks are small, carrying capacity is up to New Zealand standards, and intensive systems of rotational grazing result in high per-cow production. Grass growth in Australia is seasonal mainly because of the seasonal occurrence of rain rather than because of low winter temperatures. When irrigation facilities make water available all the year round grass growth can be controlled and maintained all year, so that neither supplementary arable crops nor hay and silage are essential, although on the Murray hay may be cured. At this distance from the larger urban markets—in the irrigated areas of northern Victoria and the adjacent parts of New South Wales—there are small semi-co-operative factories which take whole milk for processing into cheese, casein or powdered milk.

ARABLE FARMING

A third of Australia—the 'dead heart'—is unsuited to commercial agriculture of any kind. Even in the rest of Australia rainfall is rarely adequate or reliable, and the country is much more often better suited to livestock rearing than to cropping. Less than a quarter of the continent has a growing season of five months or more, during which evaporation is not more than three times precipitation (*Fig. 25*). But broken surface, high elevations, problem soils and other edaphic difficulties reduce the cultivable part of this to one-third, much of which is already the scene of profitable intensive livestock practices, including dairying and lamb-fattening. Not more than 40,000,000 acres—only two per cent of the continental area—is available in Australia under present technological and economic conditions for regular cultivation and cropping. Over three-quarters of this area was in crops (32 million acres) in 1963-1964 and of this 16.5 million acres was in wheat. The acreage of crops reached a peak in 1930-1931 of 25.2 million acres and wheat alone occupied 17 million acres. In 1956-1957 the crop acreage fell to less than 20 million acres but it has climbed steeply to a record figure in the last decade. With revived world demand and higher prices the wheat acreage has doubled in eight years. Australia has been disposing of large quantities of wheat in China and the U.S.S.R. The wheat crop normally represents from a quarter to a third of the value of all crops. Next in acreage come hay and green forage crops, oats, barley, sugar cane, orchards and vineyards, sorghums, maize, vegetables and potatoes.

In value, fruit, including citrus and grapes (15 per cent), sugar cane (a heavily subsidized crop—12 per cent), and vegetables of all kinds (8 per cent) are together less important than wheat. The 1963-1964 wheat crop was worth $467 million—38 per cent of the gross value of all arable crops. But livestock products are worth twice as much as all crops together.

Wheat

Wheat and winter cereals (oats and barley) are the most important agricultural crops. Together they occupy two-thirds of the cultivated area. They are associated in the same areas and the one economy. The Australian wheat belt (*Fig. 34*) is in three parts, all of them between the 10-inch and 25-inch isohyets; or, more accurately, between the winter isohyets of 7.5 and 20 inches, for the wheat belt is the scene of winter cropping and summer fallowing. One of the three parts is in Western Australia, another is in South Australia and the third is in Victoria-New South Wales. The Western Australian wheat area is a crescent with light but mixed soils 200 miles inland, about an arc stretching between Geraldton and Hopetoun. It has about thirty per cent of the country's wheat acreage. The South Australian sector extends east and west of Spencer Gulf. Most of the winter grains are grown in the Eyre Peninsula, Yorke Peninsula, and north and east of Adelaide as far as the lower Murray. Here there is a little less than one-fifth of the wheat acreage and one-third of the other winter cereals. The third and principal portion of wheat belt lies in the mallee, the Wimmera, and between Bendigo and Albury in Victoria (*Fig. 35*), and in the Riverina and on the western slopes of the Eastern

Figure 34

Highlands east and west of a line joining Leeton, Parkes, Dubbo and the Liverpool Plains in New South Wales. Here is found a half of the Commonwealth's total *acreage* of wheat and one-third of the acreage of oats and barley. Because of better conditions of both soil and climate, and the higher yields, a still larger proportion of total *production* comes from this south-eastern corner of the continent.

At first the production of wheat near Sydney Cove and at Parramatta was for the infant settlement a matter of food or famine, almost of life or death. The establishment of the industry in its present regions of production largely followed the laying down of roads and railways and the growth of the market created by the larger population after 1850, but its development into a great export industry owes a great deal to mechanization and to the breeding of wheats adapted to low and erratic rainfall. Wheat growing in Australia is today a highly specialized activity and comes near to being monocultural. It is characterized above all by its extensive nature, its low production per acre and its high production per man. It is made possible, despite climatic hazards, by the availability of extensive areas of relatively cheap land of easy configuration, by the maximum use of machinery, by planting suitable varieties of wheat and by the bulk handling of grain. Other essential features of the system include the conservation of soil moisture and control of weeds by the cultivation of fallow, shallow ploughing, header harvesting, and the combination in one operation of light cultivation, weed killing, topdressing and drilling on fallow.

Throughout the wheat belt sowing takes place in late autumn to obtain maximum advantage from the winter rain which, although in places very light, is fairly reliable. It is the erratic spring rains which determine the variable yield. The national average yield over a period of years in the 1930s was no more than twelve bushels to the acre, but average yields of five bushels were not unknown. Even in districts where better than average yields are usually harvested the crop was sometimes no heavier than the seeding. In the ten harvests between 1936 and 1945 the whole of the Victorian mallee had average yields over twelve bushels on four occasions (with a maximum of 14.9) and less than five bushels on three occasions (with a minimum of 0.9). But yields are rising with better seed and cultivation and intensification of arable farming. The national average yield of wheat in the 1963-1964 season was 19.9 bushels per acre—ranging from 11.3 bushels in West Australia to 24.7 bushels in New South Wales. In New Zealand the average yield in recent years has been at most fifty bushels, and annual yields have departed no more than a bushel or two from the average. It is the low costs of production obtained by the maximum use of machines and the least possible use of labour rather than

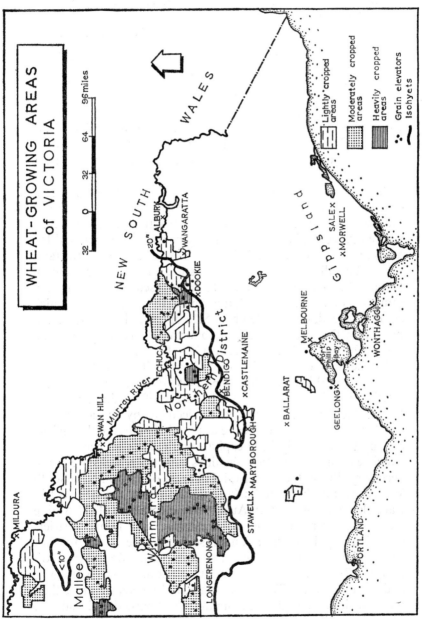

Figure 35

the high yields per acre that make production possible under Australian conditions.

The summer drought which, except in New South Wales, follows the harvesting, restricts the crops that can be used in rotation. Wheat is normally followed by either oats (for hay or green fodder for sheep), or barley (for grain for malting), or peas (a recently-introduced rotation crop), or (in Western Australia) lupins. After the second crop the paddock is left to a volunteer pasture of inferior grasses, clover and medicks which is grazed regularly by a bought-in flock of merino ewes or wethers until cultivation is undertaken in preparation for the subsequent crop of wheat.

A minimum economic holding, even in the better wheat country of the Wimmera, the Riverina or the 'western slope' of New South Wales, is not less than 1000 acres. Each year somewhere between 300 and 400 acres may be sown to wheat, and 150 acres to other crops, especially oats. Most of the rest of the farm would lie fallow, its volunteer pasture grazed by a mob of perhaps 200 cast merino ewes to be crossed with a longwool ram to produce lambs for fattening on the young crop, which is often grazed, or on oaten hay. Sale of grain, however, would, providing the season was not abnormally droughty, account for not less than eighty per cent of the farm income.

In the nineteen-twenties the wheat belt expanded inland beyond the 10-inch rainfall line. This was encouraged by the relatively high prices, by the subdivision of grazing properties to provide farms for returned servicemen, by the absence in the drier areas of trees to clear except only in parts of the mallee, and by the relatively little capital required for an economy in which elaborate irrigation facilities and deep wells were not necessary. But in the lighter rainfall areas of central New South Wales and South Australia (and on the light soils, deficient in trace elements, of Western Australia), the practice of cultivating fallow in larger proportions than in the more humid districts caused a rapid deterioration of soil structure under the hot sun, and the powdered light red soils were often carried off by wind. The dust was carried out to the southeastern seaboard, and even across the Tasman to Auckland where, on more than one occasion, it has alighted on motor cars parked in the streets. Moreover, with rainfall as low as seven inches in the growing

season, and most unreliable in such areas as the northern part
of the Eyre Peninsula and the South Australian and northern

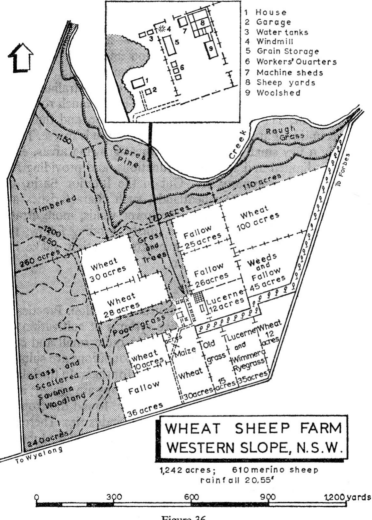

1 House
2 Garage
3 Water tanks
4 Windmill
5 Grain Storage
6 Workers' Quarters
7 Machine sheds
8 Sheep yards
9 Woolshed

WHEAT SHEEP FARM
WESTERN SLOPE, N.S.W.

1,242 acres; 610 merino sheep
rainfall 20.55'

Figure 36
(Compare with Figure 31, but notice the big difference in scale)

Murray mallee, payable crops were harvested not more than one
year in three. And in the nineteen-thirties prices slumped and

stocks accumulated. Since then the inland fringe of the wheat belt has contracted. The two-year wheat-fallow—wheat-fallow rotation has largely been superseded by a three-year rotation, often including a legume. Pastures are being sown, and, with a rise in the proportion of farm income derived from livestock, the economy is becoming less specialized—and less vulnerable (*Fig. 36*). Wherever possible, irrigation and stock water are being provided to make such diversification possible.

Acreage and yields per acre of wheat on Australian farms have both risen in recent years but there is still much room for improvement. The land is often little cared-for, and the landscape is untidy. Farms are large, and population is sparse. There are only a few small towns in the wheat-growing areas, each with very limited and specialized functions, and providing few amenities for community life. Out in the Interior Basin, on the drier margin of the wheatlands, such characteristics are more marked; and in addition the lower yields, more erratic rains, the larger acreages of bare, dusty, eroding fallow, the primitive water supplies and the greater isolation, make life harder and living standards lower.

OTHER CROPS

Australia's other crops are an unusual collection. Practically all are crops grown under intensive systems of cultivation (in contrast with the winter cereals), and in quite small and concentrated areas where rather specialized conditions are suitable for the crops, or have been made suitable for them. In the inland irrigated areas, rice, vine and citrus fruit crops are grown; and, on the Queensland coast of heavy rain, are found the tropical sugar cane, cotton, banana and pineapple industries. There are also peanut, maize, sorghum, soft fruit, sweet potato, tobacco and other unusual crops such as only the range of temperatures found on the 2000 mile-long humid east coast of the continent could make possible. In the United States Tasmania's apples, hops and potatoes find their counterpart in Maine or Washington; South Australia and Victoria, with their grapes, citrus, peach and apricot crops, find their counterpart in California; and Queensland, with its sugar cane, pineapples, bananas and sweet potatoes, has its counterpart in Florida and central America.

These intensively-cultivated crops, occupying together but a modest acreage, yet economically important both to the Australian home market and to foreign markets, may perhaps best be studied by examining the systems of cultivation and the agricultural landscapes of three sharply-contrasted regions: the moist, mild and somewhat isolated island of Tasmania; the interior, artificially-watered ribbon of intensively-cultivated land in the Murray Basin, and the discontinuous pockets of formerly-forested valley lands along the subtropical and tropical coast of northern New South Wales and Queensland.

INTENSIVE MIXED FARMING IN TASMANIA

Apples occupy almost a third of the area devoted to orchards in Australia. The acreage in apples in 1964 had reached 93,000. Of this total Tasmania, with a mere one per cent of the Commonwealth's total area, had 18,000 acres, or almost a fifth. It has a still larger proportion of the apple trees and of apple production, and furnishes half the apples exported. Only Victoria and New South Wales have a larger area of pear orchards. Soft fruit and berry fruit (including gooseberries, strawberries, raspberries, black and red currants, etc.) prefer even lower temperatures than the deciduous pip fruits, and are principally grown in Tasmania, which supplies almost eighty per cent of the crop by weight. The small island of Tasmania also has a quarter (18,000 acres) of the total area of potatoes. It supplies potatoes not only to the urban markets in Sydney and Brisbane, but also at times to the cities in New Zealand and to the port towns in the island territories of the southwest Pacific. In the production of fruit and vegetables requiring relatively low temperatures and reliable precipitation Tasmania is rivalled only by the coastal lowland areas of Victoria east and west of Melbourne, while only Western Australia competes with Tasmania in providing a considerable surplus of apples for the foreign export trade.

In proportion to its area, Tasmania is the most hilly and broken part of the Commonwealth. It is, however, the part of the country which has the most abundant and reliable rainfall. Physically, it is in many ways more reminiscent of New Zealand than of the brown, sub-humid, expansive and monotonous landscape of so much of the Australian continental mainland. High elevation, heavy rains, steep slopes and fast-flowing rivers provide water power, and much of this has already been harnessed to make electricity. But along the north coast and in the lower valleys of the Tamar and the Huon there are easier slopes, good cultivable soils and a lower, though still dependable, rainfall. Tasmania is unique in Australia in that agriculture seeks out the *drier* areas.

Tasmania displays a rich variety of physical landscape. It has glacial scenery, mountains, plains, cascading rivers (harnessed for electric power), lakes, tarns, forest, moorland, as well as smiling lowlands. The lowlands, though, are limited in extent. The central plateau and western ranges are rugged, broken, wet and forested, and the west coast is elevated, cliffed, exposed and unsettled. But from Smithton in the northwest, small basalt and alluvial plains are found on the coast east to the Tamar rift valley lowland—the largest plain and leading agricultural and pastoral district in the state. The east coast of the island is broken and population sparse. It is drier and used as sheep country.

Tasmania is relatively more important for its forest wealth, minerals, water power and fisheries than for its agriculture or livestock production. Much forest has been ruthlessly cleared, and the land sometimes abandoned to blackberry and rabbits. Here and there *Pinus radiata* has been planted on the hills and on sand dunes. Today a third of the island is forested. Eucalypts are the basis of the timber industry—stringy bark, swamp gums and gum-topped stringy bark. Much of the remaining forest is in beech trees (*Nothofagus*), known locally as myrtles, their timber being used sometimes for plywood and furniture. With timber and water power Tasmania has developed pulp and paper mills. The large mill at Boyer, northwest from Hobart, makes hardwood pulp from the local swamp gum and uses a mixture of imported New Zealand softwood pulp in its newsprint mill. At Burnie, hardboard and fine writing paper is manufactured—the hardboard from myrtle.

Among minerals, copper at Mount Lyall and zinc at Rosebery are today most important. The copper goes largely by road to a factory in Hobart for processing and the zinc by rail to an electrolytic plant at Risdon (near Hobart). Tasmania also has its ghost towns, former mining settlements lost in the mist and regrowth forest of the broken hilly western part of the state. It still produces a variety of other nonferrous metals, but no iron ore or coking coal.

It is in the Central Plateau that most water power has been harnessed. This interior 'lake district' was formerly of economic

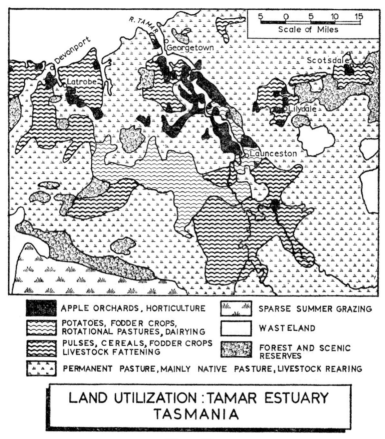

LAND UTILIZATION : TAMAR ESTUARY TASMANIA

Figure 37.

significance only for the summer grazing it provided for sheep from the Midlands and the Derwent valley. In recent decades the construction work—dams, tunnels and power stations and workers' camps—have brought activity to the area and power to the farms, factories, mines and sawmills throughout the state. Tasmania has an installed capacity of 756,000 kW (1964) and approved developments will lift this to 1,240,000 kW by 1974 (almost half the ultimate capacity of the Snowy Mountains project).

Although once the granary of the Australian colonies, Tasmania is today not markedly significant in the agricultural economy of the Commonwealth. Its agriculture, however, is diverse and its rural economies often in sharp geographic contrast to those of the other states.

Along the north coast, between Wynyard and the estuary of the Tamar (*Fig. 37*), and in the lower valleys tributary to Storm Bay in the southeast, a mixed agriculture is practised. In the north, potatoes, pulses (especially peas for canning), fodder crops and cereals are grown on the same holdings under a mixed crop-livestock economy not unlike that of New Zealand's Canterbury Plains. Both dairy and beef cattle, as well as sheep may be reared on such medium-sized mixed farms. In the vicinity of Hobart permanent pastures play a greater role, and on the low hilly country of the Midlands between Launceston and Hobart most of Tasmania's sheep are grazed on improved hill and valley pastureland. They produce some of Australia's best wool.

Sheep rearing itself illustrates the regional and local diversity of Tasmanian agriculture. The greater part of all farms, except only specialized fruit orchards and vegetable gardens, is in pasture. Improved pastures are both permanent and temporary. The permanent pastures are not unlike New Zealand's with swards of ryegrass and white clover except in the drier low and rolling hills of the Midlands and southeast where *Phalaris* and subterranean clover take over. Italian and short rotation ryegrasses and red clover feature in the temporary pastures. Elsewhere, however, there are native grasslands—dry hills and mountain sides of wallaby, kangaroo, spear and tussock grasses.

On this range of pasture types many different breeds of sheep are reared—more than a million Polewarths, 700,000 crossbreds, half a million Corriedales, and smaller numbers of Merinos, Merino Comebacks and many English breeds, including Romneys, Southdowns and Lincolns. The Polewarths and Merinos do best on the sparse hill grazings of the Central

Plateau and northeast, Corriedales on the rotational pastures of the Midlands, and English breeds on the lush permanent pastures of the damper northern coastlands. From this wide range of sheep breeds and still wider range of pastures and rearing economies come wool, which varies from coarse to fine, and stud rams and ewes from many purebred flocks for which Tasmania is famous throughout Australia.

One-fifth of the cropland is given over to fruit-growing and horticulture, and it produces a half of the net value of agricultural production. The orchards and vegetable crops are on small holdings located in the lower Tamar and Mersey valleys, and in the valleys of the hill country to the east of it (Lilydale and Scottsdale), on the coasts of the Huon estuary and of the D'Entrecasteaux Channel, and in the Derwent Valley. Apples are of outstanding importance. Pears, plums and apricots are also grown. Small fruit and especially raspberries, loganberries, gooseberries, currants and strawberries do remarkably well on hilly land in forest clearings in the south bordering the Huon and Derwent valleys and are the basis of Hobart's jam and canning industries. Hops are grown in the Derwent Valley.

INTENSIVE IRRIGATION FARMING IN THE MURRAY VALLEY

It is understandable that in a continent as short of rain as is Australia, efforts should have been made by local, State and Commonwealth authorities to collect, store and distribute water artificially. But, as was pointed out earlier, the highly mineralized underground water in the artesian basins is of restricted value, and surface supplies are scarce and unreliable. The irrigated area in the United States is thus sixteen times as large as that in Australia; in India it is nearly sixty times as extensive. Yet the 2,658,000 acres in the Commonwealth that are irrigated constitute almost nine per cent of the cultivated land, and since the irrigated cropland is very much more productive than the bulk of the non-irrigated and largely extensively-cultivated land, irrigation contributes notably to the Australian economy. Accordingly irrigation facilities and reservoir storage capacities are being extended.

Probably ninety per cent of the precipitation which occurs in Australia is lost by evaporation and transpiration. In other countries as much as sixty per cent of the precipitation is re-

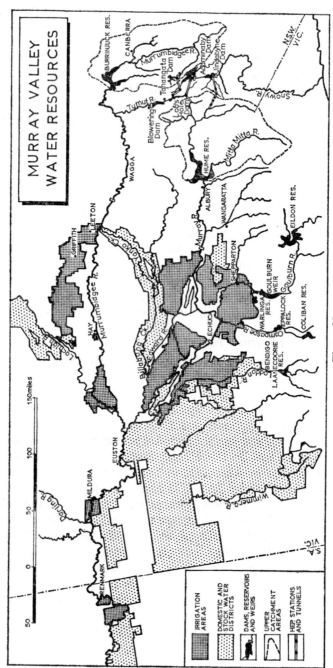

Figure 38

turned to the sea by rivers. In New Zealand the proportion could be as high as three quarters. The Murray is Australia's largest river system. The annual flow of the Murray and its tributaries, however, is relatively small. It is only one-seventh of that of the Nile, one-ninth that of the Indus, and one-fourteenth that of the Ganges or the Columbia. And the volume of its flow is very erratic. Storage reservoirs are essential, but even so the irrigated area is small in relation to the volume of storage. Yet the Murray and its tributaries provide the water for nine out of every ten acres irrigated in Australia. The main storage installations are the Hume Reservoir and Lake Victoria (serving South Australia) on the Murray itself; the Burrinjuck Dam on the Murrumbidgee; the Waranga Reservoir and the Eildon Weir on the Goulburn; the Wyangala Dam on the Lachlan; and several smaller storages on the Wimmera, Loddon and Campaspe (see *Fig. 38*).

A new and large storage dam is to be constructed at Chowilla in South Australia, six miles below the state border. It will be a 41 ft. high earth bank extending more than three miles across the flood plain; and the artificial lake will reach back 120 miles into Victoria and New South Wales. The dam will have a capacity of five million acre feet—twice that of the Hume reservoir recently enlarged to take extra water diverted from the Snowy River. (An 'acre foot' is the volume of water necessary to cover one acre to a depth of twelve inches, or 272,250 gallons.)

In the riverine plains area of the Murray Basin, above the confluence of the Murrumbidgee and Murray, water is diverted into distribution channels and on to the farmland by weirs and barrages. It is distributed widely and to a considerable distance from the river through gravity flow along earthen channels. But in the Wimmera mallee lowland section of the Murray Basin— above and below Mildura—water is lifted from the Murray by pumping. The supply is restricted and costly and the water is distributed over a small concentrated area of supply in concrete channels. Here irrigation districts are compact and close to the river. In the mallee other water, mainly from the south-flowing and erratic Wimmera River, is stored and used for domestic and livestock supply. Some 6500 miles of channels serve a pastoral area of 10,000 square miles through stock water races; and the entire domestic water supply for a score of small urban service centres comes from the same scheme (*Fig. 38*).

With the progress of the Snowy Mountains hydro-electric scheme additional water is being made available for irrigation in the Murray Basin. By dams and tunnels water from the Eucumbene River has already been diverted into the Upper Tumut and so to the Murrumbidgee; and water from the Snowy River is to be tunnelled under the Great Dividing Range to the Swampy Plain River, a tributary of the Murray. In all, almost two million acre feet of additional water will be diverted to the Murray catchment, sufficient to irrigate an extra 600,000 acres. Of the land at present irrigated in the Murray Basin, Victoria has 1,137,000 acres, New South Wales 1,060,000 acres and South Australia 118,000 acres. In a decade these figures have almost doubled.

Most of the irrigated area—but not necessarily most of the irrigation water—is used to produce annual and permanent pastures, lucerne and green fodder crops, either for fattening sheep and lambs or for maintaining dairy herds at high levels of productivity. Some is also used to raise the yields of cereals. But water is used most generously on orchards of peaches, apricots and citrus fruit, on rice crops, on fields of vegetables and in vineyards. In the Murray Valley there are 210,000 irrigated acres devoted to vines, fruit trees and vegetables—six times the area in orchards and market gardens in the whole of New Zealand. More than half this total is in Victoria. In New South Wales an additional 60,000 acres of irrigated land are used for rice cultivation. Similar intensively-cultivated crops (other than rice) are also grown in coastal areas in the southeast, in South Australia (near Adelaide and in the Barossa valley), and in smaller irrigated areas in West Australia, especially in the Swan valley and between Pinjarra and Collie. And, as is the case in other countries, the suburban and rural fringes of the large centres of urban population have their concentric rings of market-gardening, vegetable and fruit production. Sydney has its market gardens in the Botany, Mascot, Cook's River and Mona Vale areas, with more distant sources of supply of fruit and vegetables along the Nepean and Hawkesbury rivers.

THE MURRUMBIDGEE IRRIGATION AREA

Amongst the most distinctive and productive irrigated areas in the Murray Basin are those on the Murrumbidgee between Griffith and Leeton, and the Renmark, Pyap Bend, Berri and Waikerie irrigation settlements on the lower Murray, across the South Australian border (*Fig. 38*). Above Hay the Murrumbidgee flows across the eastern part of the Interior Basins at a height of about 500 feet, in an area which was formerly well-wooded savanna. Its fertile brown soils are fairly evenly-distributed, but light rainfall of not more than twenty inches made possible, after clearing, the successful cultivation of wheat and a wheat-sheep economy which, though extensive, was not frequently devastated by disastrous droughts. But with the distribution of irrigation water during and after World War I, and the subdivision of large properties for the settlement of returned soldiers, intensive, high per-acre production became possible.

Today a considerable proportion of the country's vines, stone fruit (including peaches, apricots and plums), citrus fruit (especially navel oranges), and other tree crops are grown in the Murrumbidgee irrigation area. All of the increasingly important rice crop is grown here with the aid of irrigation water from the Burrinjuck Dam, most of it near Yanco. In addition, the heavier soils of the Leeton-Griffith district produce tomatoes, beans and green peas for canning, while in the same areas the light and sandy soils are used to grow carrots and rock melons for the Sydney market. The irrigated small farms of the Murrumbidgee area are especially notable for the extent to which they make use of the latest mechanical methods in production and harvesting. Even rice is cultivated and harvested by the use of large mechanical implements. In the growing of tomatoes tractor-drawn seedling transplanters, rotary weeders and mechanical sprayers are employed. Hand picking of peas has been eliminated. Because of the distance from internal markets, much of the fruit crop (especially of peaches and apricots) and of the vegetable crop is canned. Fruit juices are extracted and tinned, and wine is made from the grapes grown. Many plums are converted locally into prunes, often for the foreign export market.

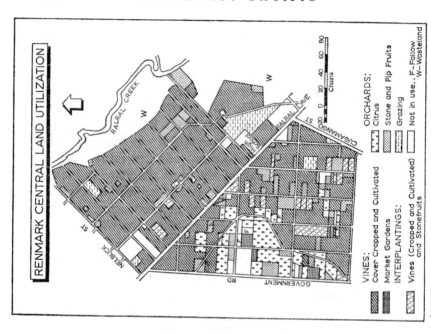

RENMARK CENTRAL LAND UTILIZATION

VINES:
Cover Cropped and Cultivated
Market Gardens
INTERPLANTINGS:
Vines (Cropped and Cultivated)
and Stonefruits

ORCHARDS:
Citrus
Stone and Pip Fruits
Grazing
Not in use. F–Fallow
W–Wasteland

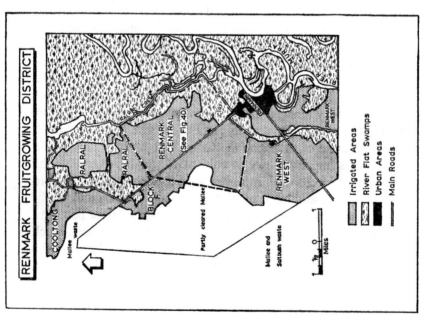

RENMARK FRUITGROWING DISTRICT

Irrigated Areas
River Flat Swamps
Urban Areas
Main Roads

Figures 39 *left*, and 40 *right* (*After* Cochrane).

RENMARK SOUTH AUSTRALIA

The lower Murray flows through semi-arid pastoral country. The annual rainfall on the South Australian border is less than ten inches. Summers are particularly hot and dry. None of the Murray's irrigated areas and attendant farm and town settlements depend so completely upon its water as do Renmark, Cadell and Waikerie. The braided network of river-beds here follows a remarkably meandering course and is incised and bounded by cliffs or steep slopes which separate the valley from the low plateau about it. The vegetation of this area was stunted mallee, she-oak and scraggy pines. In places south of the river the land was cleared for wheat, but yields were low. Elsewhere sparse sheep-rearing alone proved possible. There is now a series of eight weirs on the river, ponding back the water which is pumped up to the highest levels, whence it flows by gravity to the small fruit farms and vineyards. The irrigated farm and orchard lands are but small oases on terraces along the river, each cut off from the next and all sharply differentiated from the non-irrigable semi-desert of sand ridges and mallee all around (*Figs 39* and *40*).

Its particularly hot, dry and sunny summers give this district an advantage over others in the production of dried fruit. Specialization is more marked than in other irrigated areas in the Murray Basin. There is little intensive livestock rearing here; even milk is imported. Water is not used, as it is elsewhere, to make improved and permanent pastures possible. The vine is the chief crop. Many varieties are grown. Different varieties are used to prepare dried fruit—sultanas, currants and lexia raisins in that order of importance. Others again are grown for wine-making and as table grapes. Wine production is of fast growing importance. Apricots, peaches and nectarines are also produced—very largely for drying on racks in the open air. Pears, olives and figs are less important crops. After vines, oranges and other citrus fruit occupy the greatest acreage. These alone are marketed fresh.

The ordered rows of dark citrus groves on light soils on the slopes above the level of gravity flow of irrigation water and therefore irrigated by overhead sprays, the trellised vines on the terraces, the small enclosures, the trim limestone and red-tiled homes, the road-corner co-operative wineries, distilleries and packing and drying sheds, give these settlements a tidy, compact and prosperous appearance which is especially marked in contrast to the drab and arid aspect of the surrounding country. The newer townships serving the fruitgrowing oases, with their openness and planned layout, and their busy streets lined with cream-coloured limestone houses in irrigated gardens, have nothing of the tawdry appearance of many static or decaying country towns in the pastoral and extensive wheat-growing districts.

CANE GROWING ON THE QUEENSLAND COAST

It is a far cry from the nine inches of rain and the irrigated vineyards of Renmark to the 100 inches of rain, the hot and humid environment and the lush cultivated crops of bananas, sugar cane, papaws and mangoes of the tropical coastal lowlands of northern Queensland. Between the Tweed, Clarence and Richmond Rivers in northern New South Wales and the alluvial lowlands about Ingham, Innisfail, Cairns and Mossman (in about latitude 17 degrees south) in Queensland, is a series of discontinuous cultivated lowland areas which together constitute one of Australia's most important and distinctive agricultural regions. Two-fifths of the continent lies within the tropics, but tropical Australia supports no more than one thirtieth of the country's population. Of the 300,000 people in tropical Australia nineteen out of every twenty live on the east coast of Queensland. For this the tropical agriculture, and especially the sugar-cane growing in the pockets of land strung out along the coast, is mainly responsible (*Fig. 41*).

The coastal 'islands' of almost monocultural production of sugar cane are shut in and cut off from each other by hilly woodland and extensive beef cattle grazing hill and swamp country. This is no 'sugar coast' but a series of 'islands' of intensive cash cropping strung along an isolated and largely undeveloped tropical coast—of hurricanes and moist trade winds.

An increasing proportion of the cane crop is grown north of the tropic, and yields are higher there. A frost-free winter and a well distributed rainfall of more than fifty inches are required for higher yields of both cane and sugar. Frosts as far north as Mackay may cause serious crop losses. Because rainfall does

1.
EUCALYPT
FOREST,
WESTERN
AUSTRALIA

2.
SAVANNA
WOODLAND,
NEW SOUTH
WALES

3.
SALTBUSH,
BLUE BUSH,
MALLEE

Australian official photographs

4.
MERINO
FLOCK,
CANBERRA

5.
WATERING
PLACE,
ALICE
SPRINGS

6.
DAIRYING,
COASTAL
NEW SOUTH
WALES

Australian official photographs

7. CATTLE STATION, KIMBERLEYS

Australian official photographs

8. WHEAT, VICTORIAN WIMMERA

9. MIXED FARMING, TASMANIA

Australian official photographs

10. IRRIGATION, RENMARK

11. DRYING FRUIT, MILDURA

Australian official photographs

12. SUGAR CANE, QUEENSLAND

13. IRON ORE, SOUTH AUSTRALIA

Australian official photographs

14. MINING TOWN, BROKEN HILL

15. BROWN COAL, YALLOURN, VICTORIA

Australian official photographs

16. HEAVY INDUSTRY, NEWCASTLE

17.

RAIL
TRANSPORT,
NEW SOUTH
WALES

18.
ROAD
TRANSPORT,
WESTERN
AUSTRALIA

Photo: Australian News and Information Bureau

19.

AIR
TRANSPORT
IN THE
OUTBACK

Photo: Australian News and Information Bureau

20. EMPTY INTERIOR, WESTERN AUSTRALIA

Australian official photographs

21. RURAL TOWNSHIP, NEW SOUTH WALES

22. THE MOUNTAINS OF NEW GUINEA

23. SWEET POTATO CROP, NEW GUINEA HIGHLANDS

24. VILLAGE AND GARDENS, NEW GUINEA

Australian official photographs

25. YAM STORAGE, NEW GUINEA MAINLAND

26. NATIVE COPRA, NEW BRITAIN

Australian official photographs

27. COCONUT PLANTATION, TROBRIAND ISLANDS

28. RABAUL, NEW BRITAIN

Australian official photographs

29. GOLD, WAU VALLEY

30.
PHOSPHATE,
NAURU

31.
EUROPEAN
SETTLEMENT,
NAURU

32.
NATIVE
HOUSING,
NAURU

Photos: British Phosphate Commission

33. COCONUT PALM

Photos: Rob Wright, Fiji Public Relations Office

34. COCONUT PRODUCTS

35. COCONUT PLANTATION, SOLOMONS

Photos: Rob Wright, Fiji Public Relations Office

36. COPRA DRYING SHEDS

not everywhere reach the desirable amount, cane is grown under irrigation at Bundaberg and on the alluvial flats of the lower Burdekin near Ayr. With only forty-six inches of rain, and no irrigation, the Townsville area is not a cane-growing district. In the nineteenth century cane was grown on large estates, mainly in the southern half of its present area of cultivation. It depends on the employment of indentured Melanesian labourers. But after federation in 1901, and the adoption of the White Australia policy, the industry came to depend on the hard manual work of Europeans working in the tropics. Estates were broken up and the industry crept north. Today fifty to seventy acre holdings are characteristic. Labour is supplied by the European settler and his family except in the cutting season when casual labour, often of Italian extraction, is employed. But the industry is heavily subsidized, and the government's control of acreage is rigid. Its indirect control of cane-growing practices, of the varieties of cane cultivated, and of land use, is also notable. But the subsidy which the Australian taxpayer and sugar consumer pays is perhaps justified in view of the fact that the sugar industry is the most important in Queensland and, in its absence, it is doubtful whether any other significant use would have been found for the tropical coastlands of the state, and whether tropical Australia would have had a population larger than that of a moderately-sized secondary town in inland New South Wales or Victoria. For this reason, and to safeguard the income of one-crop cane growers, there are stringent government controls to prevent overproduction. Acreages in cane are carefully 'assigned' and tonnage quotas of cane are fixed by the mills.

Today most cane is mechanically planted and cultivated, and cane-harvesting machines are being used in the Mackay and Bundaberg areas. After cutting, the cane (mainly locally bred Trojan and Pindar high-yielding varieties) is loaded on to small trucks in the canefield, and goes by tramline to the nearest mill. To move more than twelve million tons of cane a season from nearly 540,000 acres the 'sugar coast' has 200 locomotives tugging 31,000 cane trucks along 2000 miles of tram track to thirty-four mills (all but three of them in Queensland). Each little coastal area of cane production has its mill, so that the farm is never far from the factory at which the cane is crushed

E

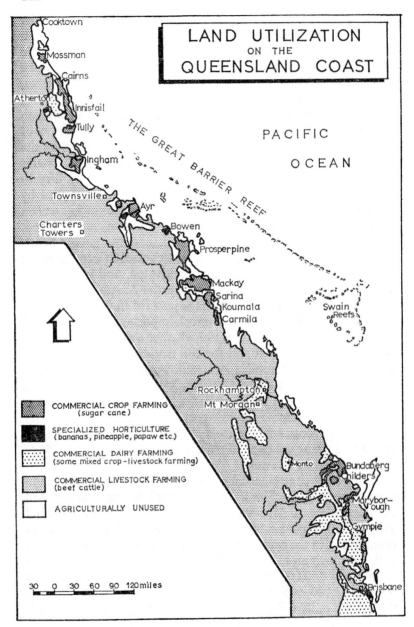

Figure 41

and processed. From the crushing mill comes not only brown sugar, which is later refined in the main consuming centres, but also molasses and the cane-fibre—bagasse. The mills and the refineries both provide employment for large numbers, and molasses and bagasse are raw material for further industrial processing. From the first are made rum, industrial spirit and other chemical products; from the latter is made an insulating wallboard.

Cane growing is often the one and only activity on cane farms, the area not in plant cane or ratooned cane being left to recuperate in fallow or a green manure crop. On some larger holdings, however, pastures of tropical grasses are sown after the ratoon cane stools have been ploughed in, and a dairy herd is run. In the southern half of the cane-growing area, cane is often only one of a number of crops cultivated. Sugar cane is there a useful cash-crop adjunct to a system of mixed farming. Maize, grain, sorghums, cotton, tobacco and peanuts may also be grown in a rotation with Rhodes grass, and beef or dairy cattle may be kept. Most of these crops are row and clean-cultivated crops: so is sugar cane. The bare, deep red soil between the rows is often subject, in the heavy rains experienced on the coast of Queensland and northern New South Wales, to soil wash, rilling and gullying. Much soil has been lost on slopes by erosion, and in the canefields this has been assisted by the practice of firing the crop before harvest and burning the trash left after cutting.

Throughout the cane-growing districts are many smaller holdings on which tropical fruits are grown for southern markets. Chief amongst these are bananas (30,000 acres, mostly in New South Wales), pineapples (11,300 acres, almost entirely in Queensland) and papaws (1500 acres in Queensland). The production of all three is dependent upon the demand of the internal market, the small banana plantations being also dependent upon tariff protection against imports of bananas from Fiji and other island territories.

AGRICULTURE *v*. MANUFACTURING

At first sight it might seem strange, in view of its vast and varied production of agricultural commodities, and in view of the fact that for many decades Australia has been one of the world's principal exporters of farm products, that the Commonwealth should in recent years have found some of her exports of primary products steady or dwindling in volume. Relative to minerals and manufactures and, with the exception of the recent spectacular expansion of exports of wheat, agricultural and pastoral products have played a decreased role in the export economy. But all this is the outcome of trends long apparent. It is the result of changes long under way, but exaggerated and quickened during and after two world wars. These trends have been the rapid growth of population (and its increasing urbanization) and the large-scale development of manufacturing industries. Farm production, which varies violently from year to year in a continent like Australia, with the unreliability of its precipitation, has not kept pace with the growth of population. In eight years after the war population grew—largely as a result of immigration—by twenty-five per cent (1,700,000), while farm and station production expanded by only twelve per cent. Meanwhile, with higher standards of living, *per capita* consumption has risen. The exportable surplus has thus declined. Already *fifty-eight* per cent of the working population is employed in the tertiary, or servicing, industries (including transport and building and construction), *twenty-seven* per cent in manufacturing, and only *twelve* per cent in agriculture, mining, fishing and forestry. Since 1948 the net value of all manufactured goods produced in Australia has exceeded that of all farms, stations, mines, quarries, forests and fisheries put together. Industrial development has gone far and fast: Australia is no longer merely a primary producer, but also an industrial nation of expanding significance.

Until World War I, industry was responsible for little more than one-fifth of the value of all production; and until that time it retained its domestic stamp. It was associated largely with the processing of the products of farm and mine. Among the long-established industries were flour making, brewing, metal refining, meat preserving, butter making and the manufacture of woollen textiles. The modern industrial structure of Australia is based more directly on the continent's mineral wealth. However, it was not the hundreds of millions of pounds amassed by the mining of gold, either in Victoria after 1851, at Mount Morgan in Queensland in the eighteen-eighties, or in Western Australia in the eighteen-nineties, that furnished the capital with which the core of the later industrial system was constructed. It was Broken Hill's fabulous wealth of silver, lead and zinc provided the foundations on which, after 1915, the industrial structure was erected. In 1915 the Broken Hill Proprietary Company blew its first blast furnace at Newcastle. From this beginning, grew the iron and steel industry, and with it a host of others. Since World War II industrial giants have grown in several fields of manufacturing.

INDUSTRIAL RESOURCES

To study Australia's manufacturing industries is to study again the southeast of the continent (*Fig. 46*). Here are most of the resources upon which industries depend, here are the factories, and here are the large industrial clusters of population—not only those people employed in manufacturing industries, but also those employed in the superstructure of tertiary industries which service both primary and secondary industries. In New South Wales, Victoria and Tasmania, seventy-six per cent of all factories in Australia, and seventy-eight per cent of all industrial workers, produce eighty-two per cent by value of all manufactured goods. In these three states live seven out of every ten Australians.

Apart from its sufficient and reliable rainfall (and the more intensive forms of agriculture and livestock-rearing associated with it), the southeast has other important physical advantages —sources of power in both coal and water; mineral deposits, especially at Broken Hill, Mt Lyell and in the Middleback Ranges; a coastal location; and good harbours. The sea provides a ready means of transport, an advantage reinforced ever since the early construction of roads and railways provided the same region with the densest network of surface routes on the continent.

COAL

Australia's resources of both bituminous and lignite coals are ample. In 1964 27.4 million tons of black coal and 18.7 million tons of brown coal were mined, and it is estimated that there are almost 6000 million tons of proven reserves of black coal and 60,000 million tons of brown coal still to mine. The coal deposits and colliery districts are shown in *Figure 43*. Sydney lies over the centre of one of the world's most valuable basins of coal, part of which extends under the sea. The coal measures are deepest beneath Sydney and rise towards the north, west and south, outcropping at Newcastle, Lithgow and Bulli. It is near the outcrops that the coal is mined. The northern field centres on Maitland, Cessnock and Muswellbrook. The Greta seam at Maitland, up to thirty feet thick, yields a valuable

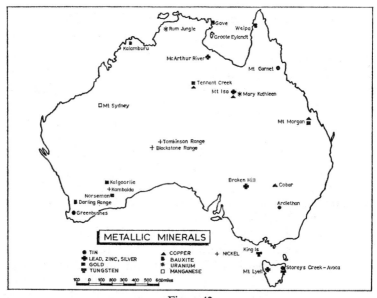

Figure 42

gas and steam coal. At Newcastle collieries, almost on the coast, produce coking coal. The northern field produces well over half the hard coal mined in Australia. The southern field, with collieries close to Bulli and Port Kembla, produces the best coking coal. Newcastle and Port Kembla annually supply coke for their own blast furnaces, for back loading to Whyalla's furnace and Port Pirie's smelters, and for export to New Caledonia's nickel smelters.

Queensland's coal deposits are not so handy. The richest seams—ninety feet thick and covered by no more than seventy feet of overburden—are in the Clermont field at Blair Athol, 250 miles inland from Rockhampton, and in the Bowen field, still further north. The chief producer at present is the Ipswich field, between Brisbane and the New South Wales border. Railways and the domestic and industrial markets of Brisbane take most of the output. Much smaller quantities of coal are mined in Western Australia, South Australia and Tasmania, most of it sub-bituminous.

In Victoria there are nearly 54,700 million tons of lignite. The

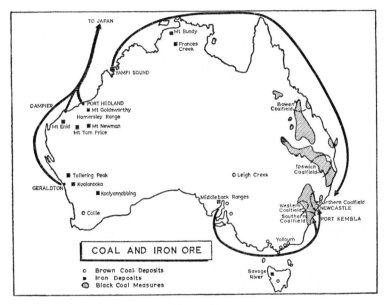

Figure 43

largest deposit lies beneath a shallow (fifty feet) overburden of sands and gravel in a trough forty miles long between Yarragon and Rosedale in Gippsland. Production is centred on Yallourn and Morwell, in the Latrobe valley, where in 1965 19,001,000 tons of brown coal were taken from State opencast workings (of a seam which is from 100 to 240 feet thick) by the massive mechanical equipment of the State Electricity Commission. The coal is used to generate thermal electric power and for manufacture of nearly two million tons of briquettes. In 1956 a gasification plant was opened at Morwell. Gas is transmitted to Melbourne through a pipeline 103 miles in length.

The thick horizontal beds of low-grade Tertiary coal represent a national asset of incalculable value, and Victoria's economy would appear to rest for many years to come on their efficient utilization. The coal and overburden are removed by enormous, electrically driven continuous excavators operating on benches within the thickness of the seams. They can each handle as much as 1750 tons of coal every hour. Both rail and conveyor belts are used to shift the coal from the opencast workings to the power plants on the bank of the Latrobe River. The Yallourn and Morwell power stations use 70 per cent of the coal mined and produce 65 per cent of the state's electricity. Yallourn has a capacity of 621,000 kW, Morwell 170,000 kW. Together they can produce more than four times the power generated by the Meremere thermal power plant near Huntly in New Zealand. A third station—at Hazelwood—will dwarf even Yallourn. It is planned to have an ultimate capacity of 1,200,000 kW. and will be completed in 1971. Hazelwood will also get its coal direct from the open-cut.

The briquetting is integrated with electricity generation. The moist, crumbly raw coal is converted into a hard, durable, compressed fuel which is readily handled and transported and which helps to meet Victoria's lack of good bituminous (black) coal. Briquettes are marketed for industrial and domestic use, and from briquettes supplied to the State Gas and Fuel Corporation at Morwell, a third of Melbourne's town gas requirements are provided as well as the needs of towns in the Latrobe valley.

PETROLEUM AND HYDRO-ELECTRICITY

In an advancing industrial nation the consumption of power rises steeply. In Australia the search for it is continuous, and costly. Like New Zealand, Australia long sought in vain for workable pools of petroleum as a second major source of fossil fuel to coal. But it had to depend on imported sources for its supply of a fuel which, in the age of the petrol engine and road transport, is indispensable. For some time the best prospect of discovering a domestic source of supply appeared to be in New Guinea or Papua, where it would be almost as readily available as if it were in some remoter part of the continent itself.

The search persisted until, in 1953, the first oil flow in Australia was struck on the Rough Range (Exmouth Gulf) in West Australia. The flow of 500 barrels a day was disappointing. But in the last decade strikes of oil, and especially of natural gas, have followed with increasing frequency—in 1961 at Tara, and Moonie in the Surat basin in Queensland; in 1962 near Roma, Queensland, also in the Surat basin; in 1963 at Richmond, near Roma; in 1964 at Barrow Island and Yardarino

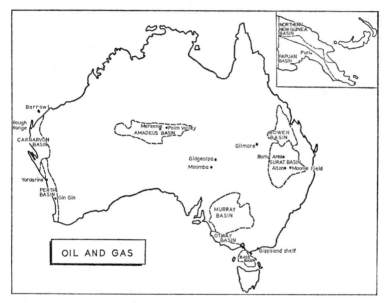

Figure 44

in West Australia and at Alton in the Surat basin. The year 1964 was the year in which Australia finally entered the ranks of the oil-producing nations. In March that year oil was first pumped from the Moonie field through a ten-inch pipeline to Brisbane for refining. Production at Moonie is quite small beside the Commonwealth's needs. It amounts to 6000 barrels a day, or 210,000 gallons—about one-fifteenth of Australia's daily consumption of all kinds of petroleum products.

Meanwhile most oil-yielding areas have been found to be

even potentially richer sources of natural gas. Gas in commercial quantities, sufficient to affect significantly the power supply situation, has been discovered in Queensland (especially in the Surat basin), South Australia (at Gidgealpa), Northern Territory (Mereenie), West Australia (Yardarino) and, most recently and most abundantly, off Victoria's Gippsland coast.

Reports dated March 1966 suggest that what might prove to be the most valuable petroleum discovery to date in Australia is the finding of oil-bearing sands, ten times thicker than those at Moonie, in the strata deep under the waters of Bass Strait on the so-called Gippsland shelf. The importance of this source could lie as much in its proximity to refineries at Melbourne and elsewhere in the populous and industrialized southeast of the continent as in its size. It is beginning to look as though Australia's investment of more than $300 million in oil exploration and development is beginning to pay off. If it does the Commonwealth's industrialization will be speeded up and its whole economy invigorated.

As compared with New Zealand, Australia has abundant high grade coal and the promise of domestic sources of petroleum; but, unlike New Zealand, has a limited development of its relatively small hydro-electric power potential.

The areas in Australia where landforms and abundant and steady supplies of rainfall combine to make water storage and the generation of hydro-electricity possible are in the east. Tasmania is best equipped. Its natural lake storage and a reliable water supply have made possible the harnessing of water power for both domestic and industrial uses. It is largely employed in the electrolytic refining of zinc and other metals and in pulp and paper making. New South Wales and Victoria share an installed capacity equal to about half that of Tasmania, while in Queensland very little power has yet been harnessed. The enormous and ingenious Snowy River project, which was started in 1948 on the borders of New South Wales and Victoria, will, when complete, be one of the major engineering accomplishments in the world, and it will change significantly the power-supply position in Australia. It will have a peak-load capacity of 3,500,000 kilowatts. (In 1963 the total installed capacity of all electric generators in Australia was 7,499,000 kW, of which hydro-electric generators accounted for only 1,850,000 kW. In the same year New Zealand hydro-electric power plants had a capacity slightly in excess of Australia's.)

On the Snow Mountains scheme there will be seventeen large dams, nine power stations and eighty-six miles of tunnels. The waters of the Snowy River and its tributaries are being diverted under the mountains to the Murrumbidgee and the Murray, providing enough water ultimately to irrigate an area four times as large as the present Murrumbidgee irrigation areas. Thus, although providing an immense addition to the Commonwealth's available industrial and domestic power, the Snowy Mountains scheme will also contribute importantly to its agricultural productivity.

In view of the rapidly changing pattern of energy supplies, it will be most interesting in the next two decades to observe the relative importance of the various old and new, domestic and imported, supplies of power. Especially interesting will be the role to be played by natural gas. In the production of electrical energy in 1963 coal was easily the most important source. Thermal power represented 72 per cent of the total installed capacity; hydro-electricity 25 per cent; and oil-driven internal combustion engines three per cent. In future petroleum, natural gas and water could become more significant sources of energy relative to coal.

IRON ORE

Iron ore is the second cornerstone of Australia's present expanding industrial structure. Since 1915 the iron and steel industry has relied overwhelmingly on iron ore from the Middleback Ranges on Eyre Peninsula, South Australia. The ore deposit is twenty miles from tidewater at Whyalla on Spencer Gulf. Of the 5,514,000 tons of iron ore mined in 1963, 4,181,000 came from the Iron Monarch and Iron Prince quarries in the Middleback Ranges. Since 1951 a second major source has been utilized. This is the Yampi Sound deposits on three small islands off the remote coast of northern West Australia. Both major deposits presently exploited for the domestic industries are distant from sources of power and from centres of industry. Both, however, are accessible from the sea. The South Australian ores are shipped 1170 miles to Newcastle. Backloading of coke from the Hunter Valley made possible in 1941 the blowing of a blast furnace at Whyalla. The Yampi Sound ores are shipped to Port Kembla.

Since 1948 iron ore has been taken from the Koolyanobbing deposits, 250 miles east of Perth, to supply the smelter and two blast furnaces at Wundowie. This source is likely to become more important with the establishment, probably in 1968, of an iron and steel industry alongside the giant petroleum refinery at Kwinana, south of Perth.

With the relaxation in 1960 of the embargo on the export of iron ore from Australia, it has been demonstrated that the iron ore deposits and reserves of the continent are among the world's largest: and a new phase of mineral exploitation is now under development. By 1970, it is estimated, Australia will be exporting as much as three times as much iron ore as is required by its own rapidly expanding iron and steel industry. This will prove a bonanza for the arid coastlands of West Australia where most of the recent discoveries of vast sources of iron ore have been made. Several consortiums of Australian, American and Japanese capital are preparing, by building roads, railways and ports, to pelletize and export to Japan enormous quantities of ore from such, until recently, unknown sources as Mount Tom Price (Hamersley Range), Mount Whaleback (Opthalmia Range), Mount Goldsworthy (inland from Port Hedland) and Tallering Peak-Koolanooka Hills. By 1970 annual exports, almost entirely to Japan, should reach 15 million tons.

In 1964 Australia had eleven blast furnaces, at Newcastle (4), Port Kembla (4), Whyalla and Wundowie (2). There are steel works at both Newcastle and Port Kembla, and the Broken Hill Proprietary Co. has announced plans to build a $60 million steel plant at Whyalla. This heavy industrial complex is not only the very backbone of Australian industrial development, but is increasingly the basis upon which New Zealand industry has come to rest as a result of its dependence upon imported iron and steel. The establishment, however, of a steel mill in New Zealand should reduce its dependence on Australia, Japan and the United Kingdom by 1967-1968.

The metal industries and the complex of closely-related industries are of outstanding importance in Australia. Almost two-fifths of the people employed in manufacture are engaged in the iron and steel industry, the manufacture of machines and the production and assembly of vehicles of all kinds. The textile and clothing industries rank second, with half as many employees, and the food processing, brewing and related industries third. Of growing significance is the group of industries associated with the manufacture of chemicals, dyes, plastics, explosives, fertilizers, paints, oils and grease. Most rapidly-growing are the new oil-refining, television, electronics and rubber industries, including the manufacture of tyres. Tin plate, aluminium, pulp, paper and electro-chemical industries are either planned or are already under development, so that during or since the war Australian manufacturing industries have assumed a diversified, broad-based and mature character. This can perhaps best be described by recognizing three major categories of industries.

MANUFACTURING INDUSTRIES

First in importance is steel-making and the complex of metallurgical, machine and heavy chemical industries technologically related to it. These are largely concentrated on the coalfields, though the refining and simple processing of some metals is often done near the mining centres, as at Mount Isa and in Tasmania. Port Pirie and Port Kembla also have smelters, the one for lead and the other for copper. The steel mills on the coalfields provide the raw materials for an array of heavy metallurgical, chemical and engineering industries. Even Whyalla has attracted shipbuilding. But the Hunter Valley is the Australian Ruhr.

THE HUNTER VALLEY

Until after 1890 the Hunter Valley depended primarily upon its mixed agriculture, and coal mining was a minor economic activity. Coal was won from the Newcastle coal seam, outcropping close to the coast from the rivermouth south to Lake Macquarie. Most of it, however, was hauled by colliers from the port of Newcastle across the Indian and Pacific oceans to Calcutta and California. But with the discovery and opening up of the rich gas coals of the Greta seams after 1886 and the growth of industry and of fuel and power consumption in the Commonwealth in the new century, the domestic demand for

Hunter Valley coal expanded steadily. Today half the coal mined—coking coal from the Newcastle field and gas coal from the Greta-Maitland-Cessnock field—is used in the valley itself. A significant proportion is shipped to Sydney for use in power stations and gasworks and as domestic fuel in the state capital. A sixth of the output is shipped interstate—mainly to Victoria or backloaded to South Australia. The local thermal electric power station at Vales Point on Lake Macquarie itself consumes more than one million of the eleven million tons of black coal mined in the Hunter Valley.

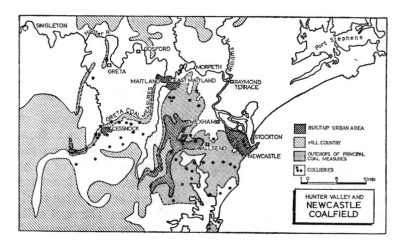

Figure 45

Since 1900 the townships of Cessnock, Abermain, Weston and Kurri Kurri have rivalled the older mining settlements nearer the coast. The mineshafts, or tunnels and adits, and the pithead buildings are sometimes surrounded by lawns and housing developments, but in many cases, and especially on the South Maitland field, by the eucalypt bush or dense scrub close in on the pithead and the railroads. Long trains of coal trucks snake their way through light eucalypt forest from mines to factories, foundries and port. The mining people live at some distance from the pitheads in towns of some size and with mixed and varied functions, like Cessnock or Weston. Miners on the Newcastle field today often live in the outer lakeside suburbs of the Newcastle urban area, as at Belmont or Toronto, alongside city office and professional workers.

The high-grade coal is not only the source of power used locally and in other states to which it is shipped, but it is also a valuable raw material from which gas and coke are produced, and upon which the heavy chemical industries of Cockle Bay, near Newcastle, depend for their production of tar, naphtha, benzol and sulphuric acid. Newcastle, the estuary port, is a B.H.P. town, like Port Kembla and Whyalla, and is the valley's chief industrial centre.

The Broken Hill Proprietary Company, which formerly owned and worked leases at the world's most productive source of silver-lead-zinc ores in the Barrier Ranges near Broken Hill, now not only operates blast furnaces and steel mills, but has its own coal mines in the Hunter valley, its own iron-ore workings in South Australia, smelters and refineries at Port Pirie and Whyalla and in Tasmania, and possess its own fleet of colliers and iron-ore freighters. It is one of the largest industrial corporations in the world. But there are a number of other large and well-known concerns in the Hunter Valley. Amongst them they manufacture black and galvanized iron sheets, tubes, axles, castings, steel rope, fencing wire, nails, coal tar and its many by-products, sulphur, cement and superphosphate. There are shipbuilding yards, and at Newcastle and Cardiff the state railway workshops make locomotives and rolling stock for railways and tramways. During the war there were a number of munitions factories; some of these have since been converted to textile manufacture, and a large factory at Hexham has been built to manufacture rayon yarn.

It was, however, the decision of the Broken Hill Proprietary Company in 1915 to site its steel mill at Port Waratah on reclaimed flats on the Hunter estuary above Newcastle that, for half a century, made the lower valley the unrivalled heavy industrial heart of the Commonwealth. Today, with the construction of an artificial harbour on the coast of New South Wales south of Sydney and near the southern rim of the New South Wales coalfield, and the rapid expansion of the iron and steel industry close to the new port, Port Kembla is challenging Newcastle as the principal base of Australia's basic heavy industries.

At Newcastle the infant iron and steel industry was initially assisted by protective tariffs; but, with the stimulus of two world wars and increasing domestic demand for its output, it has grown into one of the most efficient basic heavy industries in the world. As in other major steel-producing countries, the Australian industry is 'vertically integrated', that is, the B.H.P. Company controls not only the blast furnaces and the steel mills but also the sources and mining of the iron ore and coking coal and the finishing and fabrication of the commercial steel in rails, rods, and plates, and the drawing of wire. In the Hunter Valley this integration is most apparent on the 300 acres of former estuary swamp at Port Waratah. Here are the wharves at which the ore transporters tie up to deliver their cargoes of ore from the Middleback Ranges into storage bins. Here are the blast furnaces, and the battery of coking ovens, treating ore and coking coal and producing molten iron for the open hearth furnaces and coal coking byproducts like tar, ammonia and benzol. Here are the rolling mills, and close by a host of factories refining and fabricating the steel. Something like 15,500 persons find employment in the iron and steel industries —almost one in three of the working population of Newcastle.

Sea transport has been essential to the growth of industry in the valley. The dredged port of Newcastle is one of Australia's busiest. Only two ports have more vessels entering them. Not only is there iron ore to bring in, but also limestone (from Tasmania), ferro-alloys (nickel and chromium from New Caledonia, and tungsten from King Island in Bass Strait), and phosphate rock from Nauru and Ocean Island. In addition coal, coke, steel, fertilizers and many other heavy and bulky manufactured items are shipped out through Newcastle to other parts of Australia, to New Zealand, and to other destinations overseas. The facilities of the port have also attracted general cargo; and with its wool stores, wheat elevator and storage tanks, Newcastle also handles much of the export of wool and wheat from northern New South Wales, and also the area's imports of petroleum. In fact Newcastle handles as great a *tonnage* of cargo as Sydney, Melbourne or Fremantle. Only its great rival, Port Kembla, handles more.

Most of the valley's industries and population are clustered in its lower reaches and close to the port and city of Newcastle, which with 225,000 people, ranks as Australia's sixth city and second only to Sydney in New South Wales. Newcastle spreads from the Hunter mouth to Lake Macquarie and in its southward expansion it has overrun and absorbed some of the earliest mining villages on the Newcastle field. These now serve as rejuvenated residential suburbs. Today the urbanized area is reaching south and southwest into hills clad in eucalypts as far as Wallsend and Cardiff.

The other area of urbanization in the Hunter Valley parallels the outcrop of the Greta seam and runs from Cessnock to Maitland. It owes its development to the growing importance of the mining of steam and gas coals in the present century. The small towns here are essentially miners' towns—the homes of the men who work in the scattered mines in the eucalypt scrub all around. With adequate bus services and large numbers of private cars, miners live in towns like Bellbird, Weston and Kurri Kurri and often travel considerable distances to the pitheads. Even from Cessnock, with its larger shopping facilities and population of 15,000 people, most of its employed population travel daily to distant mines. Maitland, however, at the northern end of this axis of mining towns on the Greta seam, has other functions. It lies on the floodplain where the Hunter emerges from the upper agricultural valley. It is subject to serious flooding. It was early the commercial and service centre of the valley until superseded by Newcastle. It still serves a wider area than the miners' towns. It provides shopping and commercial facilities, not only for suburbs like East Maitland, Telarah and Lorn, but for an extensive rural area. It has a population of almost 30,000. Between Cessnock and Maitland live 70,000 people.

Rural towns like Singleton, Scone, Morpeth and Paterson depend upon agriculture, which has been of increasing importance and is being more intensively practised with the progress of industry and the growth of the valley's urban population. These and other towns service the dairy-farmers and fruit-growers in their vicinity. Some of them have meat-freezing, butter-making, timber-working and vegetable-processing industries.

LIGHT INDUSTRIES

Industries in the second major category are more varied and lighter in character. They are concentrated not on coalfields but in the large capital cities of the Commonwealth. In determining the location of these industries, power supplied by thermal electricity, which is readily transmitted, is much less important than access to markets and to labour, which even since the infant days of the Australian colonies have been con-

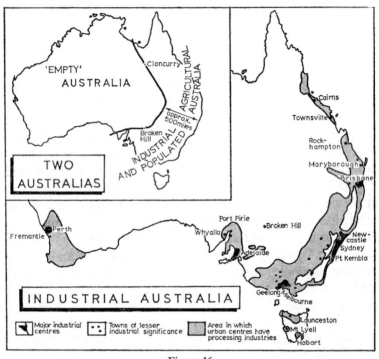

Figure 46

centrated overwhelmingly in the capital cities. Raw materials are light, partly processed already, and often imported. The tidewater location of the state capitals and the long-established road and railway patterns, focusing on the cities, give them advantages in the assembly of materials and the despatch of finished products. Textiles are representative of the industries in the metropolitan areas, although with recent labour shortages, small textile and clothing factories have been established in some country towns, and even on the coalfields, to tap the pools of female labour there. Wool, cotton and silk are spun, and a wide range of materials of both natural and artificial fibres is woven. Clothing, knitwear, hosiery, boots and shoes are all manufactured in increasing quantity and variety in all state capitals, particularly in Melbourne, and also in Geelong and neighbouring towns in Victoria. In addition to textiles a whole range of goods from radios to razor blades, from aeroplanes to plastic baby rattles, is manufactured. The major industrial groups are: light engineering; the fabrication and assembly of vehicles of many kinds, including motor cars, trucks, and tractors (especially at Adelaide and Melbourne) and aircraft (at Fishermen's Bend in Victoria); the manufacture of electrical apparatus, agricultural implements, tobacco, light chemicals and drugs, rubber and tyres, and radio and television apparatus; printing; brewing; and many others.

PROCESSING PRIMARY PRODUCTS

Most widely distributed are the industries processing the products of Australian agriculture (*Fig. 46*). These are naturally confined, however, to the small rural townships of the productive part of the continent (and to some of the larger centres). Grain milling and the manufacture of dairy products are distributed in the towns of the wheat-growing and milk-producing areas in rough proportion to the acreage of wheat and the number of dairy cows. Similarly, Queensland has the bulk of the meat works, and practically all the cane-crushing establishments. Most rural towns of any size have breweries, printing works, furniture factories and industrial establishments for the local production of aerated waters, ice cream, bread and other daily requirements. The grape-growing districts have their wineries and distilleries; the towns in the fruit and vegetable-growing areas have their canning factories, juice-extracting plants and jam works. Some towns in pastoral grazing areas have wool-scouring industries and tanneries. The scattered mining settlements usually have small plants for the refining and reduction in weight and volume of the ore they mine.

Many manufacturing industries have reached a stage of development at which they are able to satisfy the demands of the domestic market for all but a limited range of goods. The only considerable imports today are certain textiles, motor vehicles, machine tools, some chemicals, paper, crockery, china-ware, books and periodicals. Australia is therefore looking to foreign markets to absorb many factory products which it already produces in excess of internal requirements, or is likely to do so in the near future. New Zealand already takes many of these products. Some of them go to India and parts of Australia's Near North. New Guinea and the more densely-populated and better-developed island territories in the Indo-nesian 'Mediterranean' become highly important to Australia from this economic viewpoint as well as from political and strategic considerations. The raising of the living standards, of the material requirements, and of the purchasing power of the millions of people living to the north of the continent and throughout monsoon Asia is not only of humanitarian interest to the Commonwealth, but is also of direct significance to its future economic development.

TERTIARY INDUSTRIES

One-half of Australia's working population is employed in the tertiary or service industries, and provides services of many kinds rather than goods. New Zealand and Australia both have a higher proportion of their population occupied in providing services than any other countries, and this is considered a reflec-tion of the high standards of living and material comfort which their people enjoy. The tertiary industries include: finance and commerce (banks, stock and station agents, insurance, etc.); administration and professions (civil service, local body govern-ment, medicine, teaching, etc.); transport and communications; building and construction; domestic service (including hotels, boarding houses, etc.) and entertainment. Occupation in such activities occurs in all countries, but in no others do such ser-vices occupy such a large proportion of the employed popula-tion. In Australia the proportions of workers in the tertiary industries varies little from state to state. The services them-selves vary little in kind or degree from place to place within the country. For these reasons the geographic interest of the service industries is less than that of agricultural and manufacturing industries.

TRANSPORT

As much as one-tenth of the Commonwealth's labour force is employed in providing transport and communications, including transport by rail, road, air and water, and postal and telephone services. This is in part a reflection of the great distances in Australia, the mobility and high living standards of its people, and the great *per capita* volume of internal and external trade that they conduct.

The railway system is at first sight confusing, because of the variety of rail gauges involved (*Fig. 47*). Most of the railways are operated by the different states, and each has virtually a separate system running out from the capital city in radial fashion towards the state borders. Few lines penetrate the empty inland, and there is only one transcontinental line, the standard gauge line connecting Port Pirie and Kalgoorlie. Even this parallels the coast and off-coast shipping lines. Australia's population lives largely within a short distance of the sea, much of it on the coast, and a large part of its agricultural and industrial production comes from scattered parts of the coastal rimland. Railways thus have intense competition from sea traffic, especially for heavy goods consigned large distances. The recent growth of air transport has also deprived the railways of much of the long-distance passenger traffic and of the freight trade in light but valuable commodities. But the railways have undoubtedly done a great and important job in the past in opening-up the better agricultural and grazing lands and in providing access to valuable mineral deposits. In this respect the narrow gauge lines of Queensland, Tasmania and Western Australia, by permitting steeper gradients and sharper turns, have made possible the tapping of greater areas than would smaller mileages of wider-gauge line.

Since 1930 the Commonwealth Government has tried to get state railways converted to the standard gauge, but relatively little progress has been made largely because of the high cost. In 1962 however the opening of a new uniform gauge line between Albury and Melbourne completed the standard gauge link between South Brisbane and Melbourne and enabled through services to be operated for the first time from Sydney to Melbourne.

Modern road services and tar-sealed highways came after the continent's potential farm and grazing lands had already been opened up. They have, however, made possible the intensification of the use of the already occupied land, consolidated the agricultural patterns of the country and speeded its economic progress. Despite the much greater initial cost, the result largely

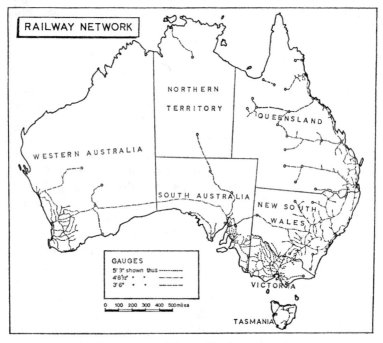

Figure 47

of freight rates and customs tariffs, and despite the high price and tax on imported fuel supplies, Australia has almost as many cars and lorries in relation to its population as the United States, though not as great a proportion as New Zealand. In 1964 there were 3,644,908 registered motor vehicles in Australia, 311 per thousand of population. In that year no fewer than 415,000 new vehicles were registered. In relation to population Northern Territory had most road vehicles. In the more sparsely-settled rural areas motor transport—especially the 'utility' truck—becomes a necessity, and the dry, hardbaked ground conditions make motor transport possible without expensive roading. During World War II, with the threat of Japanese invasion of the tropical north, government and military authorities decided to reinforce the national transport system by building roads rather than railways. Though designed primarily to meet strategic needs, many hundreds of miles of modern roads were laid down, especially in Northern Territory. They will, however, also have considerable economic and social, as well as military, value. The Stuart Highway was built from the railhead at Alice Springs north by way of Tennant Creek, Newcastle Waters, Birdum and so on to Darwin. This new highway was also linked with the railhead at Mount Isa in Queensland by 400 miles of road to Tennant Creek. An Inland Defence Road was also constructed in Queensland. It runs nearly 900 miles from Ipswich, north by way of Clermont to Charters Towers inland from Townsville. These, together with the now stock routes—twenty of them with a mileage exceeding 5000—are already making possible the extension of the beef cattle industry and giving it greater freedom from disaster when drought occurs. Cattle trucks have replaced military convoys and the weary, months-long overland trek from the 'Territory' to Adelaide stockyards has been cut to a truck journey of a few days, as a result of which cattle arrive without loss of condition.

In one aspect of its transport system Australia leads the world. In relation to its population, passenger air transport is more fully developed than anywhere else. In that they take more journeys by air than the people of any other nation, the Australians may be said to be the world's most 'air-minded' people. They are followed closely in this respect by New Zealanders. A much larger proportion of the population of the two dominions is in the habit of travelling by air, both on internal journeys and on journeys overseas, than the people of the United Kingdom, for instance, or even of the United States. This is not difficult to explain. The great distances between the large centres of urban population and the loss of time in travelling between them by surface means, the good flying weather and lack of difficult terrain over most of the continent, and the ability of individuals, governments and business concerns to find the cost of air transport, all help to explain its popularity and rapid development. The physical isolation of both Australia and New Zealand and the enormous distances which separate them from the European and American continents (with which they do most trade and have the strongest cultural ties), explain why the people of both countries take advantage of the recently-developed and highly efficient international air services available

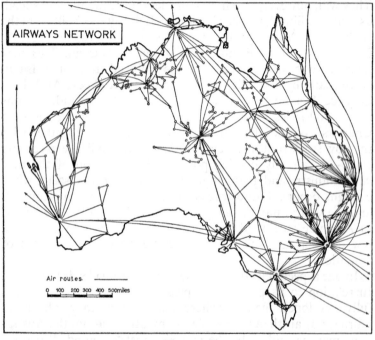

AIRWAYS NETWORK

Air routes.

0 100 200 300 400 500miles

Figure 48

to them. QANTAS is an Australian government-operated air-line. Its routes extend between Sydney and London, Sydney and Japan, and Sydney and Johannesburg across the Indian Ocean, Sydney and North America and Mexico, as well as throughout the Australian and neighbouring territories of the western and southwestern Pacific. Both the Australian and New Zealand governments had an interest in BCPA, whose services linked them both with North America until March 1954 when these services were also taken over by QANTAS. The two governments were also share-holders in TEAL (now Air New Zealand) which linked Australia and New Zealand with each other across the disturbed stretch of the Tasman Sea. In March 1954 New Zealand took over the United Kingdom's, and in 1961 Australia's, share of TEAL's services, both across the Tasman and to Tahiti. The overseas air ties of the two dominions are strengthened by the world-circling route of BOAC and the transpacific services of Pan American and CPA French, German, Italian, Indian and Netherlands international airlines also tie Australia to Europe and Asia.

One distinctive feature of the internal pattern of air services in Australia (*Fig. 47*) is the network of local routes flown by small planes, in Western Australia and Northern Territory in particular, and linking not only towns, large and small, but also isolated groups of sheep and cattle stations or remote mining camps. In addition to the regular services, many such small settlements are served by charter services and by private aircraft operated by station-holders and mining concerns, and by the Flying Doctor Service which is so widely known and publicized.

TRADE

The Commonwealth's immense volume of overseas trade, however, is carried by sea. The shipping services which link Australia with its principal markets, and especially with the United Kingdom via the Suez canal and the Cape of Good Hope, have long been a lifeline without which the young country could not have grown—if, indeed, it could have avoided death in its isolation. Vessels specially designed to carry perishable cargoes of meat and dairy produce were constructed after 1880 and have since been continually improved. The ports which handle the foreign trade are the capital cities of the states, together with Geelong and Newcastle; and like Newcastle (already described), Australia's other great ports are well-equipped with bulk-handling facilities, including giant silos for wheat, huge wool stores and refrigerated storage for dairy products, carcasses of meat and cases of fruit.

Australia's trade long continued to flow along well established

Commonwealth's trade conducted with Asian countries has expanded rapidly. The share of Australia's exports taken by the United Kingdom had by 1965 fallen to less than 20 per cent. Indeed in the following year Japan became the Commonwealth's principal customer. Otherwise only relatively slight changes in the categories of principal imports and exports, and in the list of markets for exports and sources of imports, have taken place in the last fifty years. In value the relative position of leading exports varies irregularly because of the fluctuations in prices (of wool particularly) and because of equally violent fluctuations in the amount of rain experienced in the wool-producing and grain-growing parts of the continent. But wool remains the most important export. In some years, because of phenomenally high prices, wool has accounted for three-fifths by value of all exports. In 1950-1951 the value of the export of scoured and greasy wool was over $1260,000,000, or four times the value of all exports before the war. 'Pastoral products', according to the classification of Australian statistics, include in order of value of exports (1965), wool, meat (chiefly beef but including much canned meat), tallow and livestock. In 1950-1951 these comprised together seventy per cent by value of Commonwealth exports. In more normal years they constitute a little under half. 'Agricultural products', including wheat, flour, sugar, barley, fruit (fresh, dried, canned and pulped), rice, jam and wines furnish from fifteen per cent to thirty per cent of exports, the first three alone accounting for four-fifths of the value of the group. The share of 'Farmyard and Dairy products', which in order of value are butter, cheese, preserved milk, eggs, frozen poultry and pork, has fallen from ten per cent before the war to four per cent in the last year or two.

In 1964-1965 primary produce accounted for almost 90 per cent of exports by value: pastoral products 49 per cent; agricultural products 27 per cent; minerals 7 per cent; dairy produce less than four per cent. Manufactured goods constituted ten per cent by value of all exports.

The United Kingdom and Japan are markets each for approximately one-fifth of Australian export commodities. The next largest customer—the United States—takes no more than ten per cent. In recent years the others have included New

New Zealand takes six per cent of Australia's exports and is her fourth-best customer. New Zealand buys mainly manufactured goods, especially iron and steel and machinery, and wheat and dried fruit. The United Kingdom normally supplies about the same proportion of Australia's imports as she takes of the Commonwealth's exports, although at times the United States has supplied just as great a share of the Commonwealth's requirements. Japan, Germany, Canada, France and the petroleum producing Arabian states on the Persian Gulf follow in order. It is the complaint of New Zealand that Australia buys from the Dominion much less than she sells to it. Imports from New Zealand (softwood timber, pulp, paper, fish and race-horses) amount to less than one per cent of all the Commonwealth's imports from overseas. Two major classes of imports represent eighty per cent of the value of all imports. These are: 'metals, metal manufacture and machinery' (including motor car chassis, bodies and parts, electrical machinery, cable, machine tools, special kinds of steel and cutlery) and 'apparel, textiles, etc.' (including mainly cotton, linen, silk and rayon piece goods). These come largely from the United Kingdom. Other major imports are petroleum, paper and stationery (in part from Canada, Sweden and the United States), tea (from India and Ceylon), earthenware, drugs and chemicals, surgical and scientific instruments, tobacco, rubber and timber.

ECONOMIC PROBLEMS

The rapidly rising prices paid after the war for some of Australia's major exports, especially for wool, wheat and minerals, tended for some time to hide the fact that the volume of the exportable surplus of certain other traditional export commodities was declining. Although the value of exports mounted to almost unbelievable heights, there was a rapid decline in the amount of meat and dairy produce available for shipment. In 1950-1951 the amount of beef exported was only half that of fifteen years before, and of mutton and lamb only one-fifth that of pre-war years. Indeed a greater quantity of rabbit meat was exported than of lamb and mutton. Most serious, however, was the decline in the quantity of butter exported from 262 million lb. in 1934-1935 to less than 4 million lb. in 1950-1951. Despite an improvement in the late 1950s, the production of foodstuffs in Australia has not kept pace with either the increase in population or the growth of *per capita* consumption. The progress of the manufacturing industries has tended to divert attention from the older and hitherto more important agricultural and pastoral industries. This could be a serious matter in a world in which food supplies are dwindling while population rises, and in which manufactured goods are being produced in tremendously expanded volume, range and variety, and in more and more countries.

POPULATION

In June 1954 Australia's population stood at 8,986,530. In 1959 it surged past the ten million mark. In mid-1965 it was estimated at eleven and a quarter millions. To study the growth and distribution of this population is to summarize both the geography and history of the continent.

GROWTH OF POPULATION

When gold was discovered in what later became Victoria, Australia had a population of 400,000, most of it already on the eastern seaboard. At that time Tasmania had the largest cluster of population outside New South Wales. But within a decade population had passed the million mark and Victoria already had half as many people again as New South Wales. Victoria maintained its lead until almost the end of the century, when the total population was approaching 4,000,000. At that time New South Wales had 36 per cent of the total (as against 37.1 today), Victoria 32 per cent (28), Queensland 13 per cent (14.5), South Australia 10 per cent (9), Western Australia 5 per cent (7), and Tasmania 4 per cent (3.5). The present pattern of distribution was already well-established sixty years ago. The steady growth of the Commonwealth's population from 1900 to 1940, when it reached 7,000,000, was at an average rate of about one per cent per annum. The effect of this growth was to populate still more heavily the areas already well-peopled fifty years earlier, and to swell the growth of the larger cities and ports. The population of the remoter rural areas has in the same period remained stable, or has actually declined, especially with the exhaustion of mineral deposits, deterioration of grazing and soil erosion.

But in the last few years there has been an almost explosive growth in population. In the intercensal period 1947-1954 population grew by 1,407,172, or more than eighteen per cent. In the following intercensal period (1954-1961) the additional population totalled 1,521,656, an increase of seventeen per cent. These are greater rates of growth than at any period since the 1880s. The average annual rate of increase between 1947 and 1961 was almost 2.3 per cent, a rate exceeded in few, if any, other countries of similar size and significance. The rapid rate of growth owes much to immigration and especially to planned and assisted immigration in the two decades after World War II. In the fifteen years after 1945 net immigration totalled almost a million and a quarter. In the 1960's it has averaged 75,000 per annum. Many of the new arrivals—'New Australians'—are displaced and refugee people from Europe. They comprise the largest non-British group to have come into Australia, whose people, however, are still almost wholly of British stock and, indeed, almost ninety per cent Australian-born.

It should be remembered that with all its 12,000,000 people Australia has still only one-third of one per cent of the world's population. Almost as many people live in Tokyo, London or New York as live in the 3,000,000 square miles of the Australian continent. With only three persons per square mile, against a world average density (excluding Antarctica) of fifty-five, Australia is the most sparsley peopled of all the major continents. But both Australia and New Zealand count for more in the world than their numbers would suggest. Their high levels of education and technology have enabled them to take maximum advantage of the resources at their disposal, given them a high level of *per capita* productivity and of world trade, and enabled their two countries to take a relatively prominent part in world affairs—economic, political, social and military.

Within Australia, people, like rainfall, fertile soil and power resources, are very unequally distributed. One-third of the continent has *no* people. Another third has less than one person to every eight square miles. Over ninety-three per cent of the

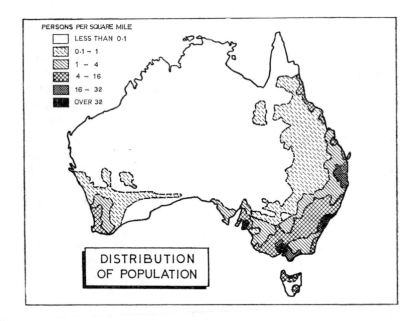

PERSONS PER SQUARE MILE
- LESS THAN 0·1
- 0·1 – 1
- 1 – 4
- 4 – 16
- 16 – 32
- OVER 32

DISTRIBUTION
OF POPULATION

Figure 49

people live, in fact, within 500 miles of the east coast, between Cairns and Eyre's Peninsula, and of these fifty-eight per cent live in ten coastal cities. Another six per cent of the total population lives in the extreme southwest of the continent, nearly sixty per cent of it in the city of Perth (*Fig. 49*).

URBAN POPULATION

After its irregular distribution, its degree of urbanization is the most outstanding feature of Australian population. Already extremely high, it is still increasing. Some fifty-six per cent of the population live in the six state capitals and the national capital, Canberra, and another twenty-five per cent in the smaller urban centres, including Darwin. No more than one-fifth of the population is described as rural. Between the two censuses (from 1954 to 1961) the population of the metropolitan centres increased by 21.1 per cent, that of the smaller provincial towns by 19.5 per cent, while the rural population increased by 2.8 per cent. Between 1947 and 1954 the rural population showed an absolute decrease. Three-fifths of the people of Victoria and South Australia live in their capital cities. In New South Wales and Western Australia the proportion is well over a half. The proportion of the total population living in the largest urban centre is less than forty per cent only in Tasmania, Queensland and the Northern Territory. In

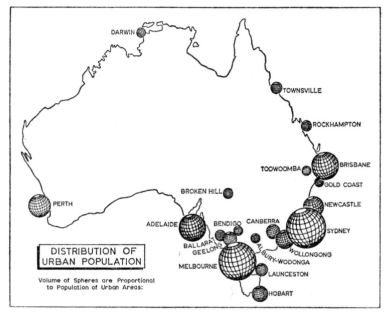

Figure 50

Tasmania this is largely because the second city, Launceston, has a population approaching in numbers that of Hobart itself; in Queensland there is a number of not inconsiderable towns, all of them secondary ports, strung out along the 1000 miles of a coast which Brisbane alone could not adequately serve. In Northern Territory three-quarters of the 'territorials' live on the cattle and sheep stations and in the mining camps scattered over the savanna. Darwin, the largest town, has not more than 17,000 people.

This high degree of urbanization is not without its problems and dangers. The vulnerability of Australia's coastal cities, their people, factories, port facilities, steam power plants and other concentrated installations was realized during the war. An effort has since been made to spread new factories through the small inland towns, but with little success. Excessively large cities, each sprawling far over the land, mean long distances to travel from home to work, loss of time and added cost in distributing goods, congestion of traffic and loss of amenities. The urban areas come to dominate the political scene, and this might be to the disadvantage of the farm and rural population and could lead to the neglect of the primary industries. In a world in which countries with surplus food supplies are becoming fewer, this could also be to the detriment of the national economy, long dependent on the export of the products of farm, orchard, vineyard and sheep station.

Most Australians are city dwellers and city workers. Nearly four out of every ten of them live in 'millionaire' cities. On June 30, 1965 the estimated populations of Sydney and Melbourne were 2,349,590 and 2,121,900 respectively. In the southern hemisphere only three other cities are as large or larger: Buenos Aires, Rio de Janeiro and Sao Paulo. At the same date the other Australian capital cities had the following estimated populations: Brisbane, 677,000; Adelaide, 614,600; Perth, 465,000; Hobart, 124,000. The Federal capital territory, Canberra, had 86,000 people.

RURAL POPULATION

Although the rural population of Australia is concentrated in the east and extreme southwest of the continent, it is still very thinly spread. Few areas of any size in the agricultural and pastoral districts of Australia have a rural population as dense even as that of the dairy lands of New Zealand. The average density of population in New Zealand, not excluding the inhospitable alpine highlands, is a little over twenty-six per square mile. The only considerable areas in Australia with a rural population of from five to twenty per square mile are the damp alluvial flats and lower valleys of the Queensland coast, southeastern Queensland and the mixed arable areas of the Darling Downs, the wheat and sheep-growing Western Slope of New South Wales, the grain lands of the Wimmera and northern Victoria with their wheatfields and intensively-cultivated pockets of irrigated land, the coastal area of Victoria with its improved permanent pastures and denser livestock populations, the coastal and valley lands of Tasmania with their richly mixed agricultural economies, the flanks of the Flinders Range in South Australia with their sloping vineyards and orchards and widespread crops of wheat and barley, and the winterrain districts of Swanland in Western Australia. Elsewhere densities of rural population are measured not in persons per square mile, but in square miles per person. The 'neighbouring' stations are far over the brown and dusty horizon, each a cluster of perhaps a dozen persons isolated in an apparently illimitable expanse of drab grazing land in glaring sunshine and shimmering dust haze, its landscape only superficially changed from what it was when still visited two centuries ago by nomadic bands of Stone Age indigenes in search of roots and insects in the parched red soil.

F

CHAPTER FOUR

Australia's
Pacific Island Neighbourhood

AUSTRALIA HAS emerged during the first half of the present century from a vigorous, hectic childhood of pioneering and experiment to a more stable, better balanced and increasingly responsible manhood. Until 1939 the Commonwealth was concerned almost exclusively with its own internal progress and development. It took for granted its traditional ties of blood, trade and culture with the parent from which it had sprung and with the family of which it was an energetic member. In time of peace it sought to develop its resources and subdue its lands while trusting implicitly in the industrial, military and naval strength of the United Kingdom to defend it and to maintain the freedom of the seas which were carrying a rapidly expanding volume of its products to distant markets. It remained little aware of the monsoon lands to the north, where lived half of mankind—people who were, in fact, Australia's closest 'neighbours'. Its gaze was directed across the Pacific to North America and to Panama, with the Atlantic and Europe beyond, or across the Indian Ocean to the Near East and Suez and the industrial markets in Europe to which this canal also provided access. Scarcely a glance was cast towards the 'Near North' and its tight-packed, miserable and often starving 1,200,000,000 inhabitants. With a policy of exclusion—the White Australia policy—the Commonwealth was content to work and play and develop its resources and living standards in a sense of false security, under the impression that a statute could insulate it from its millions of coloured neighbours.

AUSTRALIA AND ASIA

World War I temporarily ruffled the surface of this complacent and traditional attitude, especially when the Japanese moved south into the mandated islands of Micronesia. But Singapore's defences were strengthened. A second world war, however, successfully destroyed the attitudes and outlook of a century and a half. While Australia was absorbed with the prosaic and peaceful development of its agriculture and infant industries, warfare was being revolutionized with the development of aircraft and aircraft carriers, so that the Japanese were able in a month or two to leapfrog along the southeastern rim of the Asian continent, its arcuate peninsulas and island festoons, until they were established in New Guinea, and until Australia's northern coastline was under attack. It was only then at last that Australia came to realize that the continents of Asia and Australia are not widely separated and unrelated land-masses. Australia is to Asia much as is Africa to Europe. The Mediterranean has its counterpart in the Indonesian 'Mediterranean'. Singapore and Corregidor were in the 1940s not unlike Gibraltar and Malta. The coast of Northern Territory may be considered the equivalent of Tunisia, Libya and Tripolitania. The island-studded seas to the north of Australia are not as effective a zone of defence as the breadth and aridity of the continent's desert and savanna lands, which may well be compared with the Sahara and the Sudan. Since the war it has also become clear that Japan and the strategic islands in its vicinity, in friendly hands, could be an aircraft carrier for use against a continental aggressor just as were the British Isles during World War II.

After 1941 Australians also came to see how little they knew about even the nearer islands to the north. These obviously were their front line of defence. Australia had neither the military knowledge nor, alone, the power to defend them. They had been blind spots on the map as seen from Canberra. The war also demonstrated how distant London and Washington were in an emergency, and how vulnerable in modern warfare were the long sea communications across both the Indian and the

Pacific Oceans. As Japan attacked Ceylon and threatened to leapfrog south from the Solomons and Gilberts to New Caledonia and Fiji, there was a real possibility of Australia and New Zealand being isolated and cut off from all effective aid.

The people of Australia also discovered something of the broader political, social and economic, as well as of the narrower strategic problems of its Near North. In monsoon Asia, between India and Manchuria, were hundreds of millions of people. Most of them had depressed standards of living. Their technology was primitive and their economy largely a simple subsistence. But there were growing minorities amongst them that were becoming daily more aware of the better conditions to be obtained by the employment of the technical equipment of western nations, and more conscious of the standards of living already attained by the progressive but 'empty' lands in the southwestern Pacific. To many Australians, Asia's teeming millions are a great flood of humanity behind a slender dam that could easily break and inundate their country and terminate the hold they have had on their continent for a brief century and a half. Others view the situation a little more soberly, however, and are of opinion that the overcrowded lands could be assisted at home to higher levels of comfort and prosperity. If they were helped to acquire modern agricultural and industrial skills, they could be converted into more powerful and more prosperous but still friendly nations, with which Australia could trade and exist in closer association. It is with this view of the situation that the United Nations has brought aid and assistance to so many backward or under-developed countries. The more advanced countries within the British Commonwealth have also co-operated, independently of the United Nations, to devise the Colombo Plan, by means of which money, personnel and machines are being made available to India, Pakistan, Burma, Thailand, Malaysia and South Viet Nam, with a view to improving the conditions under which their people live. Hospitals, irrigation schemes, hydro-electric power plant, agricultural and industrial training establishments, scholarships which take Asians overseas to learn the western technology: all these and many other forms of assistance are being given. Both Australia and New Zealand are playing a prominent part in the operation of the Colombo Plan.

AUSTRALIA AND THE INDONESIAN 'MEDITERRANEAN'

The tropical insular territories between Asia and Australia have a remarkable diversity of physical and human conditions. Java has a population of over 70,000,000; New Guinea, nearly seven times as large, has not more than 2.75 million people. Western Indonesia has fabulous resources, many of them already tapped, so that before the last war, under Dutch stimulus and guidance, it was responsible for over three-quarters of the quinine, pepper and kapok entering world trade, over a quarter of the rubber, copra, coconut oil and palm oil, and over a fifth of the tin and tea. The outer territories of eastern Indonesia on the other hand have remained largely undeveloped, their resources little known. The whole region has a miscellany of ethnic groups and a complex assemblage of languages and dialects. On the 2000 or so inhabited islands—out of a total of 7083—in the Philippines alone more than eighty different tongues are spoken. Britain, Spain, Holland, Portugal, Germany and the United States have all at times had territorial responsibilities in the Indonesian 'Mediterranean'. The many islands, large and small, have little in common except that all of them are weak, largely undeveloped and are, or have been until relatively recently, politically and economically under alien control. Although both the Philippines and Indonesia have since the war gained or been granted political independence, they remain economically dependent. If Australia is to be safe from attack and invasion from the north, it is desirable either that the region be in the hands of strong powers or that the emergent nationalism in those lands should give rise to close-knit and well-organized local governments, able and willing to co-operate in security plans organized on a regional basis. Economic prosperity and rising standards of living seem almost equally indispensable.

Some Australians claim that the islands of the Indonesian 'Mediterranean' are as essential to the development of Australia as to its defence. The continent and the islands to the north of it are not only neighbours by location but are also economic complements. It is argued that Australian industry is already sufficiently developed to be in a position to supply these underdeveloped lands with the machinery and equipment necessary for their development. It is claimed that Australian industry, in view of its limited domestic market, can only develop beyond present levels if foreign markets are opened up. Moreover the untapped mineral wealth, the millions of acres of virgin tropical soils, both the proven and as yet undiscovered petroleum resources, the already great output of tropical raw materials and foodstuffs: all these, it is claimed, are essential to the further development of Australia itself. However, the undoubtedly great potential mineral wealth of tropical territories cannot be readily exploited—as Australia has already discovered in New Guinea; the fertility of virgin tropical soils is rarely what it seems, and western science has still to discover ways of working tropical soils on a permanent and non-destructive basis—ways which at the same time will be significantly superior to the traditional practices of the island cultivator. Moreover, a programme of this kind would require vast capital resources which neither Australia nor even the United Kingdom can at present supply. Despite a growing postwar inflow from Britain and the United States, and more recently from Japan, Australia is still sadly short of capital with which to develop further its internal potentialities and those of its own dependent territories.

AUSTRALIA AND THE PACIFIC WORLD

At different times in its history, even from its infant years, Australia has shown intermittent interest in the Pacific as distinct from the Indonesian 'Mediterranean'. From the date of its establishment New South Wales was always aware of the possibility of some European power—first of all France and later Germany—becoming established in the island territories to the east, including New Zealand. At a time when Britain was not anxious to extend its colonial commitments, the Australian colonies, singly or in concert, tried to force the hand of the mother country. But in spite of the repeated demands for British action in New Zealand, New Guinea or the New Hebrides, the Australian governments were themselves reluctant to shoulder either the responsibility or the cost of the policy they advocated. Since World War I, however, it has been clear that the threat to Australia came not from any European power in the Pacific but from Asia. Since World War II Australia has been more than anxious to meet the cost and face the responsibility entailed in maintaining its national interests in the Pacific. This is shown nowhere more clearly than in the initiative taken by Australia in suggesting and vigorously pursuing the policy which has resulted in the Anzac Pact (1944), the South Pacific Commission (1947), the Colombo Plan (1950) and the ANZUS Agreement (1951). It is revealed also in Australia's active military participation in the defence of Malaysia and South Viet Nam. If Britain is to give up its military commitments east of Suez, more and more responsibility will fall on Australian shoulders.

The Anzac (or Canberra) Pact embodied an agreement signed between Australia and New Zealand in which they acknowledged their Pacific responsibilities and clearly stated their joint intention of discharging them. It asserted their right to assume responsibility for the defence of the island arc 'north and northeast of Australia to Western Samoa and the Cook Islands', and it staked their claims to participation in any postwar changes in the Pacific, and to a voice in the interim administration and ultimate disposal of enemy territories. Australia's material strategic and economic interests make it essential that it should play a leading part in both what we have called the Pacific World and the Indonesian 'Mediterranean', but its determination to do so rests also in part on the belief that the Commonwealth (and the Dominion of New Zealand) can make a contribution, through enlightened administration, through research, technical assistance and good will, to the social, economic and political advancement of the island peoples. This objective is formally set down and shared with New Zealand, the United Kingdom, the United States, France, and the Netherlands in the agreement they signed to establish a South Pacific Commission in 1947. The Commission was subsequently set up in Noumea in New Caledonia and has now been operating for nearly twenty years.

The latest aspect of the new outlook and of the increased Australian responsibility in the Pacific was embodied in the ANZUS Pact of 1951, when, after the signing of the Japanese peace treaty, Australia and New Zealand sought and secured the promise of United States military assistance should they or their island territories be threatened with attack from any source. In return they pledged their assistance to the United

States in similar circumstances. It has been repeatedly emphasized that this does not in any way weaken the ties of the two
Dominions with the United Kingdom, but it does recognize
the predominant position of the United States in the Pacific
and the decreased ability of the United Kingdom to carry the
burdens it has so long shouldered almost alone. It demonstrates
also the determination of Australia and New Zealand to become
the legatees of British power and influence in the Pacific.

AUSTRALIAN TERRITORIES

Apart from Northern Territory and the Australian Capital
Territory on the continental mainland, and the unimportant
Territory of Ashmore and Cartier Islands (small reefs off the
northwest of the continent annexed to Northern Territory), the
dependent areas for which the Commonwealth is directly responsible are: (1) the Territory of Papua (formerly British New
Guinea); (2) the Territory of New Guinea (administered by
Australia under a trusteeship agreement with the United Nations, formerly a League of Nations mandated territory and
before 1914 a German protectorate); (3) Nauru (which in
succession has been part of the German protectorate of New
Guinea, a League of Nations mandate and a trusteeship territory administered by Australia for and on behalf of the joint
trustees—the United Kingdom, Australia and New Zealand);
(4) Norfolk Island; (5) the Australian Antarctic Territory (which
like New Zealand's Ross Sea Dependency, is part of the icy
waste of the Antarctic World and not of the Pacific World) together with Heard and McDonald Islands; (6) the Cocos
(Keeling) Islands on two atolls 2290 miles west of Darwin,
transferred from the Colony of Singapore to the Commonwealth in 1955 (Direction Island has a civil air base and makes
Cocos an important staging post on the route from Australia
to South Africa); (7) Christmas Island in the Indian Ocean, 800
miles from Singapore and 1600 miles from Fremantle, suc-
cessively administered since 1888 by the Straits Settlements, the
Colony of Singapore and by the United Kingdom as a separate
colony until in 1958 the island was transferred to the Commonwealth of Australia. With its 55 square miles and its population
of 3000 odd, Christmas Island is extraordinarily important to
Australia and New Zealand for the half million tons of phos-

phate it produces each year. Lord Howe Island in mid-Tasman is also Australian territory. It is technically a dependency of New South Wales and its population—less than 250—is entitled to vote in one of the Sydney electorates. Macquarie Island, 1000 miles southeast of Hobart, is a dependency of Tasmania and the site of a scientific base. It is a neighbour of New Zealand's Auckland and Campbell Islands.

But within the neighbourhood of Australia itself and its territories are a number of other dependent insular territories which, although in fact the responsibility of other countries, are coming more and more within the Commonwealth's enlarged sphere of influence. These lie off Australia's northern and northeastern shores. In addition to the trade which they conduct with Australia and the ties they have with the Commonwealth as a result of the pattern and arrangement of air and sea communications, they are significant also in the military affairs of the Pacific World, for they form part of the defensive screen of island territories behind which Australia shelters. They include the rest of the island of New Guinea, now under Indonesian jurisdiction; the British Solomon Islands Protectorate; the Anglo-French Condominium of the New Hebrides and the French island of New Caledonia.

NEW GUINEA

Largest and most important of all the territories within Australia's Pacific island neighbourhood is New Guinea, itself as large as the state of New South Wales and three times as large as New Zealand. Its 314,000 square miles are divided politically into three. The western half of the island constituted until 1963 the only part of the former Netherlands East Indies left in the hands of the Dutch after the formation of the independent republic of Indonesia in December 1949. But in 1963 the Dutch, in the absence of support from the United Nations, the United States or of Australia and New Zealand, were obliged to vacate the territory. For a short time it was administered by the United Nations and afterwards handed over to Indonesia subject to certain conditions including provision for a referendum among the Papuans on self-determination. The Indonesians call it *Irian Barat*. The eastern half of New Guinea falls politically into two parts, although both are administered by Australia, and since 1949 have constituted an administrative union with one administrator, one supreme court and one public service. The *Territory of New Guinea* comprises North East New Guinea (the 'Mainland'), the Bismarck Archipelago, which includes New Britain, New Ireland, Lavongai (New Hanover), and the Admiralty Islands, together with the two northernmost islands in the Solomons group (Buka and Bougainville). This is the former German territory. It is administered today by Australia under a trusteeship agreement with the United Nations. The southeastern part of the island of New Guinea became a protectorate of the United Kingdom in 1884 and was known as British New Guinea. In 1906 it was taken over by the infant Commonwealth of Australia and became the *Territory of Papua*. In addition to the mainland south of the central mountain ranges, and the southeastern 'tail' formed by the projection of the Owen Stanley Range, the Territory of Papua also includes the islands of the Trobriand, Woodlark, D'Entrecasteaux and Louisiade groups off the tail of the mainland.

THE MOUNTAINS

From the extremity of the Vogelkop (the Bird's Head) to the Louisiade Archipelago, New Guinea extends through 25 degrees of longitude, a distance of over 1600 miles. Near the Indonesian-Australian frontier the island is almost 500 miles wide. New Guinea is thus one of the few large areas outside the frozen lands of the higher latitudes which remain sparsely populated and underdeveloped. It is 'backward' in the sense that its people have little contact with the modern world and have not been drawn into the commercial system of the west. It is so large, remote and, because of its mountainous terrain, so inaccessible that large parts of it are still unexplored. In its isolated mountain valleys there still live some Stone Age tribes that have not yet seen a white man. Officers of the Australian administration are employed in exploring remote hill country and extending the area in which it can be said that the indigenous people have been brought into 'friendly relations' with the administration. Even in Papua, patrols of government officers are still attacked by hostile native bands using bows and

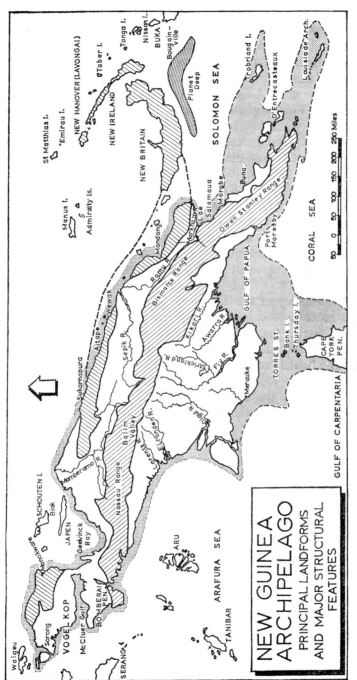

NEW GUINEA
ARCHIPELAGO
PRINCIPAL LANDFORMS
AND MAJOR STRUCTURAL
FEATURES

Figure 51

arrows. Other native tribes have not yet secured the simplest of introduced tools like knives and steel axes. They still use a pointed stick for planting and sharpened stone for cutting.

New Guinea is traversed from east to west by two distinctive series of mountain ranges (*Fig. 51*). In the north a succession of narrow coastal ranges, rising at times to 7000 feet, runs from the Vogelkop to the Huon Peninsula and is continued as a sharply curving, broken arc in the Bismarck Archipelago. On the mainland the coast ranges are broken by Geelvinck Bay, the narrow defile of the Mamberamo River and the joint delta plain of the Sepik and Ramu Rivers. Between Wewak (on the northern coast) and Rabaul (in New Britain) the ranges are paralleled by an arcuate series of young and active volcanoes, forming great piles of volcanic rock which stand usually as islands off-shore. The coastal ranges are sharply separated from the central axial mountain system by a discontinuous structural depression occupied in part by McCluer Gulf, the upper longitudinal sections of the Mamberamo, Sepik and Ramu Rivers and the valley of the Markham. This structural feature may well be continued in the trough of the Planet Deep south of New Britain. The main axial highland is a jumble of parallel ranges and elevated plateaus often separated by deep, forested furrows which might take days to cross. Some ice-flanked peaks rise to 15,000 or 16,000 feet. In the east and west of New Guinea the mass of dissected mountains—frequently snow-capped along the summit ranges—occupy the whole width of the island. The extensive lowland between the river plains of the Digul and the Fly is a fourth distinctive structural feature. It is a low plain or plateau structurally akin to the Western Plateau of Australia; but it is largely surrounded by recent alluvial, delta-like accumulations and in part covered by recent marine, alluvial and volcanic ash deposits. It is a broad lowland traversed by meandering rivers often as wide as any in the world and spreading, when in flood, to link up innumerable lakes and swamps into an enormous expanse of dirty, shallow flood water.

THE VEGETATION

Most of New Guinea is forested. The abundance of precipitation is in most places enough to ensure a dense and lush tropical forest vegetation. But rainfall is irregularly distributed in time and place. The seasonal reversal of the direction of flow of humid air masses—northwards in the southern winter and southwards towards Australia in the southern summer— makes for sharp differences in the amount and season of precipitation. Northerly coasts have a marked concentration of rainfall in the period between November and March. This is especially true of the coast between Salamaua and Milne Bay and of the north coast of New Britain. Coasts at right angles to the northwestward flow of moist air between April and October get most of their rain then. Lindenhafen (on the south coast of New Britain) with an average annual precipitation of 259 inches, has over 200 inches of rain between May and October. Inland areas cut off from the moist air masses by mountain ranges on many sides, and coastal areas, which lie parallel with the seasonal flow of air, have surprisingly little rain. Much of the northeast coast between Aitape and Madang has in some years no more than sixty inches, the goldfield settlements in the Watut valley have an average of less than sixty inches, and the Port Moresby coast as little as forty inches, with only six or seven inches in the five or six months when air masses are blowing northwestwards towards the head of the Gulf of Papua.

In addition to the rich and varied tropical rainforest with its Malayan and Australian affinities, wide areas of lower rainfall, or with their rain concentrated markedly in one part of the year, have an open savanna vegetation or a treeless cover of *kunai* grass (*Imperator* spp.) tall reed grasses and other wild grasses—*pit-pit*—closely related to sugar cane. The grassland areas of rough tropical *kunai* have also been extended in inland inhabited areas by the shifting cultivation and the burning of forest and scrub practised by the natives.

In New Guinea (as in Indonesia, the Philippines and many other tropical-forest habitats still occupied by primitive peoples) the introduction of the steel axe has shifted the ecological balance and enabled the natives to clear much larger areas of forest without the necessity of leaving burned stumps and a litter of logs not devoured by fire. Two results have followed: a rapid expansion of the area occupied by a brown carpet of *kunai* or by a sea of waving *pit-pit* plumes; and the spread of the menace of soil erosion. In the Central Highlands of Australian New Guinea recently-cleared hillsides about Mount Hagen and in the valley of the Wahgi are often bespattered with ugly slips and incipient gullies, whilst the adjacent wide valley floors have had their drainage-ways clogged with new-brought silt and have been converted into expanding swamps of cane grass and sedges.

Ill-drained coastal lowlands in New Guinea are rarely occupied by the indigenous peoples. Their vegetation is thus a little-modified expanse of swamp plants, nipa or sago palms and pandanus with a coastal fringe of mangrove on delta mudflats and of *Barringtonia* and coconut palms on higher sandspits and ridges. Such lowlands remain trackless wastes, the only highway being the wide stretch of a sluggish river snaking its way across the flat from the mountain defiles to the sea. Some valleys have oak forests, and population often follows the oak. High ridges in the mountainous interior have coniferous forests with potentially valuable ancient stands of inaccessible podocarps and hoop pines (*Araucaria*) and kauri. Higher still there is often a wet, silent moss forest of beech trees tangled with hairy mosses, lichens and creepers, and some high plateaus have a short grass cover of cloud-belt savannas. These also have been frequently extended by deforestation and shifting cultivation. The population of interior valleys, adjacent ridges and high plateaus of open, man-made parkland is usually much higher than that of the often-swampy coastlands, and in places so dense that locally there is pressure of population on resources. Here land is rotated too frequently and deforestation has been excessive.

THE NATIVE PEOPLE

The native people of New Guinea are as varied as its vegetational associations. The Papuans of the southeast, dark, woolly-haired and of medium stature, are a blend in which Australoid elements are dominant. The shorter and sometimes pygmy tribes of the interior and the west are derived from the original Negritoid invaders. Most numerous in the east, and especially in the more accessible coastal districts and throughout the Bismarck Archipelago and the Solomons, are the tall frizzy-haired Melanesians of mixed ethnic ancestry. A great variety of languages and dialects is spoken, and even the people of adjacent valleys, especially in New Britain, have no common vehicle of communication. In coastal areas, however, where contact with the outside world has been frequent—not only in New Guinea but generally throughout Melanesia—'pidgin' English has served as a lingua franca.

There are today probably almost 2,750,000 indigenes in New Guinea, almost one and a half million of them in the Territory of New Guinea, almost 525,000 in Papua, and 750,000 in the Dutch half of the island. There are about 153,000 Melanesians in New Britain and New Ireland, and in addition 56,000 in Buka and Bougainville (including groups of Polynesians in the Taku Islands). There are also over 18,500 native people in the Admiralty Islands, mainly on Manus, and these are dominantly Micronesians. Europeans in the Australian territories number about 21,500, and other non-indigenes total 5000. The Europeans are clustered in the administrative centres and plantation districts on the coast or in the isolated mining settlements, most of them in the Morobe District (Lae, Bulolo, Wau and Salamaua) of the trust territory, in New Britain, on Manus (military and defence personnel), and in the Central District of Papua (Port Moresby). The heaviest concentration of native population is in the Central Highlands districts of the two Australian territories. In the valleys and on the remote ridges and plateaus between Telefomin, Mount Hagen and the upper reaches of the Purari River there are almost 500,000 native people. Less is known, since Indonesia took over, of the composition of the population of Irian Barat. Before the retirement of the Dutch the European population reached 15,000 and the Asians numbered 20,000. Today the European population at least is much less.

No native people in the Pacific have remained so little disturbed by the civilization and technology of the world outside as have the mixed ethnic groups of New Guinea. Their lives are lived and their agriculture practised much as they were when these Stone Age people first entered New Guinea many thousands of years ago. Their tools, crops, customs and dwellings have changed little since the high, wooded valleys and the palm-fringed shores were first occupied.

NATIVE AGRICULTURE

In Irian Barat a tributary of the south-flowing Lorentz River cuts back in a deep gorge across the Snow Mountains to their inaccessible northern slopes. Here in a fifty-mile stretch of the Balim valley live at least 60,000 people who before 1937 had had no contact with the white man. They constitute the Dani tribes. The abrupt slopes of the valley rise steeply from over 5000 feet to bleak highlands beyond the tree line and standing more than 12,000 feet in elevation. Originally the valley floor was occupied by swamp patches and dense tropical rainforest. On the valley sides were forests of oaks, and above them tall forests of antarctic beech reached up to the cloudbelt short-grass savanna. In centuries of occupation the Papuan and pygmy Negritoid tribes have removed practically all the forest up to the elevation of the beech woodland. Wide stretches of the valley sides are now a dry-looking yellow-brown expanse of grass and reed and abandoned cultivation. The lower edge of the beech forest at an elevation of 8000 feet is being cleared with stone adzes and fire to provide peaty, but cultivable, land. Villages and people are found today either in the valley bottom, where agriculture is practised intensively on alluvial soils, or around the lower edge of the beech forest, where virgin forest soils are still available, after clearing, for cultivation. A few semi-nomadic folk live near the upper edge of the beech forest. They hunt with bow and arrow in the alpine grassland above and catch wildfowl in the mountain lakes. Their only agriculture consists in planting pandanus in natural clearings in the beech forest and harvesting the almond-like oily seeds of this palm.

The main crop of the shifting agriculturalists on the lower rim of the beech forest is the sweet potato. Land is cleared, logs are used as contour banks to prevent the new-cleared soil from washing away in tropical downpours, and several carefully weeded crops of sweet potato are taken from the tidily raised beds before the land is left to revert to a soil-enriching stand of second-growth forest. But at these altitudes forest growth is tardy. The land is soon required again, and after each period of cropping, second growth decreases in density until finally the land is occupied by aggressive, wind-dispersed grasses and becomes of little value for cultivation. In village enclosures small areas are devoted to sugar cane, taro, cucumbers and bananas. The gardeners' only tools are stout digging sticks, and smaller, pointed sticks used by the women in weeding. Stone adzes are used for felling trees and stone axes for splitting timber.

In the valley the deep and swampy alluvial soils are drained by a close pattern of deep ditches. Some serve as sunken roads and pathways. Black soil from other ditches is used to spread on the raised gardens alongside. Grass on adjacent hill slopes and unused flats is cut for composting. Crop yields are raised by using green manure and pig manure. Sweet potato especially but also taro, cucumbers, gourds, spinach, beans and bananas are grown, and in enclosures within the villages themselves tobacco, sugar cane and bananas are planted. This intensive, permanent and thoughtfully-planned horticulture is capable of supporting dense populations. It is of interest to notice that in the Balim valley, once densely forested, it is now necessary to plant rows of tall, slender casuarina trees along the edge of gardens or in groves on the hillsides or along the banks of the river in order to provide a hard, durable timber for making simple tools and for building material and fuel.

Until their departure the Netherlands administrators of the territory were attempting to improve communication to and within the Balim valley, not so much with the intention of modernizing the traditional economic and social life of the Dani people, as with the object of pacifying them and bringing them within the orbit of administration, law and protection. The internal Dutch airline *Kroonduif* operated a DC3 service from Sentani (Hollandia) across the maze of hills and mountains and through the mass of heavy tropical cloud to Wamena, the administrative centre of the valley. The aircraft carried occasional passengers but were more important as freighters, transporting machinery, corrugated iron, cement, soap, foodstuffs, cattle, a Landrover or two, a bulldozer and miscellaneous tools and hardware to an area with no other external links and in which lived a relatively dense population of sophisticated cultivators of elevated tropical soils not one of which had seen the coast or knew of the existence of the sea.

A road was being constructed along the valley floor westwards from Wamena, which was simply a collection of corrugated iron buildings housing the airport personnel and

government officers and temporary official visitors and research workers. Wamena was also missionary headquarters,
and to some parts of the valley access was only possible by
small planes operated by missions out of Wamena. Flights by
such aircraft at low elevations reveal not only the intensive
pattern of kumara garden cultivation but also the persistence
of inter-tribal and inter-village war. On most flights it was possible to see village huts that had been burned to the ground and
even groups of Dani youths on the warpath. What progress
has been accomplished in the Balim valley since 1963 is difficult
to say.

In other parts of New Guinea similar, if less intensive, systems
of both shifting and fixed cultivation are practised. In the dry
upper Watut valley, gardens are irrigated with bamboo pipelines and aqueducts. In different districts sweet potatoes, yams,
taro, maize and cassava are the principal food crops of native
gardeners. In some coastal districts, and on wide, lower flood-
plains of large rivers like the Sepik and Ramu, sago palms,
planted in rows and grown to a height of six feet before they
are cut and the pith removed from the trunk, provide the staple
food. Other nomadic tribes, especially in Irian Barat, merely
collect and harvest the pith of palms growing wild. Still others
collect trochus shell and catch cassowaries and birds of paradise
for their feathers. On some stretches of coast the coconut is a
principal source of food supplemented by marine foods, and
in some more accessible districts natives cure copra and sell
small quantities at the nearest trading post.

The native people of New Guinea were seriously disturbed by
the war. Scores of thousands of them were uprooted as the
war moved back and forth across the mountain ranges and
hurtled up and down remote coastlands. Crashed aircraft are
still being discovered in little trodden hills and bush. Villages
were destroyed in hundreds. Native agriculture was neglected
and customary ways of life disrupted. In an attempt to resettle
uprooted tribes and to rehabilitate disarranged economies, the
administration has in some parts of the vast territory conducted
social and agricultural experiments which—if successful—will
locally accomplish a violent revolution in native agricultural
practices and economy. Already some groups, which before the
war had little more in the way of western equipment and tech-

nology than steel knives and axes, and who were accustomed only to the garden cultivation of the traditional root crops, are now using tractors to plough virgin soils and to prepare the ground for large plots of dryland rice.

One example of this sudden shift from digging stick to tractor and from native garden culture to mechanized cultivation of grain is to be found on the lower floodplain of the St. Joseph River near the coast of the Gulf of Papua eighty miles north of Port Moresby. Here the Mekeo people are cultivating several hundred acres of rice each year with the assistance of pools of machinery provided by the administration and by co-operative organization of land and labour. The native co-operative societies have also made a start with the cultivation of soya bean, sesame, castor beans and groundnuts. In the same area, under the guidance of the territory's department of agriculture, experiments are being conducted with the native cultivation of coffee, tea, cocoa and pepper on adjacent hill land. But this revolution has affected only an insignificant fraction of the total population of the Australian territories; the vast majority of the war-disrupted native folk have gone back to their traditional way of life even though many of them have had to build new homes and have been deeply disturbed—socially and psychologically—by their experiences during the 1940s.

COMMERCIAL PLANTATION AGRICULTURE

The coconut is by far the most important commercial crop, not only in New Guinea, but throughout the Bismarck Archipelago and the Solomon Islands Protectorate. It occupies more than ninety per cent of the area in commercial plantation holdings. The other plantation crops—coffee, cocoa, rubber, rice, bananas, kapok and kenaf—occupy a minor place, and some indeed are not yet fully established, but are found largely on government experimental stations. There are nearly 500 coconut plantations in New Guinea, New Britain, New Ireland and the northern Solomons (*Fig. 52*). Coconut palms are planted in geometrical arrangement on over a quarter of a million acres, an area twice as large as that sown to wheat in New Zealand. In the former Dutch half of the island the only European 'plantations' were small holdings. They were clustered near Hollandia (Soekanupura) and Manokware, with others at Me-

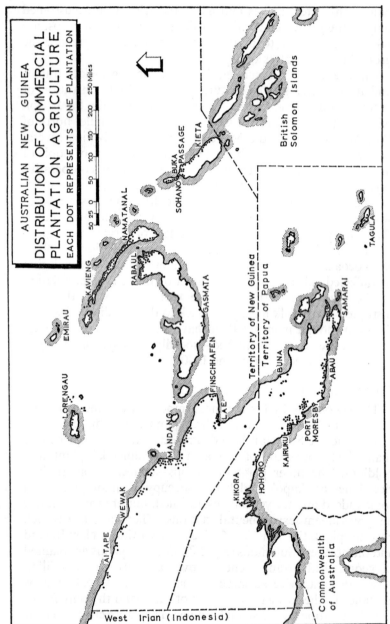

Figure 52

rauke. In Papua, with its 26,000 acres in rubber trees and only slightly more in coconuts (34,000 acres), the plantations are strung out on the narrow littoral from the Gulf of Papua to Milne Bay with the rubber estates in hilly valleys inland from Port Moresby. In the Territory of New Guinea the northern coast of the Gazelle Peninsula has half the acreage in coconuts (67,000 acres) and the two adjacent coastal strips of New Ireland have another quarter. In the Solomons, Buka and Bougainville have almost as many plantations as the mainland of the Territory of New Guinea. There most of the neatly-ordered lines of palms are found near Madang. Little rubber is produced in the trust territory, and cacao is the second most important plantation crop. Fourth in area on plantations are sweet potatoes which, together with taro, maize, rice and papaw are grown as foodstuffs for the plantation workers and for sale in the administrative centres and ports. The native labourers on the plantations, which are concentrated with few exceptions on well-drained portions of the coastline, are often recruited under close government supervision in the Central Highlands and in the hill country north and south of the Sepik valley. Throughout the Australian territories about 95,000 native workers are employed for wages. Most of them are casual workers, but some are employed on long-term or short-term agreements. Almost a third are employed by the administration; most of the remainder work on plantations with a minority on the goldfields, in desiccated-coconut factories, in sawmills, and on the wharves in the numerous small copra-shipping ports. Of the 65,000 indigenous people employed on wages in the Territory of New Guinea, 20,000 are employed by the administration and 45,000 are in private employments; 28,000 of them are general plantation workers.

There are few domestic animals in New Guinea. There are pigs and poultry—often half wild—in and around many a native village on dry and breezy hill ridges or in damp and forested valleys. Pigs are the most numerous and most important animal in all three New Guinea territories. In mountain villages almost as much care is devoted to pigs as to children and they often live in the long houses with the women and children. Cattle in villages are rare, but on commercial and government experimental holdings there are possibly 50,000 cattle, 3000 pigs and 2000 sheep. Most of the cattle are in the Territory of New Guinea: they graze the weed growth on coconut plantations. But in recent years interest has been aroused in the possibilities of rearing livestock in the drier, elevated plateau interior in the upper Markham, Ramu and Purari valleys between Lae and Mount Hagen in the southern part of the trust territory. Both privately-operated and government-operated mixed cropping and livestock-rearing farms have been established, and much experimental work is being carried out. New breeds of cattle have recently been introduced both by plantation owners and government agricultural stations in attempts to find strains and crosses suited to the varied climatic environments and pasture grasses available. Among the more successful beef breeds under New Guinea conditions are Shorthorn crossed with Brahman (Indian) cattle and with Africander. In New Guinea the former cross is called Droughtmaster. Similarly efforts are being made both on coastal copra plantations and in the highlands, where unpalatable *kunai* and *pit-pit* grass has replaced forest, to establish better grasses, legumes and pastures. Hitherto, as in other tropical islands of the Pacific, Guinea grass, para grass, elephant grass (*Pennisetum*) and molasses grass have proved the most successful tropical pasture grasses. In 1951 New Guinea's first wool clip—valued at $A9000—was exported.

In lowland New Guinea rice is the most promising commercial crop, and the wide valley floors and immense swampy and alluvial deltas appear to offer European commercial enterprise the opportunity of considerably expanding the acreage of rice, given modern methods of drainage and mechanized land clearing and cultivation. With the growth of towns on the coast, the growing of traditional and introduced vegetable and fruit crops in their vicinity is of increasing significance. Starchy native crops and green European vegetables are both produced, trucked and sold in increasing quantities. Passionfruit are of growing value to native gardeners producing cash crops. In the Territory of New Guinea they now produce more than

600 tons, sufficient to support small juice and pulp extracting and canning industries.

MINING

The only other 'development' that has taken place in New Guinea is the partial exploitation of its mineral resources. These, of course, are little known. But already New Guinea has yielded over $A60 millions worth of gold. Most of the gold comes from the Morobe District in the trust territory, especially from the valleys of the Watut and Bulolo, upper tributaries of the Markham. The Morobe field is shut away in deep, forested valleys. The deposits were opened up originally by using native carriers to take equipment into the interior. But the deposits proved so rich that it became possible to use air transport and to build airstrips and in the 1930s to fly the parts of huge dredges (some from New Zealand) and mining personnel into the valleys and to fly the gold bullion out.

Production reached a peak just before the Japanese invasion. The gold was found mainly in alluvial placer deposits. Three-quarters of the yield was won by huge electrically-operated bucket dredges like those which worked on the west coast of the South Island of New Zealand. Power was supplied by harnessing tumbling mountain tributaries of the main rivers. Today most of $A1 million worth of gold mined in the Territory of New Guinea comes from alluvial mining and lode mining at Wau, Edie Creek and Kainantu. Wau is the largest mining town, and is the urban and administrative centre of the Morobe goldfields. Other small quantities of gold are won in the Sepik valley and the upper Ramu and Purari valleys. During the Japanese invasion much mining equipment was destroyed. The industry is hardly rehabilitated even now, and production is considerably less than it was before the war, and is still declining. This, though, is partly owing to the exhaustion of the richer alluvial deposits. Before the war, gold was by far the most valuable export of both Australian territories: today it takes an inferior place after copra, desiccated coconut, coconut oil, cocoa, coffee and even plywood.

There is evidence of many other minerals in New Guinea and the Bismarck Archipelago. The only others mined at the present time in the Australian territories, however, are silver, manganese ore (from Papua) and a few ounces of platinum. But in Irian Barat petroleum is found in coastal and inland districts of the Vogelkop. Before the Dutch left the territory the flow of oil from the wells north of McCluer Gulf was steadily declining but prospecting had taken place also along the coast to Hollandia. Many test drills have already been sunk in different parts of the Australian areas but as yet without revealing payable deposits of crude oil.

Trade and Transport

The trade of the Dutch territory was until 1963 conducted mainly with Holland, Singapore and Japan; that of the Australian territories very largely with the Commonwealth. Since the Indonesian occupation of Irian Barat its only external contacts have been with Jakarta. Today the Australian territories are importing more from Japan and the United States: their exports, however, still go overwhelmingly to Australia. From Papua and New Guinea and the Bismarck Archipelago copra, desiccated coconut, coconut oil, oil cake and meal were exported in 1965 to the value of over $A20 millions, six sevenths of it from the trust territory. Next in importance were coffee and cocoa beans—all from the trust territory. Then followed in order of value rubber (which, as a result of the high prices ruling, was the chief export of Papua), timber, plywood and veneers, gold, (crocodile) skins, peanuts, passionfruit juice and pulp, and trochus, green snail and tortoise shell. Apart from rubber, these export commodities come largely from the trust territory and especially from the insular eastern part of it. The total trade of the Territory of New Guinea is more than double in value that of Papua: it is also very much more nearly balanced than that of Papua, thanks to the high productivity and greater development of the tropical agricultural resources of New Britain, New Ireland and the northernmost Solomons. In Papua imports are more than four times the value of the exports.

The trade of Irian Barat passes through Hollandia on the north coast, Merauke in the south, Biak, Manokware and the oil ports—Sorong and Steenkool. The busiest port in the New Guinea area is Rabaul, the former German capital of the Protectorate of New Guinea, on the volcano-clustered northern part of New Britain's Gazelle Peninsula (*Fig. 53*). It is followed in order of importance by Port Moresby, capital for the combined administration of the two territories, Lae, port for the Markham valley and the goldfields, Madang, shipping entrepôt for the northern mainland and the Admiralties, and Samarai on the China Strait at the easternmost tip of the mainland, serving both the mainland coast and the scattered plantations in the D'Entrecasteaux and Louisiade Islands. Small vessels call at innumerable private landings at intervals along the coasts, where plantations have produce for shipping to the main ports at which overseas vessels call to pick up export cargoes.

There are few parts of the world in which, by comparison with methods of land transport, aircraft play a greater role. The main rivers, though navigable for considerable distances, provide access only into little-settled and undeveloped districts. There are few roads. The longest stretch of road runs along almost the whole length of the east coast of New Ireland; there is another from Lae to Wau, and a small but concentrated network serves the highly-productive commercial holdings behind Rabaul, whilst other serviceable roads lead a few miles back into the hills near Port Moresby.

Air services, however, form a dense network over the whole of the Australian territories, excluding only some of the lesser island groups. This is despite some of the most difficult physical conditions in the world. Not only is the terrain difficult with its high elevations, sharp ridges and deep, narrow valleys, but the climate is such that the cloud cover is thick and changeable. Massive cloud sometimes decks the mountains and is stacked above them to a height of 50,000 feet. Coastal areas, isolated settlements, administrative posts and mining camps in the central highlands, and outlying commercialized districts on the larger islands of the eastern archipelago, are however all linked by air with the main ports, and via Lae, Port Moresby, and either Cairns or Cooktown (in Queensland) with the rest of the Australian continent. In 1965 there were over 300 aerodromes, 213 in the Territory of New Guinea alone. The social and national value of airstrips in otherwise remote and isolated valleys, served only by bush tracks and native paths, was notably displayed when the volcanic Mount Lamington in the Hydrographers Range exploded in January 1951. The moun-

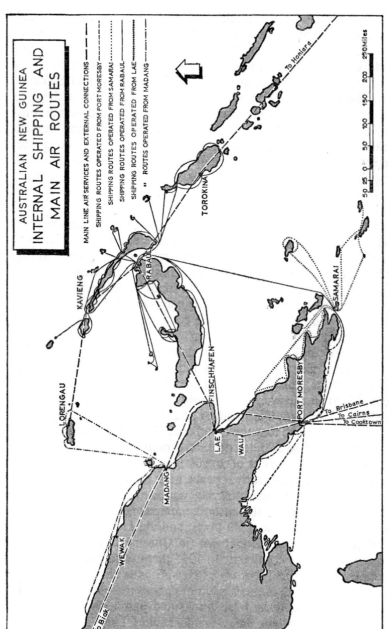

AUSTRALIAN NEW GUINEA
INTERNAL SHIPPING AND
MAIN AIR ROUTES

MAIN LINE AIR SERVICES AND EXTERNAL CONNECTIONS
SHIPPING ROUTES OPERATED FROM PORT MORESBY
SHIPPING ROUTES OPERATED FROM SAMARAI
SHIPPING ROUTES OPERATED FROM RABAUL
SHIPPING ROUTES OPERATED FROM LAE
" ROUTES OPERATED FROM MADANG

Figure 53

tain erupted with a blast that was heard as far away as New Britain and Samarai. Almost 3000 Papuans and thirty-five Europeans were killed either by the blast or the terrific heat. The Papuans perished on the slopes of the mountain where they had their villages, and the Europeans and other natives died in the administrative headquarters settlement at Higatura, which was wiped out and buried in white-hot ash or boiling mud. The eruption was first noticed and reported by aircraft in the vicinity, one on a flight from Port Moresby to Rabaul and the other coming in to land at the Popondetta airstrip ten miles from the mountain. It was some hours before the dust clouds cleared from the flanks of the Owen Stanley Range, but as soon as it was possible, doctors and medical supplies were flown in to Popondetta; and the following day the whole resources of QANTAS were organized to take in food, tentage, blankets and surgical and medical supplies. Even water had to be air-freighted. Some injured were also flown out from advance dressing stations to base hospitals. Without these operations many more lives would have been lost, suffering would have been many times more serious and prolonged, and the danger of epidemics would have been great.

PROBLEMS AND RESPONSIBILITIES

Since Indonesia took over the western part of New Guinea little information has been available and little is known of the internal effects of the change in administration. However, between 1949 and 1963, the Dutch had made impressive efforts to develop the economy, and more particularly to improve the social status of the native people and to inaugurate the political progress of the Papuans. By 1963, the Netherlands government was spending in guilders the equivalent of $A28 millions a year on agricultural research, on the development of communications—especially on airstrips in remote areas and on subsidizing air services—on mineral exploration, forestry and fishing. Effective administration was reaching into the remote interior, to the Balim valley and the Wissel Lakes district. Political development was reflected in the increasing participation of indigenes in the government, and the formation of political parties. In Hollandia and Biak and Manokware, many Papuans took an eager interest and active part in them.

The Papuans were also being trained in the defence of the territory. There were small Papuan units associated with the Dutch air forces stationed at Biak (which had a jet airstrip long before some much more advanced countries, including New Zealand) and naval units at Sorong and Manokware.

In addition money was available from the European Economic Community, of which the Netherlands is a member, for the economic development of under-developed tropical territories like West New Guinea. Mineral exploration camps in remote valleys of the Vogelkop, serviced by helicopters, illustrated the nature of the aid extended to the Dutch territory. The geologists were Germans, the helicopters French, and the pilots Dutch. (Incidentally, all spoke English as did many of the leading Papuan political figures.)

To the Commonwealth of Australia, New Guinea has also been a heavy responsibility. The Australian taxpayer in 1955-1956 paid almost $A17 millions in grants to defray the costs of administration and social services: in 1964-1965 the amount of this assistance from the Australian government was more than $A56 millions. Schools, vocational training centres, hospitals, medical services, airstrips, wharves, agricultural experimental stations and many other facilities are provided by the administration. To discharge responsibilities under the trusteeship agreement; to develop the resources of the territory; to make the establishment of plantations, factories and trading establishments attractive and profitable to private interests and without injury to the native people and without making the change from traditional ways of life too abrupt—all these present the administration with formidable problems. At the present time the Commonwealth Scientific and Industrial Research Organization is making a comprehensive survey of the resources of the territories with special reference to the development of the mixed farming and livestock industries of the elevated and cooler interior. Most tropical crops can be grown on or near the coasts of the mainland and the islands, but the main problems are not those of land and climate but rather those of capital, labour and markets. Labour particularly is short. The natives of New Guinea have not yet acquired the desire for trade goods that so many islanders in the Pacific World already have. They have their own land, village life and food crops, and have no urge to sell regular toil for trade goods. Work for wages has no great appeal to them. Without labour, and in view of the past history of violently fluctuating prices for tropical produce, Australian planters have shown little interest in taking their capital to Papua or New Guinea. There is no easy or early solution to these problems. But meanwhile the government and people of the Commonwealth are taking an increasing interest in their solution. Australia's participation in the work of the South Pacific Commission is itself evidence of this. The Commonwealth makes the biggest financial contribution to the Commission's work. Unfortunately, with the Indonesian take-over of Irian Barat, the Dutch no longer qualify for membership of the South Pacific Commission. Until 1963 however they were active participants in its activities. Indonesia is not a member.

(The political advancement of Australia's New Guinea territories is discussed in Chapter Seven.)

NAURU

Nearly a thousand miles to the northeast of Rabaul, within half a degree of the Equator, lies the raised coral atoll of Nauru, formerly part of the German Marshall Islands Protectorate. Today it is an international trust territory administered by Australia on behalf of the Commonwealth and the two other joint trustees, the United Kingdom and New Zealand. Between the wars, Nauru was mandated to the same three powers, but was occupied by Japan during World War II.

To Australia and New Zealand Nauru is the most valuable speck of territory in the Pacific. It would be difficult to say just how much their economies owe to Nauru phosphates. It is certainly a great deal. This was clearly demonstrated during the war when, with Nauru cut off and phosphate supplies difficult to secure elsewhere, depressed crop yields and decreased carrying capacity of pastures soon became evident; and this was in no small measure to be attributed to the inadequacy of the supplies of phosphatic fertilizers.

Nauru has an area of only 5263 acres, and is about three and a half miles by two and a half miles in size (*Fig. 8*). The length of the coral road around the beach is not more than about eleven miles. Offshore is a narrow reef beyond which the sea floor falls away very steeply. Between the sandy shore inside the reef and the grey scrubby cliff of coral limestone behind is a belt of light but fertile soil never more than 300 yards wide. This 'coconut land' encircles the island and is terminated inland by cliffs which may rise a hundred feet. Beyond them is the coral plateau (or *makatea*) with a maximum elevation of 200 feet. This is the former rocky bed of a lagoon, its irregular coral floor smoothed by a deposit of phosphate sometimes fifty feet deep. These phosphates have already been removed by open-cast mining from about 600 acres of the plateau surface, leaving a fantastic maze of tall misshapen coral pinnacles. In the little less than half of Nauru's surface still to be divested of its rich phosphates there remain 60,000,000 tons, less than forty years' supply at present rates of exploitation—about a million and three-quarter tons a year. Up to 1965, 35,000,000 tons of phosphate had been extracted.

PHOSPHATE MINING

The pink-brown phosphate deposits are worked by the British Phosphate Commission, an agency of the United Kingdom, Australian and New Zealand governments. The output is shipped to the two countries, Australia importing about twice as much as New Zealand. A little is shipped to the United Kingdom. The commission employs some hundreds of Chinese recruited in Hong Kong, together with Gilbert and Ellice Islanders and Nauruans and most of the male Europeans on the island. The thin scrub on a portion of the surface of the plateau is cleared and burned before a new 'field' is opened up. Then a light, narrow-gauge branch railway track is laid to tap the new area, or else roads are bulldozed to provide access for a fleet of trucks. The rock is mined by the Chinese and Nauruan employees. As many as twenty mechanical grabs are used and the phosphate rock is loaded into side-tipping trucks. Steam engines drag the rake of loaded trucks to the main line and on to the driers. There the rock is crushed, heated and dried before being taken to huge storage bins to await the mooring of one of the commission's phosphate-carrying vessels off the end of the giant cantilevers. When one of these ships —so well known in the port of Auckland—is moored in the deep water off the reef, the dried phosphate is carried on an endless carrier belt out over the beach, the lagoon and the reef, and tipped directly into the hold of the ship.

Since 1965 the rate of royalty payment has been $A1.75 a ton. The moneys are paid by the commission into a variety of trust funds supervised by the administration. Some is handed to the landowners and forms the principal source of income of the 2750 people of the Nauruan (principally Micronesian) community. Other parts of the royalty payments are held in trust for the Nauruans against the day when the island's only significant resource and sole export commodity will be exhausted. Still other sums are paid to the administration, and with these the schools, hospitals, roads, meeting houses and dwellings of the islanders are built and maintained. In this way Nauru is more than self-supporting. The British Phosphate Commission also operates in like manner on similar deposits of phosphate on the very similar raised atoll of Ocean Island, 165 miles east of Nauru, but within the British Gilbert and Ellice Islands Colony.

In June 1967 it was announced that the United Kingdom, Australia and New Zealand governments were to hand the ownership of the phosphate deposits on Nauru to the Nauruans. With the returns from the mining industry in the next three years the islanders will buy the installations from the British Phosphate Commission. Output will be stepped up to two million tons a year and in future the new Nauru Phosphate Corporation will mine the deposits and sell them to the commission.

LIFE AND LANDSCAPE

The 'flat'—as the coastal rim of deeper soils is called—is thickly shaded by a tattered peripheral fringe of waving coconut palms. But since grated coconut meat is the islanders' principal item of diet, no copra is now exported. Coconuts also cluster thickly around the shallow water of Buada Lagoon which occupies a depression in the plateau. Its waters are brackish and are divided by low embankments marking each landowner's claims to a portion of the lagoon in which fish, caught when very small in rocky holes in the fringing reef, are reared for food. All villages, except for one on the Buada Lagoon, are strung out under the palms on the island's encircling flat. The Chinese labourers are housed by the commission in a barracks compound about a mile north of the cantilever, the jetty and the European and administrative settlement, Yangor. South of Yangor an airstrip has been laid out parallel with the southeast trades, on a wider portion of the sandy 'flat'. Nauru is not as yet served by a civilian air service, but it has a good shipping service, and all imports, including freight, mail, indentured Chinese labourers and European passengers, are brought by the vessels which load phosphate.

Apart from its phosphate, the fish that can be caught on and off the reef, and its narrow coastal rim of soil, Nauru has no resources. Even water is short. As the number of modern dwellings provided by the administration has increased, clean roofs are connected with underground concrete cisterns in which rainwater is stored, but in dry periods reliance has to be placed on a large plant for condensing sea water. Nauru has an average annual rainfall of over eighty inches, but while in both 1930 and 1940 falls of over 180 inches were recorded, rainfall in the year ending in June 1950 was only 12.29 inches! The trades blow steadily from the east for eight or nine months, but they bring little rain to the relatively low island. Most rain comes in heavy torrents between November and February, when the intertropical front is south of the equator and winds in Nauru are often westerly. These rains, however, are of erratic occurrence and it is not safe to rely on them.

The thin, reddish limestone soils of the plateau are underlain by porous rock and phosphate and, with steady winds blowing, they are often dried out. They carry a vegetation of low scrub and are rarely deep enough for cultivation. Only the deeper soils beside Buada Lagoon and the sandy soils around the coasts are cultivated. Between the trunks of the coconut palms, around the villages, small patches of pumpkins are grown, together with a few trees of papaw, banana and mango. Pandanus grows wild and, with coconut fibres, its leaves are used for local handicrafts. Indigenously, and before the phosphate rock was discovered and worked, pandanus was a principal source of food. But today the Nauruans can afford to supplement their diet and clothing and knick-knacks with imports, the cost of which amounts to only a fraction of the island's exports. Under the supervision of the administration they operate a co-operative organization for importing and distributing store goods.

The Nauruans, however, have been looking for a new island home. At a conference of native peoples convened by the South Pacific Commission in 1953 the Nauruan representative asked the Commission to investigate the possibility of transferring the larger part of Nauru's indigenous population to some other island not so restricted in agricultural resources and not likely to be converted into a grey-white desert of rock by mining activity.

Since then the Australian government has sought a suitable new home for the Nauruans. The most likely prospect seemed finally to be Curtis Island, off the Queensland coast. Protracted negotiations were conducted between the government and the owners and occupiers of land on the island, and later with representatives of the Nauru Local Government Council. The island itself was held to be suitable for the proposed purpose both by the Australian government and the Nauruans. But negotiations finally broke down in 1964. The Nauruans insisted that if Curtis was to be used for their resettlement they should be selfgoverning and the island completely independent except for powers relating to defence, quarantine and possibly external affairs and civil aviation. The Commonwealth government, however, could not accept a proposal establishing an independent nation so close to its continental shores despite its sympathy with the Nauruans' desire to retain their identity as a distinct community. The Nauru representatives terminated the negotiations; and there the matter rests.

The islanders would naturally like to continue to live on Nauru. In the latest negotiations on resettlement they raised again the question of the possibility of reclaiming the worked-out phosphate land. But the Australian government is satisfied that this is a practical impossibility. It was demonstrated some years ago by officers of the Commonwealth Scientific and Industrial Research Organization that there was little hope of any widespread future utilization of the rock pinnacles on the old phosphate workings, even if suitable soil was available and the rainfall was not as erratic as it is.

G

THE SOLOMON ISLANDS PROTECTORATE

Structurally both the Solomon Islands and the New Hebrides are probably a continuation of the northern mountain system of New Guinea (*Fig. 54*). They are basically 'continental' volcanic ranges with a core of ancient lavas and an overlay of more recent rocks, both volcanic and sedimentary. The Solomons comprise a double range of high islands stretching over 900 miles from northwest to southeast in latitudes 5 to 12 degrees south. Two lines of large islands, including Choiseul, Ysabel and Malaita in the one, and Buka, Bougainville, New Georgia, Guadalcanal and San Cristobal in the other run parallel to each other. These islands are often over a hundred miles in length and rise thousands of feet above the broken surface of the Pacific. On Bougainville (which, with Buka, is part of the Territory of New Guinea) active volcanoes, Balbi and Bagana, rise to 10,000 feet. But in Australia and New Zealand the names of some of the smaller islands in the group are better known than the larger ones, largely because they were the scene of action in which troops from the dominions took part during the Pacific war, or were the places at which they were encamped. Amongst these are Vella Lavella, Florida (off which is the small island of Tulagi formerly the chief port and administrative capital of the protectorate, but badly damaged during the war), Treasury Island and the Russell Islands.

With the Solomons are also grouped for administrative purposes the Santa Cruz group to the east, the Ontong Java group of low coral atolls to the north, and the raised coral atolls of Rennell and Bellona to the south of the main island chains (*Fig. 54*). The people of the larger high islands are Melanesians, but the flanking low atolls to the north and east and the raised limestone islands to the south are Polynesian outliers.

The Solomons were discovered in 1568 by the Spaniard Mendaña on a voyage from Peru in search of the Great South Land. A quarter of a century later Mendaña left South America on another voyage intent on establishing a Spanish colony on Guadalcanal, but he failed to find the island again. He fetched up, however, on Santa Cruz in 1595 and founded his settlement there. Not long after he died, his party returned to Peru, and the first European settlement in the southwest Pacific was abandoned. It was nearly two hundred years before the islands were rediscovered, and it was not until 1893 that a British Protectorate over the southern islands in the Solomon group was proclaimed. The present boundaries of the territory were established by

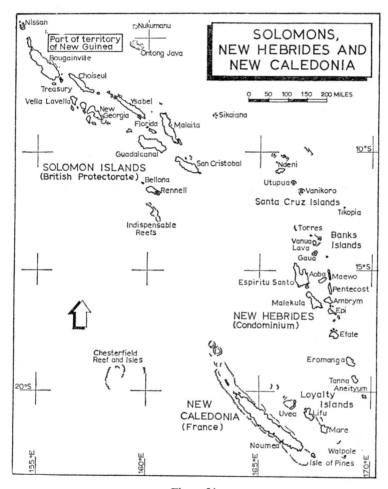

Figure 54

agreement with Germany in 1900. The Solomons remain the least developed of the island groups in the Pacific World. They are backward, disease-ridden and climatically unattractive.

ECONOMIC DEVELOPMENT

The Solomon Islands first attained some economic importance in the latter half of the last century when they proved an attraction to the infamous 'blackbirders' recruiting labour for European plantations in Queensland and elsewhere. Blackbirding was later replaced by organized voluntary recruiting of labour and in this way the Solomons provided kanaka workers for the Queensland canefields until 1903, and for plantations in Fiji, Samoa and Tonga until World War I. The physical resources of the islands were not developed by outside interests until early in the present century. In 1905 some concerns with large capital first took an interest in the group. In that year Lever Brothers took up land in the New Georgia group on a large scale, and two years later bought plantations already established on the Russell Islands. The company now has over 20,000 acres planted in coconuts in the Solomons. Burns Philp and Co. Ltd. and W. R. Carpenter and Co. Ltd. also acquired interests in the group before and after World War I.

Since the first European contacts, the population of the Solomons has declined very considerably. There are today not more than 135,000 people in the protectorate, of whom less than 1300 are Europeans and Chinese. The shortage of labour, the wet and constantly humid, hot climate of the high islands, the presence of malaria: these are amongst the factors that have retarded development. Equally potent, however, has been the hostility of the native Melanesian folk. Frequently early European missionaries and settlers were murdered: as recently as 1927 a party of government officers and native assistants was set on in Malaita and massacred. Since the last war the 'Marching Rule' movement has had a strong anti-white and anti-foreign element.

Malaita has half the native population of the protectorate, and it is from here that labour for the plantations on other islands is recruited. Plantations have not come to more populous Malaita because there the home village, brawls, disease and absenteeism makes labour less efficient and less reliable. Most of the coconut plantations are thus found on the less well-populated and the larger islands—in northern Guadalcanal and on the leeward slopes of Ysabel—and especially on some of the smaller islands like Gizo in the New Georgia Group and the Russell Islands.

COCONUT PLANTATIONS: RUSSELL ISLANDS' EXAMPLE

The commercial plantation agriculture practised on the coconut estates of the Fairymead Sugar Company (an Australian concern) and of Lever Brothers on Pavuvu and Banika in the Russell Islands is representative not only of other plantations in the Solomons but also of what is the principal commercial agricultural activity throughout the Pacific World (see *Figure 55* inset).

Only in Tonga among the island groups of the Southwest Pacific does copra constitute a larger share of the value of the export trade. The economy of the protectorate rests heavily on copra, which is responsible for 80 per cent by value of all exports.

Lever Brothers, the great soap and chemical firm, has a series of holdings amounting to about 10,000 acres on these islands. The two principal islands of the Russell group have a hilly volcanic interior and gently-sloping limestone terraces at below 300 feet. On the broad reef to the northeast of the islands are a series of smaller low-lying islets. The limestone terraces have deep, black soils. At the close of the last century the population of the Russell Islands had been reduced by disease and migration to almost nil. The natives occupied only one or two diminutive villages on the islets. The land on the two larger islands was thus available to the Crown for leasing to planters. Labour was recruited under licence and government supervision from the overpopulated coastal villages of Malaita. The native 'boys' are today registered at the capital, Honiara, before going to the plantation, where the planter is responsible for housing, food, clothing, medical care and return transportation.

The early plantations were cleared from the coastal forest by native labour using axe, spade and knife. Today bulldozers, graders and tractor-drawn ploughs speed the process. Then sprouting coconuts are planted in long rows running in straight lines up and down the gentle slope, across it on the contour and diagonally also, so that when the trees mature in seven or more years the nuts can be harvested from the ground systematically by moving the workers in any of eight directions. Once

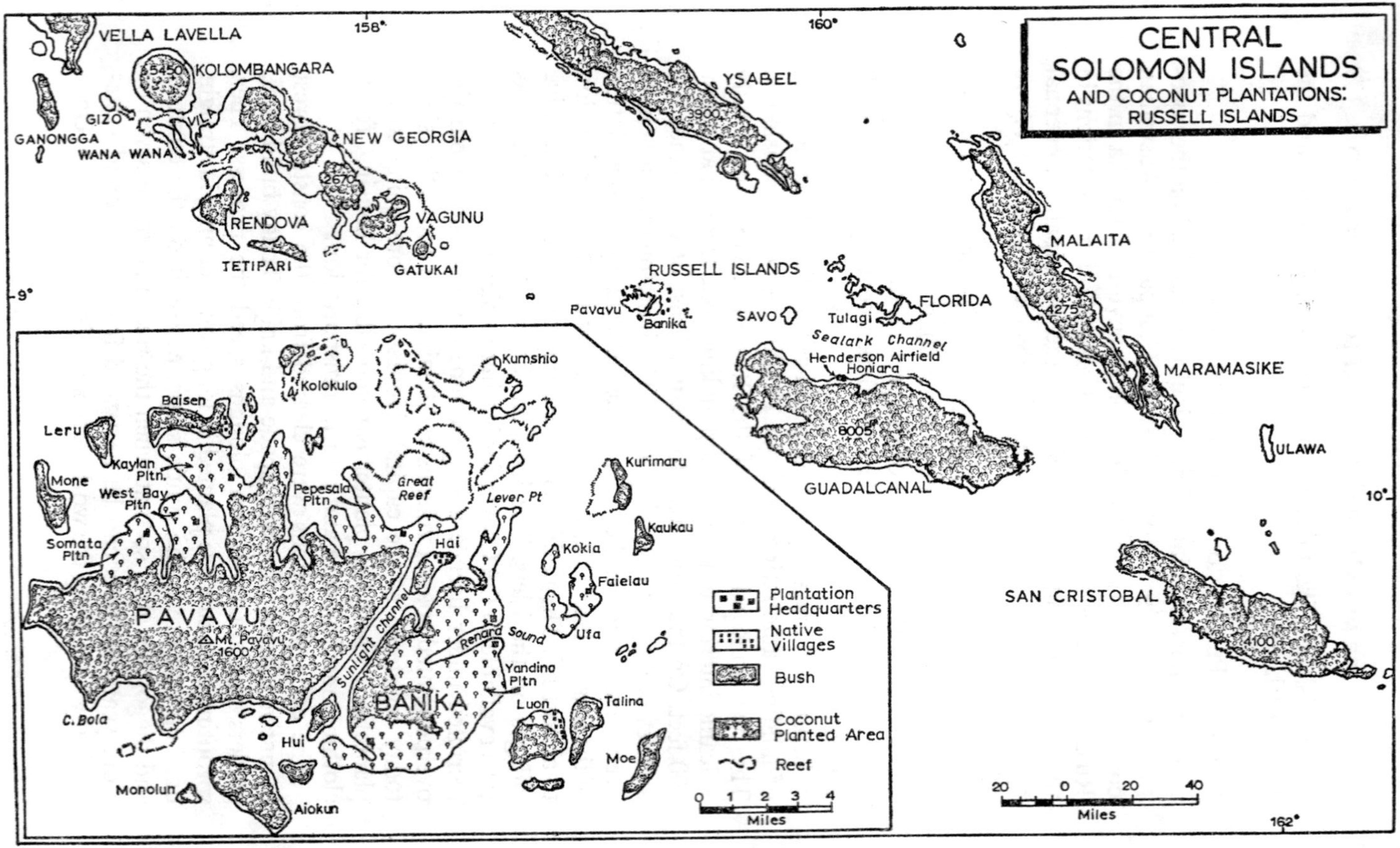
CENTRAL
SOLOMON ISLANDS
AND COCONUT PLANTATIONS:
RUSSELL ISLANDS
158°
160°
162°
9°
10°
VELLA LAVELLA
KOLOMBANGARA
5450
GIZO
VILA
GANONGGA
WANA WANA
NEW GEORGIA
2670
RENDOVA
VAGUNU
TETIPARI
GATUKAI
YSABEL
3900
MALAITA
4275
MARAMASIKE
RUSSELL ISLANDS
Pavavu
Banika
SAVO
Tulagi
FLORIDA
Sealark Channel
Henderson Airfield
Honiara
8005
GUADALCANAL
ULAWA
SAN CRISTOBAL
4100
20
0
20
40
Miles
Kumshio
Kolokulo
Baisen
Leru
Mone
Kaylan Pltn.
West Bay Pltn
Somata Pltn
Pepesala Pltn
Great Reef
Lever Pt
Hai
Kurimaru
Kaukau
Kokia
Faielau
Ufa
PAVAVU
Mt. Payavu
1600
Sunlight Channel
Renard Sound
Yandina Pltn
BANIKA
C. Bola
Hui
Luon
Talina
Moe
Monolun
Aiokun
Plantation Headquarters
Native Villages
Bush
Coconut Planted Area
Reef
0
1
2
3
4
Miles

Figure 55

the trees are established weeding is the principal activity. Some plantations are planted with palatable tropical fodder grasses and the leguminous sensitive plant so that cattle may be kept to aid in the ceaseless fight against weeds. The 20-30 nuts* which fall each year from every tree are gathered at intervals of about six weeks and carried by bullock wagon or motor lorry to the shed near the driers where the copra is cut. The coconuts are split by a gang of native boys with long, heavy, machete-like 'cane knives', whilst a number of others cut the white coconut meat from the shell. Other workers are employed processing the meat. In the drier months of the year the glistening blue-white meat is spread on great trays to dry in the sun, but this method is slow and unreliable. On most plantations today the smoking racks are on wheels running on metal rails, and are moved into a shed in which hot smoke from burning coconut husks is circulated. This method of drying is quicker, but it does not produce high-grade copra. The best method is to dry the meat over hot steam pipes in an elaborate kiln. Kiln-dried copra brings higher prices than any other.

The large plantations on Pavuvu and Banika have kiln driers. These are squat red-painted corrugated iron buildings clustered in the shade of tall, straight palms. Beside them are the open-sided cutting sheds, the great piles of nuts awaiting dehusking, and the quarters in which the native workers are housed and fed. There, too, are the storage sheds in which the copra is held in sacks until the company's vessel comes alongside the reef to load. The buildings are always on a sheltered and approachable part of the coast. The sacks of copra are carried from the sheds on to the wharf of poles and planks by an endless line of husky, dark, Solomon islanders, and are loaded into launches which lighter them out to the waiting copra boat. The headquarters of the plantation are also near the shore to get maximum advantage from sea breezes. The planter's (or manager's) house is a wooden building raised off the ground to let the air pass beneath. It has several large, open rooms flanked on all sides by a veranda with fly and mosquito screens,

---

*In many parts of the Pacific coconut palms are over-aged. The normal yield of mature and healthy palms in clean-weeded plantations is 60 nuts per palm per annum. But a large proportion of plantations date from the last quarter of the nineteenth century and are today over sixty years old and require replanting. As a result many palms produce no more than 10 nuts a year.

and is set in a garden in which are not only the inevitable coconut palms but also brilliantly coloured tropical shrubs, dark-green orange, lime and lemon trees, and the lighter shades of papaw and banana.

With the imminence of Japanese invasion in 1942, most plantations in the Solomons were abandoned. Others were damaged both by Japanese and Allied troops. On some, airstrips were laid out and military camps thrown up. The tall palms of still others camouflaged vast American supply dumps, some of which rot and rust in the reverting jungle to this day. In the Russell Islands hundreds of thousands of palms on not less than a tenth of the planted area were destroyed. Over the remainder weeds grew rife and insect pests took hold. As a result the amount of copra cut in the Solomon Islands is today not yet a quarter of what it was in the nineteen-thirties. This is partly caused also by the indirect effect of the war in profoundly disturbing the Melanesians spiritually, economically and socially. There has been a greater disinclination to work, partly the result of the high wages and savings accumulated during the war, and partly the result of the nationalistic, anti-foreign feelings that have appeared since the war and which have found expression in such disturbances as those of the 'Marching Rule' movement.

Apart from the copra of its few large coconut estates the Solomons produce little for export. The native communities are still largely self-sufficient, living in their crude fibre-roofed hutments in villages on the coasts and at times in wet, hilly and densely forested mountain valleys. Although the natives on all the larger islands are Melanesian, they speak a variety of languages and dialects, and are often unable to communicate freely with members of adjacent tribes. On Malaita tribal warfare still flares up from time to time. Only two other commodities figure in export lists—shell and timber—and neither of them is available in quantities as large as were regularly shipped before the war. Salvaged war supplies and equipment was also exported in the first two decades after 1948. Like other continental islands, such as New Guinea and New Caledonia, the larger Solomons have mineral resources, though these are as yet only partially explored. Gold, however, has been worked on a number of islands, thus proving the forecast (or substantiating the hope) of Mendaña when he named the group almost four hundred years ago. Natives on some islands, especially the outlying coral groups, collect shell to sell to traders. Formerly the fruits of an indigenous variety of sago palm, sometimes planted in swampy coastal locations, but more often growing wild, were collected and marketed as ivory nuts, which were used in the manufacture of buttons. Timber, a local island species of kauri, is cut and milled for export by an Australian company on the island of Vanikoro in the Santa Cruz group. In 1948 a survey of the forest resources of the Solomons was undertaken with the aid of a grant from the United Kingdom Colonial Development and Welfare Fund but this has not hitherto led to any extension of the exploitation of the islands' timber wealth.

ADMINISTRATION

When, after the end of the war, the rehabilitation of the administration and economy of the group was begun, it was decided to abandon the badly-damaged prewar capital of Tulagi off Florida Island, and to shift the centre of administration across to the coast of Guadalcanal at Honiara, which had been the headquarters of the American troops in the Solomons in the latter part of the Pacific campaign. The site of the new capital was alongside Henderson airfield. For some years Honiara was hardly a colonial capital. Its buildings were still in the main abandoned army sheds and shelters amidst a vigorous second growth of forest and weeds. In 1952, however, it was considered sufficiently established for the transference to it from Suva of the headquarters administration of the High Commissioner for the Western Pacific, an office formerly combined with that of Governor of Fiji.

Today, however, Honiara is a thriving and unique Pacific island port town and administrative centre. It is strung out in a narrow band along the sheltered north coast of Guadalcanal, east and west of Cruz Point. It occupies a narrow coast plain behind which sharp ridges of savanna and narrow gullies of tropical forest run inland. To the east the coast plain widens to accommodate Henderson airport and east again to provide space enough, now that road access has been provided, for copra plantations and new plantings of cocoa trees.

The town is unique in that it has been constructed in modern times. There were not even traditional Melanesian villages within its present limits. It could therefore be planned and carefully laid out. Practically all buildings, even the houses provided by the administration and commercial concerns at Kukum for semi-skilled Solomon Island workers and Gilbertese, are built of concrete blocks and other non-traditional materials. There are very few houses built of bush materials. But, because of the shortage of fresh vegetable foods and the lack of local village surplus supplies, Crown land has been made available for allotments and gardens both within the town boundaries and just beyond them.

Honiara is thus an open and pleasantly spacious tropical port centre. Its functions are principally associated with administration and transport. It is the capital and focal point of the protectorate as well as the headquarters for the British Western Pacific High Commission (responsible for the administration of the Gilbert and Ellice Islands and the British half of the Condominium Government of the New Hebrides). The port handles 70 overseas vessels a year and upwards of a dozen local vessels each day. The latter bring in produce, mainly copra, from Malaita, the Russell Islands, Ysabel, Santa Cruz, Gela and San Cristobal, and distribute imported trade goods and supplies. The airport has internal services to other islands in the protectorate and external services to New Guinea, the New Hebrides and New Caledonia—and on to Fiji, New Zealand and Australia.

There is little industrial development. It is limited to the manufacture of biscuits, and soft drinks: but there are also metal works, welding shops and vehicular repair shops. At the same time it is the educational, hospital and commercial centre of the Solomons.

In 1964 Honiara had 4650 people, seventy per cent of them Solomon Islanders. There was a European community of 400 and a Chinese community of 300. In addition there were Polynesians, Gilbertese, Fijians and part-Europeans. One interesting and distinctive feature of the population is that no section of it has deep roots in Honiara. The town is too new and has no continuity of earlier settlement. Even the Solomon Islanders are largely itinerant and temporary residents of Honiara. Equally characteristic of such a new town, still under construction, is the preponderance of men over women in its population.

Most of the trading vessels visiting the Solomons are operated by Australian island-trading firms, and as a result much of the trade of the group, especially since the war, has been diverted from the United Kingdom to Australia.

It has been argued that, because of the great strategic importance of the Solomons and the New Hebrides to Australia, the Commonwealth might by arrangement probably take over responsibility for the welfare and administration of the two groups. It is also relevant that history is likely to confirm that the critical offensive battle in the war in the Pacific—the one that finally destroyed the Japanese threat to both Australia and New Zealand—was the successful American flank attack on Guadalcanal. It might well be claimed then that, like New Guinea, these islands 'are in sober fact as essential to the defence as to the development of Australia'. If Australia and New Zealand are to assume the mantle formerly worn by the United Kingdom in the Pacific World this suggestion is strengthened. Sooner or later this question is likely to arise, although Australian eyes now gaze northwards in fixed attention and the eastern flank is ignored. At the moment the time is not the most propitious for suggestions of this kind, not only because of Australia's preoccupation with the development of New Guinea and its military commitments in southeast Asia, but also because of Australia's primary need for considerable capital expenditure in turning to account its domestic resources.

THE NEW HEBRIDES CONDOMINIUM

After a history of haphazard and lawless European contacts as disastrous in its effects upon native life and numbers as any in the Pacific, the eighty or so islands in the New Hebrides group were brought under joint Anglo-French protection in 1887. Later, by agreement signed in 1906 and modified in 1914, a condominium was established under which the two European countries have been jointly responsible for the administration of the islands and the welfare of their until recently declining population. In the mid-1950s the population was no more than 50,000. But if recent estimates are valid, it had recovered to 65,000 in 1962 and almost 80,000 in 1966, and was growing at the extraordinarily high rate of 3.8 per cent per annum. The threatened annexation of the group by France in 1886 had roused such a forceful demonstration of Australian colonial opinion that a reluctant Britain was at last forced to take a part in the disposal of a territory the strategic interest of which —in the hands of a hostile European power—had long been recognized in the Australian colonies.

The native population of the New Hebrides had already been decimated in an era of ruthless exploitation of sandalwood and of blackbird labour. Native communities had also suffered at the hands of whalers, buccaneers and escaped convicts. But before the establishment of law and order, many English, French and German traders and planters had established themselves on different islands in the group, especially as a result of the reputed high fertility of their volcanic soils. Not only had population been decimated in the first half of the nineteenth century, but intense missionary activity over a period of very many years had 'tamed' the survivors of the once warlike tribal communities of indigenous Melanesian folk. French planters and settlers from New Caledonia were actively encouraged to take up land in the group by the French government even before the establishment of the condominium, and no doubt the German traders who arrived from Samoa and New Guinea in the 1880s had the encouragement of the German government. Britain's attitude was always one of slow and studied disinclination. Under the joint administration, French interests have been dominant. Today there are three or four times as many French inhabitants of the New Hebrides as British, and French business concerns are said to conduct eighty per cent of the business of the group. Half its exports go to France and nearly one quarter to Japan. Total non-indigenous population is a little over 4000 persons, including Asians.

PHYSICAL CHARACTERISTICS

The New Hebrides continue southeastwards into higher and slightly cooler latitudes the double chain of hilly and mountain-

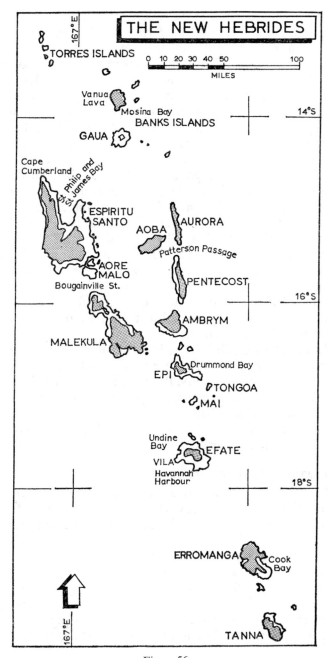

Figure 56

ous islands represented in the Solomons. The main islands of the group—they are named in *Figure 56*—are arranged in the shape of a Y. The more southerly islands of the group are in the same latitude as Townsville, Tongatapu and the Southern Cook Islands. The trades are here fresher and bring less heavy rains. Winter month temperatures fall some degrees below those of summer, whereas in the Solomons and New Guinea—within ten degrees of the Equator—there is little difference between the temperatures of the seasons. The New Hebrides, which include the outlying Banks and Torres Islands, where the continued decline of native population numbers is as marked as anywhere in the Pacific, have a total area of about 5700 square miles, which is less than half the area of the Solomons and equivalent to the area of New Zealand's North Auckland peninsula or the Canterbury Plains and downland.

The islands are volcanic. Three have active volcanoes. Mount Yasut on Tanna erupted violently in 1878 and the southeastern portion of the island was raised bodily at the same time by from sixty to 100 feet. Practically all the islands reveal similar instability, for all of them have on their eastern slopes raised coral terraces, some of which today rest at a height of 2000 feet. Rainfall is less than in the islands further north, with the result that the volcanic soils of the New Hebrides preserve considerable fertility. Precipitation, however, is enough to ensure a heavy forest cover, except only on some of the more porous coral terraces where scrub and savanna grass are found, with—on Eromanga—flocks of sheep tended by black-skinned New Hebridean shepherds.

POPULATIONS, ECONOMY AND ADMINISTRATION

The remnants of the native folk of the New Hebrides are, like the Solomon Islanders, dark-skinned, woolly-haired tribes speaking a number of Melanesian languages. Their native economies and village life were based on taro, yams, plantain and coconut, on the collecting of wild plants and (among some of the wilder and more isolated tribes on Espiritu Santo and Malekula) on the collecting of grubs and the hunting of birds. Their economy was differentiated from others in Melanesia more by the great importance which they attached to pigs than anything else. New Hebrideans bred, reared, stole, accumulated and traded pigs for both profit and prestige. Boars' tusks were the most prized and respected of native ornaments.

With the advent of whalers, sandalwood-seekers, blackbirders and traders this native economy was abruptly disturbed. Disease and death spread through the villages. Many natives were carried off. With the arrival of French and British planters and the inflow of capital and settlers from nearby New Caledonia, coastal forest was cleared and the land planted to coconuts, coffee and cocoa. Aore, especially, became a large coconut grove, and Efate's beautiful Vila Harbour was surrounded with attractive small French plantations and gardens with crops of maize, vanilla, pineapples, sugar cane and rice. By this time native labour was scarcer than it had been in the days when it was often forcibly removed to Queensland. The French half of joint administration encouraged colonization, extension of plantations and alienation of land. French settlers, but not British, were allowed to import indentured Tonkinese labour. As late as 1949, after the repatriation of many Tonkinese, the French brought in 2000 Javanese on three-year indentures. Today the non-native population of the New Hebrides totals about 4120, of whom 501 are under British jurisdiction, and 3619 (including Tonkinese and Javanese) under French jurisdiction.

Vila is the port of entry and the administrative and commercial centre of the group, and Efate is the only island with roads linking the main settlement with the scattered coastal plantations. The next largest foreign settlement is Segond (also called Luganville, or simply Santo), on the shores of Segond Channel between Espiritu Santo and Aore. Both British and French plantations cluster on the southern shore of Espiritu Santo, on Aore and on the numerous islets adjacent. The group's trade is still conducted largely with metropolitan France, and French vessels, touching Noumea and Tahiti, also call at Vila. But during and since the war, Australia took a greater share of the copra, cocoa and coffee of the New Hebrides, and supplied increasing quantities of tinned foods and manufactured store goods. It has not yet, however, won over the French settlers to acceptance of Australian wines. In the last few years Japan has taken a growing share of the Condominium's exports. The same is also true of the Solomons and New Cale-

donia. Australia is firmly established, though, as principal
source of the imports of all three territories. Shipping services
to the New Hebrides are few, and most people travel to the
Condominium today by air. Both French and Australian
services connect Sydney with Vila and Santo via Noumea.

Like the Solomons Islands Protectorate, the New Hebrides
rely heavily on copra production. As in the Solomons, copra
accounts also in the New Hebrides for almost eighty per cent by
value of all exports. In both cases commercial plantation production furnishes most of the copra for export—a higher proportion than in other groups of Pacific islands. However, the
number of indigenous individuals and villages producing copra
for sale is rising, as is the proportion of exports contributed by
the native people. In the New Hebrides the heaviest concentration of commercial plantations is on the shores of Segond
Channel; and, as a result, the small port of Santo—of post war
origin, like Honiara, and created out of American wartime
installations and with a fluctuating native population, even
of wharf workers—ships two-thirds of the copra exported. Other
exports comprise cocoa, coffee, fresh-frozen fish and sometimes
frozen meat from the cattle herds on commercial plantations.

One critic has referred to the New Hebrides as 'one of the
unhealthiest, wildest, most mistreated and most mismanaged
spots on earth'. There is much truth in the claim. The unhealthy
nature of the group is in part the product of its tropical climate and malarial mosquitoes, but in part the result of inadequate health services. Such as they are, these are largely operated
still by the missions, which appear to have been the only effective champions of native welfare. They, too, run practically all
the native schools. The 'mistreatment' is fortunately now largely
in the past, and has been referred to above. The 'mismanage-
ment' however is of the present, and is the outcome of the
condominium administrative structure which would be comic
if it were not also tragic. There are both British and French
administrations. Each maintains its own police, prisons, coin-
age (plus Australian), its own weights and measures, courts
and resident commissioners—one of these formerly subordinate
to a high commissioner in Suva (but now in Honiara), the other
to one in Noumea. It is a very unsatisfactory system but one
that provides no ready alternative acceptable at the same time

to both French and British interests, ignoring for the moment, as so often in the past, the interests of the native New Hebrideans.

NEW CALEDONIA, COLONY OF FRANCE

New Caledonia is not only one of the largest islands in the Pacific World, but it is also economically one of the most valuable, and geographically one of the most distinctive. It has little in common with its neighbours to the north or the east, excepting only its general location in the southwest Pacific, its nearness to Australia, and its structure, which is part of that common to the western margin of the ocean. Its unique hodgepodge of peoples and its bizarre assortment of cultures (Melanesian, Javanese, Indo-Chinese, Japanese and French), together with its economic dependence on large-scale mining, throw New Caledonia into sharp contrast with the coconut-dominated economies and backward, underdeveloped territories between Indonesian New Guinea and the New Hebrides. Climate, too, with its fresh and cooler winds and lower winter temperatures, distinguishes the French colony from the islands to the north, except only the southernmost New Hebrides. New Caledonia is also free from malaria, and is little affected by the host of disease-carrying and troublesome insects which are an unavoidable accompaniment of life in the islands to the north.

Administratively the French colony includes not only the main island, 250 miles long and usually over thirty miles wide, known as *la Grande Terre*, but also the Isle of Pines, thirty miles to the southeast, Walpole Island, the string of Loyalty Islands paralleling the mainland sixty miles to the east, the uninhabited Huon and Chesterfield islands to the northwest, and the Wallis and Futuna archipelagos between Fiji and Samoa. All these territories are administered from Noumea under the High Commission for France in the Pacific, who is also responsible indirectly for France's share in the administration of the New Hebrides Condominium.

PHYSICAL FEATURES

New Caledonia is a large, but long and narrow island (see *Fig. 57*). Its surface rarely rises to as much as 5000 feet but it is as broken and its slopes are as steep and its valleys as deep-cut as those on many islands with much higher maximum elevations. It is dominated by the misnamed *Chaîne Centrale*, which is not a continuous mountain chain but a jumbled series of mountain masses, steep-sided hill country and occasional plateaus of metamorphic schist and serpentine rocks which are the sources of New Caledonia's considerable mineral wealth. To the east these sharp-faced uplands rise abruptly from the Pacific, are exposed to the trades, have a heavy rainfall, and are well forested. The western slopes of the island are in striking contrast. Near the coast are softer sedimentary rocks and low plains and foothills, tidal flats and mangrove swamps, and a barrier reef offshore, broken opposite the estuary of every stream. This is a rainshadow area during most of the year, when the weather is dominated by the steady easterlies. Whilst Yaté, in the southeast, has over 130 inches of rain, Noumea, opposite on the west coast, has only forty-two inches. In many parts of western New Caledonia the vegetation and natural landscape are often more reminiscent of sub-humid areas in Australia than of the 'steamy' forest jungle of the more northerly Melanesian islands. Vegetation is often meagre, the rock is widely exposed, and open savanna, with the gnarled grey-white, eucalyptus-like *niaouli*, dominates the scene except only at higher elevations, where remnants of ancient forests of endemic species of kauri and araucaria pines are found. With the help of cultivation, grazing and fire, scrub (mainly lantana, guava and mimosa) has spread over many a hillside.

The People: Native and Alien

It has been estimated that New Caledonia originally had an indigenous population of over 70,000, numbers being kept down by inter-tribal warfare which was aggravated by struggles with invaders, including Polynesians, from the east. The natives of the island are predominantly Negroid, like those of most of Melanesia, but have many physical characteristics like those of the Australian aborigine, indicating a strong Australoid component in their make-up. Today the natives of *la Grande Terre* number only 23,500 but their number is beginning to increase again. In the territory as a whole the aliens outnumber the indigenes. At the last census (1960) Melanesians totalled 32,334, Europeans 28,454 and others, chiefly Asians, 12,016.

In 1966 the population was estimated at 96,900. The increase is chiefly due to a rise in the number of indigenes and of immigrant French Polynesians.

Cook again was the first European to visit New Caledonia. That was in 1774. He was followed by French and other explorers and by escaped convicts, runaway seamen, traders and occasional blackbirders. France took possession of the island in 1853, apparently anticipating the British by only a few hours. Not only was this mineral-rich, strategically-important island, with a climate suitable for European settlement, lost to Britain, much to the chagrin of the Australian colonies, but the Australians found the island used by the French for many years as a penal settlement, to which they took strong exception. Between 1864 and 1894 more than 40,000 prisoners were transported. Some served out their sentences and, as *libérés*, were given land and persuaded to settle in New Caledonia alongside free colonists. Most French settlers turned to cattle grazing for a living and exported hides and skins. Lack of fences, damage to native cultivations by wandering stock, and confiscation of native land led, in 1878, to a ferocious revolt, to massacres, cannibalism and military campaigning, and finally to a negotiated peace. The revolt gave the French colony a bad name, but it led to a recognition of native rights. It also became clear that the use of native labour in the mines, then being opened up, was out of the question. For a time white convicts were farmed out to both mine owners and plantation operators. But in 1883 France turned to Asia for labour, and began the process of further diversifying the island's medley of peoples by first importing Chinese, and later, Japanese, Hindu, Indo-Chinese and Javanese labourers. The economy has since been built on the use and exploitation of ill-housed, underpaid Asian labour in the mining of nickel, chrome and iron. Many of the indentured workers have, especially during and since the war, and after completing their indentured service, stayed in New Caledonia and settled there. In the nineteen-thirties there were as many as 14,000 Javanese and Tonkinese and 1200 Japanese in New Caledonia, the latter usually store-keepers and small tradesmen. Since 1948 the old system of indenture has ceased and the mining industry was for a time arrested as a result. However since 1954 the production and export of nickel have climbed steeply.

MINING AND AGRICULTURE

At one time New Caledonia was the world's leading producer of nickel, chrome and cobalt. The first two are still the colony's economic mainstay, although Canada now produces very much more nickel, and New Caledonia is not amongst the world's five leading producers of chrome. The output of cobalt has dwindled to almost nothing. But increased importance and attention was turned to New Caledonia's minerals before and during World War II. In the 1930s Japanese interests developed iron ore concessions, and ore was shipped to Japan. Nickel matte, nickel ore and chrome loaded into vessels at anchorages near the mines still account for over 90 per cent of the colony's exports. They are shipped to a number of markets, the first largely to France, and the latter in part to Australia and the United States. Crude nickel ore is largely shipped to Japan. The large mining companies, much of their capital British, and an increasing share of it Australian, retain a close grip on the economy. The mines are scattered in the hills and valleys, and many a bare, scarred hillside, especially inland from Thio and Poro, reveals the patient, little-rewarded toil of Tonkinese and other Asian labourers over the last seventy years.

The mining industry is the impermanent base of the New Caledonian economy. Its products account for 96 per cent of the value of all exports: nickel alone for 93 per cent. Such an economy, dependent virtually on one product and on world market prices, is highly vulnerable. Consequently mining activity and nickel output fluctuate violently from year to year.

Mining employs almost 5000 persons despite increasing mechanisation. The development of mining in the early years of the century depended heavily on indentured Asian labour, but since the abolition of indenture contracts and the forced repatriation of many Indo-Chinese and Javanese after 1946, there has been increasing mechanization of mining operations, an influx of French Polynesian labourers from Tahiti and Wallis islands and a greater participation of Europeans both in mining and nickel refining. In 1930 Asians formed 90 per cent of the total labour force: in 1961 they constituted only ten per cent (Europeans 49 per cent and Melanesians and Polynesians together 38 per cent).

The distribution of nickel mines and their output are shown on Figure 57. Production is concentrated on the central portion of the east coast of *la Grande Terre* (Thio, Nakety and Kouaoua) and on the west coast south of Noumea (Tontouta, Dumbea). There are smaller areas of production further north, especially at Poya. *Le Plateau*, the elevated mining area around Thio, has fifteen mines producing 30 per cent of the nickel ore (over two-thirds of a million tons). Opencast methods of mining are employed. These involve the removal of the overburden of deeply weathered red soil and rock. Ore is transported to the coast by truck and from there shipped to Noumea for processing, or directly to Japan. At Thio an aerial cableway shifts the dusty red ore from *le Plateau* to the wharf, three miles away.

The mining industry is dominated by the *Société de Nickel*, responsible not only for more than 60 per cent of the tonnage of ore mined, but also for the hydro-electric power plant at Yaté (on which domestic and industrial consumers are dependent) and the nickel refinery at Noumea.

Tiebaghi, in the far north of the island, is the only remaining centre of chrome mining.

In the long run, however, the varied agricultural resources and activities of New Caledonia will be more significant than mining. The wartime demands of military forces gave commercial cultivation a real fillip, and agricultural settlement, aided by recently-established research stations on the island and by the introduction of improved livestock from Australia and New Zealand, has made considerable progress in recent years. American-built roads have opened up new agricultural land. After minerals the most important export products are coffee, trochus shell, niaouli essence, copra, hides, sawn timber and preserved meat—indicating the range of primary production and the principal commercial developments outside mining. Apart from the exports mentioned, other crops are of local importance as food crops. After coffee and coconuts in acreage come bananas, yams, manioc and taro, maize, sweet potatoes, rice, wheat, beans and peas. In addition there are 200,000 acres

of improved grassland; and there are well over a million acres
of savanna.

LIFE AND LANDSCAPE

New Caledonia's remaining natives live largely on reserves
and still practise a simple subsistence agriculture, growing the
traditional yams and taro, but also the introduced manioc,
maize and rice. Some still live in villages in which the huts are
hive-shaped and bark-walled or have coconut thatch for roofing.
Most of the natives, however, speak a *patois* French and have
wooden and corrugated iron shacks. Others work for white
planters, a few grow coffee and some still dive for shell. The
12,000 natives of the Loyalty Islands—low or part-raised atolls
to the east—still grow their own food crops and, like so many
other indigenous Pacific island folk, cut copra for cash with
which to purchase their as yet limited requirements of imported
goods and canned foodstuffs.

Coffee-growing occupies most of the French settlers on the
land. The plantations are little more than smallholdings, usually of from ten to twenty-five acres. Very few of these *caféières*
are more than fifty acres in size or employ more than perhaps
one or two Javanese or kanaka workers. The bulk of the small
planters are also dependent on the sale of cattle and deer hides
and bananas and garden crops grown for the domestic market. A
good blend of Arabica and Robusta coffee is produced and has
hitherto been shipped largely to markets in France. In other
parts of the world coffee is grown on hill and elevated plateau
land, but in New Caledonia, with its unusual but moderately
wet, tropical, oceanic climate, the *terres à café* are the valley
bottom lands along both coasts (*Fig. 57*). Here nestle the tidy
small-holdings with their abundant leguminous shade trees to
protect the coffee shrubs in summer; and here are the French-
looking, whitewashed and stone-walled bungalows with open
spaces beside them where the family washes the coffee beans,
ferments them, and spreads them out to dry.

Cattle-raising is largely confined to the poorer valley sides
and the tablelands with their open grasslands. Shorthorn and
the French Limousin breeds are the most common range cattle.
Ouaco is the site of the one meat-preserving establishment, and
it lies near the most extensive area of scrub-invaded savanna

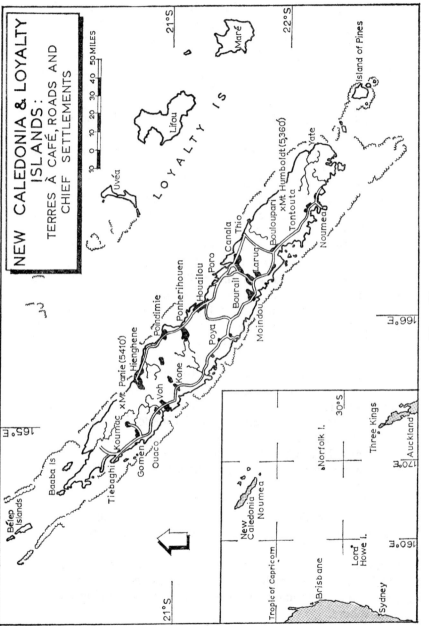

Figure 57

rangelands. Emphasis has always been on beef-cattle raising. The local market for dairy products has remained small. Dairy stock has been imported, however, in recent years—Illawarra Shorthorns from Australia and Jerseys from New Zealand, to extend the small dairy industry near Noumea and some of the mining towns, where improved tropical pastures have been established.

New Caledonia is like no other island in the Pacific World. Its climate, vegetation and mineral-bearing rocks are quite different. Its motley of different peoples, its French-looking capital and French-looking villages and small towns, set amidst coffee gardens—but with a waving fringe of coconut palms—its mines, its ranchlands and scores of thousands of cattle, its niaouli trees and the local essence-extracting activity based on them, its scarred mountain sides and its kauri stands—all add to the distinctiveness of its landscapes and economy. Administratively France keeps a firm hold on its Pacific territories in face of the demands of the white colonial population for autonomy. The French economy had not been strong in the decade following World War II; nor were French markets stable. Australia has come to supply an increasing quantity of New Caledonia's imports of food (flour, rice, preserved milk, etc.), coal and manufactured goods. But both New Zealand and Australia, with import restrictions and currency controls, have made it difficult for the French colony to compete in the import trade of the two dominions. For the future, however, reciprocal trade between New Caledonia and Australia and New Zealand would appear to offer important possibilities, and many New Caledonians feel that in such a commercial programme lies the path to further internal development and progress.

At Tontouta, south of Noumea, is a jet airport served by French international DC8s, Caravelles and smaller aircraft linking the French territories of the Pacific. It is also used by QANTAS and Air New Zealand aircraft. These air links have enabled New Caledonia to develop in recent years a significant tourist traffic, especially of New Zealanders and Australians seeking short holidays in an exotic, French-speaking tropical atmosphere.

Noumea itself is the home of half the permanent population

of New Caledonia which, with its mining towns and other urbanized small settlements, has a larger proportion of its population living in towns than any other territory in the southwest Pacific, other than Australia and New Zealand. Of the island groups, only Tahiti, another French territory, can compare with it. Noumea dominates the life and economy of the territory more than any other port town in the oceanic area. It has a polyglot population of 35,000. It is not the largest of the urban centres in the islands of the southwest Pacific, but it is probably the most industrialized, and the most unusual. In Noumea live 62 per cent of New Caledonia's European population, 71 per cent of the Vietnamese, 52 per cent of the Indonesians, 74 per cent of the Wallisians and 70 per cent of the Tahitians, but only 21 per cent of the indigenous Melanesians.

NORFOLK ISLAND

At the southern extremity of the great curtain of islands swung around the continent of Australia to the north and east is Norfolk, a territory of the Commonwealth administered through the Department of External Territories in Canberra. The island has a rectangular shape and is about five miles by three. Its 8528 acres provide no more land than does many a North Island sheep run in New Zealand. Norfolk is in fact the nearest occupied Pacific island to New Zealand. It is less than 660 miles from Auckland—almost 1000 miles from Sydney (*Fig. 57*, inset). This, and the fact that New Zealand would appear to be a better and more accessible market for Norfolk's surplus products, has prompted some to suggest that, in any more rational redistribution of island territories in the southwestern part of the Pacific World, Norfolk would be more appropriately attached to the Dominion than to the Commonwealth.

When in 1774 Cook was, in his own words, 'undoubtedly the first human being to set foot to its soil', Norfolk was a cliff-bound volcanic island and one of very few in the Pacific with good soils and a dense forest cover that had not been occupied by far-wandering Melanesians or Polynesians. Fourteen years later, when Lieutenant King landed, under the orders of the Governor of New South Wales to establish an outlying agricultural settlement of convicts, he found the island 'one entire wood' of beautifully tall, erect Norfolk pines (*Araucaria*.) The climate too was 'salubrious' and a thriving little settlement was soon producing wheat and potatoes in great quantities. In 1803 however all the settlers—the convicts had now served out their sentences—were withdrawn. But after twenty-three years of abandonment, Norfolk was again a penal station between 1826 and 1855. This time it was a convict settlement of the worst type. Riots and murders, cruelty, sickness and early death were its characteristics. Many convicts escaped, some to die at sea, others to reach New Zealand's new shore-whaling stations, or to join the riff-raff in the Bay of Islands.

But after the prisoners were finally withdrawn to Tasmania the cold limestone prison buildings and the convict-built jetty were deserted for only a few months. In 1856, 194 Pitcairn Islanders, descendants of *Bounty* mutineers and Tahitian women-folk, were brought to Norfolk from their more cramped island accommodation in the southeastern Pacific. Most of the population of Norfolk today are descendants of the former Pitcairn Islanders and bear the surnames of the mutineers. They are referred to as 'islanders' and are thus locally distinguished from more recent arrivals from Australia and New Zealand who are known as 'mainlanders'. In 1957 the island had a total population of 1059. In 1963 it numbered 853. Apart from the administrative headquarters, the jetty and small storage buildings, a few houses and boarding establishments at Kingston, there is no other township. People live on smallholdings scattered over the 8500 acres of hilly to undulating land. There are small farms everywhere, except only on the upper slopes of Mount Pitt, which rises in the northwest to more than 1000 feet.

Before the depression of the 1930s Norfolk Island was a thriving little community. Shipping services were more frequent. Bananas, oranges and kumaras were grown in large quantities and many reached the New Zealand market. Whales appeared off the coast every year and whale oil was an important source of income. A modern whaling station was established in 1956, but with the marked reduction in the number of whales it had to be closed down in 1962. Ships rarely arrive today more often than six or eight times a year, usually on the run from Sydney to Noumea, Vila and Tulagi. But the weekly air service to

Australia and the twice-weekly service to Auckland set down more passengers in a year than the total population of the island. Of these passengers two come from Auckland to every one from Sydney. Air transport has made possible a new industry, catering for visitors seeking a holiday in a not-too-distant tropical island, and has restored the closer contact that Norfolk formerly had with New Zealand.

In 1963 Norfolk's exports at $NZ187,344 were worth only about a fifth the value of its imports. This situation is made possible by 'invisible exports' in the form of services to holidaymakers. And many of the more recent settlers are retired people whose income is derived from Australia or New Zealand. Only in this way is Norfolk able to import goods more valuable than those it ships. The people of the island, other than those with overseas incomes and those who operate or work in boarding houses, live largely on and from their smallholdings. The original settlers from Pitcairn were given fifty-acre farms, but with the increase in population these have been partitioned into small, often garden size, holdings. Worked intensively, however, they are capable of supporting a family. The growing of a small acreage of cash crops for local sale or export provides income above mere subsistence. In fact the islanders live well. Many have a small car and there are fifty miles of road linking the tidy, scattered little farms with Kingston. A great variety of crops is grown. Little gardens and modest wooden houses nestle amongst the upright Norfolk pines and small newly-established plantations of gum trees, ironbarks and radiata pine. Oranges, lemons, peaches, rows of passion fruit vines, grapes and pineapples are grown alongside patches of bananas, maize, melons, yams, beans, and both sweet and Irish potatoes. Steep hillsides are covered with guavas.

Today seed is the only significant export of island origin. (Other items include 'empties', household and personal effects.) Of the seeds exported, bean seed is most important, but the list also includes palm seed (from the Lord Howe Island palm), Norfolk Island pine seed, lemon and orange seed (for growing stock for later grafting), passion fruit seed and vegetable and flower seed. In some years passion fruit pulp is extracted and shipped to Australia. The only other exports worth over $1000 in 1963 were hides from the few cattle of Norfolk's small dairy herds.

LORD HOWE ISLAND

Halfway between Norfolk and Sydney is another rocky insular part of Australia—the upstanding rock pile of Lord Howe Island, administratively part of the state of New South Wales. Of its 3000 or so boulder-strewn, palm-covered and elevated acres less than a tenth are suitable for agriculture. Its 240 people are descendants of 'Sydney-siders' who squatted on the island a hundred years ago. They still squat on Crown Land on sufferance and pay no rent. Producing seed from the indigenous Lord Howe Island (*Kentia*) palm, fishing, a small tourist trade, and gardening engage the population. Occasionally a Burns Philp vessel calls, and QANTAS operates a Sydney-Lord Howe Island air service. The chief points of interest about the island are scientific—its remarkable forest flora, its avifauna and especially its muttonbirds, its coral reef (the world's most southerly), and its strategically-located meteorological station.

CHAPTER FIVE

New Zealand

I T IS NOW more than a thousand years since man first stepped
ashore in Aotearoa. How, where, or precisely when this was,
no one knows. It is clear, however, that the islands' first human
inhabitants were Polynesians, used to the much warmer climates
of tropic islands out in the wide expanse of the Pacific World.
These first arrivals may well once have been cultivators of taro,
yams and kumara; but in the cooler climates and on the leached
soils of their new and southerly island home they seem to have
been fisher-folk and hunters of birds. It is from the evidence
they left behind, in the form of waste heaps of moa bones, that
they have become known as the Moahunters.

POLYNESIAN AOTEAROA

The Moahunters had neither domesticated plants nor animals
except the dog. They lived in either temporary or permanent
but unfortified encampments on boulder banks, sand bars and
coastal terraces near the estuaries and river mouths of the
eastern coast of the South Island. At hand was a lagoon with
wild swan (long extinct), paradise and grey duck and other
waterfowl; in the lagoon's shallows were edible shellfish and
eels, whitebait and flounders; out to sea occasional whales,
sharks, and many other fish could be caught; along the beach
the waves threw up an abundant supply of firewood; on land,
over the open grassland and in the swamps and scrub, grazed
several different species of moa. This was the habitat in which
Aotearoa's first Polynesian culture of fishing and fowling folk
developed, and these were the resources upon which it depended.

MAORI CULTURE AND ECONOMY

But with the arrival in the fourteenth century of the canoes of the 'great fleet', a later and rather different Polynesian culture was brought to Aotearoa. The newcomers settled mainly in the damp and forested coastlands of the North Island. They brought from their tropical island homes the cultivated root crops which they had been in the habit of growing there, and they were successful ultimately in selecting varieties which they were able to establish and grow satisfactorily in Aotearoa's cooler summers and often difficult soils.

In the northern part of Aotearoa the Maori's gardening skills enabled him to remain an agriculturalist. But to a greater and greater extent as he went south he found it necessary to invent the techniques of woodsman, fowler and gatherer of roots and berries. The *kumara* (sweet potato) was his principal crop, and was grown by all North Island tribes excepting only those living on parts of the bleak volcanic plateau of the interior or in the forest fastness of the mountain axis. In the South Island, the Polynesian's traditional crops could be matured only in coastal localities south to Banks Peninsula and a little beyond. In the most favoured northern localities he was also able to grow taro, *hue* (a gourd), paper mulberry and *uwhi* (yams). Although he had only a simple wooden digging stick and spadelike scoop, he was a skilled gardener, recognizing as many as thirty different soil types and appreciating the value of a number of different fertilizer materials.

Yet it was to the wildlife of forest, lake, swamp, river and sheltered coastal waters that most Maori tribes turned for food, fuel and materials for clothing and handicrafts. They provided raw materials for the manufacture of a vast range of items, from great war canoes and elaborately-carved *whare runanga* to bird snares, fish hooks and fish nets. The Maori recognized and named hundreds of different plants of forest, swamp and open scrubland. He was a most expert bird catcher. Yet his system of *tapu* and his respect for Nature gave him a reverence for trees and plants and bird life so strong and powerful that he rarely wasted and destroyed the resources with which his habitat provided him.

When Captain Cook first touched New Zealand shores the Maori tribes may have numbered half a million people. Whatever their number, it is clear that four-fifths of the Maori people lived in the northern half of the North Island. The attraction of this northerly region lay largely in its comparatively 'winterless' climate and the possibility it gave of cultivating some of the subtropical food crops brought from the Pacific. Although life was one of unremitting toil, except in the cooler season when sport and warfare demanded energy and skill of a different kind, it was, by comparison with that of the tribes along the windswept coast of Murihiku (the Foveaux Strait area in the far south) and that of the Moahunters, a life of relative ease. Large settlements, heavily-fortified *pa* with trenches, ramparts and stockaded terraces, often accommodating 2000-3000 people, were found in coastal areas from Taiamai in the north to the territory of the Ngati Porou in the east and the Taranaki coast in the west. The tribes of the north were in constant and close contact with each other. The region was threaded by a network of local tracks and routeways. Groups travelled along the rivers and coasts by canoe and through the forest and scrub by single-file track. The Tamaki isthmus was then (as now) probably the most frequented part of Aotearoa, and was the crossing place of the most often used main routes by both land and water.

The southern part of the North Island was generally less attractive and less populous. Its less powerful tribes lived mainly on the east coast and the coasts facing Raukawa (Cook Strait) and the South Island. The Tuhoe in the bush-clad Urewera were forest-dwelling hunters and gatherers. The tribes about Taupo relied heavily on birds, berries and fish from the lake. Only in coastal districts was gardening possible. In the South Island there were very few people, not more than three per cent of the total population. Its frosty and unsheltered grassland, its mountain beech forest, its rain-drenched and almost inaccessible west coast, its drier gravel basins and its snowy alpine interior were habitats that offered the Maori people limited resources and were thus of little attraction. South of Banks Peninsula the small tribes were largely nomadic; they had no cultivated crops until Europeans brought the potato, and they had to wrest a living by hunting, fishing and the gathering of berries and fern root from a hostile environment made less rewarding with the extermination in Moahunter times of the wild swan, many other large fleshy birds and the moa. The struggle for existence here left little time for the construction of large permanent settlements. The most southerly really large *pa* was at Kaiapohia. Loose hamlets or temporarily-occupied *kainga* with untidy, coarsely-thatched huts on piles were the southern counterpart of the north's elaborately-defended and richly-ornamented *pa*.

PRECURSORS OF PERMANENT EUROPEAN SETTLEMENT

The Maoris had been in undisturbed occupation of Aotearoa for three centuries when in 1642 the *Heemskerck* and the *Zeehaen* brought Tasman and his hundred or so Dutch sailors to the stormy coast of 'a great land uplifted high'. But they did not put foot ashore, and New Zealand was lost again to Europe, and the Maori culture continued to develop in isolation for another century and a quarter until the first of Cook's five visits in 1769.

It was Cook who gave shape to New Zealand on maps of the world, and it was Cook and his scientific companions who, by recording all they saw, revealed New Zealand to European eyes. Thereafter visitors came to New Zealand shores in increasing numbers and, from about 1802, fourteen years after the establishment of the colony of New South Wales in 1788, European contacts with coastal districts and with their Maori inhabitants, particularly in Murihiku to the south, and at the Bay of Islands in the north, became almost continuous. Yet it was some decades before newcomers explored the interior, and it was seventy years after Cook's first visit before permanent organized colonial settlements were established.

For fifty or sixty years after its commercial resources were first tapped by enterprising traders operating out of Port Jackson, New Zealand conducted the bulk of its trade with the Australian colonies and mainly with New South Wales. Australians, Australian ideas, Australian-developed pastoral and agricultural techniques and Australian-bred livestock all played a significant part in the development of New Zealand during the first century of its exploration and exploitation by European culture.

Early reports of good timber, tall spars, abundant seals and excellent anchorages soon attracted the attention of traders in

37. COASTAL VILLAGE, MALAITA

Photos: Rob Wright, Fiji Public Relations Office

38. NATIVE HOUSING, LISIALA

39. CANOES, MALAITA

Photos: Rob Wright, Fiji Public Relations Office

40. PLANTATION LABOURERS, SOLOMONS

Photo: Rob Wright, Fiji Public Relations O

41. LISIALA VILLAGE, MALAITA

Photo: Fred Dunn, Noumea

42. NOUMEA, NEW CALEDONIA

Photo: S. Barrau, South Pacific Commission

43. NATIVE CULTIVATION, NEW CALEDONIA

Photo: White's Aviation

44. EUROPEAN GARDENS, NORFOLK ISLAND

Photo: N.Z. National Publicity Studios

45. KAURI FOREST, NORTHLAND, NEW ZEALAND

Photo: N.Z. Dept. of Agriculture

46. DEFORESTATION, NORTH ISLAND, NEW ZEALAND

Photo: V. C. Browne

47. FIORDLAND, NEW ZEALAND

Photo: N.Z. National Publicity Studios

48. MAN-MADE PASTURELAND

49. HILL COUNTRY, NORTH ISLAND

Photo: N.Z. National Publicity Studios

50. CANTERBURY PLAINS

Photo: N.Z. Farmer

51. HIGH-COUNTRY SHEEP RUN, SOUTH ISLAND

52. TUSSOCK GRASSLAND, OTAGO

Photos: N.Z. National Publicity Studios

53. WOOLSHED, EAST COAST, NORTH ISLAND

54. DAIRYING, TARANAKI

Photo: N.Z. National Publicity Studios

Photo: N.Z. Farme

55. MODERN MILKING SHED, KING COUNTRY

Photo: N.Z. Farmer

56. WHEAT GROWING, CANTERBURY PLAINS

Photo: N.Z. National Publicity Studios

57. DAIRY FACTORY, NORTH ISLAND

Photo: New Zealand Herald

58. COAL FROM WESTLAND

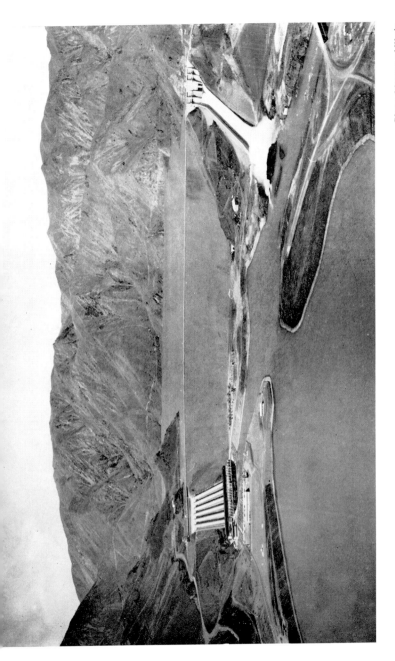

Photo: Ministry of Works

59. POWER FROM BENMORE, WAITAKI RIVER

Photo: N.Z. Dept. of Lands and Survey

60. WELLINGTON HARBOUR AND THE HUTT VALLEY (top)

Photo: N.Z. Herald

61. ORCHARDS, NELSON

Photo: Ministry of Works

62. INDUSTRY, AUCKLAND

Photo: N.Z. National Publicity Studios

63. COUNTRY STORE, EAST CAPE

64. RAROTONGA, COOK ISLANDS

Photos: N.Z. National Publicity Studios

65. THE LANDING, MAUKE, COOK ISLANDS

Port Jackson and Hobart Town to the possibilities of trans-Tasman trade, and it was not long before these resources were being exploited. In the first decade of the nineteenth century the temporary settlements of sealing gangs dotted the windswept coasts of Fiordland and Murihiku. From 1810 onwards a stream of schooners picked up mixed and growing cargoes of timber, spars, flax, potatoes, pork, firewood, bundled sealskins, pickled oysters, dried Maori heads and whale oil. By the middle of the 1830s there were shore whaling stations on the coasts of Southland and Otago, at the northern end of the South Island, on the North Island coast across Cook Strait, and on the adjacent islands of Kapiti and Mana. Kororareka in the Bay of Islands, however, was the largest of the coastal settlements visited by whaling and trading vessels. In 1839 it had a nondescript population of beachcombers, escaped convicts, runaway seamen and unscrupulous traders, probably numbering a thousand, together with haggling mobs of Maoris uprooted from their traditional tribal village homes.

But until the New Zealand Company's colonists arrived in Port Nicholson at the beginning of 1840 the European had been concerned with the resources of sea and shore, and only to a lesser extent with the products of Maori agriculture and the harvest of flax and timber from swamp and forest. He had not yet looked beyond the coastal settlements, and by far the greater part of the land was barely touched. The influence of European culture, however, had been transmitted inland. The newcomer's diseases, his muskets, his alcohol, his trade goods, his crops and animals (especially the white potato and the pig) had left no Maori tribe unaffected. European diseases had decimated the population of whole regions; and by bringing muskets and powder, the European had transformed what was formerly sporadic manly exercise and local inter-tribal rivalry into a ruthless death-dealing business and a long-range war of extermination. By 1840 there were no more than 115,000 Maoris where seventy years earlier there may well have been three or four times that number.

THE NEW LAND

In the decade 1840-1850, as colonies were planted first at Wellington and on both shores of Cook Strait and later in Otago

H

and Canterbury, and with the establishment of the first official capital on the shore of the Waitemata, Europeans began to take up land and to make permanent homes in the new and strange land, hitherto occupied only by Neolithic Polynesians and by itinerant traders and others fleeing for different reasons from European law and civilization. It was indeed a strange land. In the latter half of the century it was often referred to as 'the Britain of the South' and some still liken it to the British Isles from which by far the largest part of the colonists were to come. But it is a mistake to consider these islands in the southwest Pacific to be anything like a southern hemisphere replica of the British Isles. The physical differences are very great and have been very significant; in over a century of effective occupation people from the British Isles have failed to obliterate these differences. Indeed they never will. And now New Zealand is evolving a distinctive culture and technology which will make it increasingly different from Britain and Europe also in a human sense.

The enterprising colonists who stepped on to Petone beach, or who were passengers on small wooden sailing vessels that put into Otago, Lyttelton and Waitemata harbours, found a land like Britain only in that it was insular and of roughly the same size. It was a land of lofty alpine ranges, of torrential rain but of bright and abundant sunshine, of profuse subtropical forest, of bizarre palms and lush tree ferns, of frequent earthquakes and active volcanic cones, of 'hot lakes' and 'cold lakes', of deep fiords, of rushing mountain torrents and mile-wide shingle riverbeds such as Britain does not know. It was a land also with strange soils derived from deep clays, coarse gravel and pumice ash, with bunched yellow tussock grassland, and with semi-desert. It was a land upon which the Stone Age Polynesian had apparently made little mark except for the building of ramparts on hills and coastal promontories, and the clearing here and there of small patches of scrub or bush to make room for his kumara gardens and his clustered whares. Yet it seems increasingly clear that in fact the Moahunters, by using fire in driving and chasing the flightless birds, may have converted millions of acres of forest in the drier eastern parts of the South Island into induced tussock grassland.

SURFACE CONFIGURATION

Above all it was a land with a broken, and, for the most part, elevated surface. In Wellington and Otago the early settlements were shut in by the slopes of coastal mountains. At Nelson and Canterbury the skyline was one of snow-capped ranges. At New Plymouth the conical peak of Egmont was ever-present. Inland, except only at Auckland and Christchurch, the steep slopes of mountain and hill country were never far distant. Two-thirds of New Zealand lies at an elevation between 650 feet and 3500 feet, and nearly as much of the surface is above 3500 feet as is below 650 feet. And much of the lowland is broken and hilly; little of it lacks relief.

From *Figure 58* it can be seen that mountain landforms and landscapes make up four-fifths of the South Island and not less than a fifth of the North Island. Most of the rest of the North Island is made up of hill country, plateau and downland. There is a smaller proportion of hill country, foothills and downland flanking the mountain terrains of the South Island. In neither island do plains figure prominently. With few exceptions the plains are so small as to make it impossible to show them on *Figure 58* without exaggerating them.

THE SOUTH ISLAND

The six isolated colonies of New Zealand in the early eighteen-fifties were scattered between Auckland and Otago, cut off from each other by the mountainous interiors, and each often in better communication with Sydney than with other coastal settlements in New Zealand. Only the Canterbury settlement at Christchurch had ready access to the interior. It was established on the swampy outer edge of the largest lowland plain in New Zealand. The snow-capped and jagged ranges of the Southern Alps formed an inland skyline sixty or seventy miles away, and for forty miles the largely induced tussock grassland stretched back over flat-looking and featureless plains before it encountered and overran the surrounding foothills and downland. This grassy lowland was soon parcelled out into large sheep runs.

The Canterbury Plains are a huge accumulation of shingle waste derived from the mountains on the eastern flank of which they lie. They rise steadily but almost imperceptibly inland until

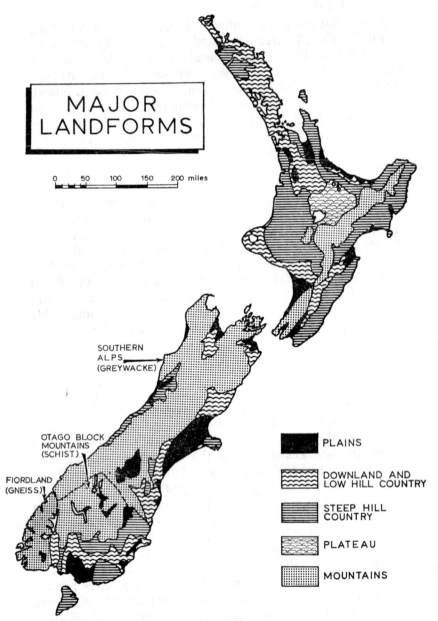

MAJOR
LANDFORMS

0   50   100   150   200 miles

SOUTHERN
ALPS
(GREYWACKE)

OTAGO BLOCK
MOUNTAINS
(SCHIST)

FIORDLAND
(GNEISS)

PLAINS

DOWNLAND AND
LOW HILL COUNTRY

STEEP HILL
COUNTRY

PLATEAU

MOUNTAINS

Figure 58

they abut abruptly against the foothills at a height of from 1100 to 1400 feet. Their smooth surface is without relief except for the gentle slope seaward and the deep, mile-wide trenches cut across them by the rivers from the inland mountain highland. The trenches are occupied by the many braided channels of the rivers running between grey-white stretches of riverbed shingle.

To the first agricultural settlers and the sheepmen—many of these pastoralists coming from Australia—the plains were a dusty yellow-brown sea of bunched tussock grasses (*Fig. 59*) stirred into waves and rustled alternately by the cold, gusty wind from the southwest, and the hot, dry and steady nor'wester blowing out of the inland mountain gorges. The parched, windswept gravel plain was ideal sheep country, and when later its brown loess soils were first disturbed by the plough they yielded for a time heavy crops of wheat and oats.

The tussock grassland stretched also over the bordering downland and foothills and deep into the mountain highland itself. The eastern side of the South Island was sheltered from the moist air masses off the Tasman Sea by the alpine barrier. Only on the mountainous coast of Marlborough, Banks Peninsula, Otago Peninsula and on the southern coast round to Fiordland, does rainfall amount to forty inches or more, and here the forest was intact or the low ground was occupied by swamp and peat. Elsewhere east of the alpine highland rainfall is between twenty-five and thirty-five inches, and it is associated with frequent drying winds, with high summer temperatures by day and frequent frost by night. Where inland basins, like those of Central Otago and the Mackenzie Country, are shut off not only from the west but from the south and east as well, these climatic conditions are accentuated. In such basins rainfall may be as little as twelve to fifteen inches; frosts may occur on 200 nights every year, but in the clear, dry air midday summer temperatures are the highest in the country. The south central part of the South Island is New Zealand's 'continental interior'. Here the low grassland of small tussock species was probably in place when the first Polynesian drifted upon some New Zealand shore.

There were 17,000,000 tussock-clad acres in 1840 (*Fig. 59*). The virgin grassland consisted of tall and vigorous tussocks, with their foliage interlocked and no bare ground between. Beneath the foliage of robust poa and fescue tussocks a thick carpet of damp, decaying grass conserved the light rain and was an additional protection for the soils against the dry winds, the intense sunshine and the sharp frosts. But since the runholders first turned out their small flocks of emaciated Merinos, the tussock grassland has deteriorated greatly. The plains and the easy, rolling slopes of the adjacent downland were ploughed out of the tussock after 1860. Over 4,000,000 acres were used in this way, their thinning cover of indigenous grasses being replaced by arable crops and rotation pastures of introduced grasses. But where the tussock grazing land was too elevated, too broken or too dry for the plough, fire and grazing have reduced—and sometimes virtually destroyed—the grassland.

THE MOUNTAIN HIGHLAND

The South Island highland falls into three distinctive parts, distinguished from each other by their rocks, their landforms and their geological history. The southernmost portion (*Fig. 58*) is the ancient crystalline mass of Fiordland with its deep vertically-walled canyon-like valleys occupied, in the west by outward-radiating salt-water fiords, and occupied inland by the fresh-water arms of the 'cold lakes'—Te Anau, Manapouri and Monowai. This mountain region is the wettest in New Zealand. Milford Sound sometimes has over 300 inches of rain in a year. Except on the rock walls of the valleys, where there is not even any soil, and at high elevations, where the open upland surface between the fiords rises into a belt of sub-alpine shrubs and grasses, the region is one of constantly wet and dripping forest.

East of Fiordland is the mountain interior of Otago. Here the mountain blocks of foliated mica schist stand apart from each other. They are separated by terraced, gravel-floored basins, some of them occupied in part by moraine-dammed lakes. The surfaces of the terraces are flat and straight. The walls of the purple-brown mountains rise sharply, but often smoothly, to wide, open, grass-covered summits broken by projecting tors of schist. By contrast with Fiordland—and despite its proximity—this is the driest part of New Zealand. The basin floors are especially arid and desert-like. But the alluvial gravels and the wash of rivers in Central Otago had rich pockets of payable gold, and in the 1860s the pioneer graziers had the company of a motley array of immigrant diggers.

To the north of the frosty, windswept saucer of the Mackenzie Basin and from there to Cook Strait extends a different kind of mountain terrain. This is the tussock-clad, greywacke 'high country'. It is a succession of lofty alpine ranges, often over 10,000 feet high and reaching 12,349 feet in the cloud-piercing summit of Mount Cook, built of an indurated but much-jointed blue-grey sandstone called greywacke. The frost-fretted stony ranges are separated by deeply penetrating U-shaped valleys cut by glaciers. Their slopes are often deceptively smooth where enormous screes of angular rock waste have accumulated on their flanks. On the narrow flat floors of the valleys braided ribbons of blue-green melt-water swing from side to side of the white riverbed of rounded shingle, and between the river-bed and the mountainside are sprawling symmetrical fans of rock rubble covered with tussock and matagouri (*Discaria*) scrub. The dun-coloured tussock runs part way up the steep slopes and gives way to grey talus or to a green-black contour strip of beech forest, above which towers the jagged outline of snow-capped rock ridges. Such mountains run out to sea along the Marlborough coast. In the Sounds they are largely bush-clad, and in Nelson they are divided off into separate blocks by fault-depressed lowlands.

Fiordland has been put to little use and still remains unoccu-pied except for a few deerstalkers, lighthouse-keepers and hydro-electric power station operators. But the rest of the South Island's mountain interior was taken up by sheepmen soon after the tussock plains. By 1860 it was being grazed back to the beech forest and up to the snowline by Merino sheep. And its vegetation was being burned. The first occupiers—the pioneer runholders—set whole watersheds alight, the blood-red glow of the fires they lit in the mountain valleys being visible at night from Christchurch sixty miles away. They did this to rid the grassland of the spiny shrubs growing amongst the tussocks, and to provide palatable fresh green growth from the burned-back grasses. In the early days the fires were a regular—almost an annual—procedure, and the tussocks were reduced in height, density and vigour. Add to this the effect of over-grazing, not

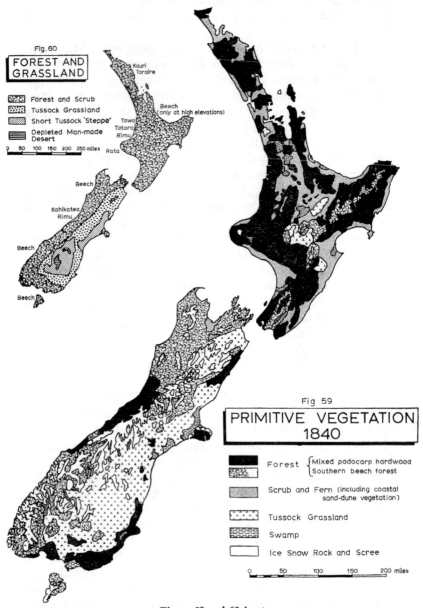

Fig. 60

FOREST AND
GRASSLAND

Forest and Scrub
Tussock Grassland
Short Tussock 'Steppe'
Depleted Man-made
Desert

0   50   100 150 200 250 miles

Kauri
Taraire

Beech
(only at high elevations)

Tawa
Totara
Rimu

Rata

Beech

Kahikatea
Rimu

Beech

Beech

Fig 59

PRIMITIVE VEGETATION
1840

Forest { Mixed podocarp hardwood
         { Southern beech forest

Scrub and Fern (including coastal
                 sand-dune vegetation)

Tussock Grassland

Swamp

Ice Snow Rock and Scree

0   50   100   150   200 miles

Figure 59 and 60 *inset*

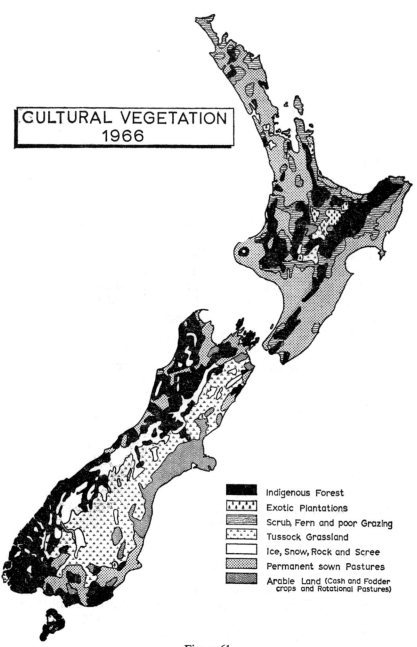

CULTURAL VEGETATION
1966

Indigenous Forest
Exotic Plantations
Scrub, Fern and poor Grazing
Tussock Grassland
Ice, Snow, Rock and Scree
Permanent sown Pastures
Arable Land (Cash and Fodder crops and Rotational Pastures)

Figure 61

only by sheep but also later by millions and millions of rabbits, and it is not difficult to see why so much of the grassland deteriorated, and especially that in the drier, hotter and frostier basins. Indeed in Central Otago and parts of the Mackenzie Country the parched floors of gravel basins were converted into 'man-made deserts'. The soil was often bared, and it began to erode. It was loosened by frost, washed by rain and lifted by wind. In later days, especially with the use of the high country for the generation of hydro-electric power, this has become a serious problem.

THE WEST COAST

The main divide of the Southern Alps lies well to the west. From it the land falls away rapidly towards the Tasman Sea. It has been customary to speak of a Westland 'plain', but there is no such thing. For most of its length the west coast of the South Island is made up of mountain slopes. This is true of Fiordland from Puysegur Point to Abut Head and again most of the way from Cape Foulwind to the base of Farewell Spit. Only in the central waist of the island is the mountain rampart set back a little from the west coast, and here the coastal lowland is made up of broken hill country, each tumbled section of which is separated from the others by gravel terraces and riverbeds. But one or two dark, forested valleys have cut back into the highland. The western wall of the mountains is rain-drenched, cloud-banked and forested. Only the richly-rewarding alluvial gold brought people into this region in a hectic but arduous rush after 1865. Later coal, timber, the scenery of forest, lakes and glaciers, and occasional pastures on valley flats have supported a small population strung out thinly and patchily between Karamea and the Fox Glacier, and recently extended further south with the opening of the road to Haast Pass and over the ranges to Central Otago.

THE NORTH ISLAND

The North Island is characterized above all by its once forested hill country. The mountain highland here is narrow and lies to the east. The mountains are a continuation north of Cook Strait of the South Island's greywacke highland, but their deep

V-shaped valleys have not been glaciated and the narrow ridges are clothed to their summits in vegetation. They have little of the expansive grey rocky appearance of the South Island high country, and the tawny tussock is replaced here by dull green rainforest and scrub.

EASTLAND

On the eastern flank of the mountain axis lies a plaster of softer and younger rocks. From Hawke's Bay southwards these are separated from the Rimutakas and the Ruahines by the elongated Wairarapa lowland, but further north the steeply corrugated hill country, cut into the less resistant mudstones and sandstones, lies immediately on the flank of the mountain ranges to the west. The hill country is sheltered by the ranges from air masses off the Tasman, and is in general a rain-shadow area with some of the North Island's lowest rainfalls. But between a quarter and a third of New Zealand's weather approaches from the east and south. When such meteorological conditions exist the North Island east coast is exposed either to cool squally southerly weather with showers, or to moist saturated warm tropical air masses from the northeast. When warm air masses, heavily laden with moisture, are driven against the hills and mountains, heavy rain is precipitated, and the districts from mid-Hawke's Bay north to East Cape are liable to experience some of the heaviest rains that occur in New Zealand. Three-day totals of over thirty inches are not unknown, and three-day totals over ten inches are almost an annual event in some part or other of this region. After such rainstorms hillsides for miles around in Hawke's Bay or Poverty Bay are pitted with ugly yellow slips and whole valley-sides slip, slump or flow downhill.

The wetter parts of this hill country were heavily forested and some of them were not cleared until well on in the present century. But drier districts, including those with a thin mantle of volcanic ash on their steep, short slopes, had a vegetation of bracken fern and manuka scrub. Some sheltered lowland areas had patches of tussock grassland. The Wairarapa, and later the lower hills of southern Hawke's Bay, were the first part of the North Island to be extensively occupied by Europeans. Sheep were brought into the Wairarapa in the infant years of the settlement at Port Nicholson, and the hill country further north was taken up in the 1860s and 1870s. The forested papa hill country inland of Poverty Bay and north to East Cape was not cleared until still later—much of it after 1900. Here much land is still Maori land.

THE VOLCANIC PLATEAU AND WESTERN HILL COUNTRY

West of the ranges extends the wide sweep of the Volcanic Plateau. Above it to the southwest rise the masses of the volcanic piles of Ruapehu, Ngauruhoe and Tongariro. This plateau was on the arrival of the first Europeans a drab expanse of stunted grey-green scrub and grey-white pumice soil, bleak and cold and exposed. For many years its soils remained sterile and unworked. The only European settlement was alongside the 'hot lakes' and other thermal oddities near Rotorua. But after World War I many thousands of acres were planted in North American conifers, which, today, impatiently await harvesting as one of New Zealand's major untapped resources. And in the last thirty years it has been discovered how to utilize the pumice soils by the lavish use of phosphatic fertilizers mixed with minute quantities of cobalt. Farms are now creeping on to the plateau's fringes, and the Lands Department is employing heavy machinery and great amounts of aerially distributed fertilizers to convert a wilderness into green and productive pasture land.

Deep-cut hill country, with short but steep slopes, razor-back ridges, streams in rock-walled papa gorges and no flat land, occupies most of the rim of the Volcanic Plateau, but especially the large block of land between the Manawatu plain and the northern edge of the King Country and the middle Waikato valley. Its elevation decreases and its slopes become gentler towards the coast in the west. There is little coastal lowland, and where it is widest—in Taranaki—the volcanic pile of Egmont rises well over 8000 feet above the sea, and 7000 feet above the undulating downland and low hill country immediately to the east of it. In pre-European times all was densely forested with tawa, totara, rimu and a great variety of other trees, and threaded only with occasional Maori tracks. It was not cleared until after 1880, and much of it is still in forest, or is reverting through scrub and second growth to forest again (*Fig. 59*).

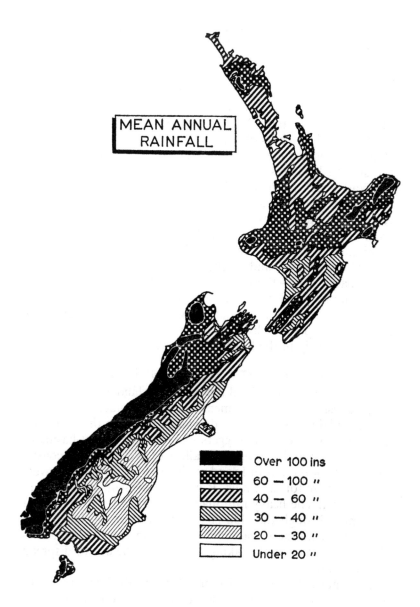

MEAN ANNUAL
RAINFALL

Over 100 ins
60 — 100 "
40 — 60 "
30 — 40 "
20 — 30 "
Under 20 "

Figure 62

THE NORTH

The narrow northern peninsular section of the North Island reaches north almost to latitude 34 degrees south. It is narrow and rarely elevated, though it is often broken and irregular of surface. Land and sea interpenetrate, and at the Tamaki isthmus the Manukau and Waitemata harbours and the Tasman Sea and Pacific Ocean are separated by no more than a mile or two of land. Rolling low hill country of papa and sandstone, higher hills of greywacke, low volcanic cones, small coastal plains and mangrove flats, and—south of the isthmus— the swamp lowlands of the Hauraki and the peaty basins of the Waikato: these are the 'winterless' north's characteristic landforms. Wet and humid, warm and largely frost free, this region carried an indigenous vegetation of subtropical forest and swamp, and a dense Maori population. Much of the forest was dominated by the giant kauri which has given to many areas a grey-white, leached and sterile soil. Poor gumland soils and fertile basalt soils—the latter indigenously carrying a forest of puriri, taraire and pukatea—alternate with bewildering frequency. Most important today, however, are the former peaty, organic swamp soils, drained, reclaimed and put down in rich pastures, largely in the last half century.

PROGRESS OF SETTLEMENT IN THE NORTH ISLAND

While in the South Island the open grassland and the alluvial gold deposits invited settlement, while runholders spread out over the plains, foothills and downland and into the mountain high country, and while diggers explored the frosty basins of Central Otago and the forested valleys of Westland, the coastal settlements of the North Island made little headway. They were hemmed in by forested hills. Roads out of them were difficult to construct. The heavy rain made the best of them ribbons of deep mud through the chill shade of the dripping bush. And for many years there was opposition from the still numerous Maori population to the taking of land and the outward spread of settlement.

It was not until after the Maori Wars and the introduction of refrigeration (1882) that an assault was made on the forest of the North Island; in the period from the 1880s until the 1920s the forest was cleared at the rate of thousands of square miles each decade, and in some cases it was cleared from such steep hill country that it was impossible to replace it with stable pasture, so that the land was subsequently abandoned. In much more of the steep hill country the occupier still wages a constant two-way struggle with soil erosion in the form of slips and slumps, and with the everlasting effort of the indigenous forest to re-establish itself first as scrub, fern and aggressive weeds, and later as second growth.

With the development, however, of new grazing techniques, the breeding of new grasses and better stock, and with the construction of roads and the growth of motor transport in the last thirty-five years, settlement has subsequently made phenomenal progress in areas of lower elevation and lesser relief and especially since it has proved possible to reclaim many swampy lowlands and the pumice soils of areas of plateau and low hill country. And even on the steep mudstone hills, since the advent in the early 1950s of aerial topdressing, pastures have been improved, stock numbers expanded and weeds and soil erosion banished. Indeed many hilly country stations, once breeders and suppliers of store stock, are now able to fatten sheep, lambs and beef cattle.

In the 1870s the South Island had two-thirds of New Zealand's population, although the North Island was still the home of the bulk of the Maori people, at that time declining rapidly towards a minimum of little over 40,000. But within twenty years of the first shipment to the United Kingdom of refrigerated produce, the population of the two islands was equal, and since the turn of the century the North Island's superior resources and more efficient livestock industries have enabled it to prosper until it now has almost seventy per cent of the Dominion's people.

FARMING

Like that of Australia, the economy of the Dominion of New Zealand is dominated by its pastoral industries. Even to a greater extent than the Commonwealth, New Zealand is a producer of livestock products for export. A much larger proportion of its annual output is surplus to domestic requirements, and its pastoral export products have a wider range, so that its overseas trade is not dependent so markedly on one livestock product as is Australia's on wool. Whereas the great pastoral industries of Australia are based largely on the grazing

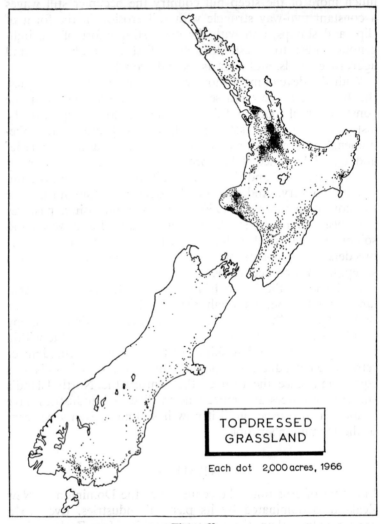

TOPDRESSED
GRASSLAND

Each dot 2,000 acres, 1966

Figure 63

of the herbage of natural grass and shrublands, or are associated with the extensive cultivation of wheat, New Zealand's rest upon man-made pastures of introduced grasses of the highest quality which have replaced subtropical forest, tussock grassland or raupo swamp. The real history of New Zealand is the history of a largely successful struggle to replace Nature's indigenous vegetation with one of man's designing: upon the outcome of this struggle are based the high standards of living, leisure and comfort which are enjoyed today by more than 2,650,000 New Zealanders—both *pakeha* and Maori.

With more than 53,748,000 sheep and 7,169,000 cattle in 1966 New Zealand has, in relation to its *population*, a greater number of livestock than Australia: in relation to its *size*, it has at least ten times as many sheep and cattle. Indeed New Zealand pastures support more livestock units in relation to farm area and total population than any country in the world. Pastoral farming is much more intensive, and production per acre and *per capita* are both very much greater than in Australia. And whilst in recent years New Zealand has been able to maintain, or even increase, the volume of its exports of meat, butter and cheese despite a rapidly growing population, the export surplus of many branches of the Australian livestock industries has declined to a fraction of that shipped to world markets from New Zealand ports. For its fortunate situation, in a world increasingly short of food, New Zealand has to thank not only its more abundant and reliable rainfall but also, more especially, its advanced pastoral farming technology, and also to some extent its restraint in not pushing too far the fostering of manufacturing industries for which its domestic resources do not well equip it.

In estimating the respective importance of the different branches of a country's farming, much depends upon the significance attached to each of a number of different considerations. There are in New Zealand more dairy farms than farms of any other kind, and more people are employed on them than on other kinds of farms. But the value of the production of sheep farms, even when wool prices are not high, far exceeds that of dairy farms. The value of 'agricultural' products—the wheat, oats, barley, seeds, fruit, vegetable, hops, and tobacco which come from mixed crop-livestock farms and from highly specialized small orchard and garden holdings—stands behind that of both sheep and dairy products. A third consideration is the amount of land that each of the major categories of farming occupies, and from the geographic point of view this is perhaps the most important, for the patterns of land use so largely give the landscape its differences of appearance and character. The various kinds of sheep farming occupy the greatest area in New Zealand, and so help to give the greater part of the occupied regions of the country its characteristic appearance (*Figs 64* and *65*).

SHEEP REARING

Nearly sixty per cent (30,000,000) of New Zealand's sheep are in the North Island, nearly three-quarters of the island's total in two hill-country regions, and the rest largely in dairying districts and often on dairy farms. It is sometimes claimed that sheep are reared in the drier east of the North Island and cattle in the heavier rainfall districts west of the ranges. But there are, in fact, as many sheep on farms to the west of the mountain axis as to the east. Of the two hill country sheep-rearing regions delimited in *Figure 65*, however, the Eastland region has more sheep and a denser sheep population than the Wanganui-Taranaki hinterland. It also has many more beef cattle.

Both regions have deeply dissected terrains of steep-sided hills and valleys cut into soft youthful sedimentary rocks. Both have had their vegetation transformed (often within the present century) from forest and—in Hawke's Bay—from scrub and fern. The indigenous cover has been replaced, not always successfully, by second-class and third-class pastures of English grasses. Ryegrass and cocksfoot were often sown on the ash-littered surface after the bush burn, but pastures today are dominated in the wetter hill country by browntop, and in drier districts—east of the Wairarapa, for example—by the aggressive native danthonia. The wetter and steeper hill country between Wanganui and Raetihi, and Stratford and Ohura, and that tributary to the east coast north of Wairoa was not only more difficult to clear but more difficult to fence and to keep in grass. It is still littered in part with blackened stumps of forest giants. Pastures tend to run to hard fern and second growth. Scrub has to be cut or burned. Often after heavy rain hillsides are scarred by soil erosion. Run cattle are often kept alongside the sheep to graze rough gullies and to keep down the second growth. But in the last decade phosphate and seed distributed by air-

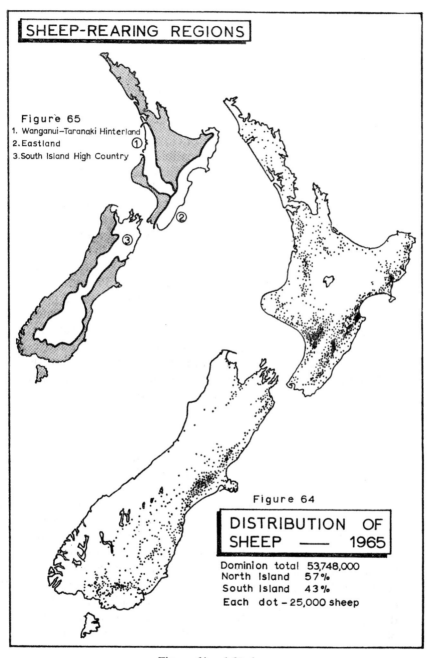

SHEEP-REARING REGIONS

Figure 65
1. Wanganui–Taranaki Hinterland
2. Eastland
3. South Island High Country

① ② ③

Figure 64

DISTRIBUTION OF
SHEEP —— 1965

Dominion total 53,748,000
North Island 57%
South Island 43%
Each dot – 25,000 sheep

Figures 64 and 65 *above*

craft have converted thousands of acres of poor grass pasture and weeds to ryegrass and clover and made possible carrying capacities double those of earlier years.

In the hill country of the North Island the sheep stations often run to some thousands of acres, but are most frequently from 750 to 2500 acres in size. Only the easier and lower country has land on which hay crops can be harvested. Here lambs may be fattened. Elsewhere aerial topdressing of hill pastures with superphosphate and aerial sowing of clover and species of lotus have made the fattening of stock possible. But in general these are breeding and rearing districts. They act as giant inland reservoirs of store stock from which the lowland farmers with first-class pastures and abundant hay and silage draw old ewes and store lambs. Each autumn there is a wholesale exodus of store sheep. They come off the hills of the East Coast and from Hawke's Bay and are driven through the gorges of the mountain axis—huge droves of up to 15,000 sheep or 3000 store cattle —on their way to the Waikato or the Bay of Plenty. If the summer is especially dry, this migration of stock takes place earlier and is accentuated. But in recent years giant articulated three-decker trucks and trailers have replaced the drover and his horses and dogs. In the Taranaki-Wanganui region the move-ment of store sheep and lambs is through the great stockyards at Stratford, Raetihi and Feilding, where autumn sheep sales are a special feature. Cartage is here often by rail.

In details no two farms are alike. It is, however, impossible to describe them all. The details of one sheep station repre-sentative of the North Island's two large regions of hill-country sheep rearing must suffice (*Fig. 66*). This station is at Parihau-hau, twenty-three miles from Wanganui. It lies in the deep-cut valley of a tributary of the Mangawhero, itself a branch of the Wangaehu, though it is approached by way of the main road inland from Wanganui. Its 1255 acres lie awkwardly astride a 200 ft. gorge notched in the blue papa. The 300 acres across the gorge can only be reached by means of a suspension bridge of multiple strands of fencing wire slung across the vertical-walled chasm. Sheep have to be driven in single file over its narrow swaying planks to the other side. This part of the station gets little attention. It is divided into only two large blocks where the wethers and dry ewes are left with little supervision. Many of its steeper slopes have reverted to manuka, despite frequent burning and, in days of more abundant labour,

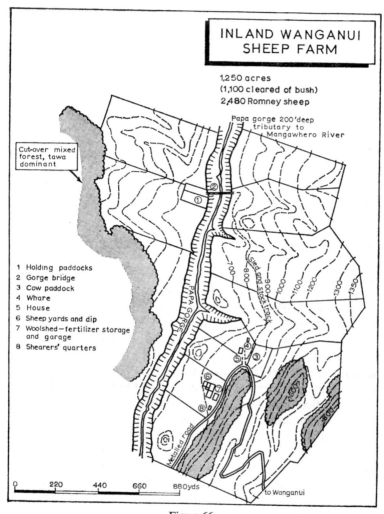

INLAND WANGANUI SHEEP FARM

1,250 acres
(1,100 cleared of bush)
2,480 Romney sheep

Papa gorge 200' deep
tributary to
Mangawhero River

Cut-over mixed
forest, tawa
dominant

1 Holding paddocks
2 Gorge bridge
3 Cow paddock
4 Whare
5 House
6 Sheep yards and dip
7 Woolshed — fertilizer storage
  and garage
8 Shearers' quarters

PAPA GORGE

sled and stock track

700
800
900
1000
1100
1200
1300
1350

Metalled road

0   220   440   660   880 yds

to Wanganui

Figure 66

frequent hand-cutting with slashers wielded by gangs of Indian scrubcutters.

The rest of the farm—on the near side of the gorge—is fenced into eight paddocks with one or two smaller ones near the homestead where the house cows are kept, and near the sheepyards, where mobs of sheep are often held for short periods at shearing or crutching time. It is wild-looking country, strewn with ghostly, black, burnt forest remnants, with evidence of massive slumps of ancient origin, all of it deeply cut by small streams rushing down towards the gorge, alongside which, here and there, are the only fragments of near-flat land on the property. But with hand topdressing in earlier days and aerial topdressing in the last decade this rough and steeply-sloping country carries a fair sward of ryegrass, vernal, browntop, white clover and lotus. Only in the rougher spots does it run rapidly to bidi-bidi and to hard and silver fern, but this is kept under control by a mob of ninety Polled Angus breeding cows which also provide an annual saleable surplus of two-year-old steers.

The station carries just over 2500 Romney ewes and 500 wethers. Each year more than 1500 lambs are sold off, most of them fat and ready for the works. And 400-500 ewes are annually culled from the flock and sold. Both Romney and Southdown rams are kept. Each year wethers are bought to replace those that are sold off in small batches as they become fit for the butcher. But the main source of income is wool, over a hundred bales of it, worth in recent years anything from $NZ10,000 to $NZ16,000. These 5000 head of livestock and 1255 hilly acres of land are cared for by two men—the working manager (the owner is primarily a stock-buyer and lives in Wanganui) and a boy. Additional temporary help is provided for scrub cutting, fencing, topdressing, crutching and, of course, for shearing in October, when a gang of ten itinerant Maoris— shearers, fleece pickers, floor sweepers and cook—takes possession of the woolshed. This pastoral economy is thus extensive. Apart from the land and stock, there is relatively little capital investment, but production per man is extremely high. The only buildings on the station are the large woolshed with its six stands of machines driven by a petrol engine, the surrounding sheepyards and dip, the house in which the manager lives, three whares for casual and seasonal labour, a garage and a makeshift cowbail. Yet this one property provides wool enough to clothe thousands of people in distant lands and meat enough to satisfy two or three hundred families for a whole year.

In the South Island, sheep rearing is of a quite different kind and more reminiscent of Australia. The economy of the high-country sheep run has much in common, though not its mountain terrain, with the outback Merino station of New South Wales or South Australia; and the rearing of sheep on mixed crop-livestock farms in the eastern lowland areas of the South Island has at least some features not unlike those of the Australian wheat belt. Of the 24,000,000 sheep in the South Island many more are to be found on rotational pastures in arable lowland areas than on the tussock grassland of the mountain interior. But no region is as completely dependent on sheep, and on fine wool in particular, as is the high country of Marlborough, Canterbury, Otago and inland Southland.

In this high country a tenth of New Zealand's sheep still graze, and rely almost entirely upon the modified remnant of the indigenous steppe grassland. Whilst the damp hill country of the North Island has been transformed in appearance with the clearing of the forest largely in the last seventy years, the South Island high country is still much as it was when Maoris trod barefoot or in flax sandals over its rocky passes, and when the immigrant Scottish and Australian shepherds first mustered its lofty slopes and high cirque basins. It is still largely Crown land, leased to the runholders in great blocks, ranging in size up to 80,000 acres. It has been repeatedly burned, but in most places the fescue tussock and the hardy snowgrass persist. Fire has removed some beech forest, and the poa tussock has replaced it. Inferior English grasses and clovers—and numerous weeds—have been carried into much of the grazing land, but the dry, tawny hue of the tussock landscape remains.

Although Merino blood is still dominant in the high country flocks, few are today pure Merino flocks. The runs produce a medium-fine wool which commands high prices. But they have few, if any other, products for sale. Rarely is the lambing percentage and the survival rate high enough to produce a surplus of young store stock after the needs have been met of replacing culled ewes and wethers. A few runs carry a small herd of beef cattle. Apart from the fine wool and the small number of store stock which it produces, the high country's other saleable products are confined to deer skins. Both deer and rabbits are caught by professional hunters.

The high-country run lies isolated by mountain ranges and by swift alpine torrents, often unfordable. The station is a cluster of buildings picked out at a distance most easily by its attendant dark clump of exotic conifers which contrasts sharply with the dominant browns and greys of the tussock landscape. Near the homestead and giant woolshed there are usually one or two small fenced enclosures in which stock is held after a muster of the mountain grazings, but for the rest the run is divided into a few 'blocks' of tussock, beech forest, alpine scrub and elevated rocky waste, not by fences, but by such natural barriers to stock as wide riverbeds and inaccessible rock gorges. A 'block' may be 10,000 acres in size. High on the flank of a mountain grazing block there may be a musterer's cabin which provides shelter for men and dogs during the twice-yearly musters. The roughest and most elevated land is grazed only in summer. In winter it may lie for long periods under a deep cover of snow. From May on, the station livestock are grazed on the lower, sunnier 'winter country' which is often within view of, and accessible from, the homestead. But even here large numbers of sheep may die from exposure or from being buried under snow if not rescued in time by snow 'raking'.

DAIRY FARMING

There are few farms in New Zealand on which a small number of dairy cattle are not kept. Many a sheep farm or cropping farm will have a handful of cows in milk and will probably produce small surpluses of cream for the butter factory: others, with one or two dairy cows, will provide a domestic supply of milk for the household, pet animals, dogs and other young livestock. But four regions—all of them small in area —support eighty per cent of the 2,100,000 cows in milk. Here indeed are nearly half (38,000 out of 80,000) of the Dominion's farm units. Since these same small regions are also the home of half the country's non-dairy cattle, a fifth of its sheep and three-quarters of its pigs, they constitute the principal source from which come New Zealand's exports. The four regions are picked out clearly in *Figure 68*. All are in the North Island. They include the areas popularly known as Northland, the Waikato, the Hauraki plains, the Bay of Plenty, Taranaki and the Manawatu. Here farming is intensive by comparison with the hill-country and high-country grazing areas of New Zealand and

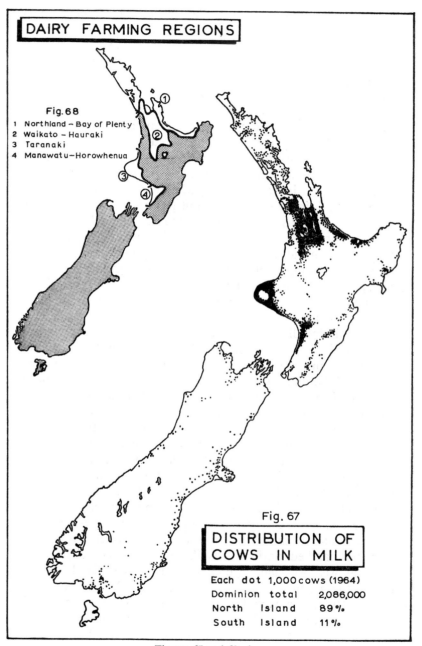

DAIRY FARMING REGIONS

Fig. 68
1 Northland – Bay of Plenty
2 Waikato – Hauraki
3 Taranaki
4 Manawatu–Horowhenua

Fig. 67

DISTRIBUTION OF
COWS IN MILK

Each dot 1,000 cows (1964)
Dominion total   2,086,000
North Island   89%
South Island   11%

Figures 67 and 68 *above*

the open grasslands of Australia. Whereas the high country carries about one sheep to five acres, the typical dairy farm carries the equivalent of eight sheep or more to the acre. Farms are smaller. Even including the occasional sheep farms within the dairy regions and the patches of unused swamp and scrub, holdings average less than 200 acres. In some counties the average is less than 100 acres. The closely divided checkerboard of small pastures, carefully fenced with wire or bounded by box-thorn and barberry hedges and sheltered by belts of pines and cypresses, have swards of ryegrass and white clover. In the warmer parts of Northland and the Waikato paspalum is also frequent, whilst in Taranaki and Manawatu cocksfoot, crested dogstail, and timothy are important pasture constituents. With few exceptions—as for example on the rich alluvial soils of the lower Hauraki plains—heavy topdressing with superphosphate is the rule. In fact most dairy farms on pumice and gumland soils depend almost entirely for their productivity upon the phosphate rock of Nauru and Ocean Island. Occasionally a few acres of root crops are grown; but on all farms hay and silage are made.

The dairying districts, now occupied by some of the world's most productive pastures, were not indigenously grassland. When the European found them, and until they were occupied between 1880 and 1925, they were either in dense subtropical forest or in swamps of raupo, flax, niggerhead and manuka. The lowlands of Taranaki were first cleared of their forest, then the Manawatu plain. The swamp basins of the Waikato and the peaty flats of the Hauraki were not reclaimed until after 1910, and indeed many thousands of acres are still the marshy undrained habitat of ducks and waterfowl. The gum-lands of Northland were not transformed from sterile scrub of manuka and umbrella fern until still more recently, and the pumice soils of the low, rolling hill country in the upper reaches of the Waihou, the Piako and the Waikato could not be properly handled until it was discovered in the 1930s that the soils were deficient in cobalt. Both in Northland and on the northern fringe of the Volcanic Plateau, hitherto unused, land is still being won for dairying and for other forms of intensive pastoralism. These pasture lands are all man-made.

Most dairy herds are of from fifty-five to one hundred and ten cows, and about seventy-five per cent of all cows in milk are grade Jerseys. The Jersey is favoured because of the high butter-fat content of its milk and because of the emphasis placed hitherto on the production of butter. It is also a small and economical cow and adapted to the moist warm to mild conditions characteristic of the New Zealand dairy lands. On most dairy farms sheep also are kept and fat lambs are produced, although dairying is sometimes a completely specialized activity with farm income derived exclusively from the production and sale of butterfat and bobby calves. In the Manawatu especially, dairy cows and sheep and lambs graze the same pastures in rotation, and here too there are amongst the lowland dairy farms a considerable number of specialized fat lamb farms of slightly larger average size, on which beef cattle (and not dairy cows) are also pastured. Here many farms breed pedigree stock.

Only a small part of the output of milk is consumed fresh in urban markets. The rest is processed in factories in the dairying districts. A close network of good roads is an essential feature of the intensively farmed pastoral regions. Along them whole milk or farm-separated cream is collected from each holding by teams of motor tankers every day—sometimes twice daily —during the dairying season. The dairy factories are also characteristic—either the closely-grouped, small cheese factories at crossroads (especially in Taranaki) or the large butter factories and dried-milk factories, more widely spaced and usually in small townships. The large modern factories for producing butter, dried milk and casein, so characteristic of the Waikato and the Hauraki-Piako lowland, are amongst the largest and most efficient in the world. Today they are capable of switching from the production of butter to dried whole milk, skimmed milk or buttermilk powder, or to casein. Most produce an increasing diversity of products; and some are today almost wholly automated. Several enormous new factories are being build to cope with the swelling flood of milk.

A representative dairy farm on, say, the Hauraki plains is a tidy, close-knit and highly efficient unit of specialized farm production (*Fig. 69*). Its 108 acres run back from a narrow road frontage in the form of a long rectangle, and are divided into fifteen small grassy paddocks most of them accessible from a central race. Near the road is the small modern bungalow,

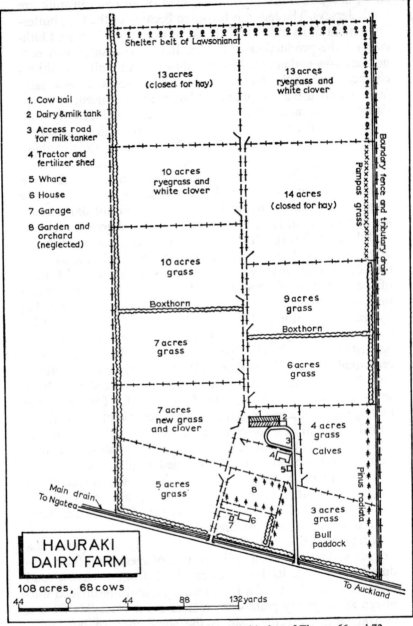

Figure 69. Compare the *scale* of this map with that of Figures 66 and 72

garage and tractor shed and not far away are the yards and the milking shed from which a light railway track leads to the cream stand on the road. The factory lorry formerly collected the full cream cans from this stand, but for some years now whole milk has been delivered to a stainless steel vat close to the dairy, and a turning circle has been laid down so that a giant road milk tanker can collect the milk direct from the steel vat. Between the front of the farm and the road is a deep drainage ditch, and to reach the farm you cross a timber bridge over this main roadside drain. Subsidiary drains follow the boundary fences and run back at right angles to the main drain. But despite this elaborate artificial drainage, the land is often wet and muddy, especially in winter, so that the yards and cowbails are concreted, and so also very often is the main race which gives the herd access from the yards to all the paddocks. These are all in grass, mainly ryegrass and white clover. All pastures are topdressed annually in autumn, not from the air but by bulk topdressing trucks equipped with powerful blowers. The main problems are to avoid the growth of buttercup and pennyroyal and to avoid poaching and breaking of the sward by stock when the ground is very wet. The first problem has been solved in recent years by the use of hormone weedkillers. The second problem is avoided by some dairy farmers who own or lease a 'run-off'—an area of rougher grazing within reasonable distance of the home farm and to which dry stock are taken in winter and on which sheep or young in-calf heifers may be grazed in summer. No crops are grown, but hay is harvested from two or three fields during the flush of early summer growth. Alongside one of the tributary drains is a hundred-yard hedge of planted pampas grass with its waving plumes, which is to provide some auxiliary fodder. Grass growth persists all year, but is less in late summer if the weather is dry, and also in winter, especially if ground frosts are more frequent than the annual average of about twenty-five.

On this farm the milking herd comprises eighty-eight Jersey cows. Twenty-five heifer calves are kept each year for replacement. The cows are milked by machine from September to May. The butterfat in the milk is the only source of farm income except for the money derived from the sale of fifty or more few-day-old bobby calves. But this is a family farm. No outside labour is employed. By dint of early hours and the monotonous routine of milking eighty-eight cows twice daily for nine months, the farmer and his son ensure a gross income of $7600 which, after all expenses are met, furnishes a high standard of living, much higher than that of farmers in other countries with a similar capital investment and land area.

MIXED CROP-LIVESTOCK FARMING

Agriculturally, as in so many other ways, there are striking contrasts between the North and South Islands of New Zealand. But in general, if not in detail, the North Island's surface-sown hill country has its counterpart in the alpine tussock high country, and the four lowland dairying regions are matched in the drier, lowland, eastern areas of the South Island by two regions in which arable farming and a mixed economy dependent on grass, cash crops, fodder crops and livestock are characteristic. These are the South Island's most productive and most intensively-farmed districts. The gravel and loess-strewn Canterbury Plains, the adjacent undulating downland, the formerly swampy and red tussock-clothed lowland of Southland, and to a less extent the confined alluvial plains of the Awatere, Wairau and Waimea in Marlborough and Nelson are the scene of this mechanised mixed crop and livestock farming. Although in New Zealand the total area in field crops is little over 1.3 million acres—no more than 3.0 per cent of the occupied land—nearly four-fifths of it are concentrated in these lowland areas of the South Island's drier eastern side. A wide range of crops is grown. Apart from the cash grain crops—wheat, oats and barley—the principal crops grown in order of acreage are: turnips, swedes, rape, kale, chou moellier, peas and potatoes. But together these account for less than one-fifth of the overall acreage of the farms in these districts. Most of the rest is in pasture—either temporary, rotational or permanent—so that grasses and clovers still constitute the most important 'crops'. They are of course mainly used for grazing, but hay is harvested and grass and clover seeds are often valuable cash products.

In the same regions over one-fifth of the country's sheep are kept and almost one-tenth of the dairy cows, beef cattle and pigs. Livestock densities higher than those on the plains and

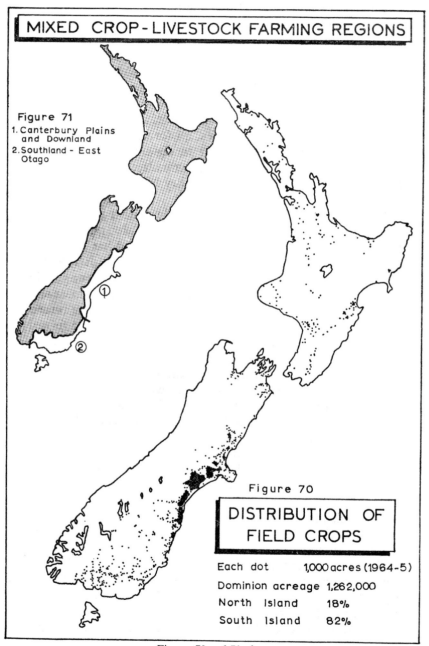

MIXED CROP-LIVESTOCK FARMING REGIONS

Figure 71
1. Canterbury Plains and Downland
2. Southland - East Otago

Figure 70

DISTRIBUTION OF FIELD CROPS

Each dot	1,000 acres (1964-5)
Dominion acreage	1,262,000
North Island	18%
South Island	82%

Figures 70 and 71 *above*

downland of Canterbury, Otago and Southland are found only in the rich dairy lands of the North Island. On the damp plains of Southland dairying is part of the mixed arable economy. Swedes, turnips and oats are grown as stock feed and, with good, heavily-limed pastures, support both dairy herds and fat lamb production. Southland's dairy factories process cheese, condensed milk and baby foods. It is on the Canterbury Plains that crops are largely cash crops—wheat, malting barley, oats for breakfast foods, and potatoes, all for the internal market, and peas and grass seed for sale in distant lands. But chou moellier, lupins, lucerne and turnips are also grown, and, with hay and rotational pasture grasses, they help to fatten Canterbury lamb (*Fig. 70*).

For a number of years after the establishment of the Otago and Canterbury settlements, the plains and downland of the South Island were utilized, as the high country has continued to be utilized, as extensive Merino sheep runs. But with the Australian gold rushes in the 1850s and the scramble for gold in New Zealand in the next decade, a demand arose for meat and flour. Runholders on the dry, sunny Canterbury Plains turned to wheat growing. They ploughed the tussock sod and turned the grey-brown earth. In the 1870s and 1880s some of them harvested each year many thousands of acres of grain, and New Zealand had a wheat acreage almost four times as large as it has been in recent years. Single wheat fields were, like those of South Australia and the Victorian mallee, many hundreds of acres in size, with a dozen or more reapers and binders busy working in them at one time.

But the over-cropping and the extensive methods of that time rapidly exhausted the fertility of the soil and often led to its serious erosion by the strong, dry nor'-wester. Meanwhile water-races had been dug across the plains, bringing water —for stock but not for irrigation—from the downs and foothills to parched grassy land which, because of its porosity, was not crossed by streams; and in 1882 New Zealand made, by the sailing ship *Dunedin*, its first successful shipment of refrigerated cargo to London. In the 1890s the Liberal Party was elected to power and there followed high land taxes and policies of acquiring land for subdivision. As a result many extensive runs were converted into family farms and land-hungry farm workers were settled on small farm settlements clustered here and there on the plains. In the 1890s an agricultural revolution was worked out both on the plains and the downland. Mixed

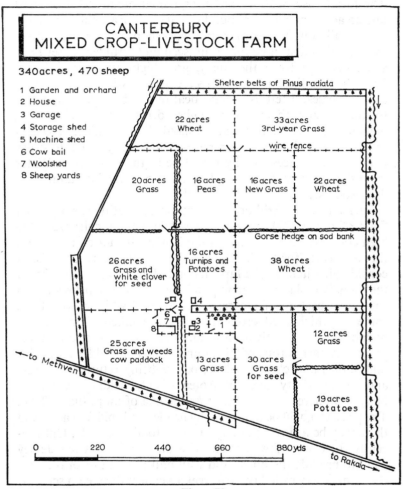

Figure 72

farming, increasingly efficient and intensive, has been the rule ever since.

Today a representative farm on the Canterbury Plains is one of 340 acres (*Fig. 72*). It is rectangular in shape and divided into fourteen paddocks by wire fences, gorse and sod-bank

I

hedges and tall, dark shelter-belts of radiata pine. Along one side of the farm is a chain-wide shingle road, and the chances are that it runs for miles, possibly twenty miles, without a bend. The farmhouse, with a garden and small unattended orchard and an adjacent cluster of buildings, including a small woolshed, a two-bail cowshed, garage and workshop, tractor and implement shed and storage for grain, seed and fertilizer, is set back some distance from the dusty, grey highway. It is sheltered from the 'howling' nor'wester by a clustered windbreak of gums and cypresses. There is a great deal of machinery. In addition to the tractor there are ploughs, drills, harrows, mowing machine, header harvester and a hay-baling machine. A system of yard-wide, shallow water races brings stock water to every paddock. The races usually run close to the fence lines. Water from the race may be pumped by electric motor into a tank for domestic use.

Such a farm in Ashburton county, near Methven, supports a flock of nearly 500 ewes, purchased largely as culls from the high country. Their wool, and the lambs which are fattened on the farm early for the butcher or the freezing works, furnish a considerable item in the farm income. Each year a majority of the ewes is replaced by new purchases. Most enclosures are in rotational pasture of ryegrass and red and white clover, from some of which seed crops and hay are taken. Four or five paddocks are in cultivation in any one year. For two or three years they carry crops of wheat and peas, and fodder crops like blue lupins and chou moellier, before being returned to grass and clover. Forty acres of Aotea wheat, yielding over forty bushels an acre, represent a gross income of more than $2000. The peas, too, will be harvested by header and sold for cash. And there may be a surplus of hay or other fodder for sale. Until recently there were few farmers who did not keep a few Jersey cows to provide the household with milk; and most of the year the cream lorry called twice a week to collect the cream separated from the milk that is surplus to farm requirements. Today, however, most Canterbury farm households get their milk in bottles and pasteurised. It is delivered from the town milk treatment plant by the mailman. The harvest, which closely follows shearing, is the busy time of the year, and additional labour may be required, although the header harvester has eliminated the stooking and stacking of wheat sheaves, so that today two men can convert a standing crop of waving golden wheat into heavy sacks of dry harvested grain in a few hours.

INTENSIVE CULTIVATION

Many other crops are grown in New Zealand, most of them intensively on smallholdings; but only locally do such activities as orcharding and market gardening contribute to the character and personality of the landscape. With the exception of apples, the orchard and market-garden crops are for the domestic market. Before World War II New Zealand exported almost a million and a half cases of apples each year, largely to the United Kingdom. During the war few were exported, and the trade has hardly yet surpassed its prewar proportions.

Since the market is an internal one, and the perishable products are largely for local consumption in a fresh condition, specialized smallholdings growing fruit and vegetables are, more often than not, located handy to the main urban centres or to good transport facilities. In some cases, however, unusual climatic conditions or especially fertile soils play a part in their localization. Both Auckland and Christchurch have a large acreage of orchards and market gardens within their metropolitan boundaries. In Auckland there are not only vegetable farms, but also vineyards, citrus and apple orchards and strawberry patches, operated variously by Chinese, Maoris and Dalmatians at Henderson, Mangere and Tamaki. In the sunny valleys running up into the Port Hills overlooking Christchurch are gardens, glasshouses and small orchards producing early tomatoes, celery, winter flowers and cherries (*Fig. 73*). In both cases however rapid housing development and so-called 'urban sprawl' are pushing the intensive smallholdings ahead of them out of town and into the adjacent counties.

Other specialized crop-producing districts are at a little distance from the urban markets, but on or near to the railway or main highway linking them with the cities. Such is Pukekohe producing on its gentle volcanic slopes early potatoes and onions, Ohakune with its Chinese vegetable gardens, Otaki and Greytown serving the capital, and Waimate with its farms growing seed potatoes and its strawberry patches. For twenty-five of the thirty miles to the wholesale market in Auckland,

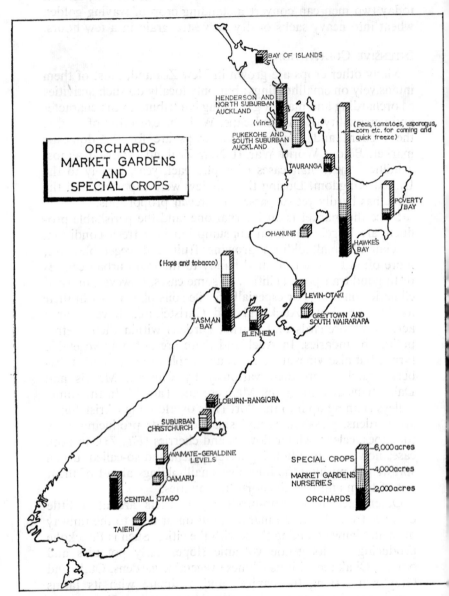

ORCHARDS
MARKET GARDENS
AND
SPECIAL CROPS

BAY OF ISLANDS

HENDERSON AND
NORTH SUBURBAN
AUCKLAND

(vines)

PUKEKOHE AND
SOUTH SUBURBAN
AUCKLAND

TAURANGA

(Peas, tomatoes, asparagus,
corn etc. for canning and
quick freeze)

POVERTY
BAY

OHAKUNE

HAWKE'S
BAY

(Hops and tobacco)

LEVIN-OTAKI

GREYTOWN AND
SOUTH WAIRARAPA

TASMAN
BAY

BLENHEIM

LOBURN-RANGIORA

SUBURBAN
CHRISTCHURCH

WAIMATE-GERALDINE
LEVELS

OAMARU

CENTRAL OTAGO

TAIERI

SPECIAL CROPS

MARKET GARDENS
NURSERIES

ORCHARDS

6,000 acres

4,000 acres

2,000 acres

Figure 73

Pukekohe now has the advantage of express motorways. Two especially sunny districts, Nelson and Hawke's Bay, produce most of the fruit exported, especially apples; but both are more and more dependent on the home market for the disposal of their increasingly varied production of special crops. Nelson glasshouses and the light, sun-drenched soils of part of the Waimea plain across to Motueka and Riwaka produce a wide range of products, including tomatoes, green peas, soft fruit and vegetables for the internal market and especially for Wellington, apples and pears for export, and hops and tobacco for processing in different parts of New Zealand. In the Napier-Hastings district sweet corn, asparagus, peas, beans and tomatoes are being grown in increasing quantities for canning. Such crops are found alongside the longer-established apple and peach orchards and the vineyards where grapes are grown for wine. Hawke's Bay and the Poverty Bay flats at Gisborne also today produce under contract to the processing firms rapidly growing quantities of vegetables for quick-freezing. Citrus fruits—New Zealand grape-fruit and lemons in particular —are grown commercially, especially near Kerikeri, Henderson (Auckland) and Tauranga. These largely frost-free northern districts are also growing more of the less familiar, exotic, subtropical fruits like tree tomatoes (tamarillos), Chinese gooseberries, passion fruit, and guavas. The local market has hitherto taken all their output. Most unusual and surprising is the location of intensive orcharding in the frosty basins of Central Otago, which although lavishly supplied with sunshine, have a rainfall barely enough to support the sparsest grassland. Fortunately frosts at blossoming and fruit-forming time are usually restricted to a very shallow layer of the atmosphere, at most a foot or two deep. They are, however, sufficient to reduce fungous and virus pests to a minimum, whilst not often harming the tree and its crop; so that, with occasional resort to the burning of oil in smudge pots and with abundant and brilliant sunshine, the Cromwell, Clyde, Alexandra and Roxburgh districts are able to produce New Zealand's best cherries, apricots and peaches. Irrigation is usually necessary, and the fruit can stand the cost of air transport to distant internal markets. The most recent development in the marketing of crops grown intensively on smaller holdings is the air freighting of strawberries and flowers to Sydney, Singapore, Hong Kong and even London and of tamarillos, 'Kiwi fruit' (Chinese gooseberries) to Hawaii and California. This holds great promise of rapid development.

EXTRACTIVE INDUSTRIES

Agriculture, even in the widest sense, is not the only 'primary' industry. Underground mining, open-cast mining, timber-winning, quarrying of building stone and road metal, reclaiming riverbed sand and shingle, dredging gold, gum-digging and the harnessing of water power resources: all these are also primary industries and all are characteristic of different parts of New Zealand. They do not provide work for large numbers of people, but they are of mounting importance to a maturing country whose economy is increasingly dependent upon coal and water power (as well as imported petrol and fuel oil), upon timber for housing and manufacturing, and upon stone and cement for constructional and road-building industries. Unlike agriculture, however, many of these are extractive industries, relying on resources that are exhaustible and non-renewable.

On the arrival in Aotearoa of the first Polynesians, forest and scrub may well have occupied by far the greater part of the country up to an elevation of 4500 feet. When the Europeans first came in considerable numbers, dense forest still occupied well over half the country. In it was some of the world's finest softwood timber. Kauri spars and matai timber were amongst the earliest exports. But to the pastoralist, especially after 1882, when it became possible to ship frozen produce to England, the bush was a nuisance, an enemy to be vanquished with the utmost speed and efficiency. The bush-burn technique was soon developed, with the result that between 1870 and 1925 hundreds of thousands of square miles of forest were burned and ravaged with the waste, in many cases, of all the timber. New Zealand has today less than a sixth of its area in 'forest', and a mere fraction of this is millable timber. Two of the most valuable native timbers—kauri and matai—are no longer generally obtainable. Rimu, the most widely available timber for many decades, is increasingly difficult to obtain, and kahikatea, from which millions of butter boxes and cheese crates have been made, is no longer to be secured for logging. (Compare *Figs. 59, 60* and *61*.)

TIMBER RESOURCES

From the earliest days of settlement, however, some people planted trees, if only to have around their houses the kinds of trees they had been used to—the deciduous trees of western Europe, so unlike the heavy, dull evergreen trees of the New Zealand bush. It was not long before shelter trees were planted on the open grasslands of the South Island, and it was soon discovered that North American conifers—especially the Monterey pine (radiata) and Monterey cypress (macrocarpa)—and the Australian eucalypts grew much more rapidly and provided better windbreaks, particularly in winter when the European deciduous trees dropped their leaves. The dark black lines and serried outline of shelterbelts of *Pinus radiata*, macrocarpa or Lawsoniana have become characteristic features of all but few New Zealand farm landscapes. And from late in the last century, and especially between the two world wars, these and other exotic trees, including Douglas fir, maritime pine, ponderosa pine, and European larch, have been set out in large plantations, both by private companies and by the government. There are small plantations in different parts of both islands but the largest exotic plantations—claimed to constitute the world's largest 'man-made forest'—are on the pumice ash soils of the Volcanic Plateau in the interior of the North Island. Here there are 800,000 acres of softwoods rapidly approaching maturity. The former widespread prejudice against radiata pine timber is disappearing, and in the absence of indigenous softwoods its wider use, even for constructional purposes and for furniture, is being rapidly established. In 1965, 473 million board feet (63 per cent) of the New Zealand total timber production was exotic softwood timber. For some time this timber has been widely used for the manufacture of wallboard, paper containers, cartons and fruit boxes. It is now rapidly becoming the basic raw material of some of New Zealand's largest industries. Not only have improved methods of treatment and preservation become available, but establishments designed to manufacture pulp and paper, multiwall paper containers, cardboard, veneers and plywood have been constructed. On the industrial fringe south of Auckland city there are new industries based on this softwood timber; timber mills have sprung up in many parts of the Volcanic Plateau, especially near

Rotorua; and new towns like those at Kinleith-Tokoroa and Kawerau have mushroomed. Board mills at Whakatane have been responsible for its rapid growth. The exploitation of this new-found resource of soft-wood timber and the blossoming industries and new towns based upon it, and its conversion to pulp, paper and newsprint are one of the main reasons for the continued growth of the population of the northern half of the North Island at a rate considerably in excess of the Dominion average. In 1966 Tokoroa and Kawerau, the location of the new integrated timber milling and pulp and paper processing plants, had 11,231 and 5765 people respectively. Immediately before World War II, at the 1936 census, Tokoroa had 460 people and Kawerau practically none. It was not listed as a 'locality' at which the population was separately enumerated.

POWER RESOURCES

Another reason for the rapid growth of both the urban and rural population of the northern half of the North Island is the fact that in the last decade some of the most significant development of the country's power resources has taken place along the Waikato River, in the sub-bituminous coalfields of the Huntly district and in the Wairakei area where vast underground reservoirs of geothermal steam have been tapped by boring and harnessed to drive electric generators.

Broadly it may be said that New Zealand's inanimate power resources are in kind and availability the reverse of those of Australia. By comparison New Zealand has relatively little coal, especially coal of high quality. But, on the other hand, it has for its size large amounts of harnessed and potential water power.

However, in view of the spectacular development of New Zealand's hydro-electric power resources in the last half century, and especially since World War II, it is easy to underestimate the contribution of coal to the total energy used in the country and to the economy as a whole. Although the relative importance of coal is declining, it still furnishes well over a quarter of all the energy consumed in the Dominion. Both water power (including geothermal steam) and oil (still practically all imported) each contributes relatively little more than coal to the total consumption of power—39 and 35 per cent respectively. If one excludes the energy used in motive power (chiefly hydro-electricity, petrol and diesel oil), and considers the power used for heating, then coal remains the principal heating fuel.

HYDRO-ELECTRICITY

Of the electric power used in New Zealand homes, on the farms, or in factories practically all is hydro-electric power. Steam generation of thermal-electric power is limited to stand-by plant at King's Wharf, Auckland, and Evans Bay, Wellington, and to the Meremere (Mercer) thermal station (180,000 kW) fired with Huntly and Maramarua coal. However, to service Northland without additional long and expensive transmission lines and consequent leakage, it has recently been decided to build an oil-fired thermal station of 240,000 kW capacity near the oil refinery at Marsden Point, Whangarei. This first produced power in June 1967.

Water power is consequently one of New Zealand's most valuable natural resources. Because of its abundance and the success in harnessing it on a large scale, New Zealand is able to claim one of the highest *per capita* consumptions of electric energy. For this enviable achievement and the relatively low cost of the power produced the Dominion has, above all, four things to thank: its high general elevation and broken surface; its abundant and reliable precipitation; the skill of its engineers and constructional workers; and its ability to finance the importation of hydro-electric equipment and reinforcing steel, which itself depends upon the productivity of its export industries.

With its often excessively heavy rain, its lofty mountain catchments, its tumbling rivers, its fault-bounded depressions and moraine-dammed glacial valleys, both often occupied by lakes, the country has resources of water power adequate for some years yet if only they can all be harnessed. One unfortunate aspect of the matter, however, is that whilst the North Island has built up the denser population, the greater industrial development and by far the heavier demand for power, the South Island has much the larger part of the undeveloped water power resources. It also has most of the reserves of coal.

To overcome this maldistribution of power supply and power demand a submarine cable has been constructed across Cook Strait. Interisland transmission of power commenced with the completion of the cable and with the large-scale generation of power from the Benmore station in 1965. The year 1966 was the first full year of operation. With heavy winter rain, the North Island sources of water supply—the Waikato (and Lake Taupo) and Lake Waikaremoana—can come close to meeting the demand. But in summer lake and dam storage is run down. A particular advantage of the Cook Strait cable is that, in interconnecting the supply systems of the two islands, it will allow the excess spring and summer supply of the South Island (when rivers run full from snow-melt and heavy rainfall in the alpine watersheds) to relieve the North Island demand, and enable the North Island's reduced spring and summer river flows to replenish lake storage.

With the completion in the 1960s of the Atiamuri, Whakamaru, Ohakuri and Aratiatia dams, the decision to proceed at last with suspended work at Maraetai II, existing plans for generation of hydro-electric power from below Lake Taupo will be completed. The stations on the Waikato River have an existing capacity of more than 750,000 kW—representing in 1966 approximately two-fifths of the total New Zealand installed hydro capacity, and more than four-fifths of the North Island's installed capacity. However, plans have been prepared, and work commenced, on a complex project for building tunnels and diversions to tap extra water to augment the supplies reaching Lake Taupo. Power stations will be built on the Tongariro River and elsewhere in the lake's artificially extended watershed. The project will cost many millions of dollars and take a decade to reach completion. Turangi, headquarters of constructional operations, will meanwhile become a town with a population of 7000 persons.

In the South Island, harnessing of the extensive water power potential proceeds apace. Benmore station, on the Waitaki River, was completed in 1965. It had a capacity of 360,000 kW in 1966, with an ultimate capacity of 540,000 kW. It has already superseded Roxburgh (335,000 kW) as New Zealand's largest hydro-electric power station. Between Benmore and the older Waitaki station, an earth and concrete dam is being constructed at Aviemore. The station there will have an ultimate capacity of 220,000 kW and will produce its first power in 1968. By that time the Waitaki catchment will be furnishing considerably more power than the Waikato.

But the most important hydro-electric power project in New Zealand lies still further south in Fiordland, where the country's greatest untapped potential of waterpower is to be found. The Manapouri scheme—the first to be tackled in the region—involves raising the levels of Lakes Manapouri and Te Anau and diverting the lake water underground to Deep Cove, an arm of Doubtful Sound. The water will plunge 700 feet down a shaft to a power station built in a huge underground rock chamber now being excavated. It will have a capacity of 700,000 kW and will discharge the water through a 30-foot diameter concrete-lined tailrace tunnel to Deep Cove.

With the completion of the Waitaki River and Manapouri schemes, now under construction, the South Island will be generating almost twice as much hydro-electric energy as the North Island. As a result, and despite the completion and operation of the Cook Strait cable, power planners are turning their attention in the North Island to thermal electric supplies. Investigations of the Wanganui and Motu rivers have revealed that high costs and engineering difficulties would be involved in harnessing them. Apart from the Tongariro project and the Matahina earth dam and station on the Rangitaiki River, now in operation, other plans and investigations are concerned with coal and oil burning stations, and prospective nuclear power stations, to be erected especially in the Auckland region.

New Zealand has another most unusual source of electric energy—geothermal steam. In the interior of the North Island, and especially in a belt running northeast from Lake Taupo, the structural instability of New Zealand reveals itself in a 'thermal zone' of hot springs, fumaroles, geysers and mud pools. In the 1940s and 1950s investigations revealed a deep source of energy readily tapped by boring. After thorough testing it was decided to drill wells, to tap the underground source of heat and steam, and to use the energy of the roaring geothermal steam jets to generate electric power at Wairakei. Steam is conveyed in pipes to the powerhouse on the bank of

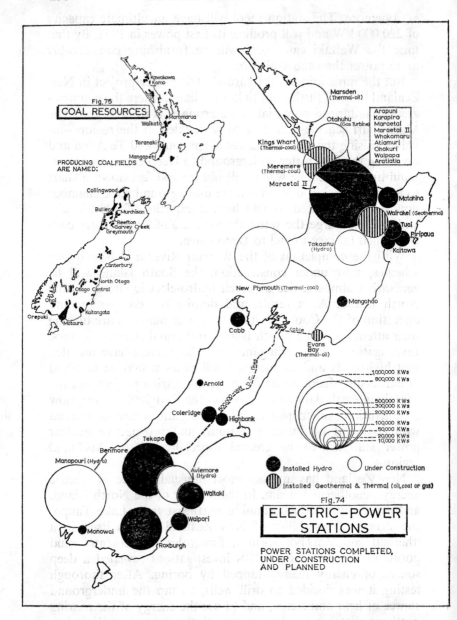

Fig. 75
COAL RESOURCES

PRODUCING COALFIELDS
ARE NAMED:

Kawakawa
Kamo
Maramarua
Waikato
Taranaki
Mangapehi
Collingwood
Buller
Murchison
Reefton
Garvey Creek
Greymouth
Canterbury
North Otago
Otago Central
Ohai
Kaitangata
Orepuki
Mataura

Marsden (Thermal-oil)
Otahuhu (Gas Turbine)
Kings Wharf (Thermal-coal)
Meremere (Thermal-coal)
Maraetai II
Arapuni
Karapiro
Maraetai
Maraetai II
Whakamaru
Atiamuri
Ohakuri
Waipapa
Aratiatia
Matahina
Wairakei (Geothermal)
Tuai
Piripaua
Kaitawa
Tokaanu (Hydro)
New Plymouth (Thermal-coal)
Mangahao
Cobb
cable
Evans Bay (Thermal-oil)
Arnold
Coleridge
Highbank
Tekapo
Benmore
Manapouri (Hydro)
Aviemore (Hydro)
Waitaki
Waipori
Monowai
Roxburgh

D.C. lines
500,000 K.W.

1,000,000 KWs
800,000 KWs
500,000 KWs
300,000 KWs
200,000 KWs
100,000 KWs
50,000 KWs
20,000 KWs
10,000 KWs

● Installed Hydro   ○ Under Construction
▨ Installed Geothermal & Thermal (oil, coal or gas)

Fig. 74
ELECTRIC-POWER
STATIONS

POWER STATIONS COMPLETED,
UNDER CONSTRUCTION
AND PLANNED

Figures 74 and 75 *above*

the Waikato River, the water of which is used for cooling. The station has a capacity of 166,000 kW—more than the Arapuni or Karapiro hydro stations—and, although it has produced power since 1958, the supply of steam from the deep underground geothermal source shows no significant sign of variation or diminution.

COAL

The Dominion is not richly blessed with what is in so many other countries the chief energizer. Its coal resources are small, poor and fragmented (*Fig. 75*). It has been estimated that New Zealand has 'inferred' coal reserves of 926 million tons, of which only 93 million tons are 'measured' or 'proven'. Of the 'measured' coal only 28 million tons, or less than one-third, is bituminous. The United States produces half as much bituminous coal every year as New Zealand has 'inferred' reserves of bituminous, sub-bituminous and lignite coal. The United Kingdom mines the equivalent of the Dominion's total recoverable reserves of bituminous coal every two or three months. New Zealand's *annual* output is equal in quantity (but not in quality) to little more than the *daily* production of United States mines. This has long been one of a number of fundamentally important handicaps in the way of the development in New Zealand of heavy metallurgical industries.

Against Australia's annual output of almost fifty million tons of coal of all kinds, New Zealand produced in 1965 2.66 million tons, most of it sub-bituminous coal and lignite. This is a *per capita* output less than half that of the Commonwealth. The coal is produced in small quantities from a number of different 'pockets'. Most of New Zealand's coal is Cretaceous and Tertiary, not Carboniferous. The seams are much folded and fractured, and there are no extensive 'coalfields' in the sense in which that term is used in England, or coal 'basins' in the sense in which that term may be used of the coal seams under Sydney. All New Zealand's hard coal comes from mines on the West Coast of the South Island. As elsewhere, the mining settlements in the Buller, Reefton and Grey districts are few, small and scattered. They are among New Zealand's few settlements with specialized functions. They are found in hilly and broken country, often isolated and hemmed in by bush. Most of Westland's hard coal is shipped through Greymouth and Westport, largely to the North Island where it is used on the railways, in gas production and for certain industrial purposes. The West Coast produces a little more than a quarter of the country's coal, most of it hard bituminous coal. Its share of the national output is steadily falling.

The coal output of the Waikato is of growing importance. Here there are thick seams of soft, sub-bituminous coal in the low hill country fringing the Waikato's largely reclaimed swamp basins. Underground mines have long been in production in the area round Huntly and Taupiri, and there is a group of specialized but small mining towns west of the river. But during and since the war new open-cast methods of working accessible pockets of coal have been introduced in order to speed and increase the output of fuel. An increasing portion of the Waikato's output—now almost sixty per cent—comes from deep, crumbling seams of brown coal from which the overburden of clay has been stripped by very few men using giant American earth-moving equipment. At Kimihia a lake has been partly removed, its floor stripped off, and the coal from twenty to seventy feet below is now being loaded mechanically on to a conveyor belt for removal to the bins and railway trucks. Open-cast mining of small near-surface deposits of coal like these gives rise to no town, however small, but only to a group of temporary hutments and small houses to accommodate, not miners, but machinery operators and motor mechanics. Like logging camps they are only temporary settlements, without the shops and the other facilities of even the smallest towns. Open-cast mining, not unlike gold-dredging, leaves in its wake a countryside laid waste, a tumbled hummocky expanse of clay without soil, but soon a nursery of weeds. It would seem that if such methods of winning coal are to be extended, some provision should be made by the State (which is principally responsible for these operations) to preserve and re-spread the topsoil and avoid the creation of ugly, useless landscapes in areas which formerly were in forest or pasture, or were the site of pretty lakes and home of fish and waterfowl.

The largest consumer of Waikato coal is the Meremere power station. It is proposed to install a seventh coal-burning generating unit at the station; and the Waikato mines will supply coal for the New Zealand iron and steel industry at Glen-brook (Waiuku) when in operation. The relative importance of Waikato coal production will thus continue to grow.

Apart from the Waikato and West Coast fields, the rest of the coal comes from many small, scattered workings, both underground and open-cast—in Northland, inland Taranaki, Canterbury, Otago and Southland (*Fig. 75*). In Southland and Otago much of the coal produced is lignite. Here and else-where many small mines are operated by groups of miners working co-operatively; and since each has an annual output of a few thousand tons, together they contribute a not insignificant proportion of the Dominion's total annual production. The principal users of coal in New Zealand are small industries. Dairy factories, hospitals and hotels, for example, together take over forty per cent of the output; railways take another twenty per cent, domestic users consume nearly a quarter of the output (but waste most of its heat and energy), whilst gasworks, the most efficient users of coal, take one-seventh of the annual production, all of it bituminous. The future may well see a more efficient use of dwindling supplies. The erection of the Mercer thermal electric power station on the Waikato, using open-cast coal from Maramarua, was completed in 1958. The extraction of gas and oil from coal in Westland, and the greater production and use of by-products are under investigation. New Zealand may well be forced in future to make more efficient use of its coal resources.

PETROLEUM AND NATURAL GAS

New Zealand is poorly endowed with minerals. Most serious is the lack, or virtual lack, of petroleum. Near New Plymouth oil wells have been in production for many years, but their annual output is equivalent to no more than an hour or two's petrol consumption of the vehicles on New Zealand roads. New Zealand continues to import its requirements—from the Middle East and Central America. In recent years imports of petroleum products have exceeded 400 million gallons and cost more than $60 million. Consumption of petrol and oil products is indispensable in many phases of the country's economic life—on the roads, railways, farms and in homes and factories. It continues to rise steeply. It is therefore not surprising that the search for petroleum deposits within New Zealand has been stepped-up since World War II. But such is the structure of the country, with its much faulted strata and lack of extensive gently folded basin structures, that the prospects of rich discoveries seem remote.

However in 1961 a consortium of oil companies drilling for petroleum in Taranaki discovered a pool of natural gas at Kapuni estimated to be capable of producing more than 30 million cubic feet of gas a day, plus a 'condensate', for not less than twenty years. From the oil 'condensate', shipped via New Plymouth to the new oil refinery at Marsden Point, Whangarei, sufficient petroleum could be produced to meet about a fifth of New Zealand's present requirements. The volume of gas available is in excess of twenty times the present production and consumption of coal gas in Auckland and Wellington together. It is, however, an insignificant fraction of the gas produced by each of many sources in the United States, or of the deposits discovered in recent years at Lacq in France, at Schlochteren in the Netherlands, in North Africa, under the North Sea, or in Bass Strait. The United States produces every three or four weeks as much gas as Kapuni will produce in its estimated life of from twenty to thirty years.

New Zealand's problem since 1961 has been to decide what to do with the new-found natural gas. Five years after its discovery the issue had not been resolved. There were four possibilities. The gas could be used to drive gas turbines and produce electricity on the gas field: but this would produce no more electricity than one small hydro station (120,000 kW) and would waste 75 per cent of the thermal value of the gas. The gas could be used largely as the raw material of petrochemical industries to produce ammonia, acetylene, carbon black, ethylene and polyethylene. But the supply of gas, especially of ethane and butane, was so small as to make the enterprise uneconomic, and the internal domestic demand was so restricted as to make overseas markets necessary.

The gas could be piped to Auckland and Wellington. The estimated cost of the pipelines ($30 millions) meant that the price of the gas distributed to Auckland and Wellington homes and factories would have to be subsidized by the government;

and the demand was so small that it would be many years before pipeline distribution would become economic.

New methods of distributing gas have recently been developed. The chief of these is to cool the natural gas to minus 150°C thus condensing it to a liquid with a volume 1/630th of the volume of the gas. The United Kingdom is already importing liquefied natural gas from Algeria in ocean-going tankers. Gas could be liquefied in the relatively small quantities New Zealand presently needs; and the liquefied gas could be transported flexibly by road, rail or sea-going tankers in the amounts required, and when required, to *all* parts of the country.

In April 1967 the government announced that it had reached agreement with the consortium on the price to be paid for Kapuni gas, and that it intended to build pipelines to Auckland and Wellington. Gas will be available to industrial and domestic consumers in these cities and other cities and towns en route by 1970. During the early stages of distribution, while demand is building up, gas will also be used to fire the gas turbine generators at the new Otara (Otahuhu) thermal power station. Kapuni natural gas will be a most useful addition to the variety of power resources in New Zealand at a time when hydro-electricity is becoming rapidly more expensive to harness. The important thing is to make the most efficient and economic use of it.

OTHER EXTRACTIVE INDUSTRIES

Many metallic minerals occur in New Zealand, and the official publications issued in the Dominion list no fewer than twenty-two that are worked. Apart from gold none of them, however, is of even minor economic significance. All the others occur in minute quantities, and, although they may be worked here and there, they have not given rise to a real mining industry or to an output of economic importance. Strictly speaking it is true to say that iron ore, petroleum, tungsten and platinum, for example, are mined in New Zealand, but none of them is of any importance. In minerals the Dominion is a very poor relation of Australia.

Mining in all its forms employs only 6080 persons, over 4580 of them producing coal. Although in the early development of the country gold was very important, it plays practically no role in the present-day economy. As was also the case in Australia, gold contributed powerfully to the progress and settlement of the country in early pioneering days. It brought immigrants in a succession of rushes and in a greater flow than would otherwise have come to this isolated colony in the southwest Pacific, and it contributed wealth which assisted the progress of agriculture, road-building and government. Although the value of the output of gold has shrunk since World War II to insignificant proportions, the value of the metal won in New Zealand since Gabriel Read discovered a gully full of gold near Lawrence in Otago in 1861 has exceeded the value of all the coal mined to date.

The 1860-70 decade was a fabulous one. In a short, exciting period millions of ounces of gold were won by simple methods, using tin dish and shovel to work the alluvial earth of the gravel terraces of Otago's basin floors and the forested flats of Westland's tumbling rivers. Before the glory departed, whole river valleys blossomed overnight with tents, and a stream of small sailing ships disgorged successive cargoes of diggers from California and Australia and of inexperienced immigrants from different parts of Europe. The red shirts and knee-tied moleskin trousers of the miners gave different parts of the southern provinces of the infant colony a colour which long ago either faded under Central Otago's sunshine or was soon washed out by Westland's phenomenally heavy rain. It was also in the 1860s that the lodes of quartz in the Thames and Coromandel districts of the Hauraki field were first worked, primitive crushers being erected to facilitate the extraction of the metal. Gold continued to be produced at Waihi until the mines there, and the great batteries, ceased operation early in the present decade. But the tide of men and goods brought to the country at a critical era in its development was far more important in the long-run than the value of the bullion itself.

The pan and cradle were succeeded late in the last century by wooden dredges, or in the Hauraki by deeper mines and more efficient methods of extraction. Today, gold production has dwindled again almost to nothing after a revival which resulted from the introduction of giant, floating, metal-constructed, bucket dredges operated by electricity. For two or three decades such enormous mechanism—amongst the world's largest—operated in Westland and Otago. They were capable of handling millions of cubic yards of alluvial gravel in a year and of raising it from depths of almost a hundred feet. But increasing costs and diminishing returns have led not only to the closing of the Waihi mines but also to the dismantling of all but one of the dredges. The dredges left behind them along the valley bottom in which they worked a hummocky desert of gravel tailings. It is doubtful whether the value of the gold won was worth the destruction of alluvial land which the dredges caused. In 1965 no more than 12,136 ounces of gold were produced, this being only one-tenth of the export in the early years of the last war, and but a fraction of the fabulous shipments of nearly a century ago. It would not be any real loss to the country if the gold-mining industry disappeared. It employs only a few score men and, although all the gold is exported, its export value in 1965 was considerably less than that of much minor agricultural exports such as pea seed, clover seed or edible tallow.

MANUFACTURING INDUSTRIES

Manufacturing began in different parts of New Zealand soon after the first settlers were put ashore. Artisans as well as farmers and farm workers were sent as colonists, with a view to the manufacture of goods which could not readily be imported and for the production of which raw materials were at hand or could soon be produced in the infant settlements. The preserving of food, the erection of buildings for shelter, and the printing of newspapers in which to criticize the government of the day, all had an early start. Small flour mills, pickle factories, jam factories, bakeries and biscuit-making establishments were founded in the early towns, and in the rural environs of the coastal settlements timber was milled, bricks were baked and pipes, tiles and other clay products were manufactured. Simple furniture was also made. Coach-building and the manufacture of implements and their repair, using in part imported metal, followed. In Canterbury the manufacture of hardier ploughs and new kinds of harvesting machinery earned the early engineering industries a reputation outside the country. Tanning of hides and skins, the production of cloth, blankets and woollen rugs, and the manufacture of soap and candles from local tallow accompanied the expansion of the pastoral industries. Most of these developments were in the South Island, where Christchurch and Dunedin were the largest manufacturing centres, and where Dunedin, thanks largely to the stimulus of the gold discoveries, was for some decades the largest centre of population in the colony.

But it was refrigeration and the depression in the primary industries in the decade after 1882 that gave manufacturing in New Zealand its first great fillip. From that time dates the establishment of the great processing industries which have ever since remained the most important and characteristic in the Dominion's economy. They are dependent, as have been no other New Zealand industries either before or since, on export markets.

Since early in the present century the growth and diversification of manufacturing industries have been in part dependent upon the expansion and increasing efficiency of the farming industries, but also, more significantly, upon the effects of two world wars, the depression of the early 1930s, and, since 1936, upon the encouragement and protection of manufacturing by government action. This action has worked through tariff barriers and customs duties on imported manufactured goods, but more effectively through import restrictions and control of overseas currency. The effect of this policy has been to encourage the establishment of a very wide range of industrial activities for which the country has few, if any, advantages. They are dependent very largely upon imported raw materials or partially-processed commodities, and compete severely with existing and long-established industries for scarce capital, labour, factory sites, power and other services.

Because of the rapid growth of industrial employment, especially with the return of servicemen and the beginning of the recent flow of immigrants in 1946, the number of persons employed in manufacturing has for some years exceeded the number employed on farms. Today farming, fishing, forestry and mining account for fourteen per cent, and manufacturing for twenty-six per cent of the total labour force, while more than one-half of the people gainfully employed are employed in the tertiary industries, including building and construction and the armed services. Increasing *per capita* production of agricultural and pastoral products, and the continued mechanization of agriculture, have also contributed to this situation, though it cannot be claimed that manpower on farms is adequate. Nor does the land get the human attention that its most productive and conservational use really requires. The amount of eroded and weed-infested farmland is evidence enough of this.

New Zealand's working population in 1964 had reached 960,000. Of these over 256,000 worked in the manufacturing and processing industries, and over 134,000 in primary industries, including mining, forestry and fishing. On this basis manufacturing appears to be more important than agriculture. But from figures, prepared by the Government Statistician, to show the value of production of the different branches of economic activity pursued in the Dominion, a more faithful picture is obtained of the relative significance of agriculture in the wider sense. The table on page 260 shows that the value of production of the different farming industries is still more than 36 per cent greater than the value added to goods in the process of factory manufacture, even if more people are employed in the factories. On the other hand the figures also demonstrate that during and since World War II the volume of production in the factory industries has expanded much more rapidly than that of the farm industries.

Compared with the industrial countries of the northern hemisphere, and with Australia, industrial units in New Zealand are very small. The average number of workers per factory is only twenty-one. Almost two-thirds of the industrial establishments each employ less than ten persons, and only 300 have more than 100 workers. This alone distinguishes the industries of New Zealand from the factory industries of most other countries. It reflects the lack of a large internal market and also the absence to date of heavy industries, both of which would be prerequisites of really large-scale industrial development. New Zealand industries are not only small, but they are also what are known as 'light' industries. Most of them, unlike heavy metallurgical industries for example, are what might be called 'foot-loose'. They are not inevitably located at the source of supply of power or raw materials. Indeed many of the small factories in the four main centres draw their raw materials

VALUE OF PRODUCTION OF MAJOR ECONOMIC ACTIVITIES IN NEW ZEALAND. VALUE OF PRODUCTION IN $M

Year	Value of Production in $M				Index of Volume of Production—all Farm Products	Value of Production in $M			Manufacturing Value of Net Output (Net value added)	Index of Volume of Factory Production
	Agricultural	Pastoral	Dairying, Pigs, Poultry & Bees	Total Farming Group		Mining	Fisheries	Forestry		
1938-39	16.6	75.0	66.6	158.2	100	8.8	1.2	8.0	61.0	100
1949-50	41.6	236.0	137.8	415.4	123	16.4	2.8	21.8	169.0	174
1956-57	50.8	431.4	215.4	697.6	140	37.8	5.8	42.2	339.0	253
1965-66	NA	NA	NA	846.8	199	NA	NA	NA	621.8	440

NA: Not available

from overseas and their power from distant hydro-electric power stations. Almost complete reliance upon hydro-electric power is thus a third characteristic feature of these factories. They employ small electric motors to operate small machines rather than steam boilers and shafts driving great machines at which scores of operatives work. Over ninety per cent of engines used as motive power in New Zealand factories are electric motors and they average no more than seven horse-power.

Manufacturing industries have two other general characteristics: lack of specialization and lack of notable regional concentration. Even though (with a few exceptions) factories are small they usually produce a variety of goods, and frequently switch from the production of one item to another. For example, the woollen mills, although among the few large establishments, both spin and weave, produce both woollens and worsteds, both suitings and blankets and sometimes both cloth and the finished garments. In the textile towns of Lancashire and Yorkshire each mill often performs only one process or specializes in the production of but one class of goods. Nor has New Zealand its 'manufacturing belt', like Japan's industrial area adjacent to the Inland Sea, or Germany's in the Ruhr.

The manufacturing centres are spread out from Invercargill to Whangarei (*Fig. 76*).

This characteristically wide distribution of manufacturing activity is due to a variety of factors. Many raw materials originate on farms, and others come from mines, quarries, forests and market gardens. All these are widely scattered. The electric power used is produced in many parts of the country and is easily distributed. The New Zealand coalfields have attracted no agglomeration of industries as have those in New South Wales. Population is widespread, and so too, therefore, are markets and supplies of labour. Thus all New Zealand towns have factories and factory workers in much the same proportion to their total population. Finally, internal transport is neither easy nor cheap. It is not surprising, then, that many manufactured items are produced locally in small quantities and in small establishments, and that there is no marked regional concentration of manufacturing activities. Although, with its large market and supply of labour, Auckland is the most important manufacturing centre, there are a number of small South Island towns that are relatively more highly industrialized. Factory production per head of population is higher, for example, in the woollen-mill towns of Mosgiel, Kaiapoi and Milton.

Perhaps the most important groups of industries in New Zealand from all points of view are those processing exclusively, or almost exclusively, the products of the farms, either for export or for home consumption; those manufacturing other indigenous raw materials (from forests, swamps, quarries, etc.); and those utility industries producing gas from New Zealand coal or electricity from both water power and coal. Together, these account for over forty per cent of the value added by manufacture to raw materials, and for thirty-five per cent of the people employed in industry. The processing of farm produce is the backbone of New Zealand industries and of the export trade. The great export industries—meat-freezing and preserving, and the production of butter, cheese, and other milk products—together account for twenty-six per cent of the value of total industrial production. There are thirty-seven freezing works in the country and more than 300 dairy factories. These house the Dominion's best-known industries, although some of their characteristics are not representative of industry

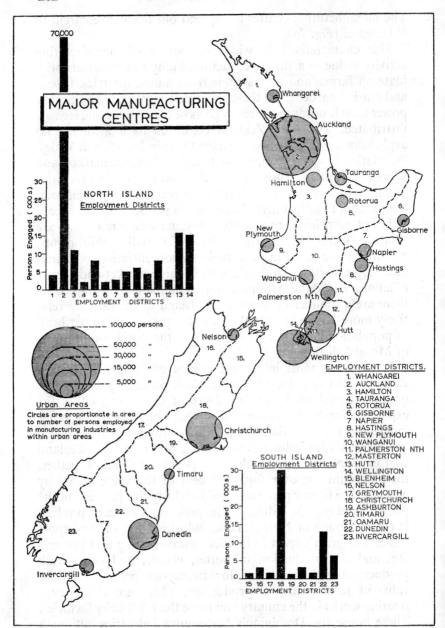

Figure 76

as a whole. The freezing works are large-scale, highly specialized and employ mass production methods, including the endless moving chain. They are often the Dominion's largest industrial plants. They follow an efficient routine. A 'chain' of twenty-six men can kill and dress 2000 sheep or lambs a day. The meat is then frozen at the works, taken in insulated railway wagons to the wharf and thence into the ship's refrigerated holds. Whilst the dairy factories, both the large modern establishments and the older, small cheese factories, are scattered through the dairy-farming districts, freezing works are on the outskirts of the main urban centres and near the export ports. Milk and cream are perishable products that will not stand transport over long distances, but livestock can be walked, railed or trucked many miles. They can thus be assembled at the works, all of which have good rail and road access. They are outside the cities, rather than inside them, partly because of their noxious character and partly so that holding paddocks can be provided in which stock may be held after travelling long distances and before they can be accommodated inside the works. The fastest growing cities, like Auckland for example, have sprawled housing and other industries around and beyond these noxious zones and engulfed the freezing works in their outward tide of urban growth.

Other industries processing farm products of domestic origin include fellmongering, wool scouring, tanning, glue and manure manufacture, candle making, wool manufacture, grain milling, ham and bacon curing, jam making, brewing, wine making, and the quick-freezing and canning of fruit and vegetables.

Apart from farm products, other domestic raw materials which are processed and manufactured are timber, clay, limestone, pumice, *Phormium* flax, and fish. Of these timber is the most important, and is rapidly becoming the basis of important, large-scale and expanding industrial enterprises. In terms of persons engaged, sawmilling already stands second to meat freezing and preserving. With the expansion of the harvesting of radiata pine plantations, the revival of softwood exports, and the development of pulp and paper industries, it will become even more important. On it are already based industries concerned with the manufacture of veneers, sashes and doors, joinery, paper bags and cartons, wallboard and building sheets, furniture, and cabinet work, as well as the giant new pulp, paper, newsprint and tissue industries. Sawmilling is increasingly concentrated in the southern part of the Auckland province, where there are not only the largest remaining stands of indigenous timber in the North Island but also the great exotic pine plantations; but typically small mills are found in many parts of the country cutting out the diminutive pockets of native softwoods that remain. The manufacture of pulp and paper products now employs in excess of 6000 persons and the value added (more than $50 millions) greatly exceeds that of any industrial group other than meat freezing. Gas is manufactured from New Zealand coal in the four main centres and a number of secondary towns, and gasworks, together with the electric power generating plants mentioned earlier, employ more than 5500 persons.

New Zealand's other industries are of great variety. They are those based on the 'true' manufacture of partly-processed raw materials which have received treatment within the country (for example, the manufacture of biscuits from New Zealand-milled flour but using also some imported ingredients), or on imported materials either raw or partly processed (for example, the manufacture of nylon hosiery from nylon yarn processed since 1964 in New Zealand but from imported polymer chips.) It would be impossible to list here all the industries involved. They are in general small-scale, and show no great concentration in any one part of the country, though most of them are located in the four main centres, where they have their markets, find their labour supply and are close to the ports importing many of the raw materials used. It is amongst these industries that are found those which rely heavily upon artificial supports and import control.

Within this large group two sub-groups are outstandingly important: the engineering industries and the clothing industries. (With the latter may also be included the following: the manufacture of hosiery, knitwear, footwear, and the leather and rubber industries.) The metal and engineering industries, relying entirely upon imported materials, or scrap (which is now reworked into merchant bar products, including reinforcing rods by Pacific Steel at Otahuhu), are the most numerous in the country, and employ over 40,000 persons. The group embraces sheet metal working, general engineering (including the railway workshops, which are among the largest establishments and heaviest industries in the Dominion), radio and electrical engineering, the manufacture of kitchen ranges and appliances, the manufacture of agricultural machinery, and the building, assembly and repair of motor vehicles. The assembly of motor vehicles in the Hutt Valley, at Newmarket and Otahuhu (Auckland), and in Christchurch from parts brought in great crates from Windsor (Ontario), Detroit (Michigan), or from Coventry, Dagenham, Luton, Oxford, Wolfsburg (Germany)—and most recently from Tokyo—is carried out in a few small plants on a limited, mass-production basis; but motor repair is a small-scale activity carried on in thousands of small workshops and garages, and is found in practically every small township. The motor repair shop has in these days of tractors and headers taken the place of the earlier village smithy.

Industries making innumerable items of clothing and apparel are representative of the light and foot-loose industries which have sprung up in New Zealand in recent years of import restrictions and shortages. Other than the few factories treating woollen materials, they depend upon imported materials down to the last button and the last inch of thread. Small, attractive, new, reinforced-concrete factories housing these industries have been built in recent years in many parts of the larger cities, usually in districts where other industries have not yet congregated and where female labour can be recruited. Branch factories have invaded the secondary centres and some country towns, especially towns like Huntly, Waihi and Greymouth, where male labour is largely employed in mining and in other industries which do not themselves provide employment for women. The lightness of the imported raw materials and of the finished goods, and the transmission of electric power widely through the country, have assisted this dispersal.

Other characteristic New Zealand industries not hitherto mentioned include printing and publishing, often small-scale and widely spread; the production of chemical fertilizers, a large-scale and heavy industry, and dependent on Nauru and Ocean Island phosphate rock and North American sulphur; the production of light chemicals, including medicines, soap, toilet preparations and plastics, and often using imported materials; and the paint and varnish industries. There are in addition a host of diminutive 'industries', often in backyard sheds or other makeshift premises, operating on a small and inefficient scale, using home-made machinery and small electric motors, and producing luxury rather than essential goods. They grew up especially during and after World War II, and in recent years they have experienced increasing difficulties. They have been materially assisted by the conditions and policies of the time, but are by no means necessarily a permanent feature of the Dominion's industrial economy.

With repeated balance of payment crises and tightening import restrictions in the 1960s, and official encouragement to 'import replacement industries', manufacturing has developed more rapidly than in any previous period. Among new industries are more elaborate manufactures, operating necessarily on a larger scale, and serving a Dominion-wide market. A number have already been established: others are planned and projected. Some are basic industries. They may become the foundation upon which closely related, or allied, or dependent manufactures may subsequently become established.

In 1964 New Zealand's first oil refinery at Marsden Point came on stream. It already refines most of New Zealand's petroleum requirement from imported crude. In future it will refine also the condensates from Kapuni. Most of the annual output of two million tons of refined products is distributed by tanker to ports around the coast of both islands.

No new pulp and paper factory has been established, but the existing mills are being extended to meet overseas demands and the rapidly expanding domestic market for pulp, paper, board and packaging materials. In addition specialty products— laminated papers, tissue papers, wallpaper etc—are now being produced. In addition to the exports of logs to Japan and sawn timber to Australia and the Pacific Islands, some seventy per cent of the newsprint produced is shipped overseas.

South of Auckland—at Otahuhu, and in the new industrial zone set aside at Wiri (between Papatoetoe and Manurewa)— there have recently been established steel merchant bar and aluminium fabricating industries. The one uses New Zealand steel scrap and the other imported aluminium ingots. In future years both could secure their raw material requirements from New Zealand smelters. Work has already been commenced at Glenbrook, near Waiuku, thirty-five miles from downtown Auckland, on the construction on a 1000 acre site of the New Zealand Steel Limited's iron and steel mill. The plant will employ titanomagnetite ironsands from immense coastal sand-dune deposits only ten miles away, north of the Waitako River mouth, Huntly coal and Raglan limestone. The ironsands will be worked by open-cast methods. They will be transported by rail, but may later be flushed through a pipeline. Conventional blast furnace treatment of the ironsands is unsuitable, and a new reduction process will be employed with lower capital cost and technical superiority. Electric energy will be the principal source of power. Billets will be made by 1968. Stage II will produce welded pipes and cold rolled strips by 1973. By 1978 total output will exceed 400,000 tons of steel products a year.

Aluminium smelting in New Zealand is still only the proposal of a giant overseas corporation. The plan is to process alumina imported from Queensland. The alumina itself would be reduced in Australia from the immense bauxite deposits in the Cape Yorke Peninsula. The aluminium thus produced—250,000 tons of ingots a year—would be sold on world markets and to New Zealand fabricators of aluminium products. The advantage New Zealand offers for aluminium smelting is cheap hydro-electric power. For this reason, and also for ease of import of alumina, the smelter would be at Bluff and it would draw a huge block of electric energy from the Lake Manapouri underground power plant now under construction. The smelter would cost $120 million and directly employ 6000 persons. Its ingot exports would be the first significant addition to export production and to the earning of overseas funds since the establishment of pulp and paper industries in the North Island interior in the 1950s. There is, however, no firm assurance that these proposals will be carried out.

INDUSTRIAL AUCKLAND

The industries of the Auckland metropolitan area may be taken to illustrate the industrial characteristics of the country. Auckland and the adjacent urban boroughs between New Lynn and Otahuhu comprise the largest urban area in New Zealand and accommodate the largest and most important industrial concentration in the Dominion. But Auckland has no monopoly of factories. Its share of the manufacturing activities is no greater than its share of the population. It has other functions. It is not an industrial city in the sense in which Sheffield, Lille, Barmen-Elberfeld or Buffalo are so predominantly industrial cities. It owes its growth largely to the development of the dairy lands of the Waikato and the Hauraki and, more recently, of the peninsula to the north. It is not surprising that Auckland's growth, slower before 1900, has since then been much more rapid than that of the other large urban centres. The natural advantage of its harbour and its position in relation to Pacific shipping routes, and the man-made facilities of its port, have also hastened and encouraged the growth of both the city and its industries.

Almost a third of the employed population of metropolitan Auckland—totalling more than 170,000 people—work within the central core of the city. This is an area less than a mile deep and no more than a quarter of a mile wide. It has a narrow frontage of wharves on the Waitemata Harbour and runs back from there up the narrow Ligar valley. Queen Street runs north-south and marks the course of a stream which city dwellers today do not know exists. It is the main retail shopping, administrative and commercial street in the city, and within a short distance of it are all the main transport terminals. Yet within the same confined area are the places of employment of nearly a quarter of all the *factory* workers in the whole of the metropolitan area. It is characteristic of the small scale of New Zealand industries that these many factories in 'down-town' Auckland can find room enough in this small and busy area. As often as not they are located above ground-floor level in Queen Street and above shops, warehouses, offices and administrative buildings in the immediately surrounding area. More than half of the factory workers are engaged in the clothing industry, the rest in a variety of other light industries—printing, furniture-making, tobacco manufacture, light engineering, radio assembly and the making of children's wear.

However, this concentration of industrial work within the heart of the metropolitan area is not as marked as it was in the decade after World War II. Since then much of the Queen Street area has been redeveloped. Multistoreyed bank, insurance, office and administrative buildings have replaced single or double-storeyed structures built in the 1870s and 1880s. The small factories at the rear of, or on the second storey of, such century old buildings have been displaced. The manufacturer has joined the flight to the suburbs where he can spread his single-storey factory, design it for the function it has to perform, surround it with lawns and gardens, and tap suburban reservoirs of (especially female) labour.

As a result the commercial core—in the case of Auckland, the axis of Queen Street—has assumed more specialized functions. With the removal of manufacturing and the relative decline even of retail shopping, banking, insurance, entertainment, airline booking offices and travel bureaus have taken over. The jobs done in Queen Street have changed as markedly as its buildings and skyline in the last decade.

Outside the central core but within the surrounding built-up older residential sections of the city are a number of other smaller industrial concentrations. These are Newmarket (engineering, motor-car assembly and repair, brewing, and the manufacture of aerated water, pickles and preserves), Mount Eden (joinery and woodworking, general engineering, and footwear manufacture), Parnell (engineering, metal working, footwear and confectionery manufacture), Freemans Bay (jam, condiments, metal working, clothing), Western Reclamation (ship repair, boat-building, and general engineering), and Morningside (joinery, cabinet-making, furniture, chemicals, and footwear). After the central core, Newmarket has Auckland's second-largest assemblage of small and varied industrial activities. Like the central core its industries are handy to, but not directly on, the railway; but it differs from the central core in that its industries occupy separate buildings and are outside the retail district and away from the shops of Broadway.

The other industrial nodes are, or were until recently, outside the residental districts, but they are being rapidly submerged by the outward-flowing tide of rapid recent residential expansion. These outer industrial areas have fewer but larger industrial establishments and somewhat heavier industries. They often have indispensable and direct access to the railway, and many are immediately adjacent to either the main north or the main south road exits from the city. The most important concentrations are along the Great South Road between Ellerslie-Penrose and Otahuhu, including also Te Papapa and Westfield (*Fig. 77*).

Ellerslie-Penrose, a postwar Auckland industrial suburb, is still the most rapidly growing one. The factories are of recent construction and modern design, and are often large by New Zealand standards. Outstanding are the well-equipped modern establishments producing plywood, building board, joinery, glass, paint, concrete pipes, brushware, and rubber goods. At the head of the Manukau Harbour, at Westfield and Otahuhu, industry is distinguished by the large size of its units, by the fact that they are characteristic New Zealand industries processing the products of the farms of the Auckland province, and by their noxious features. Here are three freezing works, forming the biggest concentration of its kind in the country. Alongside are factories treating hides and skins, glue works, wool-scouring plants and organic manure works. There are also phosphate-fertilizer works with their great yellow outdoor dumps of imported sulphur. The district is also characterized by its blemished and blighted appearance, its overgrazed holding-paddocks, its repugnant smell and the unsightly appearance of the discharge pipes, refuse areas and the nearby fouled mud-flats. It is a not very attractive approach to the Dominion's largest city. Further out at Otahuhu are the railway workshops and a large modern brewery. Here, too, is the merchant bar mill and the steel scrap reclamation plant of Pacific Steel.

Other industries are at Onehunga and New Lynn (pottery, earthware pipes, bricks, tiles, tanning and textiles). On tide-water across the Waitemata Harbour there are sugar refineries at Chelsea and naval repair and workshops at Devonport.

It is a sign of Auckland's growing industrial maturity that even before the decision to establish the iron and steel industry at Glenbrook, factories were established, relying on scrap, or on iron and steel imported from Japan and Australia, to produce steel bars, steel wire and steel rope. These have all been established to the south of Auckland in recent years. The recently zoned industrial area at Wiri already has aluminium fabricating, and instant coffee manufacturing industries, and a giant new wool store is under construction. Contemporaneously with this industrial development and diversification, the metropolitan area's residential zones have spread southwards.

66.
EUROPEAN
PLANTATION,
RAROTONGA

67.
CITRUS
NURSERY,
RAROTONGA

68.
ORANGE
GROVE,
AITUTAKI

Photos: Kenneth B. Cumberland

Photo: N.Z. National Publicity Studios

69. PACKING ORANGES, TITIKAVEKA

Photo: N.Z. National Publicity Studios

70. IRRIGATED TARO PLANTS, MAUKE

71. TOMATO CROP, RAROTONGA

Photos: Kenneth B. Cumberland

72. PACKING SHED, AVARUA

73. ONEROA, MANGAIA

Photos: N.Z. National Publicity Studios

74. COASTAL ROAD, NIUE

75. MANIHIKI ATOLL

Photos: Tudor Collins

76. PUKAPUKA, NORTHERN COOK GROUP

77. NATIVE AGRICULTURE, TONGA

Photos: Kenneth B. Cumberland

78. EUROPEAN PLANTATION, TONGATAPU

Photo: N.Z. National Publicity Studios

79. PREPARATIONS FOR A FEAST, TONGATAPU

Photo: Kenneth B. Cumberland

80. NATIVE PIONEERING, 'EUA

81. TONGAN VILLAGE

Photos: Kenneth B. Cumberland

82. GIRLS FROM NIUAFO'OU, TONGA

83. SAMOAN *FALE*, SAVAI'I

Photos: Tudor Collins

84. VILLAGE SCENE, APOLIMA, SAMOA

85. APIA, WESTERN SAMOA

Photos: New Zealand Herald

86. PAGO PAGO, AMERICAN SAMOA

87.
DRY ZONE,
VITI LEVU,
FIJI

88.
CANE
HARVEST
MBA

89.
TRANSPORT
OF CANE,
LAUTOKA

Photos: Rob Wright, Fiji Public Relations Office

90.
LAUTOKA
SUGAR MILL,
VITI LEVU

91.
CANE
GROWER'S
HOME,
SINGATOKA

92.
CATTLE
RANCH,
YANGGARA,
VITI LEVU

Photos: Rob Wright, Fiji Public Relations Office

93. FIJIAN *KORO*, WET ZONE,
VITI LEVU

94. MELANESIAN FROM FIJI

95. CHIEF'S HOUSE, FIJI

Photos: Rob Wright, Fiji Public Relations Office

96. TRANSPORTING BANANAS, REWA RIVER

Photos: Rob Wright, Fiji Public Relations Office

97. YAMS, TARO, TURTLES, LAU GROUP

98. GOLDMINING, VATUKOULA, FIJI

Photos: Rob Wright, Fiji Public Relations Office

99. SUVA, FIJI

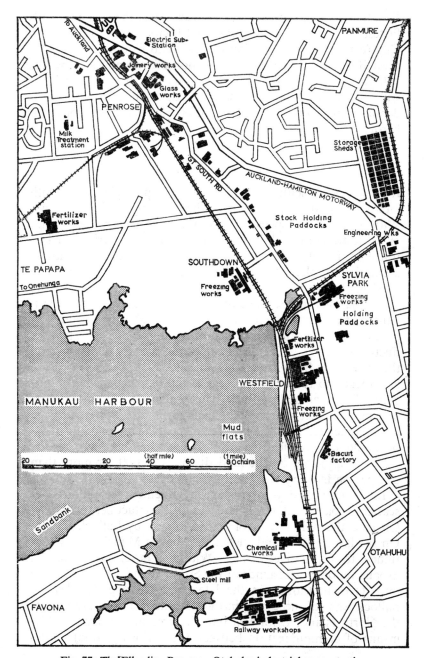

Fig. 77: The Ellerslie - Penrose - Otahuhu industrial concentration

Papatoetoe and Manurewa were a decade ago the urban region's fastest growing boroughs. Now that honour goes to Manukau City (a recent amalgamation of Manukau County and Manurewa Borough). With the construction of iron and steel works still further south, and the related and ancillary industries it will attract, the southward surging tide of industrial and residential expansion of the Dominion's largest metropolis can hardly be halted this century.

TRANSPORT

It would be difficult to overestimate the part played by both internal and external transport in the economy of New Zealand. With its economic specialization, and a larger *per capita* share of world trade than all but one or two other countries, efficient transport facilities to and from the Dominion, and within it, are indispensable. Internally, the broken upland interior of the two islands, the small amount of near-flat land and the scattering of population around the coast, add to the importance of the systems of transport which put these dispersed urban centres in touch with each other, and each of them in touch with its productive hinterland. The wellbeing of the country depends upon the movement from farms and stations to works and factories, and thence to the ports, of large quantities of perishable agricultural and pastoral products. The significance of the operation and maintenance of transport facilities is also apparent when it is appreciated that the number of people employed in transport and communications is well over half as large as the number employed on the land. It totals 95,000, or more than one person in every ten gainfully employed.

In the earliest days of European settlement people lived in scattered coastal villages. There was little contact between them. On land the only means of transport was by bullock wagon. On the larger rivers and sheltered estuaries Maori canoes continued to ply a lively trade. With the development of the expansive, open grasslands of the South Island, the horse came into its own, though in the later bush-clearing decades the bullock was still necessary in the deep mud and heavy rain of the North Island. Until well into the present century the chief means of communication between the various growing settlements, even within the same island, was by sea. Not until after 1910 did people go from Auckland to Wellington all the way on land. Before that time one took a carriage or went by boat train from Auckland to Onehunga wharf and then by a small passenger vessel from there to New Plymouth; from New Plymouth the railway line had been put through the recently cleared forest land to the capital. Today, however, few coastal shipping services survive. The only passenger services are between the islands—from Wellington to Picton, from Wellington to Lyttelton, and from the Bluff to Oban in Stewart Island. Coastal cargo vessels still link the main ports together, and the minor ports with the overseas export ports, and colliers still distribute coal by sea from Westport and Greymouth.

Railways came first—in the 1860s—to the more extensive lowland areas of the South Island. Bridging the milewide gravel riverbeds was the main problem. Later, in the North Island the broken surface of hill country, rainforest and mud made construction difficult. Tunnels, bridges, embankments and spiralling curves are characteristic. The main trunk line between Wellington and Auckland was completed not long before World War I and not very long before railways were faced with the competition of road transport. The North Island had until recently a smaller mileage of railways than the South Island. In 1954 it had 1683 miles against 1843. But with the closing of little used branch lines the respective mileages ten years later were 1647 and 1618. Not until the 1960s did the North Island have as large a mileage of railways open to traffic. From Picton to Invercargill is 584 miles, whilst there are 626 miles of line between Opua and Wellington. The South Island, however, still has a greater portion of its mileage on branch lines (*Fig. 78*). Today the railways carry twenty-five million passengers a year, including suburban traffic, and the number is declining. Their importance lies in the transport of heavy freight. The greater productivity of the North Island, the industrial importance of the Auckland and Wellington terminals, their large population and their great volume of maritime trade, are reflected in the fact that the North Island main trunk line carries forty per cent of the total rail traffic of the country— considerably more than the whole of the South Island system. By tonnage the principal freight hauled by rail has long been

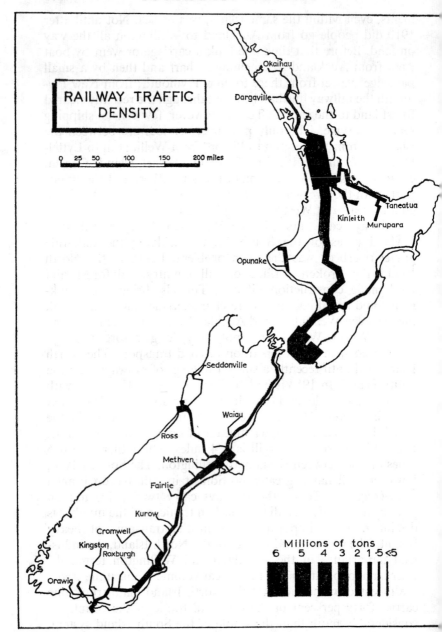

RAILWAY TRAFFIC DENSITY

0 25 50 100 150 200 miles

Okaihau

Dargaville

Taneatua

Kinleith

Murupara

Opunake

Seddonville

Waiau

Ross

Methven

Fairlie

Kurow

Cromwell

Kingston

Roxburgh

Orawia

Millions of tons
6   5   4   3   2 1 ·5 <5

Figure 78

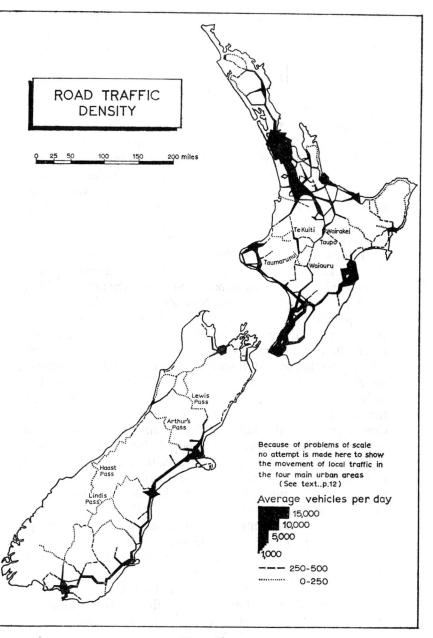

ROAD TRAFFIC
DENSITY

0   25   50   100   150   200 miles

Te Kuiti
Wairakei
Taupo
Taumarunui
Waiouru

Lewis
Pass

Arthur's
Pass

Haast
Pass

Lindis
Pass

Because of problems of scale
no attempt is made here to show
the movement of local traffic in
the four main urban areas
(See text..p.12)

Average vehicles per day

15,000
10,000
5,000
1,000
— — — 250-500
·········· 0-250

Figure 79

coal. But with the development of the exotic timber milling and timber processing industries of the North Island interior, logs (ex Murupara especially), sawn timber and pulp mill products now comprise the heaviest and bulkiest commodity hauled by rail. Then follow in order fertilizers, frozen meat, lime, livestock, petroleum and grain. Coal is hauled from the Waikato coalfield to Auckland, from the West Coast mines to Greymouth and Westport, and through the Otira tunnel to Christchurch. Timber is carried greater distances. It is loaded principally at Murupara and Rotorua, and indigenous timber chiefly at Tuatapere (Southland), Ross (Westland), and at Putaruru, Taumarunui and National Park in the North Island interior. Petrol supplies and fertilizers move in the opposite direction to timber and farm products—from the ports inland to rural townships for distribution to farms.

Motor-bus services on the increasingly numerous and well-surfaced roads now carry each year eight times as many passengers—again including suburban services—as the railways. Many more travel by private cars. New Zealand has in proportion to its population more motor vehicles than any country outside North America, almost as many as Canada and considerably more than Australia. Freight haulage by road is complementary to that by rail. It serves especially to link city factories, warehouses and retail establishments with the wharves and the railway, and to tie the individual farm to the dairy factory, to the stores and warehouses in the nearest town, and to the closest point on the railway. Today tar-sealed highways run between all the major centres of population, and few farms do not have roads sufficiently well surfaced to make them accessible to powerful motor lorries (*Fig. 79*). Road transport is thus able to bring in lime and fertilizers and take out loads three storeys high of wool bales and of fat lambs. But the network of metalled roads is not always dense. There are only twenty-seven people to every square mile in New Zealand and much of its surface is made up of mountain and hill country cut by deep gorges and traversed by rivers difficult to bridge.

New Zealand is almost as air-minded as Australia. The development of internal and external air transport traffic since 1946 has been the most spectacular feature of its transport system. Internal airlines, linking towns and cities having a popu-

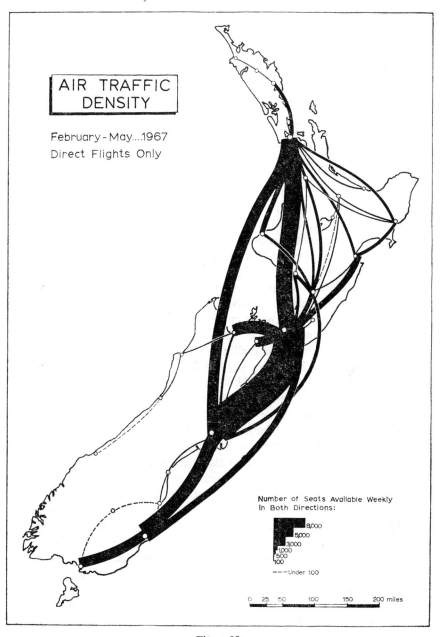

AIR TRAFFIC DENSITY

February - May....1967
Direct Flights Only

Number of Seats Available Weekly
In Both Directions:

8,000
5,000
3,000
1,000
500
100
---Under 100

0   25   50   100   150   200 miles

Figure 80

lation of over 20,000 as well as many smaller towns in isolated areas in the far north or on the west coast of the South Island, have taken the bulk of the long distance passenger traffic, much of the postal traffic, and some of the freight from the railways (*Fig. 80*). In 1966 the New Zealand National Airways Corporation carried more than a million passengers on internal services. Of the persons entering or leaving New Zealand today many more travel by air (mainly on Air New Zealand, QANTAS and BOAC services across the Tasman) than by ship. Trans-Tasman air traffic continues its remarkable boom: the number of passengers carried to and from Australia increases every year by from 20 to 25 per cent.

Of the internal air services the main trunk route between Mangere (Auckland), Rongotai (Wellington), Harewood (Christchurch), and Taieri (Dunedin) is by far the most important. It carries over half of all the National Airways Corporation's passengers on one or more of its sectors and three-quarters of the mail and freight. The competition of air travel with internal shipping services is also apparent in the fact that sixty per cent of passengers carried by air in New Zealand cross Cook Strait, mainly of course between Rongotai and Harewood, but also between Wellington and Nelson and Wellington and Blenheim. The ferry service by sea from Wellington to Nelson was withdrawn in 1960 in face of this competition. But there has been a remarkable revival of sea communications across Cook Strait. The rail-road ferry *Aramoana* commenced services between Wellington and Picton in 1963. Within two years she was carrying more than 200,000 passengers and almost 50,000 vehicles annually. She also carries railway rolling stock and thus links North and South Island railway systems. So successful—and so profitable—has been this venture that the *Aramoana* was joined in 1966 by the *Aranui*, and the Wellington-Lyttelton passenger ferry boats *Maori* and *Wahine* have both been converted to roll-on roll-off ferries carrying road vehicles of all kinds. As a result of these developments, the traffic of Straits Air Freight Express between Rongotai and Nelson and Rongotai and Blenheim has declined.

Auckland, Christchurch and Wellington are all terminals of overseas international air services. Christchurch is linked with Melbourne and Sydney and serves as the base from which

Unites States Deep Freeze operations to Antarctica depart. Wellington has trans-Tasman services. The new Auckland international airport at Mangere, however, has the greatest variety and number of overseas connections. In addition to trans-Tasman services to Sydney, Melbourne and Brisbane operated by BOAC and QANTAS as well as Air New Zealand, it is the home base of Air New Zealand services to Hong Kong, Singapore and Los Angeles. Through Auckland also pass trans-Pacific services operated by Pan American, Canadian Pacific, UTA and BOAC. So rapidly is international passenger traffic growing and especially in the Southwest Pacific that it is likely that other foreign airlines may soon operate giant jets through Auckland—Air India, Alitalia and Japanese Airlines.

It is also from Auckland that both Air New Zealand and QANTAS serve Pacific Island territories—often through Nandi.

The aeroplane has also come into its own in other ways which are peculiarly associated with New Zealand's primary industries and their particular problems. The aerial spreading of super-phosphatic fertilizers has been expanded phenomenally in a few years. Today there are many large operating companies and in 1965 almost a million tons of fertilizer were spread on more than eight million acres of (mainly) hill country pastureland by aircraft. Aerial-work operators have also used their light aircraft in the last year or two in such other activities as aerial spraying of crops with insecticides, spraying weeds, like gorse, with hormone weed-killers, spreading of poison bait for rabbits in the South Island high country, distributing trace elements deficient in some soils, sowing seed, and dropping supplies to musterers, deer stalkers and others in isolated terrain.

As a result of the fact that the Dominion conducts a greater *per capita* share of world trade than all other countries excepting only Iceland, the oil states on the Persian Gulf, and one or two of the smaller countries of Western Europe, its ports are busy places. This is especially the case since overseas trade is restricted to very few ports. Ten handle ninety-nine per cent of the overseas trade. Five ports—Whangarei, Auckland, Wellington, Lyttelton (the port of Christchurch) and Tauranga—handle three-quarters of the manifest tons of all cargo, both coastal and overseas, passing through New Zealand ports, and two (Auckland and Whangarei) alone handle nearly half.

K2

The really surprising thing about these statements is the high ranking of Whangarei and Tauranga. Traditionally the important overseas ports have been Auckland, Wellington, Lyttelton, Dunedin-Port Chalmers and Bluff, with Napier, New Plymouth and Timaru performing a minor role. But recent changes in the economy and in industrial localization and resource development have disrupted the traditional ranking. Measured by the tonnage of cargo handled Whangarei is now the first port in the Dominion, exceeding Auckland's 4,103,000 manifest tons of cargo in 1966 by no less than 1,774,000 tons. Of Whangarei's total cargo tonnage (5,877,000 tons) a half is inward overseas freight, practically all crude petroleum for the new refinery at Marsden Point; and another 2,550,000 tons is outward coastal freight, practically all refined petroleum products distributed by tanker to other New Zealand ports. In 1950 1081 vessels used the harbour facilities at Whangarei, and they had a net tonnage of only 122,000. In 1966 fewer vessels—907—used the port but had a net tonnage of 2,440,000.

Tauranga's port traffic has grown since 1957 with the exploitation of the *Pinus radiata* timber resources of the Volcanic Plateau. It has approximately the same number of vessels entering and leaving as it had a decade ago, but their tonnage has increased almost tenfold with the improvement of facilities and new wharves at Mt Maunganui. Meanwhile overseas outward cargo—logs to Japan and pulp, timber and newsprint to Australia—has exploded from 70,000 tons to 680,000 tons.

Wellington is much the most important *entrepôt* port in the country. It receives overseas imports for redistribution to coastal ports and collects from them exports for overseas shipment. Nelson apples are an outstanding example. It is also the most central of the ports and the terminal of daily inter-island ferry services to Lyttelton and Picton, so that the tonnage of shipping entering Wellington is half as much again as that entering the Waitemata. Auckland, however, handles a greater tonnage of *cargo* than Wellington and has a very much more diverse trade than Whangarei, and from this point of view can claim to be the most important port in New Zealand. Its overseas imports are particularly large; and it handles a larger volume of dairy products, canned meat, tallow, and hides and skins for export than any other port. The amount of coastal cargo at Auckland is much less than that at Whangarei with its heavy outward flow of refined petroleum products but is slightly higher than at Wellington which stands third with Lyttelton fourth. Closely following Lyttelton are the two West Coast coal ports, Westport and Greymouth. In their case traffic is one way—outwards. Their imports of coastal cargo are less than that of fifteen or more other small ports, but in terms of total cargo (in and out, coastal and overseas) Westport and Greymouth have a tonnage exceeded only by that of the big five and by Napier and New Plymouth, which are both secondary overseas ports. Another recent development has been the spectacular growth of Onehunga's coastal trade. With the development of the iron and steel industry and the continued industrial development on the southern margin of the Auckland metropolitan area, this traffic should continue to increase.

The world over, significant changes are pending in the handling of shipping cargoes. To obviate frequent handling of small lots of cargo—bundles of carcases or boxes of butter— the tendency is to pack cargo in giant steel containers at the point of production. Here it stays until unpacked at its destination. As a result, road haulage vehicles, railway wagons, wharfside facilities, and even ships are being redesigned to handle the containers, which hold from ten to twenty tons. New Zealand has been recommended to equip two container ports—Auckland and Wellington. Its total trade is not sufficient to justify the heavy expenditure necessary at more than two existing ports. Auckland is preparing for 'containerization' by building a new wharf and setting aside fifty acres of land for holding containers in transit.

OVERSEAS TRADE

New Zealand's trade has a simple pattern and has not changed appreciably in its basic character since the earliest decades of permanent European settlement. It may still be described as a 'colonial' pattern of trade, with the Dominion shipping foodstuffs and raw materials, and importing in turn manufactured or partially-manufactured goods. Its most outstanding feature is its large *per capita* value. In the calendar year 1964 New Zealand imports were valued at $690 millions and exports at $772 millions. The value of total overseas trade was no less than $540 a head.

New Zealand's reliance upon grassland farming is clearly demonstrated by its exports. In the last thirty years the proportion of the total value represented by pastoral exports has fallen below ninety per cent only during the years 1943-1946, when, under abnormal wartime conditions, considerable quantities of meat and dairy produce were diverted to feed American servicemen in New Zealand and the southwest Pacific, and were not classed as exports. Since World War II the figure has been over ninety-three per cent, or higher than ever before. In 1964 wool accounted for thirty-seven per cent of the value of exports, and dairy produce (butter fifteen per cent of all exports, cheese five per cent, and dried, condensed and evaporated milk, including casein, four per cent) for rather less than a quarter. Frozen, canned and other preserved meat provided a quarter of the value of exports, and hides and skins four per cent. Together tallow, fruit (mainly apples), seeds, gold and timber furnished little more than another three per cent by value. The two largest groups of manufactured products exported, 'machinery' (mainly dairy machinery) and 'chemicals, drugs and druggists' ware' provided together no more than a mere fraction of one per cent of all exports. In 1964 timber products—mainly newsprint and wood pulp—accounted for three per cent of the value of all exports.

Imports are much more varied. They may be generally classified into three groups. By value, goods wholly or mainly manufactured (apparel, footwear, piece goods, machinery and metals, glassware, chinaware, paper, instruments, petroleum products, chemicals, motor vehicles, etc.) account for upwards of eighty per cent of imported merchandise. Processed foodstuffs, fresh fruit, tobacco, sugar, tea, coffee and alcoholic beverages and other foodstuffs together represent about twelve per cent of imports by value, and raw materials (as distinct from finished parts, machinery and partially processed materials) for use in the Dominion's growing small-scale manufacturing industries another five per cent.

The destination of exports and the origins of imports change little from year to year. The flow of trade has for a century been mainly along one track—to and from the United Kingdom. Since 1940 the United Kingdom has annually taken from sixty five to eighty-eight per cent of all exports and supplied from thirty-five to sixty per cent of all imports. In 1956 the percentages were respectively sixty-five and fifty-five. There has, however, in the 1960s been a greater and more pronounced change in the direction of New Zealand's overseas trade than at any time since the infant days of settlement. By 1965 the share of the Dominion's exports going to the United Kingdom had tumbled to forty-five per cent, and of imports to thirty-six per cent. With the relatively static nature of Great Britain's economy, the 'threat' of her entry into the agricultural protectionism of the European Economic Community and the impressive expansion of livestock numbers and pastoral production in New Zealand, the establishment of alternative markets had become urgent and imperative. Small quantities of primary products were being shipped to a variety of new markets. Among them Japan, the United States and Canada showed most promise. Attempts were made in 1965, through a freeing of trade, to correct the imbalance of trade with Australia by expanding New Zealand exports to the Commonwealth. A promising development was the growth of airfreighting of beef steaks, strawberries and other high quality perishable primary products to Singapore, Hong Kong, London, Honolulu and Sydney. After the United Kingdom—but still a long way after—the Dominion's best customers in 1964 were the United States (15 per cent of all exports), France (6 per cent), Japan (5 per cent), Australia (4 per cent), West Germany, Italy and Belgium.

POPULATION

In September 1952 the Dominion's population reached two millions. In 1967 it had already reached 2,700,000. It grows by 2.1 per cent a year and should reach three millions by 1970. Since the war the rate of growth has been from two to two and a half per cent per annum, which is in excess of that of the overcrowded nations of eastern Asia. It took nearly seventy years from the planting of the first permanent settlements for the population to climb to the first million. The second million took forty-four years, but if present rates of natural increase and of immigration are maintained, the third million may well take less than twenty years.

In several respects the populations of Australia and New

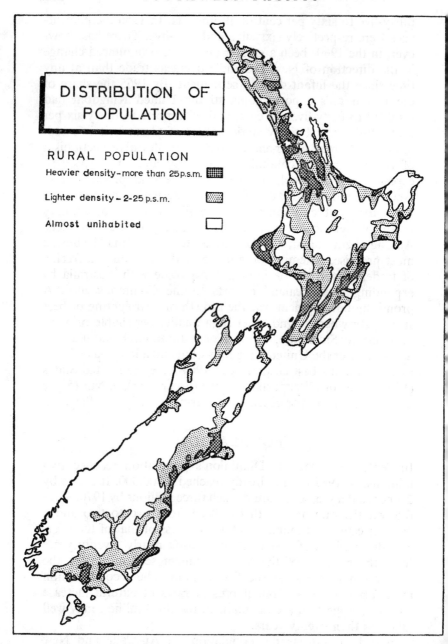

DISTRIBUTION OF POPULATION

RURAL POPULATION

Heavier density—more than 25 p.s.m.

Lighter density — 2–25 p.s.m.

Almost unihabited

Figure 81

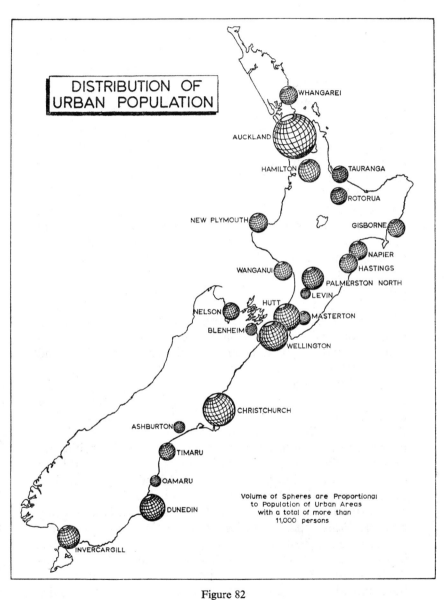

DISTRIBUTION OF URBAN POPULATION

WHANGAREI

AUCKLAND

HAMILTON — TAURANGA

ROTORUA

NEW PLYMOUTH

GISBORNE

NAPIER

WANGANUI — HASTINGS

PALMERSTON NORTH

LEVIN

HUTT

NELSON — MASTERTON

BLENHEIM

WELLINGTON

CHRISTCHURCH

ASHBURTON

TIMARU

OAMARU

Volume of Spheres are Proportional
to Population of Urban Areas
with a total of more than
11,000 persons

DUNEDIN

INVERCARGILL

Figure 82

Zealand are alike. Both are growing fast, both are still over-whelmingly of British origin, both are predominantly urban and both are increasingly concentrated into a few major urban units.

There are not more than twenty-seven New Zealanders to every square mile of territory. This density is a mere fraction of that of Great Britain or Japan, but it is nearly seven times greater than that of Australia. The density and distribution of population (*Fig. 81*) reflect all the other features of the geography of the country. Distribution is very unequal. Large parts of the country, the upland and mountain areas, are practically unin-habited and have less than two persons per square mile. More than two-thirds of the South Island, in an unbroken stretch from the Marlborough Sounds to the southern fiords, has very few people. In the North Island the sparsely populated area is much smaller. It is mainly in the east central interior; but with the slow inward extension of pasture establishment and with the growing importance of the man-made forests of the Volcanic Plateau this little-occupied area is being reduced in size. Apart from the totally unoccupied mountain districts, the areas with fewer than two persons per square mile correspond closely with the extent of the most extensive systems of sheep grazing, and are otherwise occupied only by deer stalkers, pig hunters and those whose job it is to maintain communications and hydro-electric power installations in these 'back-blocks'.

A density of from two to twenty-five persons per square mile is representative of rural New Zealand. These are the areas of easier hill country and more intensive forms of sheep rearing, the mixed crop-livestock farming areas and the lowland dairying districts. In the South Island such moderate rural densities are found mainly to the east and south—in coastal Southland, Otago and Canterbury. In the North Island they are mainly to the west in the Manawatu, Taranaki, Northland, and the Waikato, but also in the Bay of Plenty, southern Hawke's Bay and the Wairarapa. Densities of more than twenty-five per square mile are found in the few areas of really intensive farm-ing—market gardening, livestock fattening and city milk pro-duction—and also in the areas into which the urban centres have spread their suburban overflows. These higher densities are more prominent in the North Island.

In 1881, the year before the first shipment of refrigerated

farm produce to England, six out of every ten New Zealanders lived in the South Island. Today seven out of ten are in the North Island. In this sense at least, the North Island became the 'mainland' in 1900. For more than eighty years, since refrigeration made possible the great export industries, since the Maori wars were terminated, and since techniques of bushburning were first applied on a large scale, the population of the North Island has been growing more rapidly than that of the South Island. This tendency reached a peak during and just after World War II, but since then the so-called 'drift north' appears to be abated to some extent. Even in the North Island there is a tendency for population to become more and more concentrated in the northern part. Since 1901 the proportion of the total population of New Zealand living in the Auckland province has increased from less than twenty per cent to more than forty per cent.

The apparent northward movement has been accompanied by a tendency for people to live more and more in towns and cities. In 1881 less than four in ten lived in towns large and small; today between six and seven out of every ten do so. The trend has been for people increasingly to prefer to live in towns and especially northern towns, Auckland above all. This is related specially to the growth of the dairy industry, the development of the Waikato's power resources, the establishment of manufacturing industries and the increasing number and importance of the services (the tertiary industries) which are so predominantly urban services.

The urban population does not show the same concentration in one or two 'millionaire' cities as is the case in Australia. Yet over forty per cent of the people live in the 'four main centres' as they are known—the four metropolitan areas of Auckland, Wellington, Christchurch and Dunedin. Auckland, with twenty per cent of the total population, is the largest urban unit, and alone of New Zealand cities has the busy, cosmopolitan characteristics of overseas cities of equal or larger size. This urbanization is largely explained by the following facts: the high degree of farm mechanization; the world's highest production per man on farms; the employment in industry of more people than work on farms; the employment in transport, commerce, professions and public service of as many people as work in agriculture, mining, fishing and industry put together; and the high standards of living and the early retirement (to the cities) of farmers, timber-workers, miners and others whose work has been done in rural areas.

There is a large gap between Dunedin (108,680 in 1966), smallest of the 'four main centres', and the largest of the 'secondary towns'. These form the second well-marked layer in the urban hierarchy. They are Whangarei, Hamilton, Tauranga, Rotorua, New Plymouth, Gisborne, Napier, Hastings, Wanganui, Palmerston North (in the North Island) and Nelson, Timaru and Invercargill (in the South Island). They range in size of population from 27,630 (Nelson) to 63,330 (Hamilton). With the exception of Hamilton, Rotorua and Palmerston North, which are the Dominion's only inland cities of any size, they are coastal or near-coastal, and most of them are ports. All of them have regional importance. Below them are a whole range of centres with some urban functions, down to those of the small mining or dairy factory townships, of which few have more than local importance. They include mining towns, recreational centres, timber towns, hydro towns, and others with rather specialized functions, but most of them are country towns serving a farming community and functioning principally as wholesale and retail trading centres.

The relative rates of growth of the population of different rural areas, and of different cities and towns, may be appreciated by considering the changes that have occurred in the last generation and which are recorded by the censuses taken in 1936—just before the war—and in 1966. In 1936 New Zealand had a total population of just over a million and a half. Since then the population of the whole country has jumped to 2,676,919, an increase of just over 70 per cent. This figure—70 per cent—provides a useful measuring rod. In the same period the North Island's population increased by 86 per cent: the South Island's by only 40 per cent, less than half the North Island's rate of expansion. While numbers in the Auckland province grew by almost 100 per cent. Otago's were relatively steady and showed a growth of only 16 per cent. (Incidentally, within the thirty year period Auckland province came to accommodate itself more than 200,000 more people than the whole of the South Island.)

The 'four main centres' show the following percentage growths in the last three decades: Auckland, 159 per cent (with 547,915 people in 1966); Wellington (including the Hutt), 88 per cent (282,583); Christchurch, 86 per cent (246,773); Dunedin, 32 per cent (108,680). With the exception of 'new' towns, like Kawerau and Tokoroa, it was the secondary centres and some smaller towns in the South Auckland area that showed the most 'explosive' growth. Tauranga grew by more than 800 per cent, Rotorua by more than 400 per cent, and Hamilton by almost 225 per cent. Whangarei, the fastest growing secondary centre in the 1960s had more than tripled its population since 1936. Meanwhile, with the exception of Christchurch, the larger towns in the South Island have barely held their own, and, like Dunedin, have grown more slowly than the Dominion's total population, and still more slowly than the urban population of the country as a whole.

The North Island's population growth has, however, not only been in cities and towns. Its progress has not only been a matter of expanding opportunities of employment in manufacturing industries, commerce, professions and local-body administration; it has also been solidly based on the land, on the development of farming techniques, the drainage of swamplands, the fertilizing of inherently infertile pumice soils, the topdressing of pastures, and the use of improved pasture species and livestock. Despite the mechanization of farming, some counties, excluding the boroughs within them, have shown a remarkable growth of population. Amongst these Matamata, Piako, and Waitomo show percentage increases in thirty years of from 67 to 185. Meanwhile many South Island counties show absolute decreases of population. Not the least in size or population is Ashburton, the centre of the mixed crop-livestock farming area of Canterbury, sometimes called 'the granary of New Zealand', in which in thirty years the population has fallen by eleven per cent.

The Maori people add an unusual, attractive and Polynesian-Pacific note to the Dominion's population. Their numbers after falling to less than 40,000 in the later decades of the last century, have recovered steadily and in the last thirty-five years have begun to grow at an increasingly rapid rate. There were in 1966 198,188 people with half or more than half Maori blood. The

Maori population is moreover a young population, three-quarters of it under thirty years of age. Less than half the 'Maoris' today are of full Maori blood. In 1966 the Maori people constituted 7.5 per cent of the population; but within twenty years, if present trends persist, this proportion will have increased to possibly fifteen per cent, and the Maori population may well total many more than at any time since they first trod the surf-fringed shores of Aotearoa over six hundred years ago.

The Maori, too, is moving into the towns. This again is more particularly noticeable in northern towns. In 1936, 1766 Maoris lived in the Auckland urban area: in 1966, 33,261. Today Rotorua has 7109, compared with 669; and Wellington (including the Hutt) 10,194 compared with 589 thirty years ago. Including Maoris and Pacific islanders (who are migrating to New Zealand in a steadily expanding stream), Auckland has the largest urban grouping of Polynesians anywhere in the world.

CHAPTER SIX

New Zealand's
Pacific Island Neighbourhood

I T HAS been even more difficult for New Zealanders than for
Australians to realize the strategic threat to the two dominions from southeast Asia across the Indonesian 'Mediterranean'.
Between New Zealand and the Asiatic mainland there have not
only been the 1200 miles of the Tasman Sea, but the broad mass
of the Australian continent, the island-studded Indonesian
'Mediterranean' and the great imperial base of Singapore. Nor
did the Japanese invasion of New Guinea and the bombing of
Darwin have the same awakening effect in New Zealand as it
did in the Commonwealth. New Zealand watched with more
interest and greater apprehension the island-hopping of Nippon-
ese forces through the Carolines, Marshalls and Solomons
towards Fiji and New Caledonia.

NEW ZEALAND AND THE PACIFIC WORLD

New Zealand's interests in the Pacific have always lain a
little to the east of Australia's. Australian territory is confined
to the western margin of the Pacific: New Zealand's stands
astride the Marshall line, and the Cook Islands and Samoa,
where until recently New Zealand had direct responsibility, are
out in the central structural province of the Pacific. The dependent territories of Australia form part of the screen of 'continental' islands off the north and east of the continent, and they
fall entirely within Melanesia: New Zealand's Pacific island
neighbourhood is a mixed domain partly of 'continental' and
partly of both 'high' and 'low' oceanic islands, partly in
Melanesia and partly in Polynesia. The native people of the

Commonwealth of Australia have no close relations in the Pacific: the New Zealand Maori has cousins in the Cook Islands and other relations throughout Polynesia. Australia lies close to Asia and has a back door opening on to the Indian Ocean: New Zealand is set entirely within the watery immensity of the Pacific.

Neither the earlier colonial nor the later dominion governments of New Zealand have shown more than sporadic interest in the country's Pacific island neighbourhood. The people by and large have shown even less. Official interest has in the past been only that of prominent individuals in the government of the time, individuals with both foresight and ambition, men like Grey, Vogel, Seddon and Fraser. Not often, whilst fighting the bush, cursing the mud, firing the tussock, or scratching for gold, has New Zealand been inspired with a sense of humanitarian mission in the southwest Pacific, or imbued with the prospect of commercial profit. Still more rarely has it appreciated the strategic possibilities of insular outposts to the north. Despite occasional precocious appeals in the latter decades of the nineteenth century to the United Kingdom Government to make sure that the Pacific became, apparently as of right, a British domain, the New Zealand purse was rarely opened to make the suggestion possible, or to help to finance the naval administration and defence of the territories already in British hands. It was rather by accident than by design, and almost without knowing it, that New Zealand, after the turn of the century, came to acquire responsibility for territory extending almost from the pole to the Equator and almost half-way from Wellington to San Francisco.

No one would claim that on a world scale the New Zealand territories in the Pacific are of very great importance. Although well over two-thirds of all Polynesians lived until the 1960s in insular territories under New Zealand administration, the total population of the territories (outside the Dominion itself) amounted to little more than 100,000, or less than a quarter of the population of metropolitan Auckland. Even if the people of the territories under other than Dominion administration, but within its Pacific island neighbourhood, are included, the total is still only half a million, or no more than that of metropolitan Wellington and Christchurch put together. Yet within the many scattered islands in question most of the peoples and problems of the Pacific World are represented, and the variety of life, landscape and economy is almost as wide as that of the Pacific as a whole.

NEW ZEALAND TERRITORIES

It is doubtful whether one New Zealander in a hundred could list accurately all the territories in the Pacific for which his country is, or was until recently, directly or indirectly responsible, and describe their status and the nature of their political connection with the Dominion. The list is much longer and the territories are more numerous, if economically, strategically and politically less important, than those of Australia.

The term 'New Zealand' is used most frequently to relate simply to three islands—the North Island, the South Island and Stewart Island—tucked away in a remote southwestern corner of the Pacific. But the term may also be applied to an extension, predominantly oceanic, which includes scores of scattered islands, a considerable portion of the Pacific's broad face, as well as a slice of the Antarctic continent. This wider 'New Zealand' extends through nearly 90 degrees of latitude and over 45 degrees of longitude. It is 3500 miles from Wellington to the frigid plateau at the polar apex of New Zealand's Ross Dependency, and nearly 3000 miles to the distant tropical atoll of Penrhyn (Tongareva), within nine degrees of the Equator and almost half-way from Wellington to the shores of North America.

The Dominion proper includes the North Island, the South Island, Stewart Island and the Chatham Islands together with the *outlying* (or *minor*) islands. Of the outlying islands, the Three Kings and the Kermadecs lie to the north, and Campbell Island, Solander, Bounty, the Snares, the Antipodes and Auckland Island lie to the south. The rocky southerly islands are often popularly referred to as the *sub-antarctic islands*. Of all the outlying islands only the Kermadecs and Campbell Island are now regularly inhabited, and then only by a handful of meteorological and other government officers (*Fig. 83*).

New Zealand's island territories (the *annexed* islands) comprise the Tokelaus and the Cook Islands (the Southern Cook

Group, the Northern Cook Group and Niue).* Also under New
Zealand's jurisdiction is the Ross Dependency which comprises
that part of Antarctica and of the off-shore islands lying between

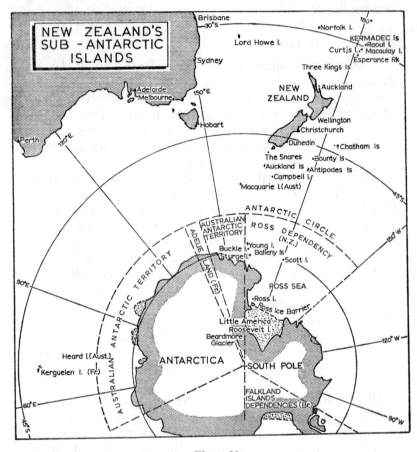

Figure 83

longitude 160 degrees east and 150 degrees west and extending
south of latitude 60 degrees south to the pole.

In addition to these territories, all of which comprise New
Zealand territory, there are others in which the Dominion
has formal responsibilities. The islands of Western Samoa

*A list of the islands which comprise the different groups is to be found in
Appendix I, together with details of their area and population. (See also *Figure 84*)

were administered by New Zealand from 1920 to 1946 as a mandate of the League of Nations. In 1946 a trusteeship agreement for Western Samoa was approved by the General Assembly of the United Nations, and under it New Zealand continued to assume responsibility for its administration. On January 1, 1962, the Trusteeship Agreement was terminated and Western Samoa emerged as the first fully independent Polynesian state. New Zealand, however, retains its friendship and certain moral and financial responsibility for the island country. Finally New Zealand is jointly responsible with the United Kingdom and Australia for the administration of the Trust Territory of Nauru. Administration and official appointments are largely delegated by the two other powers to the Government of Australia, but New Zealand appoints a representative to the British Phosphate Commission which was until 1967 responsible for the working of the island's phosphate deposits and largely in control of the island's economy. (See Chapter Four.)

Excluding the Ross Territory, which is part of the continent of Antarctica, and the island of Nauru, which falls within the Australian sphere of influence, a line drawn on the map of the Pacific to include all the other New Zealand territories defines and delimits 'New Zealand's Pacific Island Neighbourhood' (see *Fig. 13*, Chapter Two). Within it fall some other insular territories which, whilst not New Zealand's administrative responsibility, are in other ways dependent upon the Dominion. They have the same kind of interest for, and connection with New Zealand that the Solomons and New Hebrides, for example, have with the Commonwealth. These other territories include the Crown Colony of Fiji (together with Rotuma to the northwest), the French islands of Wallis and Futuna, administered from New Caledonia but with a population of Polynesians closely akin in language and culture to the Samoans, and the Kingdom of Tonga, a protectorate of the United Kingdom.

NEW ZEALAND'S OUTLYING ISLANDS

Apart from the off-shore islands, there are within the proclaimed limits of New Zealand proper (from latitude 33 to 53 degrees south and between longitude 162 degrees east and 173 degrees west) a number of scattered islands—all of them rocky 'continental' islands—which have played a larger part in the early history of the colony of New Zealand than they do in the contemporary economy of the Dominion. Together with the Kermadecs, which lie outside the proclaimed boundaries of New Zealand proper and are, technically, separately annexed territory, they are—apart from the Chathams—of no economic significance today, although in the past their off-shore fish and whaling grounds, and the seals and birdlife on their coasts attracted temporary visitors. Their principal interest today is scientific and (in times of war) strategic. Only the Chathams are permanently inhabited and they are officially part of the Dominion proper. They constitute one of its 129 administrative counties and form part of the electorate of Lyttelton.

The *Chatham Islands*, consisting of two main islands—Chatham and Pitt—and a series of small rocky outliers with attractive names like the Pyramid, the Forty-Fours, Star Keys and the Sisters, have structural and geological affinities with Southland and Stewart Island. They lie less than 500 miles to the southeast of the mainland, nearer to Napier than to Wellington or Lyttelton. Their area—375 square miles—and their climate and plant and animal resources have been sufficient to enable them to support a considerable population for more than a thousand years, ever since the first Polynesians arrived in the New Zealand area. To form Chatham Island, broken hilly knobs of schist have been tied together by great sand-bars encircling a grey, peaty lagoon. Although the climate is bleak and raw, with frequent low cloud and persistent humid winds from the southwest, frosts are rare. Low, wind-shorn forest covered the hills, and scrub and swamp vegetation occupied the sandhills and the borders of the lagoons. Fish, especially blue cod and crayfish, and birds were the basis of the economy of the Moriori. After a period of destructive exploitation, during which Waitangi in Petre Bay was the resort of whaling vessels and their crews, and during which the original Chatham Island natives were enslaved and decimated by invading Maoris, the island swamps and low forested hills have been converted into sheep runs. Despite the cost and difficulty of marketing wool and animals on the mainland, sheep-rearing has remained the principal economic activity. With fishing it is the basis of the livelihood today of a population of a little more than 500 persons, mainly of Maori or part-Maori blood. The last so-called, pure-blooded 'Moriori' died in 1933.

Of the 'sub-antarctic' islands, only *Campbell Island* is occupied today. Since 1941 it has accommodated parties of government officers and has been the temporary home of scientists studying sub-antarctic meteorology, the ionosphere and the island's plant and animal life. Yet not only Campbell Island but the *Snares*, southwest of Stewart Island, the twenty-five mile long 'mainland' of the *Auckland Islands*, and the little-known *Antipodes* and *Bounty Islands*, have in the past been the scene of both enforced and voluntary settlement. Soon after their discovery at the beginning of the last century sealing gangs were landed, and often stranded, on many of their inhospitable, rocky, storm-swept shores, and there was an attempt at organized settlement, complete with lieutenant-governor, on the Auckland Islands in 1850. In the days when sailing vessels followed the route from Australia to Cape Horn, well to the south of New Zealand, wrecks were frequent and an unknown number of castaways lived, and many died, on the sub-antarctic islands. Both Auckland Island and Campbell Island were in the 1890s the scene of pastoral farming—in both cases only short-lived. On Enderby Island, in the Auckland Islands, wild descendants of the Shorthorn cattle introduced in the 1890s still survive. Pigs, cats, goats and rabbits persist on other islands in the group. But since the hectic ruthless era of sealing and whaling early in the last century, the sub-antarctic islands have been little visited. Their flora and fauna have largely recovered from the despoliation of the earlier period. The seals are coming back; off-shore, whales are increasingly numerous. In and about the various islands to the south of New Zealand are millions of birds: sooty shearwaters (muttonbirds), petrels, mollymawks, penguins and albatrosses. The Snares and Bounty Islands in particular, less seriously disturbed than the others, are of very great scientific interest; and although none of these islands is likely to be of economic benefit to New Zealand, the Dominion is fortunate to possess in these isolated, wind-swept southern territories a scientific asset of inestimable value. Their proper preservation and regular inspection should be a national duty. The sub-antarctic islands present New Zealand with a wonderful opportunity of studying not only their plant life but also the oceanic resources of the little-known high latitudes and the vast population of birds and mammals which the southern waters support. The *Three Kings* lie to the northwest of North Cape and were discovered and named by Tasman. There is evidence that they may have once been occupied or regularly visited by Polynesians, but apart from occasional temporary occupation by Maoris during the whaling period, they have had no population since the beginning of European settlement. Landing is difficult on their vertical rock shores. However goats were liberated to provide food for any seamen who might be wrecked on them. These goats soon transformed the vegetation and multiplied to a total of several hundreds. But since the last war the goat population has been exterminated by the New Zealand Department of Internal Affairs and within a very few years the manuka scrub is being invaded by the forerunners of a rich forest flora.

The *Kermadecs*, in much the same latitude as Lord Howe and Norfolk islands, lie about 600 miles to the northeast of Auckland, nearly half-way to Tonga. Of the four islands comprising the group, Raoul, or Sunday Island, is the largest and most elevated, being more than 7000 acres in extent and reaching over 1700 feet. Like Curtis, Macaulay, L'Esperance and the smaller Herald Islands, Raoul is of volcanic origin. Thermal activity still occurs. The group is perched on the summit of a great submerged crustal upthrust—the outer rim of the continental western margin of the Pacific—overlooking the profound depths of the Kermadec Trench to the east. It has a pleasantly cool subtropical climate and a forest vegetation including *pohutukawa*, *nikau*, *karaka*, tree ferns and other species with close relatives in the North Island of New Zealand. Most useful tropical and temperate fruits and many root crops and grasses have been introduced at different times, and parts of Raoul are occupied today with a thicket of guava and cape gooseberry.

Polynesian voyagers stayed in the Kermadecs some time and left behind them stone artifacts. The islands inevitably became a rendezvous for whalers, and it was the opportunity of growing produce to sell to the whaling crews that gave rise, from 1827, to sporadic settlement by a few families of Europeans. For thirty-six years the cultivation of potatoes, yams, taro, maize and bananas continued. Later, from 1878, members of the Bell family lived on Raoul and, with the help of Niue islanders, stayed there until advised to leave after the outbreak of the 1914-1918 war. Further attempts at settlement were made again between the wars, but none was long-lived.

In 1964 there were only nine persons on Raoul. They were government officers engaged in operating the radio and meteorological stations and in maintaining the emergency landing strip built during the war.

THE COOK ISLANDS

The Cook Islands are at one and the same time the most remote from Wellington of all New Zealand's territorial responsibilities in the Pacific, and the group for which the Dominion is exclusively and most directly responsible. They were declared a British protectorate in 1888 and proclaimed part of New Zealand in 1901. In the crafty chessboard manoeuvring by which European powers acquired their Pacific island territories, the niceties of geography had little significance: as a result unlike islands were grouped indiscriminately. Few groups illustrate this better than the Cook Islands.

They have in common little more than the fact that they are all 'oceanic' tropical islands out in the broad expanse of the central structural province of the Pacific, and that their people have common Polynesian origins. Structurally and geologically practically all kinds of 'oceanic' island forms are represented. Some islands in the group are practically devoid of soil; others have amongst the most productive tropical soils in the Pacific. Some are low, minute specks with little cultivable land whose inhabitants live almost entirely on fish and the fruits of the coconut and the pandanus; others are lofty basaltic islands with a variety of soil, vegetation and environment, and had a richly diverse native economy. Still others are raised, rocky coral platforms with thin soil and dry-type scrub vegetation of intermediate attraction as the homes of either Stone Age or Atom Age men. The scattered northern islands in the group, typical small atolls, are much more akin to, and have much greater affinities with, the atoll outliers to the north and west of Samoa (the

Tokelaus) and again with the still more remote Line Islands to the northeast of the northern Cooks. The larger southern volcanic islands have closer cultural connections and greater geographical identity with the Society Islands to the east, and the Austral Islands to the southeast, than they have with the still more distant atolls to the north with which they have, however, been tied by political disposition.

Only Niue, the largest of the Cook Islands, has been given separate administration, ostensibly because of the distance which separates it from the others, although it is several hundred miles nearer Rarotonga than some of the northern atolls. Two years after the New Zealand annexation (in 1903), Niue was accorded separate treatment. It is administered by a resident commissioner directly responsible to the Department of Island Territories in Wellington. The remaining islands in the group (both the Northern Group and the Southern—or Lower*— Group) are administered from Rarotonga, which is the seat of the Cook Islands government. In 1965 the Cook Islands were granted full internal selfgovernment. Its legislative assembly now appoints a Leader of Government Business (or Prime Minister) and the Executive Committee appointed by him constitutes a 'cabinet'.

NORTHERN ATOLLS

The Northern Group consists of seven islands. Penrhyn, the most distant and most northerly (latitude 9 degrees south), is a forty-mile-long atoll of coral around a lagoon no less than 100 square miles in extent (*Fig. 6*). It provides the only land-locked shelter within the group for inter-island copra schooners. Its numerous *motus*† have together an area of only 2400 acres, although some of these narrow low ridges of sand run for as much as five miles along the coral rim of the lagoon. They accommodate, and, with the marine resources of the lagoon and the reef, support a population of 628 people—a density of well over 150 per square mile and considerably in excess of anything found in Australia and New Zealand outside the urban areas. Rakahanga and Manihiki are close neighbours, and

---

* Because of the inappropriate nature of the term 'Lower' as applied to those of the Cook Islands which are 'high' islands the alternative designation ('Southern') will be used here.
† See Chapter 1, especially pp. 8-11.

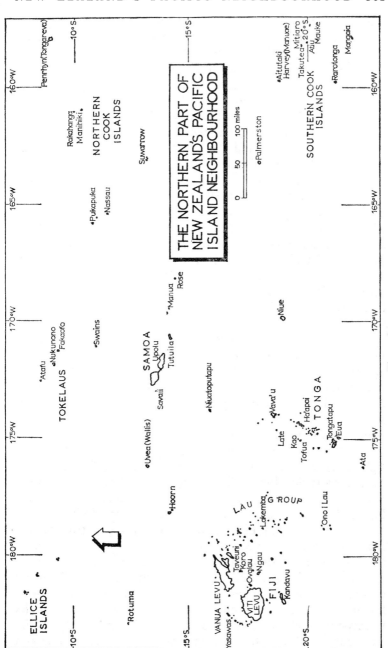

THE NORTHERN PART OF
NEW ZEALAND'S PACIFIC
ISLAND NEIGHBOURHOOD

Figure 84

stand astride the latitude of 10 degrees south. Both are typical atolls with small *motus* amounting in all to about 1000 acres. The lagoon at Manihiki is five miles across and is dotted with rocky islets on which dark waving palms stand out sharply against the placid blue-green expanse of the waters of the lagoon. The multi-coloured coral floor of the lagoon at Manihiki is particularly famous for its pearl shell, which in recent years has sometimes constituted the principal export of the whole group. Both islands have neat well laid-out villages, in which live Rakahanga's 319 people and Manihiki's 1006.

Further west stand Pukapuka, Nassau and Suwarrow. All are atolls, the first rising unusually in one place to over 100 feet. Pukapuka has a population which, though Polynesian, is somewhat different in language and culture from that of the other islands in the group. In 1961 the population totalled 718 people, and had a density of over 380 per square mile of dry land. Suwarrow was not inhabited. The 300 coconut-clad acres of Nassau are, however, visited by Pukapukans who go there to cut and dry copra. In 1961, 109 were living there. Suwarrow was formerly operated as a coconut plantation, first by Lever Brothers and later by the Auckland firm of A. B. Donald. Unlike Pukapuka, it lies low in the waves of the Pacific and is sometimes swept entirely by great seas whipped up by hurricanes as was the case in 1942 when the lives of some visitors to the atoll were saved only by the fact that they lashed themselves high in the storm-tossed coconut palms.

Palmerston lies in the track of aircraft en route from Upolu to Aitutaki or Tahiti. It was probably one of the few islands sighted by Magellan on his historic voyage over four centuries ago. It is a typical low atoll, with eight irregularly-shaped sandy *motus* threaded along its coral reef. Unoccupied until 1862, Palmerston became the home of an Englishman, William Marsters, who took with him to the island three native women from Penrhyn. They became the forebears of a future population of over a hundred Marsters, more than seventy of whom still live at Palmerston collecting shell, drying fish and cutting copra, and speaking a strange eighteenth-century English. Twice hurricanes have swept the whole island, swamping even its twenty-foot high 'hill', as a result of which parts of the family have gone forth to other islands in the group. Their name and curious speech are met today in Rarotonga, Aitutaki and Penrhyn.

Together the northern islands have a sixth of the area of the Cook Group (excluding Niue) and a similar share of the total population. In 1956, however, they surprisingly provided over forty per cent by value of the exports of the group, including practically all the pearl shell and most of the copra, which in that year were, with tomatoes, the most valuable exports. Subsequently its has become necessary to conserve pearl shell by restricting the amount collected, and the high islands of the Southern Group have found new export commodities. In 1964 the northern atolls furnished only one-eighth of the value of all exports.

RAISED ATOLLS

The islands of the Southern Group are vastly different. They are high islands, both volcanic piles and raised atolls. They are still largely and richly forested. There is room for commercial as well as for subsistence agriculture. These islands accommodate more people. They are visited less frequently by hurricanes and have a more regular and more reliable rainfall, and, unlike the northern atolls, where water has to be stored in concrete tanks, have no seasonal water supply problems.

Four of these islands—Mangaia, Atiu, Mauke and Mitiaro —are much alike in origin, structure and landforms. All are raised atolls. They vary in size and elevation, but in all cases a large part of their surface is made up of the rough and broken coral rock which was formerly the floor of the lagoon of an atoll. Mangaia is the second largest island in the group, and the most southerly. It has an area of 12,828 acres and is almost thirty miles in circumference. Parallel to the fringing reef, with its few and dangerous boat passages, is a narrow sandy strand. This is overlooked by high and broken cliffs of limestone. At the landing at Oneroa, steps have been cut in the coral cliffs to provide access to the main part of the settlement which is perched up on the edge of the *makatea*. The *makatea* circles the island and forms a plateau at times a mile wide whose surface is rough and jagged, its undulating grey-white slopes pitted and underlain by caves and only partly covered with red, residual soils and a dry-land vegetation of casuarina, ferns and introduced guava. This plateau varies in height between 200 and 300 feet. It is terminated inland by another series of rough but lower cliffs, inside which is a ring of deep soils and discontinuous taro swamps at the base of the dissected volcanic slopes beyond. The low hills reach an elevation of over 500 feet and form the centre and the structural core of the island. Here are streams of running water and rich, deep soils developed on the easy basaltic slopes. Most of the crops are grown here and in the nearby swamps, but the settlements are perched on the outer edge of the *makatea* platform, midway between the soil and water resources of the land and the marine resources of the reef and of the narrow off-shore lagoon.

Atiu (6654 acres) and Mauke (nearly 4600 acres) are smaller. At Atiu the *makatea* is less imposing, not so broken and of lower elevation (*Fig. 9*). The core of low volcanic hills has the same plateau-like appearance as the *makatea*. It provides Atiu's productive garden soils. Apart from Taunganui, which is the principal landing point, the volcanic area also provides sites (close to each other) for the five settlements and centres of population. Good roads across the coral plateau link the villages with the landings and the fishing places. Mauke has not been raised nearly so high, and its *makatea* rises not hundreds but merely tens of feet above the unbroken fringing reef. Again the deep dark soils are near the centre of the lemon-shaped island; and, of its two villages, one is in this central area and the other on the more sheltered (northwestern) coast. Mitiaro is lower still, the former floor of its lagoon standing today no more than a few feet above the sea—a rocky, long, narrow stretch of coral covered in part with blown coral sand and with only small pockets of volcanic rock and red-brown soil. In 1961 the population of these raised coral islands was as follows: Mangaia, 1877; Atiu, 1266; Mauke, 785; and Mitiaro 307. Tukutea is a low atoll swept by both hurricane waves and *tsunami* (mis-named 'tidal waves') and is not regularly inhabited. Manuae is also an atoll planted in coconuts and leased to a private plantation operator. Its temporary population in 1961 amounted to eighteen people.

HIGH VOLCANIC ISLANDS

Rarotonga, with its towering pile of volcanic peaks, rising 2100 feet above its fringing reef and the wind-ruffled ocean off-shore, is the 'metropolitan' and administrative centre of the group (*Fig. 4*). On the quarter-mile-wide coastal fringe of coral-sand and rich, volcanic soils, and in the few narrow valleys that cut a little way back into the steep tree-lined basalt slopes of the interior, live 8676 people, almost half of the Cook Island total. Most of them live in the town of Avarua and the contiguous villages of Avatiu, Tukuvaine and Tupapa. The road round the roughly circular island runs near the coast all the way. Its twenty-two miles represent a comfortable afternoon bicycle run. Since missionary days the villages, their houses built of burnt lime or of *purau* sticks, and thatched with coconut leaves or roofed with corrugated iron, have been built along this road and near the coast. Formerly they were a quarter of a mile inland at the foot of the steep volcanic slopes and were connected by the ancient, narrow, paved highway—the *ara metua*—which can still be traced today. The lofty interior is difficult of access and is uncultivated, although much of the timber has been cut out, and on some ridges the bush has been burned so often that it is now replaced by a low mat of fern, and soils are in parts severely eroded. (See *Figure 85*.)

Aitutaki lies 140 miles north of Rarotonga. It, too, is a volcanic island, with the form of an irregularly shaped almost-atoll. Most of its 4000 acres are made up of a dissected mass of basaltic hills at the northwestern corner of a roughly triangular lagoon. The reef runs along the western margin of these hills; to the southeast stretches the varied-blue sweep of the lagoon. Most of Aitutaki's 2582 people live on the coast to the west of the volcanic hills, and here there is a deep passage through the fringing reef to a good wharf. There are one or two low sandy *motus* on the eastern part of the reef. The landing strip for aircraft is laid out on one of these stretches of coral sand joined to the northern end of the main island. With its expanse of lagoon Aitutaki has access to marine resources which are richer and more varied than those of all other islands in the Southern Group. It also has rich volcanic soils. It was formerly a calling point on the National Airways Corporation Dakota service, which until 1951 linked Auckland, Fiji, Tonga, Samoa and the Cook Islands, and terminated at Rarotonga. Then it was more fortunate than its 'metropolitan' neighbour in that its lagoon provided for some years a port of call on the Tasman

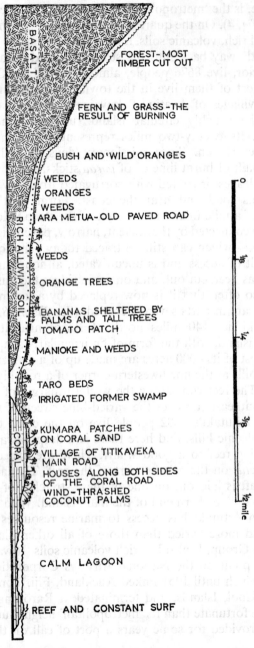

Figure 85: Rarotonga's coastal fringe in cross-section

Empire Airways flying-boat Coral Route which went on to Tahiti, but which, by avoiding Rarotonga, left the administrative centre of the Cook Islands more isolated again than at any time since before the war. Today the airstrip close to Avarua is being extended to enable larger land-based aircraft to provide a regular air service.

TRANSPORT PROBLEMS OF THE ISLANDS

Shipping is a most serious problem in the Cook Islands, and derives in part from their physical features. Indeed, shipping problems are widespread in the Pacific World, and are especially characteristic of the groups of widely scattered coral islands or of volcanic islands enclosed by a dangerous fringing reef. Nowhere in the fifteen islands of the Cook Group is there a good harbour. Even anchorages outside the reef are not available at Mangaia, Mauke, Mitiaro and Atiu, where the seaward face of the off-shore reef descends abruptly to great depth.

At both Avarua and Avatiu on Rarotonga the coral reef is sufficiently broken to admit small trading vessels to harbours of very restricted capacity. But the *Moana Roa*, which is by no means a large vessel, has to anchor off the reef in a roadstead, although this is sheltered under most conditions of weather, and is adjacent to the boat passage across the reef. In the harbour there are sheds at the landward end of a short wharf, and cargoes are loaded from it into small lighters which are then towed by motor launch through the reef passage to the vessel anchored outside. At Mangaia and Mauke, in the absence of even an anchorage, quite small inter-island trading schooners are obliged to sail up and down, off the reef, whilst cargo is taken ashore, or brought off, in rowing boats which are at times capsized as they cross the wave-swept reef. Bad weather may often cause delays which not only add to the cost of shipping but also result in the deterioration of perishable cargo.

Inter-island transport in the Cook Islands is provided by local trading vessels—one or two only—operated by the companies established at Avarua for the purpose of buying and selling copra and shell. Recently the administration has also operated a small ketch with both passenger accommodation and cargo space. These vessels call at the outlying northern atolls, rarely more than two or three times a year, to land stores and to collect copra and pearl shell. During the hurricane season—in summer, from December to March—the inter-island vessels seek shelter in the wider lagoons of the northern atolls. At this time the *Moana Roa* is also withdrawn from its monthly run, so that during a period of more than two or three months traffic is at a standstill and each island must depend upon the goods it has in store or upon its own resources.

The principal link between the Cook Islands and New Zealand (and the world beyond) is provided by the restricted passenger and cargo space of the government-operated vessel *Moana Roa*, which is not large enough to cope with either the passengers or the export cargo offering.

Certain trans-Pacific freighters—operating usually between New Zealand and the west coast of North America—call erratically at Rarotonga on their southward voyages if they have vacant cargo space. However, their schedules are not co-ordinated with the timetable operating under the slightly more regular services of the *Moana Roa;* and it often happens that these vessels call within a day or two of the *Moana Roa's* own arrival. Then it may be two months before another vessel appears to lift export cargo: meanwhile the crop of tomatoes or oranges may well have matured—and rotted. The provision of more frequent shipping is essential not only to the welfare and agricultural progress of the Cook Islands, but also to that of many other insular groups at present under a handicap roughly similar to that of New Zealand's dependency. A regular scheduled air service between New Zealand and Rarotonga is also an imperative requirement.

LIFE, LANDSCAPE AND ECONOMY

Cook first sighted some of the southern islands of this group; but others, including Rarotonga, were not brought to European attention until they were visited and reported on by John Williams, the missionary, after 1820. But although they were discovered late and have always been well off the beaten track, the disintegration of the traditional way of life and of the native economy of the larger southern islands has proceeded further than in Fiji, Tonga, Samoa and the other islands in New Zealand's Pacific island neighbourhood. Through the nineteenth century, missionary rule was almost complete, and the rigid 'Blue Laws' persisted well into the present century. But missionary rule brought prosperity, outside contacts and hard work. Small European plantations were established, especially in Rarotonga, and they prospered with their production of oranges, copra, bananas, vanilla, mandarines and pineapples. The native economy, too, was missionary-modified and partly commercialized. The volume of production and export (largely to New Zealand) climbed to a peak in the middle 1920s when as many as 178,000 cases of oranges and scores of thousands of cases of bananas were shipped in a year. Since then shipping shortages, low prices, high cost of fruit cases (imported from New Zealand), deterioration of the orange trees, uninspired administration and unimaginative agricultural policies have brought neglect of the still rich basic soil resources. And this has been accompanied by both economic and spiritual depression amongst the Cook Islanders. Most European plantations have gone out of production. Not even the higher postwar prices brought a revival. With the lack of shipping over the years since the war, thousands of cases of fruit and of the newer, risky catch-crop tomatoes, have been left to rot. However, the recent erection of a central cool store and packing shed in Avarua has helped to avoid losses due to lack of shipping.

For years native food plants, on Rarotonga especially, have been haphazardly cultivated, and much fertile land carries only a tall tangled growth of lantana, elephant's foot and other weeds. Taro terraces and the accompanying irrigation facilities have been neglected. Pandanus has disappeared as a result of the attacks of a white scale. The walls of many a burnt lime and mortar house stand grey and gaunt and roofless. There has not been money to replace the rusted sheets of roofing iron. Many Rarotongans have reverted to the use of their traditional type of house—a *kiekau* whare— with walls of *au* (a hibiscus) and a roof of thatch. But since pandanus is not available for thatch coconut leaves have been used with the result that many palms have been defoliated. Defoliation and the damage done to green nuts by rats, and the lack of new planting, have made coconuts insufficient for local needs. Except on Aitutaki, copra is no longer a significant export from the Southern Group. Yams and breadfruit are rarely seen. Back in the sheltered valleys out of the wind, where bananas were cultivated, land has been unused for many years, and hibiscus hedges have spread, and with guava and lantana occupy many acres of the richest land.

Neglecting their gardens, the Cook Islanders have sought employment on wages. Many have gone to Avarua, not only from the villages of Rarotonga but also from other islands. Here some find work on the wharves, some with the departments of works and agriculture and some in small factories, recently established, making slippers and knitwear for the New Zealand market. The output of these small factories has continued to grow, so that in 1964 manufactured goods constituted the second most valuable item in the Cook Islands' export list. Over 3000 Cook islanders have meanwhile taken passage to Auckland and found work in the growing factories there. Moreover, with the neglect of native food crops—kumara on the coral sandy soils, taro in the irrigated swamps, bananas and breadfruit in the gardens and coconuts around the coastal rim of the islands—and with the diminution of the export trade, not only housing but also diet and health have suffered.

ORANGE PLANTING

It was not until the mid-1940s that the administration sought, belatedly, to remedy the unhappy state of the Cook Island life and economy. It then devised and put into operation an orange replanting project to replace the old and diseased trees by small citrus orchards of late navel and Rarotonga seedless oranges budded on to citronella stock in government nurseries. Most of the fruit still exported at that time came from seedling trees growing wild, often in the bush, and first introduced by the missionaries. But the replanting scheme ran into difficulties over questions of land tenure. Community ownership of land remains a serious obstacle to economic progress. It is very difficult to secure agreement from the many Maori 'owners' of a small piece of 'customary' land for its lease to Europeans, or for one of their own number to have the individual use of it. But with patient negotiation the native land court has made it possible for the government to plant 300 acres of oranges in Rarotonga, Aitutaki, Atiu and Mauke in the names of individuals, and in 1952 it was announced that another 500 acres were to be planted, assuring by 1960 an annual crop of not less than 300,000 cases. This estimate proved optimistic. In 1964 there were over 1000 acres in citrus trees. Only 87,000 cases of oranges, however, were exported. This was largely because of the building in Avarua by Dunedin interests of a juice extracting plant. So successful has this been that fruit juice is now the most valuable export of the Cook Islands; and canned 'Raro' orange and pineapple juice is known throughout New Zealand.

The revenue of the Cook Islands Government, derived from import duties, postage stamps and income tax, is insufficient to meet expenditures. The New Zealand Government has long found it necessary to meet the deficit, and continues to make subsidies and grants available—especially for transport, health, education and other social services. In 1963-64 these amounted to $1,550,000, or $80 a head for all Cook Islanders resident in the group. It has been argued that it would be cheaper for the New Zealand taxpayer to transport all the islanders to the Dominion and find for them remunerative employment there. This, however, is no practical solution to the problems of the Cook Islands and would be unacceptable to the people themselves. It is part of the 'burden' of all countries responsible for the welfare of dependent people in underdeveloped territories to subsidize their social and economic progress. New Zealand, like Australia, is no exception; and, spread over all New Zealanders, the 'burden' of caring for the welfare of the Maori people of the Cook Islands costs only $0.58 per head per year.

NIUE

Niue lies nearer Tonga and Samoa than Rarotonga, and, although within the political boundaries of the Cook Islands, it is administered separately from them. It consists of the one island only and is larger than Mangaia, the largest island in the Cook Group. Like Mangaia and Atiu and Mauke, it is a raised atoll. Its extensive bulk of coral has been raised above sea level at least twice so that its plateau surface is stepped. A cliff of broken coral lies inside the fringing reef. It is forty miles round the island by a road which for the most part follows the precipitously cliffed coast. Above the cliffs is the first limestone terrace at a height of ninety feet. From this there is a steep rise to the upper and older plateau surface at a height of 220 feet. This occupies the bulk of the interior, its coral surface being more deeply weathered and its soils sufficient to support a heavy forest growth. There are, however, no running streams and Niue has (at the surface) no core of volcanic rocks.

Most of Niue's 4864 (1961 census) people live in villages which are situated near the coastal edge of the lower terrace in the west. Of these Alofi, with its off-shore anchorage, unsatisfactory but the best available, is the largest, and has almost 1000 people. It is the administrative centre. The other villages, amongst them some of the largest, are in the eastern part of the island and up on the higher terrace.

The Niueans are Polynesians, and are thought to have come to Niue at least a thousand years ago from both Tonga and Samoa. They are thus not as closely related in either blood or culture to the Cook Islanders or to the New Zealand Maoris as these two Polynesian groups are to each other. Cook discovered Niue in 1774, but the hostile reception then given him caused him to name it Savage Island, and partly because of this it was not until 1849 that missionary endeavour met with any success at Niue. It was native missionaries, Samoans mainly, who converted the Niueans, and so complete was the formal religious conversion that even in recent years of very infrequent shipping connections the islanders have refused to load bananas on Sundays, even when this meant missing one of the very few favourable opportunities in the year of getting their crop away to the New Zealand market.

The economy of Niue is a simple modified native one. Practically all the land passes from generation to generation by blood descent; none is held for European plantations and only a little is leased for missionary purposes. Each family grows food crops in the pockets of deeper soil scattered over the broken surface of the *makatea*. Rarely is the authority of the native village policeman required to ensure that every able-bodied male shall plant sufficient food crops to provide sustenance for his family. In order of acreage planted, the food crops are: coconuts, taro, yams, tapioca, bananas and kumaras. Most intensively used is the lower terrace along the east of the island, where a heavier rainfall supports a richer forest cover, and where more organic matter is incorporated in the *makatea* soils. To the subsistence economy is added the production of cash crops. Copra is sun-dried and is the principal export. A belt of well-cared-for palms encircles the island. Bananas are grown both as food and cash crop. Export bananas come principally from small clearings in the shelter of woodland growth inland of the eastern villages, which are linked with Alofi not only by the coastal road metalled with *makatea* but also by others which radiate from the landing across the plateau surfaces. The administration operates a small fleet of trucks over these roads and thus provides the economic lifeline between the point of call for shipping and the more productive and heavily-populated villages eight or nine miles away.

The only other source of cash income with which store goods are purchased is plaited ware. The Niueans make attractive hats, baskets and table mats from coconut leaves, and for the last two New Zealand provides a good market. Plaited ware accounts for from a fifth to a third of the value of exports.

Like the Cook Islands, Niue is not self-supporting. Its imports are three times the value of its exports. The administration's expenditure is usually two or three times greater than its receipts. In 1963-64 the subsidy from New Zealand was nearly $600,000, or $120 a head for all Niueans. Hurricane disasters frequently hit Niue hard, causing damage not only to buildings, houses, schools and churches, but destroying food and export crops, thus retarding production for years ahead. The disasters of February 1959 and January 1960 are estimated to have caused damage amounting to $2 millions. For an island community of less than 5000 persons, and with an annual revenue (excluding subsidies) of only $380,000, such losses are calamitous.

TONGA

The independent kingdom of Tonga is geographically distinctive in a number of ways. Its structure and the combination (in its 160 islands) of volcanic, coralline and sedimentary rocks, of active volcanoes, of raised coral islands and atoll reefs gives it a physical character all its own. But it is in its cultural geography—its stable and successful economy, its Europeanized system of land tenure, its social progress and political cohesion —that Tonga is most strikingly distinctive from the other island groups of the southwest Pacific.

Of all the Melanesian and Polynesian peoples in the Pacific island neighbourhoods of Australia and New Zealand, only the Tongans have managed to preserve for themselves independence and self-government during a century and a half of European expansion and imperialism in these extensive oceanic areas. No other group has yet adapted its economy so successfully to the modern commercial system and at the same time retained the essential family subsistence basis of its pre-European society and economy. No other group is so completely independent of outside financial assistance. Whilst from New Guinea to the Cook Islands the welfare of the dependent territories of the southwest Pacific is a charge on the taxpayers of Australia, New Zealand or some other administering power, Tonga has very considerable amounts of capital invested in Australia and New Zealand and ranks as one of the world's few 'creditor nations'.

LAND TENURE

Traditionally Tonga had a feudal system. Chiefs were constantly at war with each other but had time to exact fealty, labour, produce and military service from the village cultivators in exchange for permission to use land. Over the years 1830-1860 a young chief from Ha'apai, converted to Christianity by a Wesleyan-trained native missionary, made himself king of all Tonga by methods which were not exactly a credit to his teacher. Under missionary influence the chief set himself up as constitutional monarch and took the name George I Tubou. The people were emancipated from semi-serfdom and a completely alien system of land tenure was instituted—a system which has been the foundation on which was built the subsequent economic and social progress of the kingdom. Since 1862 every male Tongan on reaching the age of eighteen has been granted for life and at a nominal rental the leasehold of an *api*—a bush section of eight and a quarter acres—and a 'town allotment' on which to build his village home. Such a garden and house site guarantee the Tongan family both social and economic security. Before

1900 some land had been leased to Europeans, especially on the largest and metropolitan island in the group—Tongatapu. There are still a handful of plantations, some of them operated by Germans whose forebears came to the Pacific before the turn of the century.

Tonga became a protectorate of Great Britain in 1900. A British agent and consul, responsible formerly to the High Commissioner for the Western Pacific in Suva but since 1952 to the Governor of Fiji, acts as adviser to King Taufa'ahau Tupou IV, formerly Prince Tupouto'a-Tungi, elder son of the late Queen Salote. The consul has responsibility for foreign relations and has a veto in certain financial matters and in the appointment of Tongan civil servants recruited overseas. Most of the foreign officers of the government, including teachers and engineers, come from New Zealand.

The many islands of the group are distributed in two parallel chains and fall into three latitudinal groups—a northern group (Vava'u), a central group (Ha'apai) and a southern group (Tongatapu). These islands are all part of the great structural arc which runs from the North Island of New Zealand through the Kermadecs and Tonga towards Samoa. It is paralleled by deep ocean trenches to the east. It is a region of great structural instability, of recent elevation and of active vulcanism. The total area of the islands, most of which are not inhabited, is about 160,000 acres, or nearly three times the surface area of the Cook Islands. The population, according to preliminary census results (1966), is over 77,000 and is growing rapidly. In 1939 it was 34,000 and in 1946 it reached 43,000.

The western chain of islands is volcanic. The eastern string consists of coral atolls and raised coral islands. Some of the volcanic islands are oddities that are better known to the world at large than the larger coral islands on which the bulk of the Tongans live. Amongst the oddities is Niuafo'ou, better known as Tin Can Island, because the mail was formerly sent ashore in sealed biscuit tins. This island has long suffered from violent eruptions and when, in 1946, a severe volcanic outbreak destroyed the administrative centre and the homes of the sturdy Niuafo'ouans, the entire population, 1300 of them, was transferred first to Tongatapu and later to new homes cut out of the bush on the hitherto thinly occupied island of 'Eua. Kao

is an extinct volcano with a perfect conical peak rising to 3400
feet. Late is a dormant volcanic pile and uninhabited. Tofua
has a steaming crater lake. But Falcon Island is the oddest
oddity. It is the summit of a cone which periodically erupts
ash and cinders. At such times its summit rises above the level
of the blue sea only to disappear again as waves and weather
destroy the unconsolidated pile. The island may be seen and
is entered on the chart by one ship but is likely to have disappeared before the next vessel arrives to investigate it.

Practically all the people live in the eastern coralline islands
—a quarter of them on the raised, dissected, hilly island of
Vava'u and its smaller neighbours; almost as many on the
much smaller area of the many *motus* strung out on an elongated, partly-submerged reef which constitutes the Ha'apai
group; and almost a half on Tongatapu, the largest island, on
which is Nuku'alofa the chief port, the capital and the largest
town in Tonga. On the diminutive sandy *motus* of Ha'apai
people are crowded—more than 500 to every square mile. There
is already some pressure of population on the land, and numbers
are still rising rapidly. It is impossible to find eight and a quarter
acres in Ha'apai for every youth attaining eighteen years and
they are reluctant to go to Tongatapu where land is still available.
Tongatapu (*Fig. 86*) is a raised coral island, but it was tilted on
being raised so that the land slopes up inappreciably from sea-
level in the north (where the reef extends away off-shore and is
dotted with beautifully wooded *motus*) to almost 200 feet in
the southeast (where a high cliff with spectacular blowholes
overlooks the fringing reef and the stretch of ocean across to
the high mass of 'Eua). The smooth, almost flat surface of
Tongatapu has a deeply weathered ginger-brown, sandy coral
soil in which volcanic ash, drifting in the air from erupting
islands of the group, is richly incorporated. The soil is very
productive.

AGRICULTURAL ECONOMY

The Tongan is a garden cultivator. He grows a profuse variety
of root crops, fruit and fibres primarily for the sustenance of
his family. For this his garden allotment is more than enough.
He goes out from the clustered *kolo*, or village, to his *api*
perhaps twice a week. He may have a mile or two to go to

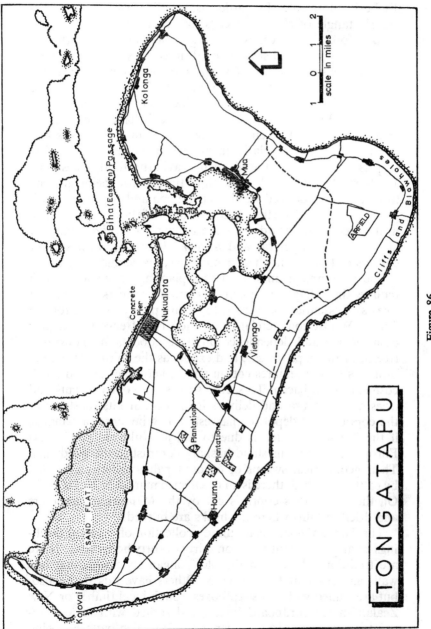

Figure 86

his bush allotment. His garden is, to alien eyes, a most disorderly tangle of shrubby weeds, tall coconut palms, second-growth forest, with crops growing in a jumble beneath and between the trees and shrubs and dead stumps. Before the yam planting season it is the Tongan gardener's custom to fire a small portion of his holding to clear it of rough growth. The fire determines the size, shape and location of the patch to be cultivated. From the air these 'cultivated', handkerchief-sized areas give the dull green-brown landscape of scrub, trees and waving palms an irregularly pock-marked appearance. The first crop is one of yams, the Tongan's favourite food and staple. The burned patch may be used three times before being allowed to revert to introduced weeds like lantana and guava and indigenous shrubby growths. Amongst the variety of crops grown in the second and third years are bananas, taro, *kape* (a giant taro), *kumala* (kumara) and *manioke* (cassava), with smaller clusters of kava plants, paper mulberry, maize and melons.

The government annually issues planting ordinances which require the villager to plant minimum numbers of coconut trees and essential food crops to ensure plenty of food for the family. Whilst commercial production is not encouraged (nor cash income and dependence on store goods), the Tongan is free to grow crops for sale and export as the spirit moves him, or as his family requires cotton goods, kerosene, canned meat, cosmetics or tobacco. To secure such store goods he cuts and dries a little copra and delivers it in coconut kits (baskets) to the copra board depot, or harvests a few bunches of bananas if the *Tofua* or *Matua* is due to call at Nuku'alofa. The few European plantations stand in sharp contrast to the weedy *api*. Their geometrical sweeps of coconut palms are clean weeded by cattle, for which there is an unsatisfied market in Nuku'alofa. On the plantations copra is cut by the Melanesian labourers and dried in kilns where the husks are burned.

The Tongan village is an untidy collection of assorted dwellings arranged without order on thirty or forty house sites. There are traditional houses in the old Tongan style with thatched walls and roofs and round ends. Others have this shape also, but are walled with old soap boxes, rough local timber or New Zealand-made cardboard boxes, and roofed with rusted, unpainted corrugated iron. Others are of an alien pattern—being in lean-to style and constructed often in recent years of salvaged iron matting from wartime runways. Around and behind the houses are small thatched, open-sided shelters, cookhouses, privies, primitive copra driers and usually an unpainted large round-ended missionary church.

WESTERN SAMOA

In direct contrast to the Cook Islands or Tonga, Samoa presents the example of a group of high volcanic islands, with smaller islands off their shores, all close together in terms of Pacific distances, with similar geological, climatic and biological characteristics and inhabited by Polynesians of similar culture, history, language and tradition, and yet arbitrarily divided and set apart under two strikingly different administrations—now the independent Western Samoan administration and formerly the New Zealand administration at Apia (Upolu), and the United States administration at Pago Pago (Tutuila). (See *Fig. 89*).

CHEQUERED HISTORY

Western Samoa was until January 1, 1962, a United Nations Trusteeship Territory. Its political history has been chequered and unhappy. Discovered in 1722 by the Dutchman, Roggeveen, and visited later by the French navigators, Bougainville and La Perouse, the Samoan group was not adequately reported on until visited by the ubiquitous John Williams in 1830, more than one hundred years after Roggeveen's voyage round the world. Williams was immediately welcomed by the native faction then in power. The Samoans accepted only such of the new religion as they could fit comfortably into the *fa'a Samoa*, or traditional Samoan custom and way of life. A few pagan customs were discarded but there was no revolutionary change in native morality or outlook. Great mission churches, later including Roman Catholic churches of German design and architecture, were built in all the villages, and these are a characteristic feature of the coastal landscape to this day. And copra was cut to fill the church boxes with coins and to support the new edifices. The Samoans accepted the commercial system of the west much as they had accepted its religion, choosing

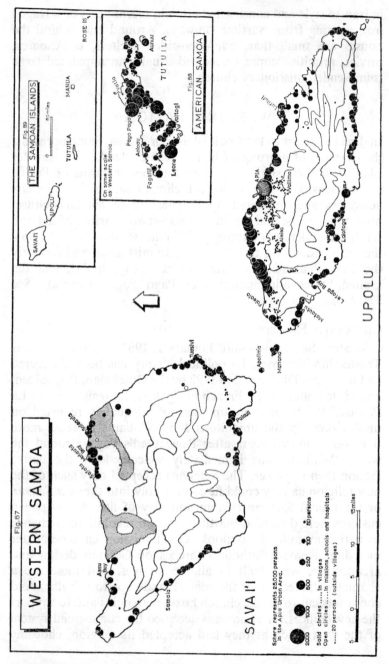

Figures 87: WESTERN SAMOA (showing distribution of villages); 88 *lower inset*, AMERICAN SAMOA and 89 *top inset*, the SAMOAN ISLAND GROUP.

what they liked and scornfully rejecting what they disliked. They retained their subsistence economy and saw to it that they had time free from their gardens for their age-old political rivalries and the practising of their proud Polynesian customs.

In many ways the embittered political, strategic and commercial rivalries of the foreign powers—especially Britain, Germany and the United States—left the Samoans little disturbed. Their island home is still the nearest approach to the colourful, lush tropical paradise popularly supposed to constitute the south sea island. This international rivalry may have culminated in naval action had it not been for the hurricane of 1889. Hurricanes are quite rare in the group. Their more usual track lies to the south in higher latitudes. But this hurricane found seven warships—three German, three American and the British warship *Calliope*—in the roadstead at Apia on Upolu. The *Calliope* forced her way out in the teeth of the hurricane, but the others were lost. The broken, rusted hull of the *Adler* can still be seen on the coral reef at Apia and is witness to the wreck of the hopes and intentions of the powers, and of Germany in particular, to establish an administrative and commercial empire in the south Pacific. German commercial interests were already dominant. The Hamburg firm of J. C. Godeffroy and Son and its successor, the so-called 'Long Handle Firm' (*Deutsche Handels- und Plantagen-Gesellschaft der Sudsee Inseln zu Hamburg*), established some of the largest and most efficiently-operated plantations in the Pacific on the island of Upolu, and captured much of the lesser trade of the group. To operate these plantations, whilst the Samoans sat and slept and smiled in their open-sided, cool and shaded *fales*, the Germans and other smaller plantation operators brought in Chinese coolies and Melanesian labourers from the Solomons. By agreement in 1899 Samoa was partitioned between the Germans and Americans, the Americans taking Tutuila and its naval base and coaling station at Pago Pago, and the Germans retaining the economically more attractive Upolu and Savai'i. Britain withdrew.

German rule was thorough and rigid. Firmness drove native political feeling and intrigue underground and laid the foundations of the later resistance of the *Mau*. The planters were government-sponsored and their economic programme was similarly thorough and vigorous. Samoa was to become a rich and productive tropical garden. Science was brought to the aid of tropical plantation agriculture. Few crops were not experimented with. The plantations were enlarged and the labour force ran to no less than 4000 Chinese and over 1000 Melanesian 'black boys'. This was a period of prosperity.

NEW ZEALAND ADMINISTRATION

But German rule was short-lived. In 1914 New Zealand troops were landed in Western Samoa, and occupied it until 1921, when New Zealand restored civil administration to a territory which was then constituted a C class mandate of the League of Nations and conferred on His Britannic Majesty to be administered on his behalf by the Government of New Zealand. Until 1936 New Zealand ran into difficulties in Samoa. Its intentions were good, but its tactics deplorable. Discontent grew amongst both Europeans and Samoans. New Zealand officials were not trained for the administration of dependent tropical territories, and still are not. They had little knowledge or understanding of native ways and customs. The German plantations were taken over and were operated and managed as the Reparation Estates. Prices fell and the smaller European planters ran into financial difficulties. Importation of labour was prohibited and the numbers of Chinese and Melanesians were reduced. The discontented Europeans fomented native dissatisfaction and helped to fan Samoan opposition to an administration which was primarily intent on protecting native interests against those of the Europeans. The *Mau* embarked on a programme of civil disobedience and at times, until 1936, force appeared necessary to restore order, but it was against the humanitarian attitude of the government and the people of New Zealand to use it. Finally, in 1936, agreement was reached with the Samoan leaders, and after that rapid progress was made towards self-government and towards satisfying the ambitious political aspirations of the Samoan chiefs and village leaders. In 1946 Western Samoa became the first trusteeship territory of the United Nations. In 1953 the Prime Minister of New Zealand announced proposals which would give the territory and the Samoans' accepted leaders complete control of internal affairs.

By 1961 all the preliminaries had been completed, including the writing of a constitution and its acceptance at a plebiscite by the people and its approval by the United Nations and the Government of New Zealand, for the termination of the Trusteeship Agreement. On January 1, 1962, Western Samoa became a fully independent Polynesian state. By treaty arrangement with the new state New Zealand still assists Western Samoa in the conduct of its international relations; and the Dominion also helps by providing finance and training facilities in an endeavour to improve educational facilities and to ensure the smooth operation of the new Samoan civil administration. But none of this assistance detracts from Western Samoa's sovereign independence.

PHYSICAL GEOGRAPHY

Upolu and Savai'i are very models of the Pacific World's upstanding volcanic islands. They have close physical similarities with those of the Hawaiian group. They lie within 13 or 14 degrees of the Equator and have a warm, wet tropical climate. Monthly average temperatures vary no more than three degrees through the year; and in forty years the thermometer has not fallen to 60 degrees or risen to 95. Most of the year the trade winds blow from the east and bring a steady rain, but from November to May, when the inter-tropical front reaches south the trades are interrupted by northerly and westerly winds and by a still wetter period. Over most of the islands rainfall is at least 100 inches a year.

Western Samoa has an area over 700,000 acres. (Compare New Zealand proper with sixty-six million acres and the Cook Islands with 63,000 acres.) Savai'i is half as big again as Upolu. Both are rugged mountainous islands, Savai'i reaching over 6000 feet and Upolu 3600. Both are built up from a succession of great flows of basaltic lava. Like giant fans these flows spread out from the elevated interior towards the coasts. Geologically they are all young, but on Upolu some have weathered to provide here and there near the coast pockets of dark soil between the black stretches of rock and scoria. On Savai'i two great flows are little more than fifty years old. There was an eruption in 1902; and another, which lasted from 1905 to 1911, spread a broad tongue of lava over plantations, roads and villages and poured the black molten mass over the reef on the north coast into the sea. Except where it has been buried or destroyed by the most recent flows the islands are circled by a fringing reef. Primarily because of the recency of these flows, the roughness of the rock surface and the lack of soil, Savai'i, though half as large again in area as Upolu, has little more than a quarter of the total population of the two islands—32,000 out of 131,500 (1966 estimate). But even on Upolu population and settlement are almost exclusively confined to the coast, and especially to small parts of it, because of the rugged, rocky and elevated nature of the forested interior (*Fig. 87*).

COASTAL VILLAGES

The organized village community is the basis not only of Samoan social life and economic well-being but also of the pattern of distribution of Samoan population and settlement. Apart from Apia, in the centre of the north coast of Upolu, the only port and point of entry into Western Samoa, with its rapidly growing population of European officials, part-Samoans and Samoans now totalling more than 25,000, the population of the territory lives in over 270 compact village units. Ninety of them are on the coasts of Savai'i, one each on the islets of Apolima and Manono in Apolima Channel between the two main islands, and the rest on Upolu. But the villages are not evenly strung along the coast. Some stretches are devoid of settlement and others are overcrowded with villages and people. More than anything this reflects the pattern and age of the lava flows, for the coastal margins of the younger flows, roughly-surfaced and soil-less and without a sheltered reef for fishing, do not provide suitable sites for settlement.

The densest village population is on the north coast of Upolu, west of Apia, where villages are strung tightly like beads, almost touching each other, on a slender thread of tar-sealed road. From the air-strip at Faleolo (formerly used by NAC Dakotas) and the flying boat base at Satapuala (used for many years by TEAL Solents) fifteen miles in to Apia the road follows the coast through a succession of thirty villages, closely huddled and densely populated. The road is thronged today with American cars and modern buses—a reflection of post-war prosperity and of Samoa's favourable balance of trade with the dollar area—while in their cool, opensided *fales*, with their bodies and worldly goods exposed to the passing world, the Samoans laze away the hotter part of the day.

The villages are trim, tidy and colourful, and consist of scores of round or oval *fales* raised on piles of scoria rubble two or three feet above the ground. During the day the detachable mats of coconut leaves, which at night serve as walls to keep out chill breezes, are tied up, and the interior is open to the full view of the village. Little iron or other imported material has as yet replaced the traditional materials used in house-building; nor have age-old building skills deteriorated. Native dress is of traditional form but the fabrics used are colourful imported Manchester cottons. Men wear the traditional *lava-lava* wrapped around the lower part of their portly frames. The rocky ground between the houses is covered by carefully trimmed grass with here and there flowering hibiscus, frangipani and dwarf decorative coconuts. Behind the coastal villages, extending up the lower easier slopes of the lava flows to an elevation of about 700 feet, are the native cultivations, in a wilderness of shady bush and irregularly planted coconut palms. Evidence of the occasional commercial agriculture of the Samoans is to be seen in their villages in the mats spread around the *fales*, on which blue-white strips of coconut meat and purple-red cocoa beans are spread to dry in the hot and plentiful sunshine. In front of the villages are the sandy shore and the off-shore reef of coral from which the Samoan derives some of his sustenance. On the beach are the village canoes. On narrow, single-file wooden piers, run out over the shallow water inside the reef, are the communal latrines. In all the larger villages there are massive missionary churches with distinctly 'continental' architectural forms, built of stone and concrete with white-washed walls and red roofs. These, together with the modern road and the traffic on it and the village store and copra and cocoa collecting depots (operated today by Morris Hedstrom and Co. or Burns Philp and Co.) are the only bizarre and exotic notes in a densely-populated, coastal landscape which comes near to the popular ideal of a south sea island paradise, much nearer than anything in Tonga or the Cook Islands.

AGRICULTURAL PROSPERITY

For more than a decade after the end of the war Western Samoa enjoyed almost unprecedented prosperity. In the last year or two the territory has conducted an international trade worth more than $NZ12 millions (compare Tonga $NZ 25 millions and the Cook Islands $NZ4.8 millions), and has had a considerable surplus of exports. Cocoa has been the great bonanza in recent years, with high prices ruling as a result of depredations of plant diseases in the West African producing areas. In 1951 the value of cocoa exports exceeded that of copra for the first time in forty years. There are over 9500 acres in cocoa with several hundred shrubs to the acre. Coconut palms—forty to seventy to the acre—occupy over 37,000 acres and bananas 14,000 acres; but these two are basic food crops as well as the source of cash income. In the last twenty years there has been a significant increase in the native production of commercial crops. Today eighty per cent of the copra exported, seventy-nine per cent of the cocoa beans and ninety-four per cent of the bananas are provided by Samoan villagers and small-scale native planters. Together these three crops account for over ninety-eight per cent of all exports. One danger of the economy is its overwhelming dependence upon copra and cocoa, the prices for which have at times fluctuated violently. Another danger, more serious, is that the volume of export production has not been keeping pace with the rate of growth of population. Only rising prices maintain the appearance of prosperity. At times in the 1960s prices for copra and cocoa have fallen and the new state's finances have not been sound.

Apart from the Western Samoa Trust Estates, the profit from the operation of which is devoted to the social and economic welfare of the Samoan people, plantation agriculture is today on a very small scale. A few Europeans and part-Samoans operate small, leased holdings in the neighbourhood of Apia. The estates operated by the Western Samoa Trust Estates Corporation,* mainly in western Upolo, are the only large units. They provide also an important part of the taxes upon which the government of Western Samoa depends for income. Above

---

* To which the former Reparation Estates (taken over by the New Zealand Government in 1919 as reparations from the Germans) were transferred in 1957 by the New Zealand Government in trust for the Samoan people.

all they serve as an object lesson in scientific tropical commercial agriculture for the Samoans, who now have accepted responsibility for their own economy, government and welfare. The tidy, ordered rows of coconuts and the carefully-sheltered stands of cocoa shrubs, sweeping over the intermediate slopes of the more deeply weathered lava flows, stand in sharp contrast to the neighbouring native gardens and the unused rough land higher up the slope. To weed the coconut plantations herds of Hereford and Angus cattle, numbering 10,000, are kept on the estates. Each year over 2000 head of cattle are slaughtered for local consumption. The Trust Estates Corporation also operates on Savai'i one of the only two sawmills in Western Samoa. Since the war the estates have also operated desiccated coconut and banana-drying industries. Both prospered during the disrupted period of international trade after 1945, but both have since become uneconomic and ceased operation in the mid-1950s.

GROWING POPULATION

But for all the spectacular and prosperous development of commercial agriculture the Samoan economy is still overwhelmingly a subsistence economy. A large part of the land cultivated by Samoan villagers is devoted to food crops, and most of their working time—two or three days a week—is absorbed in the leisurely cultivation of their gardens and the growing of crops of taro, yams, ta'amu (a species of taro), bananas, breadfruit and papaws. In a haphazard fashion they also 'keep' pigs and poultry as a source of food, especially for entertaining and for ceremonial occasions. Fishing is less important than it was formerly.

The Samoans retain most of the land. The Western Samoa Trust Estates comprise a little over 32,000 acres, and another 16,000 acres are owned by Europeans, including the missions. The rest is held by the Government of Western Samoa (formerly the Crown) for the native people, but fifty-five per cent of the total area of the islands is too steep, or is too broken and rocky to be made productive. Some land has already been seriously eroded and little of the forest is virgin or contains millable timber. Already there is population pressure on the land along the north coast of Upolu and locally in other parts of the island. Meanwhile population in Samoa is growing as fast as anywhere in the world. Since 1921 it has expanded by no less than 230 per cent (from 34,000 to 131,500—Samoans and part-Samoans). Between 1945 and 1951 the increase was nearly 15,000, or twenty-two per cent in six years. It has continued since then to expand at a rate exceeding three per cent per annum. Some villages are overcrowded and insanitary, others have scarcely enough village land to provide adequate food. There is still room for the siting and establishment of new villages, especially on Savai'i, but a serious problem is looming up in view of the rapid and unrestricted growth of population.

AMERICAN SAMOA

To the United States the convention of 1899 awarded the island of Tutuila (seventy miles east of Apia), the three small hilly islands which comprise the Manua Group, and the isolated uninhabited Rose Island. To these was added Swain's Island, occupied for many years by an American, but considered part of the Gilbert and Ellice Islands Colony until it was handed over to the United States by Britain in 1925 (at the same time as the Tokelaus were transferred for administrative purposes to the government of Western Samoa).

Because of the earlier importance of its naval base at Pago Pago, a port of call for ships of the Matson line which once again operate between the west coast of North America and the British dominions in the southwest Pacific, eastern Samoa has rarely been considered in other than strategic and naval terms. But more than 22,100 (1964) Samoans live in the American territory, 3300 in the Manua group, 65 on Swain's Island and the rest on Tutuila, most of them in Pago Pago (the administrative centre) or its vicinity. Although in the 1950s an estimated 5000 people, mostly trained young adult Samoans, left the territory to seek greater economic opportunities mainly in Hawaii and California, there was immigration from Western Samoa and Tonga which kept the total population fairly stable. In 1965 there were approximately 5000 aliens in American Samoa in addition to the native population of 21,000. The territory was administered until 1952 by the United States Department of the Navy but has since been transferred to the

Department of the Interior. A similar change took place at the same time in the administration of the more recently acquired United States Trust Territory of the Pacific Islands in Micronesia.

Throughout the period of naval administration emphasis was placed on two things—on the maintenance of the naval base and airstrip, and on native welfare. The two went hand in hand, for many Samoans found employment at the base and a market there for their garden produce. White settlement and economic enterprise were discouraged and the naval administration even marketed the natives' copra. It was a paternalistic rule, on the face of it benevolent and generous enough; but it has failed to prepare the Samoans for self-government or for the competitive commercial world in which they will have to live (with the diminished strategic importance of the islands) unless they are to become museum pieces. Subsidized living standards are higher than in adjacent territories. This is what attracts Western Samoans as temporary and permanent visitors to their kinsfolk in American Samoa. Half the employed population are non-agricultural workers. A quarter work for the government. These proportions are both higher than in any other territory.

Second only to its reliance on American subsidies and government employment, the economy of the territory depends upon the canning of fish. In 1953 it was ruled that fish caught by the Japanese and landed in American Samoa for processing and canning could be subsequently shipped to the United States without payment of tariff. Later that year an American company began canning deep-swimming tuna landed by Japanese fishing boats at Pago Pago. A second company began canning albacore (a white fleshed tuna) in 1963. It also processes fish meal, fish oil and pet foods. The following year a company was established to supply cans for the two canneries. These are cut and shaped from sheets of tinplate imported from California. In 1963 the export of canned tuna and fish by-products was worth $U.S.11.4 millions ($N.Z.8.2 millions), and the three factories employed 830 persons. Fish products comprise 99 per cent by value of all exports from American Samoa.

Tutuila is an elevated, mountainous, volcanic island, with a coastline more broken and its lava flows more deeply dissected than in Upolu or Savai'i. It is twenty-five miles long. The naval base is at the head of the deep indentation in the south coast forming the spacious harbour of Pago Pago. The island has predominantly steep slopes, heavily wooded to their summits. The coast is cliffed and irregular so that villages are often at the head of inlets and at times in fertile inland valleys. The general economy and the subsistence agriculture of the eastern Samoans are not unlike those of their western neighbours. Taro, yams and breadfruit are the chief native food crops, and pineapples, oranges and bananas are grown for sale in Pago Pago. Otherwise copra is the only commercial product. The islands of Tau, Ofu and Olosega, which comprise the Manua group, are steep, conical, volcanic islands with few villages and a little-disturbed native population. Swain's Island, on the other hand, is a coral island raised fifteen or twenty feet above sea level, so that its lagoon is partly dry land and only partly occupied by a shallow sheet of brackish water (*Fig. 7*). It was long the home of an American and his chiefly Samoan wife and family. Today its three small villages have a total population of 65. The villagers cut copra from the coconuts growing profusely in the deep coral sand on the island's low, flat surface. Pandanus and taro supplement their diet of coconut and fish.

THE TOKELAU ISLANDS

Some 270 miles due north of Apia, visited each year by an occasional cutter collecting copra and until 1966 by flying boats of the former R.N.Z.A.F. establishment at Lauthala Bay, Fiji, are three isolated atolls—Atafu, Nukunono and Fakaofo—which comprise the Tokelau Islands (or Union Group), the latest addition to New Zealand's Pacific island territories. Formerly part of the Gilbert and Ellice Islands Colony, and under the jurisdiction of the High Commissioner for the Western Pacific in Suva, the Tokelaus were handed by the United Kingdom to New Zealand for administration through Apia in 1925. In 1949 they were annexed to New Zealand. All are geomorphologically and structurally perfect coral atolls. Nukunono comprises thirty *motus* on a broad, flat reef of coral, six miles by eight miles in size. The *motus*, including the largest in the whole group—four miles long and 300 yards wide—have a total area of 1350 acres. Fakaofo's sixty-one minute islets total only 650 acres, and Atafu's nineteen occupy a mere 500 acres. The total population of the three atolls is over 2175, almost a thousand on Fakaofo and more than 500 on each of the others. These comprise some of the densest populations in the Pacific World, for in all cases settlement is confined to one sandy *motu* on the leeward (western) side of the atoll, where a passage in the reef provides at best dangerous access for small native boats working trading vessels standing off in deep water outside. The islets adjacent to the one on which the village is situated on each atoll are used for planting food crops. At low tide they are accessible on foot along the reef.

The Tokelaus stand in an oceanic borderland between Polynesia and Micronesia. Whatever their earlier population may have been, the islands have been invaded, since their first discovery by Quiros at the beginning of the seventeenth century, by Polynesians from Samoa, with whom the Tokelauans retain linguistic and cultural ties. Their present-day culture, however, has been given a distinctive mould by the atoll environment in which they have lived for two or three centuries. Apart from a little sun-dried copra, all agricultural products are subsistence crops. They consist of *pulaka* and *ta'amu*—two different species of taro—and papaws. In addition the coconut and the edible fruit of the pandanus provide food. The islets are covered with a coarse, rubbly coral sand devoid of humus and organic matter. It supports only pandanus, the coconut palm and a dry scrub vegetation including *tauanave* from which short lengths of timber are secured. All three are used for building houses, while canoes are made from several pieces of *tauanave* lashed together by sennit made from the husk of coconuts. Bananas are a luxury because of their need for a humus-rich soil. They are grown occasionally on Fakaofo. Fish are available both in the lagoon and off the reef. Tuna, trevalli, bonito and mullet are all caught in considerable quantities. A few poultry and pigs are kept and fed on coconut.

On receipt of news of the impending despatch from Apia of a trading schooner chartered by the Trust Estates Corporation (which since the war has conducted the trade of the group because the usual companies found it unprofitable) copra is cut, dried and bagged. Between the calls of vessels the people devote their time to securing food from the gardens, the reef and the lagoon, to the maintenance of their dwellings and tidy settlements, to house-building and to the manufacture from pandanus leaves of woven floor mats, fans and table mats. The craftmanship they exhibit in their handicrafts is of a high order. The three villages in the group are well planned and tidily laid out. The Tokelauans take great pride in the appearance of their homes and villages. The ordered rows of houses under a cluster of waving palms are constructed of *tauanave* and pandanus timbers with walls and roofs of woven pandanus fibres. Their design is quite different from that of the round Samoan *fale*. The gabled roofs and occasional verandas show affinities with the Gilbert and Ellice Islands.

The Tokelau group, because of its small size, limited importance and isolation, presents a difficult constitutional problem. Because of the intensified pressure of population on very limited resources there are also acute economic and social difficulties. New Zealand, as administering authority, is attempting to find solutions to both questions.

Since the Tokelaus are too small to stand in isolation it was suggested in 1965 that the people might like to associate politically either with an independent Western Samoa or a self-governing Cook Islands. Representatives from the Tokelaus visited both Apia and Rarotonga. They decided, however, at an inter-island conference to reject both suggestions for amalgamation and asked instead for continued direct association with New Zealand.

In 1966, at the insistent request of the islanders themselves, New Zealand launched, first, a pilot project, and then a three-year plan (1966-1968) of transferring Tokelau islanders to New Zealand in order to relieve the pressure of population there. There is already a Tokelauan community of 300 persons in New Zealand. They have come, via Apia, in the postwar years on their own initiative and at their own expense. The new plan proposes to bring an additional 200 islanders to the Dominion in a period of three years. The first contingent—of single young people—arrived early in 1966. Later it is intended, under the plan, to assist family groups to resettle in New Zealand with special arrangements for their housing and welfare. Single women are provided with work and accommodation in hospitals and other institutions. Family groups will be housed in a settling-in area near Taupo and work will be provided for the men in nearby forestry projects.

At the same time improved educational facilities are being provided in each of the three atolls, especially facilities for adult education. The intention is to prepare future immigrants to New Zealand with training before their departure, and to equip those who remain in the isolation of the mid-Pacific so that they may better handle their island problems and take an increasingly effective part in their own administration. It is intended that three island *fonos* (councils of family heads) should assist in deciding priorities for government expenditure in the Tokelau Islands and should give further consideration to the islands' future constitutional evolution.

It will be interesting to watch not only the progress of the resettlement plan but also the future development of this miniature example of the movement of a dependent Pacific island territory towards independence and fuller participation in both its own affairs and in the life of the world outside its ocean-isolated environment.

WALLIS AND FUTUNA
(ÎLES WALLIS ET FUTUNA)

Between Fiji and Samoa, and south of a line joining Rotuma and the Tokelaus which outlines the northern fringe of New Zealand's Pacific island neighbourhood, are the French-controlled islands of Wallis and Futuna (Hoorn). They constitute a colony of France and are administered from Noumea, New Caledonia. The Wallis group consists of the islands of an 'almost atoll'. An off-shore encircling reef, almost fifty miles round, encloses a lagoon in which stands the volcanic island of Uvea. There are also twelve small islets, mainly of coral sand, either on the reef or within the lagoon. Uvea has an area of nearly 15,000 acres and rises to a height of 470 feet. Small lakes occupy the crater of the extinct island volcano. Its slopes are well wooded.

This small group provides a variety of soils and agricultural situations. On Uvea are soils derived from the volcanic rock, from alluvium and from coral limestone. Copra and trochus are the main exports, but coffee, cocoa, and vanilla are grown spasmodically for sale, and taro, tapioca, citrus, bananas and breadfruit for local consumption. Tapa cloth is still made from the paper mulberry. Uvea and the islets have a population of nearly 5750 persons, all but thirty-five of them natives. Mata Utu on the east coast of Uvea is the largest village. It is the seat of the French Resident and administration, and from it roads radiate westwards over the hilly island linking all the villages by motor transport.

Futuna and Alofi, which comprise the Futuna or Hoorn group, are both isolated upstanding volcanic islands, rising respectively to the substantial elevations of over 2500 and 1250 feet. Both are hilly, well-watered, wooded islands. Futuna has an area of over 16,000 acres and Alofi, five miles to the southeast, is less than half that size. Like the islands of the Wallis group their native population is Polynesian and appears to have links with both Samoa and Tonga. The population of 2700 is almost exclusively indigenous. There are small coconut plantations but the natives practise a subsistence agriculture of diversified character, as befits the varied environments of the high volcanic islands of the Pacific World.

FIJI

The British Crown Colony of Fiji is not only a valuable asset and perhaps the best example of British colonial endeavour in the Pacific, but it is also the insular hub and crossroads of the southwestern part of the ocean. Fiji is to the southwest Pacific and to Australia and New Zealand what Hawaii is to the north Pacific and to the North American continent. Like Hawaii, Fiji is a considerable source of tropical produce, a market for manufactured goods and processed foodstuffs, first stop on trans-Pacific journeys either by jet or passenger ship, strategic outpost, advanced air base and winter tourist resort. Just as traffic for North America diverges at Honolulu for Vancouver, Seattle, San Francisco and Los Angeles, so traffic for Australia and New Zealand diverges at Nandi and Suva. And going the other way, Nandi and the port of Suva are the jumping-off places for 'points east'—the scattered island territories of Polynesia

—as is Honolulu for 'points west'—the minute island specks of Micronesia as far west as Tokyo and Manila.

Excluding only Hawaii, Fiji is economically the most important island group in the Pacific World as here defined. Together, the territories of New Guinea and Papua have an area which is twenty-six times as large as that of the 320 or so islands of the Fiji group, but the value of their total trade is no more than two-thirds that of the Crown Colony. Fiji stands third amongst the island territories of the Pacific World in the size of its population. Australian New Guinea has an uncounted indigenous Melanesian population of possibly two millions and a quarter; Hawaii has a polyglot population of over 800,000 and Fiji a rapidly expanding population—more than half Indian—of 500,000. Moreover, its problems are as varied and as fascinating and as difficult of solution as those of any other dependent territory in the Pacific.

PACIFIC CROSSROADS

Fiji owes much to its actual location within the Pacific. Suva, Auckland, and Brisbane form the corners of a roughly equilateral triangle. The main islands of the group lie centrally amongst the larger and more important insular territories of the southwest Pacific. Tonga and Samoa are Fiji's more important neighbours, but New Caledonia and the New Hebrides are not much further away, and the Solomons, Gilbert and Ellice Islands, and the Cook and Society Islands are as close to Suva, or closer, than is Wellington. Many of these groups are now linked by the services of Fiji Airways. In Fiji, Melanesia and Polynesia come together and merge. Within the group at Rotuma, and especially in the outlying Lau group to the east, there has been a diffusion and exchange of Polynesian and Melanesian culture and custom, and a mingling of people themselves.

Since early in the period of European exploitation of the Pacific island territories, Fiji has been an important calling point for shipping, and a place at which goods were collected and transhipped. First Levuka, on Ovalau, and later Ngaloa on Kandavu (at which for a decade goods, mail and passengers were transhipped from vessels on the San Francisco-Sydney service for New Zealand and the islands) were the Fijian points of call. Finally the well-equipped harbour and port of Suva took over the expanding *entrepôt* traffic. In more recent times the jet airport at Nandi, the flying-boat base at Lauthala Bay and the Suva airport at Nausori have added to the important routeways converging on Viti Levu and to the functions of Fiji as a Pacific crossroads, although New Zealand has now decided to close down the base at Lauthala Bay and finally scrap its flying boats. Fiji has also had a central position politically and administratively. Suva is not only the centre of administration for the Fiji island group, but until 1952 was the headquarters of the High Commission for the Western Pacific, through which were handled Britain's interest in the Solomons, New Hebrides, Tonga, the Gilbert and Ellice Islands and other smaller groups. Moreover Suva is also the medical, educational and military centre of the island territories of the area. From New Guinea to Tahiti students go to Suva to school or to train as medical practitioners. It will before long be the site of a southwest Pacific university. There appears to be a real possibility of a university utilizing the Lauthala Bay buildings and teaching its first courses in 1968 or 1969. It seems a great pity that the head-quarters of the South Pacific Commission could not have been placed in Suva rather than in the less central and less accessible New Caledonian capital of Noumea.

The colony's crossroads location in the southwest Pacific, and its increasing accessibility with the development of inter-continental jet air services, have contributed significantly to the recent rapid growth of its tourist trade. Two other things have been important: the scenery of the islands and their palm-fringed tropical reefs and strands; and the colour and life provided by the multiracial population and culture, and es-pecially the preservation of much of the indigenous village life, culture, songs, dances and ceremonies of the Fijians. So suc-cessful has been the drive for tourist traffic and the building of hotels in Suva and at strategic coastal points on the King's and Queen's roads (which together encircle the island of Viti Levu) that tourism now stands second only to the export of sugar as an earner of foreign currency. In each of the years 1962-1965 inclusive there was an increase of between 24 and 33 per cent in the number of visitors to Fiji. Ninety-four per cent of them arrived by air, and approximately equal proportions came from New Zealand, Australia and the United States.

STRUCTURE AND CONFIGURATION

The archipelago is one of 'continental' islands lying on two partly submerged platforms which are joined northeast of Taveuni and which represent the outermost edge of the continental structure of the western margin of the Pacific (*Fig. 90*). In the numerous islands of the archipelago continental sedimentary and volcanic rocks are represented as well as the coral limestone and basaltic lava. The latter, of course, are more commonly the materials of which the truly oceanic islands of the central Pacific are built. On the broad northern shelf stand the larger islands of Viti Levu, Vanua Levu, Taveuni, Kandavu, the islands of Lomaiviti (Ngau, Ovalau and Koro) and the Yasawas. The narrower eastern shelf, elongated and running almost due north and south, has on it the scores of small volcanic, limestone and coral islands which constitute the Lau group. Between the two platforms are the deeper waters of the Koro Sea, and east of the 300-mile sweep of the Lau Islands the ocean floor falls away rapidly to considerable depths.

Like New Zealand, New Caledonia and other continental islands, Viti Levu and Vanua Levu (with together almost four million acres—Viti Levu two and a half millions and Vanua Levu one and a half millions) have a complicated structure and geological history. Both are large 'high' islands mainly of ancient volcanic and more recent andesitic rocks, but also partly of Cretaceous and Tertiary sedimentary rocks mixed in an almost indecipherable jumble. The interiors are elevated, broken, cut by deep valleys, wet and forested. The tumbled skyline is often broken abruptly by the up-thrust, almost vertically-walled, 'thumbs' or 'spikes' which are the remnant necks or plugs of volcanoes, the main mass of which has been removed by denudation. In both cases lowland is restricted in area, though valleys lead back deep into the confusion of hills and dissected plateaus of the interior. Some rivers, however, fed by heavy tropical rains, and much larger than one would expect from the limited area of their catchments, have built up deltas around the coasts. In Viti Levu the lower valleys and deltas of the Rewa, Navua and Mba provide low-lying cultivable land, though much of the

Rewa and Navua deltas are still swampy, undrained and fringed with mangrove thickets. The occasional lowlands of Vanua Levu are mainly on the dry (northwestern) side and are broken into separate small pockets by projecting ranges of low hills.

Ovalau and Taveuni are both high volcanic islands. Ovalau is roughly circular and its outer slopes rise steeply to a concentric series of peaks 2000 feet in elevation overlooking the

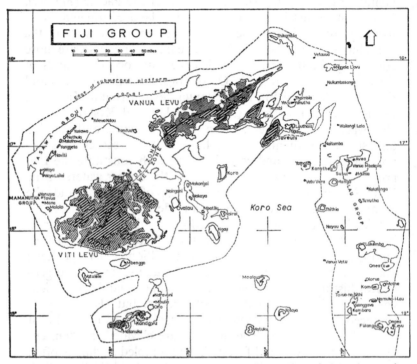

Figure 90: The Fiji Group, showing surrounding reefs and the submerged shelf on which the group lies

deep crater of the old andesite volcano. Taveuni is twenty-six miles long and has a 3000-4000 feet high backbone formed by a line of volcanic cones of recent origin and activity. In cross-section it is like the gable of a roof, and the surface of the basaltic lava flows have steep but unusually uniform slopes to the sea in both the east and the west. The innumerable smaller islands of Fiji have an almost infinite variety of form and structure, and they are strewn indiscriminately over a quarter of a million square miles of ocean, mainly but not entirely, to the east of the larger units. The same expanse of sea is threaded with a maze of coral reefs, flanking closely all the sea lanes and closing all but a few approaches to the centre of the group (*Fig. 90*). The menace these reefs present to shipping in part explains why Tasman and Cook, who both touched at the group, failed to investigate and chart it, and also why Bligh, in an open rowing boat with six oars (after the mutiny of the *Bounty* in 1789), was the first European to penetrate deeply amongst the islands of Fiji. Very few of the islands in the group are coral atolls. Most of the lesser islands of Lau have a complex structure and consist of volcanic materials or of uplifted bedded limestones which rain and waves have at times cut into fantastic shapes.

WET AND DRY ZONES

Meteorological conditions in Fiji are not, in general, different from those of neighbouring groups in similar latitudes. The trades blow steadily and with little interruption during most of the year. But from November to March or April winds are more variable, and may often have a westerly or a northerly component. This is the season when both the 'heat equator' and the intertropical front reach farthest south. It is the season in which intense tropical storms are most likely to develop just south of the Equator and speed along a curved track which takes them first to the west then southwards and finally off in a broad sweep to the southeast. To Fiji this is both the 'wet season' and the 'hurricane season'. Such terms are, however, liable to be misleading. At any one place many years may pass without a tropical storm of unusual intensity; and the so-called 'dry season' is in fact by world standards often very wet.

Suva—on the windward side of Viti Levu—has an annual average rainfall of 121 inches, but annual totals have ranged between 73 and 221 inches. Normally most of this rain falls in the summer half-year when winds are most variable, with maximum monthly totals between December and March. July is the driest month but may have anything up to eighteen inches of rain, which is more than the average *annual* total of most of Australia and indeed of some parts of the South Island of

New Zealand. Suva is representative of the windward or 'wet zone' not only of Viti Levu but also of Vanua Levu, Taveuni and Kandavu. Temperatures, cloudiness and relative humidity are all high and vary little through the year.

Both Lambasa and Lautoka are representative of the rather different weather and climate of the 'dry zone'. The larger islands are sufficiently large and elevated to create a rain shadow on their leeward side, and especially on lee coastlands. Here the seasons are more sharply differentiated. Between November and April, when variable winds blow, Lautoka has three times as much rain, and Lambasa four times as much, as during the 'dry' season when the trades dominate the situation. Whereas June, July and August at both stations average only two inches a month, both February and March have over twelve inches at Lautoka and over 14 inches at Lambasa. In the 'dry' season the rain-shadow areas, especially on Viti Levu and Vanua Levu, have clear skies, lower humidity and greater variations in daily temperature so that the evening air can feel quite cool: in January, on the other hand, tropical downpours are often accompanied by hot, sultry weather with both temperatures and humidity higher than in the wet zones to the east.

The interiors of the large islands have much heavier rainfall, with totals over 300 inches, higher humidity and almost constant mist and cloud. On the other hand the small islands with their restricted elevation have the least variation in weather and climate from season to season, the most equable temperatures and a moderate rainfall which is more evenly distributed through the year.

PLANT COVER

Most of Fiji was originally forested, and more than half the total area, mainly on wet, windward slopes, still has a cover of tropical rainforest, with mountain rainforest on the cooler, mist-shrouded upper slopes of the larger islands and many thousands of acres of mangrove on ill-drained deltas and littoral fringes. Much of the forest however has been burned or had its timber extracted. Even before Europeans arrived the Fijians cleared forested slopes to cultivate their food crops, and abandoned them subsequently to second growth forest, bamboo, hibiscus and even reeds. The first Europeans combed the islands in search of sandalwood, and found much of it on Vanua Levu. Later traders and settlers have accelerated the exploitation of timber—*ndakua* (Fijian kauri), *vesi* and *mbuambua*, the most durable of Fijian timbers.

In both Viti Levu and Vanua Levu the transition from wet to dry zone is abrupt, not only on the coast but also in the broken mountainous interior. The dull green of the rainforest, relieved only by flashes of lighter green in the valleys, is replaced sharply by the brighter yellow-green of grassland and the arid brown and red colours of the parched savanna. Only here and there in the moister upland interior does a stunted forest and shrubland persist in the drier halves of the two islands. It is a matter for investigation to determine what the original vegetation of the dry zone was. Today it is predominantly a grassland vegetation, often dominated by a variety of introduced tropical grasses or the indigenous reed grass (*ngasau*). To the driest-looking lowland areas, with a short-grass vegetation, broken here and there by parched patches of fern, harsh low scrub and stretches of bare red soil, which is usually eroded, the Fijian gives the name *talasinga*, signifying sun-drenched or sun-burned country. Elsewhere in the dry zone the grassland has the form of savanna; the undulating low hills are covered with tall grass and reeds interrupted occasionally by small clumps or isolated trees of feathery *nokonoko* (casuarina), wind-rustled pandanus and introduced acacias. This is the *vanua singasinga* or open country. It is possible that the present vegetation of this area is an induced cover, replacing a denser, taller, natural vegetation after clearing and burning in pre-European times, and after the repeated firing of the parched grassy carpet by Indian tenant farmers and cattle rearers in more recent decades.

As one goes further east within the Fiji group the flora becomes poorer and poorer, partly because of the smaller size and more limited environments of the lesser islands, but also because of the increasing distance from the Malayan and Indonesian source regions. Many of the coral and limestone islands of Lau have a very restricted natural vegetation. Coconut palms, pandanus trees, and shrub growth constitute the most permanent plants in a vegetative covering which is discontinuous. All these are adapted to the relatively dry conditions produced, not by low rainfall, but by the thin, sandy soils.

VARIETY OF LANDSCAPES

The islands of Fiji thus present a great variety of environments and many sharply contrasted landscapes. There is the reef-fringed shore with its dark foliage and its golden strand, then the blue lagoon and the vivid white surf of the reef beyond. There are the deep, quiet valleys of the wet zone, with rain-drenched forest hiding the yellow residual clay soils of the hillsides, the thickets of grey-green mangrove over the flat stretch of the delta of the Rewa and its many meandering distributaries, the brown sun-drenched hills of the dry zone, the coastal *talasinga* with its sparse vegetation, its cool, clear nights and scorching hot days, the coral islets thick with palms but devoid of drinking water and the fantastic shape and strangely-eroded surface of low limestone islands.

This physical diversity of Fiji is reinforced by the cultural variety which now characterizes the Crown colony. Not only Melanesians but also Polynesians contributed to the indigenous culture of Fiji, and to this must now be added the cultural contributions of an alien Asian majority from a number of different parts of India, of a distinctive, if small, group of Chinese, and of an influential minority of Europeans. Today not only is the peace of an inland, riverside Fijian *koro* characteristic of Fiji, but also the hive-like activity of the Indian bazaar, the bustle of the sugar mill in the cane crushing season, the ordered pattern and commercial motivation of the European plantation, the drab workers' lines and massive machinery of the Australian-operated gold mine and the quietly efficient air of the isolated government outpost presided over by the District Officer of the British colonial administration.

THE INDIGENIOUS CULTURE AND ECONOMY

At the time of its discovery by Europeans the archipelago was occupied by tall, dark-skinned Negroid Melanesians. In the eastern islets, and even on the eastern mainland of Viti Levu, an admixture of Polynesian blood and culture, probably mainly from Tonga, was also evident. The Fijians lived most often in forested coastal districts of the main islands and in the coconut-dominated reef islets of the Lau group. Their villages were tight compact communities of inter-related families. Small-scale feuding was chronic among rival chiefs and associated groups of villages. Settlements were therefore originally sited with an eye to defence and to security from attack. Off-shore islands like Mbau and Serua were often favoured, and so, too, were hill fortresses and moated sites in the mangrove-threaded deltas. But most of the people lived on the shore and in forested river valleys that penetrate deeply into the hill country of the wet zone.

Access to water was important, not only because both river and lagoon provided a source of food, but also because most transport was by water. River communities had dug-out canoes, and also, for exchanging goods with coastal villages, rafts of lashed bamboo. Coastal communities had their fleets of out-rigger canoes which they used not only for coastwise transport but also for fishing in the lagoon and on the open sea. Transport by land was confined to single-file bush tracks, knee-deep in orange-yellow clay, climbing steeply over from one valley to another. Off the main roads (see *Fig. 92*) communications are still much the same today, and it is the duty of the village labour force to maintain the trackways within each acknowledged village area.

Each family had its house site, together with proprietary rights to the land on the valley flat and on the steep forested slopes, where food was grown in small garden clearings or *teitei*, by a primitive system of shifting cultivation. Some few villages, however, had permanent irrigated *ndalo* (taro) beds. The forest was an important resource. It provided timber for building and for canoes, and fuel for cooking. Fibres, dyes and medicines all came from different forest species. In old clearings edible roots were collected, including especially the wild yam. The Fijian had at hand materials in variety with which he built some of the sturdiest dwellings found in the Pacific. In the wet zone his *mbure* is still framed with very heavy timbers, with walls and roof coverings made of the stems and leaves of reeds or possibly of sago or coconut fibres, all lashed together in a most thorough manner with sennit dyed in many colours. In the dry zone stout timber is used more sparingly, and is often replaced by bamboo. Split bamboo, plaited to form attractive patterns, is used for walls, and a thick tight thatch, tidily-trimmed at the edges, is carried on a light bamboo trellis. In the coral and limestone islets greater reliance had, and still has, to be placed on coconut and pandanus.

Three all-important traditional concepts permeated both the economic activities and the social life of the Fijian community. The first was the mutual aid and the communal work rendered by all physically fit members of the community. The building of *mbure*, the tidying of the village, the maintenance of the canoe fleet and of footpaths were communal responsibilities assigned by the village council and headman. *Kerekere* referred to the reciprocal sharing of goods and food and the entertaining of visitors. *Kerekere* was a method of protecting the needy, an indigenous system of social security found in a variety of forms throughout the Pacific. The third concept was the chiefly right—*lala*—to extract tribute, especially from outsiders allowed to settle on the land of a community. This contributed to the political cohesion of associated villages and made for larger political units.

European Impact

Much of this traditional way of life is still found amongst those Fijians who live on the outlying islands and also on the large islands away from the coastal trading points and growing towns as well as in the valleys remote from the coastal roads. These districts have not been penetrated to any extent by the immigrant Indians and remain predominantly Fijian in economy and custom (*Fig. 95*). It has been a general attitude of British colonial policy to preserve the ancient way of life of native peoples in so far as is reasonably possible, and the majority of the Fijians live and work and play basically much as their forebears did, although the recent war and the economic, social and political developments of the last twenty years have brought changes as rapid and as fundamental as in any earlier period of Fijian-European contact.

The European penetration of Fiji falls into three distinct periods: first a period of early trading after the initial exploration; then a period of large-scale economic exploitation; and thirdly a current period in which the tendency is towards the break-up of the large estates and plantations, towards the spread of a small-scale commercial agriculture practised by both Fijians and Indians, and towards a growth of towns and industries and a general diversification of the economy of the colony.

Sandalwood and *bêche-de-mer* were the goods first sought

after, but before European settlement began in the 1860s visiting traders were collecting a wide range of native-grown agricultural products for shipment, including bark, rattan canes, yams, candlenuts, ivory nuts and tapa cloth. The American Civil War, and the high prices for cotton which resulted from it, first gave stimulus to the plantation economy, to the purchase and leasing of Fijian land and to the inflow of capital. But in 1870 the demand for Fiji-grown cotton disappeared, and for a number of years the planters had economic difficulties during which they sought for an alternative crop. Meanwhile internal warfare and political unrest culminated in the Deed of Cession in 1874, which encouraged commercial enterprise, although planters lived from hand to mouth for another twenty years. But by the 1890s, what are today Fiji's outstanding agricultural products—copra, sugar and green fruit (bananas) —were the principal exports. Experimentation with a great variety of crops had revealed the most successful lines of development. Once the most profitable crops had been found, labour became the crucial problem. The Fijians were at this time in the early stages of their struggle for survival after the inter-tribal warfare of the middle of the century and the ravages of introduced diseases. Their numbers were in decline. Nor were they accustomed to the regular routine of labour in commercial activities. In the 1870s Solomon islanders were introduced, but were later repatriated. The first Indian labourers were brought in under indenture in 1879. This was an experiment that proved highly successful, at least from the point of view of the establishment of large-scale commercial plantation agriculture; and up to 1916, when the system was abolished, over 60,000 Indian labourers were brought to the colony—Hindustani-speaking peasants from the United Provinces, tall bearded Sikhs from the northwest, Punjabis, Madrassis and Gujeratis from near Bombay. And many of them chose to stay.

THE ROLE OF INDIANS IN FIJI

It was the Indians who laid the foundations of the sugar industry, and it is their rapidly increasing number of descendants who today grow most of the cane and supply the labour force in the crushing mills. Now, too, they operate much of the road transport system of the colony, are busy artisans and shop-keepers, and provide the bulk of the urban population. Visitors to Fiji, seeing only the largest towns and ports, especially Suva, Nandi and Lautoka, may well have the impression that Fiji is a 'Little India of the Pacific'. The Australian Colonial Sugar Refining Company Limited (C.S.R.) established interests in Fiji in 1880, and by 1920 had absorbed the other planting companies and was milling all the sugar cane produced in the colony. It still has larger financial interests in Fiji than any other concern. Today, however, this subsidiary of the Colonial Sugar Refining Company operates in Fiji under the name of South Pacific Sugar Mills.

The copra plantation industry was the other which survived the experimental stages. Whilst cane-growing became established mainly in coastal lowland areas of the dry zone on both Viti Levu and Vanua Levu, coconut plantations were located mainly on the damp windward littoral fringe of Vanua Levu and on the lower basaltic slopes of Taveuni and on many a smaller island (*Fig. 91*). They did not compete with the sugar estates for Indian labour. Work on coconut estates proved more congenial to the Fijian because it proceeds at a slower pace and lacks the compelling grind of seasonal operations found in the cane-growing industry. With the subsequent decline of the large estates, Fijians have become responsible for almost two-thirds of the copra output of the colony, but they produce only an insignificant proportion of the sugar cane.

The large-scale cultivation and export of bananas also persisted, reaching a peak during World War I, when in one year no less than 1,650,000 bunches of green fruit were shipped to Australia and New Zealand. But with the exhaustion of soils by this gross-feeding crop, together with the spread of plant diseases, and above all with the penal duties imposed in Australia to protect the banana growers of Queensland and New South Wales, there was a decline of European plantations in the 1920s, and much of the land in the southeast of Viti Levu, formerly in bananas, was given over to dairying, and the growing of sugar cane and rice. In recent years all the bananas exported have come from native Fijian gardens, mainly in the deep, sheltered middle valleys of the tributaries of the Rewa. Today only one-third of the copra amongst the major crops, and only pineapples amongst the minor crops, are produced by large-scale operations on the plantation system.

SUGAR CANE

The economy of Fiji is today based upon three export products—sugar, copra (and coconut oil) and gold—upon a rapidly developing tourist industry and upon the production of domestic foodstuffs. Gold is only of temporary interest and importance, so that agriculture is the major industry and the basis of the welfare of a population now approaching half a million. Sugar is increasingly the single most important crop. In 1964 it accounted for 77 per cent of the value of all exports. After the termination of the indenture system it was necessary to evolve a method of cane-growing by small farmers. Land, owned or leased by the Colonial Sugar Refining Company, was allocated to Indian tenants on the basis of a farm unit of about twelve acres, that being the area capable of being worked by an Indian family. By 1930 this system was well established and has proved highly successful. Today all but three per cent of the cane is produced by small farmers and supplied by them to the company for crushing.

The cane is grown on more than 130,000 acres, and the annual crop weighs 2.3 million tons. The 1964 crush produced a record of 307,000 tons of sugar. Cane has done best in the dry zone (*Fig. 91*). Here the larger alluvial lowlands from the valley of the Singatoka round to Viti Levu Bay in the northeast, and the near-flat land in western Vanua Levu look like miniature seas of varying colours of green, rich and dark in the case of the ratoon crop and light and yellowish in the case of the plant cane. They stretch discontinuously along the coast and reach back to the dry-looking, brown, grassy hills behind. The small-holding of each industrious, patient, plodding Indian family has in any one year one part devoted to newly-planted cane, one in ratoon cane (from which one crop has already been taken), one in rice or a leguminous crop, usually beans for ploughing in, and a fourth which is officially fallow (according to the land-use regulations laid down by the company) but which is these days used increasingly, without reducing subsequent cane yields, for family food crops—rice, *dahl* (lentils), peas, beans, millet and vegetables. The cane lands present trim and tidy landscapes with thousands of small unfenced areas of crop, the tall cane almost hiding the low thatched dwellings in which live the peasant families.

In addition to buying and crushing the cane, the company also advances money to its tenants, purchases their fertilizers and machinery, lays down good husbandry regulations, conducts research and provides new varieties of cane, and organizes the co-operative harvesting of the crop and the transport of the cane to one or other of the four crushing mills. These mills

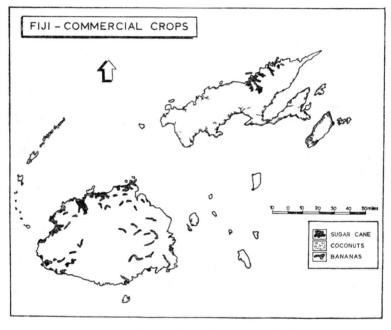

Figure 91

are in the centre of the largest areas of continuous cane cultivation. There are mills at Lautoka, Mba and Penang (in the Viti Levu dry zone), and at Lambasa (in Vanua Levu). The company has 440 miles of permanent light-railway track and 160 miles of portable line, this being used in the season to connect the individual producers' fields with the main line. The largest single stretch of line runs 120 miles from the east bank of the Singatoka, through Nandi, Lautoka, and Mba to Tavua. Free rides are available to passengers throughout its length. It is significant that this railway serves practically the whole of the dry zone of Viti Levu, in which (except for Suva and the lower Rewa) the Indian population is most densely concentrated, and in which Indians overwhelmingly exceed Fijians in numbers (cf. *Figs. 94* and *95*). The mill towns—marked by the tall stack of the mill chimney—and also the other towns in the dry zone cane-growing districts are essentially Indian settlements. Their streets are thronged with a busy crowd and lined with the

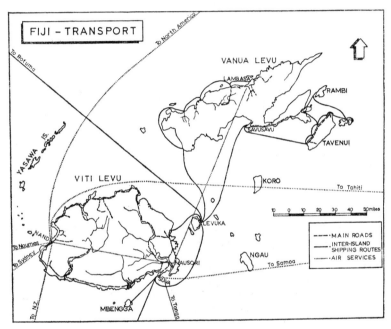

Figure 92

small shops of Indian vendors and artisans, and their residential quarters are rigidly zoned, with company executives and engineers living usually in a select European quarter on a hill overlooking the collection of Indian hutments below. On Vanua Levu, Lambasa is linked with its cane-producing hinterlands by ninety miles of permanent track and, like Nandi or Lautoka, is an Indian town.

SMALL-SCALE COMMERCIAL FARMING

Even before the termination of the indenture system many Indians chose to stay in Fiji and leased or purchased land, usually on the low slopes in the dry zone. Here they built one-roomed shacks walled and roofed with reed grass and here they cultivated in primitive fashion their minute holdings. Today they grow rice, *dahl*, *mungh*, pigeon peas and maize for food and occasionally small patches of peanuts, rice or sugar cane for sale. On poor land they plod on patiently day after day and eke out a miserable existence. Some of these poverty-stricken peasants have 'holdings' of no more than an acre or two, which they lease or sub-lease from other Indians who have managed to buy or lease land from Europeans who obtained title to it before the Deed of Cession. Because of the hopeless indebtedness of the Indian peasant—often the result of having to find marriage dowries for his daughters—his land is badly treated and overcropped. The surface soil is a deep red in colour. Much of it is being rapidly eroded. Raw gullies are beginning to cut across many a gentle slope. Crop yields are already desperately low, and are falling.

But the most serious wastage of the soil resources of the colony is taking place within a few miles of its capital. In the broken, low, hilly country between Suva and Nausori most of the soil has already gone from an area which once carried a tropical forest with great stands of *ndakur*. Indians, Chinese and some Fijians are cultivating shallow soils on short but steep slopes and are growing row crops and also other crops intensively, and without fallowing. Their produce is destined for the Suva market and for export to Auckland on the *Matua* or *Tofua*. In many instances the cultivation of pineapples, taro, *yanggona* (the root of which is dried and powdered and used to make the beverage and ceremonial drink *kava*), Chinese cabbage, bananas, tomatoes, tobacco and a range of European vegetables, has changed a district that scarcely more than a generation ago was a little-disturbed extent of rainforest. It is now an untidy expanse of low hills with minute gardens often built up from soil retrieved from lower down the slope, with bare raw stretches of soapstone, and with abandoned rocky tracts of noxious weed growths. The outward expansion of the urban population of Suva is invading these untidy garden areas and forcing the cultivation of market garden crops further from the city market.

COCONUTS AND COPRA

Of the 130,000 acres in cane on the coastlands of the dry zones of the two main islands, about half is harvested each year in a six-month period of hectic activity in both canefield and crushing mills. But from the 168,000 acres of coconuts spread throughout the islands and islets of the colony, a steady flow of nuts is taken from almost every acre throughout the year. Coconut-oil, copra and coprameal in 1964 represented 12 per cent of Fiji's exports. One half of the copra is cut in Fijian villages and the other half on European plantations, large and small. Coastal soils, wetter climates and Fijian population go together with copra production in Fiji, excepting only that on this basis the coastal areas of Viti Levu do not have the production they should have. (See *Figures 91* and *95*.) This is because until thirty-five years ago coconuts on Viti Levu and Ovalau suffered from the depredations of a purple moth which make the palm's lofty clump of foliage yellow and fruitless. After 1925, however, entomologists introduced from Malaya a fly which, as a parasite, soon effectively controlled the moth. Since then new planting has taken place, and Fijian village production on Viti Levu is increasing. But in 1953 the dreaded rhinoceros beetle was found on palms in Suva Harbour and in other parts of the southeastern districts of Viti Levu. The beetle was presumably imported accidentally by some vessel calling at Suva. The beetle has already done very great damage to copra production in Samoa and has recently extended its ravages to Vava'u in Tonga. Drastic measures are being taken in Fiji to restrict the spread of the beetle and if possible to exterminate it.

Most of the plantations are on the coastal fringe of the Vanua Levu wet zone and on the accessible and roaded west coast of Taveuni. Many of the coconut plantations in Vanua Levu are on moderately-sized holdings of a few hundred acres running back into the hills near the coast. Some *ndakur* and *vesi* and other timber is still being cut out. Coconuts were planted on the easier coastal slopes before the turn of the century. The major characteristics of such plantations are illustrated in *Figure 93*. Across Somosomo Strait, along the coastal rim of the great flows of basalt of which Taveuni is built, is a succession of large plantations dating from the 1880s, some of which were started as sugar plantations, and today extending twenty-six miles without interruption from Vuna at the southern tip

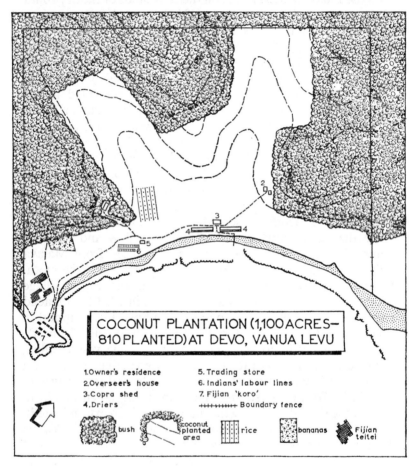

COCONUT PLANTATION (1,100 ACRES— 810 PLANTED) AT DEVO, VANUA LEVU

1. Owner's residence
2. Overseer's house
3. Copra shed
4. Driers
5. Trading store
6. Indians' labour lines
7. Fijian 'koro'
++++++++ Boundary fence

bush   coconut planted area   rice   bananas   Fijian teitei

Figure 93

to Naselesele in the north, and then across to the smaller islands of Nggamea and Lauthala. The measured ranks of palms sweep inland for about a mile—and up to an elevation of 500 feet—and appear from the deck of a copra boat off-shore like a smooth rich green carpet against the rougher texture and darker shade of the rain-drenched bush on the higher slopes beyond. Some holdings run to 8000 acres, with half their area in trees, and produce as much as 500 to 1000 tons of copra a year (at almost $100 a ton). At least one plantation has its own picture theatre near the workers' lines and its own airstrip. Both Indians and Fijians provide labour, but in recent years adequate labour has been difficult to find. The palms are already getting beyond the age of bearing and, with weed infestation increasing, many nuts are not being recovered. A third of the palms on the European operated estates are more than fifty years old. On some plantations both cattle and goats are kept, and wild cattle roam the forested slopes above the plantations. There is room, however, for many more cattle on the estates. But the bulk of Fiji's copra is cut from scattered trees on coral strands or around native *koros*, especially in the smaller islands of Lomaiviti and Lau, and is collected in innumerable places by the monthly or bi-monthly copra boat, but ten bags at a time rather than hundreds.

The inter-island shipping provided by the small fleet of copra boats is the economic lifeline of the smaller islands (*Fig. 92*). These assorted small vessels are operated often by the trading companies. The *Yanawai* is typical if somewhat better equipped. Four times a year it makes a government-subsidized trip to Rotuma to collect copra there, but it sails frequently from Suva to Levuka (Ovalau), to Savusavu (Vanua Levu), to the string of plantations on the coasts of both sides of Somosomo Strait, to Rambi (where live a colony of Banabans from Ocean Island), to Kioa (with its colony of Ellice islanders), to Nggamea and to Lauthala. Its crew is Gilbertese. Its outward cargo includes dressed timber, mechanical equipment, softboard, petrol, biscuits, soap, sharps, onions and assorted store goods. It has passenger accommodation for half a dozen planters returning from business visits to Suva or holiday trips to New Zealand and Australia. Its inward cargo consists principally of copra (as much as 4000 bags, possibly 250 tons) but also includes twenty or thirty live cattle and a deck 'cargo' of Indians and Fijians with their bedding, kits of bananas, yams, papaws and avacado pears, crates with pigs, roosters, turtles and turkeys—gifts for relations in Levuka or Suva.

BANANAS

Third amongst Fiji's commercial agriculture products—but a long way behind sugar and copra—stand bananas. Like the coconut, the banana is both a food plant and an export crop. The export crop of from 150,000 to 250,000 cases (worth from $350,000 to $600,000) comes from a very small fraction of the innumerable tiny patches of banana plants—amounting in all to 5000 acres. As a commercial crop the banana is in decline. Today for example rice for sale in Fiji is more important. Its acreage has increased to more than 30,000.

Banana-growing for export is today almost exclusively an extension of native village agriculture—a small-scale commercial graft on a subsistence economy. It is confined largely to the rich deep alluvial soils of the river terraces in the valleys of the Waindina, Wainimala and Wainimbuka—tributaries of the Rewa in the Viti Levu wet zone. Here at irregular intervals neatly-ordered clusters of *mbure* are sited in trim short-grass clearings on the river terraces. All around hills of forest and of bamboo and second growth, marking former clearings, hem in the valley settlements. Adjacent slopes, with their yellow-red tropical clay soils, provide land for the rotation of food-crop gardens by repeated clearing. Amongst the taller trees and the burned remnants of the smaller ones the *matanggali* has its steeply-sloping patches of over-burned and eroding gardens (*teitei*). Here the village families grow yams, *ndalo* (taro), tapioca and occasionally *kumala* (kumara). Immediately around the *koro* are coconut, breadfruit and papaw trees and *yanggona* plants. And at a distance from the village along the terrace, usually at some well-sheltered bend of the river, and almost lost in tall reeds and grasses, each family has its banana plants. After the *Tofua* was put on the islands run from Auckland, and after the disastrous hurricane of January 1952, these areas in bananas were extended. As a result Fiji's export of bananas doubled in the year 1953. In the 1960s however there has been a steady decline in the number of cases exported. This is due in part to the recently discovered black-leaf streak disease. Two or three days before a vessel is due to leave Suva for Auckland (or, at times, for Vancouver), the village picks its bananas, builds bamboo rafts, and poles its crop down-river to the open-air packing stations on the river bank, where the bunches are broken into 'hands', and the 'hands' into 'fingers' (or single fruit), and then packed in cases of native timber. From the packing stations the export crop is taken by lorry or is lightered on small barges down the Rewa and so on to Suva where final inspection takes place before shipment.

LIVESTOCK

Pastures and livestock are not conspicuous features of the agricultural landscapes of even the larger tropical islands of the Pacific World. The savanna lands of Fiji and New Caledonia are the only significant exceptions. Only in Viti Levu (and more recently also in the upland valleys of New Guinea) have serious official attempts been made to establish pastoral industries. But despite the employment by the administration of veterinarians and livestock officers, together with the provision of extension services for pastoralists, the supply of milk and meat available in Viti Levu—even in Suva itself—is insufficient to meet the present demand, and quite inadequate (in the estimation of medical authorities) for the dietary requirements of the rapidly growing population. In the wet zone—especially at Navua and Tailevu—there are examples of both large-scale and small-scale dairy farms operated by both Europeans and Indians, and butter and ghee (butter, clarified by boiling so as to resemble oil in consistency, used by the Indian community for cooking) are made in two factories. There are also examples of beef cattle ranching on the open grasslands of the dry zone *vanua singasinga*, notably the Yanggara ranch of the Colonial Sugar Refining Company near Tavua, with its 17,000 brown, hilly acres and 3000 head of Hereford cattle. In addition, thousands of Indian peasants have a dairy cow or two tethered on the roadside and graze zebu-cross working bullocks on the trash in the canefields; many Madrassis have herds of goats which over-graze the grass and shrubs of the savanna; and all Fijian *koros* have their pig and poultry population, sometimes sharing the *mbure* with the people themselves. But there is much room for improved stock-raising and for better tropical pastures in the farm economy of both Fijians and Indians.

MINING AND MANUFACTURING

Although predominantly dependent upon the soil, Fiji's economy is not as narrowly or overwhelmingly agricultural as that of the other territories within New Zealand's Pacific island neighbourhood. Today the mining of gold is of front-rank significance. In value, gold ranks third after sugar and coconut products among the colony's exports. In the 1950s manganese became Fiji's fourth most valuable export. In 1957 it had half the value of gold exports and nearly twice the value of bananas shipped. But mining is a temporary and a robber economy which must ultimately disappear as the ore is exhausted, and in Fiji it seems likely to continue to be restricted to gold and silver. Manganese has already virtually disappeared from the export lists. Timber now stands fourth after sugar, coconut products and gold. It is followed by bananas and biscuits.

The Emperor, Loloma and Dolphin mines on the Tavua gold-field near Vatukoula in Viti Levu produce gold and silver worth more than $2,850,000 a year; but, at the rate at which it is being mined and treated at present, the gold-bearing ore would appear likely to be exhausted within ten or twenty years. The gold occurs in very finely-divided particles and the ore is already being mined at a depth of over 2000 feet. The mines are therefore operated by large capital concerns, mainly Australian. Vatukoula is one of the largest settlements in Fiji, with carefully-planned but unattractive residential areas set in a disorderly landscape on the edge of a wilderness of mine buildings. Of its 6045 people the majority are Fijian, with significant minorities of Europeans, part-Europeans and Rotumans.

Apart from cane crushing, gold refining, rice milling and butter manufacturing, the colony's manufacturing industries are concentrated largely in Suva. Here both domestic and imported raw materials are processed in increasing quantities. Oil mills crush copra and extract coconut oil. Some oil is used in the manufacture of soap and margarine, but most of it is shipped to the United Kingdom. Cigarettes are made in two factories. Biscuits—large, thick ship's biscuits—for which there is a market throughout the dependent territories of the Pacific World, are also made from imported ingredients. Suva also has factories in which starch is made from tapioca (cassava). Island trading vessels are built in Suva and vessels up to 1000 tons can be repaired on the slip there. Large engineering workshops service not only the colony but also other insular territories in the neighbouring part of the Pacific. In other factories cement, nails, barbed wire, matches, soap and clothing are manufactured. Today Suva also has its own brewery.

Suva is also the headquarters of island trading firms. Its streets are lined with Indian drapers' and tailors' shops and with Chinese stores and eating places. The drapers' shops are like dark caves, tiered with rainbow-coloured bolts of cotton and rayon from Bombay, Manchester and Macclesfield; while the tailors' shops are the scene of endless activity, their sewing machines whirring throughout the night. They are always brim-ful of tireless, suave, bare-footed assistants admirably at the customer's service. Suva's open-air vegetable market and street bazaar with their varied array of Indian, Chinese and Fijian products and foodstuffs rank as one of Fiji's most colourful tourist attractions. Tourism is becoming one of Fiji's important industries.

POPULATION PROBLEMS

Fiji's problems are large and varied, but social and political issues are more serious than economic questions. Most hinge on the growing pressure of population on resources, and especially on the extraordinarily rapid expansion of the immigrant Indian majority. Since 1936—not long before World War II—when it stood at less than 200,000, Fiji's population has increased by 150 per cent. In September 1956 it was already 345,737, and in 1967 will reach half a million. With 7000 deaths from the influenza epidemic of 1918, the native Fijian population reached its lowest total in 1919. This was a little over 80,000, but still represented nearly sixty per cent of the colony's total: by 1966 it had climbed quite spectacularly to 200,000, but then represented only forty-one per cent of the total population. In the same period the Indian population climbed much more steeply from 57,000 to 240,000—from not more than thirty-five per cent to just over fifty per cent of the total. The Indian people—no longer 'immigrant' or 'alien', since ninety-five per cent of them have been born in the colony—are growing in numbers much faster than the indigenous Fijians. Hitherto there has been a great disproportion of males to females amongst the Indian people. For the first time the proportion has become normal in the course of the last decade. Between 1941 and 1961 Indian birth rates per thousand of total population averaged 44 and the Fijian rate only 38. On the other hand crude death rates averaged 8.5 (Indian) and 14.0 (Fijian). Meantime, however, the crude death rate for the people of the Colony as a whole has fallen to seven per 1000, and that of the Fijian people

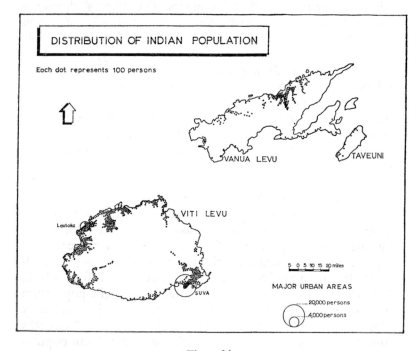

Figure 94

is now almost as low as that of the Indians. Recent trends must inevitably persist, if they do not, indeed, become more pronounced, so that the total population seems likely to continue to grow at the unusually high rate of three per cent per annum, with Indians outpacing the Fijians—at rates of 3.2 per cent and 2.1 per cent per annum respectively. The ability of the population to reproduce itself is evident in the fact that today a third of it is under ten years of age (nearly forty per cent in the case of the Indian population) and nearly two-thirds are under twenty-one.

With less than sixty per cent of the total land area of the archipelago, Viti Levu has over seventy per cent of the colony's population. Most people live close to the sea. The population has a peripheral (or marginal coastal) distribution while the interior chaos of misty green hills and valleys is sparsely peopled. Vanua Levu has less than its share of people—only fifteen per

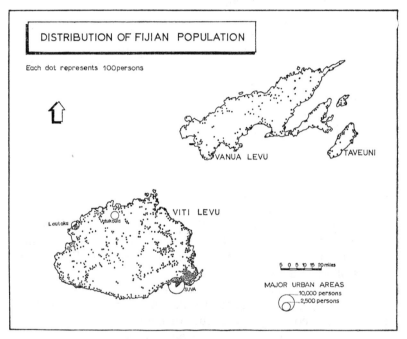

DISTRIBUTION OF FIJIAN POPULATION

Each dot represents 100 persons

VANUA LEVU

TAVEUNI

VITI LEVU

Lautoka

Mtukoula

SUVA

5 0 5 10 15 20 miles

MAJOR URBAN AREAS
......10,000 persons
......2,500 persons

Figure 95

cent on thirty per cent of the total area. But the small islands of Lau and Lomaiviti have an average density of population that is twice the average of the colony as a whole. Moreover, the population of these scattered insular areas is more than ninety-five per cent Fijian. Although they form the largest ethnic and cultural group in the colony, the Indians outnumber the Fijians only in Viti Levu, where they are so largely concentrated on the dry zone sugar lands, the hilly savanna and in the coastal mill towns and ports (*Fig. 94*).

In view of the threatened—almost inevitable—growth of population, greatly increased production and extended use of the land is essential if standards of living are not to decline. By the Deed of Cession the United Kingdom undertook to reserve their land to the native people. About eighty-three per cent of it remains in their hands, and their interests in it are safeguarded again by legislation passed in 1940. In that year an ordinance set up a Native Land Trust Board to administer and preserve native land and stimulate interest in its wider and more efficient use and conservation. In some cases land leased to Indians is being resumed when leases fall due. In coming years it will be necessary to re-settle many Indian families and to find land for the expanding Indian population if that which they now cultivate is not to be destroyed by over-use. Hitherto little has been done to meet the imminent danger.

The future of the Fijian seems reasonably clear. Despite the ease with which he can now secure the commutation of his traditional communal chores and responsibilities to the *koro*, and despite the efforts made to introduce him to individualized commercial agriculture, he remains at heart a subsistence agriculturalist, with a simple conception of life embracing above all his clan institutions, the thatched house of his boyhood, his family's hillside *teitei* and the peace and leisurely ways of the *koro*. In the use of the land he remains a long way behind his industrious and acquisitive Indian neighbour. But in the words of Ratu Sir Lala Sukuna he is 'beginning to learn what to do in order to keep his place in the surge of civilisation. . . he has a gentle willingness to learn, a friendly attitude and he preserves his courtesy and beauty of manners.' Meanwhile, as he makes haste slowly, his basic economic asset and one significant physical resource—the land—is being surveyed, consolidated and reserved. But for the increasing thousands of Indian 'Fijians' land becomes scarcer and scarcer. Here lies Fiji's dilemma.

This dilemma has serious political implications. Fiji has been moving steadily towards self-government. But the Fijian community and the much smaller European section of the population have frequently expressed satisfaction with progress and have resisted any suggestion of independence, or any interference with the continuation of the British connection and the link with the Crown.

The Fijians claim, and enjoy, a 'special position' in the colony. This is based on their status as the indigenes of the islands, on their ownership of the land, on the fact that they ceded Fiji to the United Kingdom and that Fiji became a colony by cession and not by conquest. Moreover, unlike the Indians, they have participated in the colony's defence and have served in the British cause overseas. Some Indians object to this privileged 'special position' of their partners in the colony, especially in view of the Indians' numerical superiority and their more active and successful participation in the economy of the country. They demand equality with the Fijians and fear that the 'special position' could lead to a national Fiji communal movement to claim Fiji for the Fijians and to oust the Indians. Many Indians, however, seeking above all security, and not strife, in the land of their adoption, would be quite happy and content to accept the Fijian community's privileged status and title to 83.6 per cent of the land, providing the Indians had better access to it, were allowed to use and develop it, and could secure long-term leases of it and compensation for their improvements.

This, in brief, was the background to the constitutional conference called in London by the Secretary of State for the Colonies in August 1965. The conference, and the debate held later in the Legislative Council in Suva on the decisions of the conference, revealed the political cleavage between Fijian (and European) and Indian views on constitutional development.

The conference decided that the Legislative Council should have an elected membership increased from twelve to thirty-six, and that the number of members nominated by the Governor should be reduced from ten to four. The Indian representatives wanted members elected on a common roll, which would have assured them of a big majority. Fijians and Europeans demanded continuation of communal rolls—each racial community electing its representatives separately. The conference decision was a compromise acceptable to the Fijians, Europeans and Chinese, but unacceptable to a majority of Indian politicians. Of the elected members of the Legislative Council, fourteen are Fijians, nine elected on a Fiji communal roll (by Fijians, Rotumans and other Pacific islanders), two elected by the Council of Chiefs and three elected by a cross-voting system. Twelve are Indians, nine from communal voting and three from cross-voting. Ten are Europeans, seven elected on a communal roll (including Chinese and any other minority groups) and three by cross-voting.

The Indians are opposed to the Fijians' 'special position' claim, with some justification, that this arrangement is undemocratic and that it favours especially the Europeans (who are much fewer in number and who will hold the balance of power) and the Fijian chiefs.

Elections were held in September-October 1966 under the new system. They were contested by two political parties: Alliance, dominated by the Fijians and Europeans, but with support from a section of the Indian community (especially the Moslems) as well as minor communities; and Federation, better organised, actively political, and representing perhaps 80 per cent of the Indian population. The Alliance party won the cross-voting seats and has a safe majority. From it comes the Leader of Government Business (Ratu K.K.T. Mara) and the Executive Council, or 'cabinet'.

The latest development on the difficult Fijian road to ultimate autonomy is a resolution of the United Nations Security Council in December 1966 urging the United Kingdom to grant independence to Fiji, and advocating the calling of another constitutional convention. The newly independent African and Asian nations are not happy with the absence of a common roll and the continuation of a 'special position' for one community, one that is no longer a majority group.

The colony still has some distance to go along the road of political development to a destination which, if strife, bloodshed and racial discord are to be avoided, must ultimately involve a partnership between Indians and Fijians in all affairs, but particularly in the use and development of limited island resources for the maximum benefit of a fast-growing population, and which must finally be based on the acceptance of the view that the two largest communities in Fiji are complementary and not competitive.

CHAPTER SEVEN

Prospect and Retrospect

I N THE main body of this book attention has been directed very largely to only a part of the Pacific World—the part which for convenience may well be designated *Southwest Pacific*, a term that has been used to provide the book with its title. The Pacific World, however, extends north into the middle latitudes of the northern hemisphere and east to within a relatively short distance of the coasts of the central American mainland. Very broadly it may be said that the interests of Australia and New Zealand in this insular Pacific World decrease with increasing distance from Wellington and Canberra. Australia's immediate territorial interests extend no further than Manus and Nauru; New Zealand's reach no further north and east than Nauru, the Tokelaus and Penrhyn. Their commercial and military interests reach only a little further among the islands themselves, although they do extend, of course, beyond the islands to the continental shores on the rim of the ocean. There are thus several island groups within the Pacific World beyond the limits of what have here been referred to as the 'Pacific island neighbourhoods' of the two British dominions. See *Figure* 13.

THE NORTHERN PART OF THE PACIFIC WORLD

North of the Equator are practically all the American island territories within the Pacific World excepting only American Samoa. Here is the large, lofty and predominantly volcanic group of Hawaii, its original inhabitants Polynesians, but now a complex commercialized agricultural area, producing sugar and pineapples worth hundreds of millions of dollars for the markets of the continental mainland. In 1958 Hawaii produced a million tons of sugar from more than 200,000 acres of cane as well as 65 per cent of the world total production of canned pineapple from 75,000 acres under this crop.

Hawaii is also urbanized. Honolulu is a city as large as Auckland. It has important processing industries and is a cosmopolitan, much publicized tourist centre with a dense cluster of modern, multi-storeyed, plush tourist hotels at Waikiki. Hawaii and Alaska were admitted as the fiftieth and forty-ninth states of the union in 1959 and 1958.

The small surviving indigenous population, hardly recognizable as such, is lost today amidst a polyglot English-speaking and thoroughly 'Americanized' population of Chinese, Japanese, Filipino, Portuguese, Puerto Rican, English and American extraction. The Hawaiian 'chain' extends 1600 miles west-northwest from Hawaii, the largest island in the group. The island of Hawaii has for neighbours the six other permanently-settled islands in the group—Maui, Lanai, Molokai, Oahu (with Honolulu and Pearl Harbour and a population of over 550,000 out of a total of 755,000), Kauai and Niihau. Further west the group deteriorates into a series of volcanic rock pinnacles and ultimately into low coral islands without visible trace of volcanic materials. Here the island of Midway alone is inhabited and it is almost solely a military outpost, air base and staging post for civil airliners.

From Midway to Wake, the next military outpost and port of call for passenger aircraft, is a long flight over ocean unbroken by islands. But westwards beyond Wake, almost as far as New Guinea, the Philippines and Japan, the ocean is spattered with the myriad coral reefs and atolls and the occasional volcanic piles of Micronesia, together with the volcanic island festoons of the Bonin and Volcano Islands, which because of their long occupation by Japan, are considered part of the Oriental rather than of the Pacific World. The larger Micronesian islands have had a longer and more varied history of European contact than most of the island groups of Polynesia. They have in turn been part of the empires of Spain, Germany and Japan. American control dates only from the later phases of World War II. Today the Marianas, the Carolines (including the Palaus, which reach as far west as New Guinea's westernmost projection in the Vogelkop) and the Marshall Islands comprise the United States'

Trust Territory of the Pacific Islands. Also part of Micronesia are the Gilberts. They lie on both sides of the Equator in the central Pacific and, with the neighbouring over-populated atolls of the Ellice Islands, further south and astride the ethnic and cultural boundary between Micronesia and Polynesia, they comprise a British colony administered by the High Commission for the Western Pacific.

The United States' principal interest in the Micronesian trust territory is strategic, and for almost six years after the end of the war the islands were the responsibility of the United States Navy. But, like American Samoa, their administration has since been transferred to the Department of the Interior. Many of the larger islands—Saipan, Truk and Guam (which has been American territory since 1898 except for a brief period of occupation by the Japanese during World War II)—are heavily-fortified naval and air bases. They are stepping-stones from the Pacific to the Asian mainland, and have been retained by the United States with a view to the prevention of renewed Japanese incursion into the central and south Pacific, and with the object of resisting aggression from any other part of the eastern rimland of Asia. As the Japanese well demonstrated, these islands could be powerful weapons in the hands of an aggressive Asian power. But just as Australia and New Zealand have, since colonial days, viewed the islands to the north and east of them as essential to their defence, so too might the U.S.S.R., a resurgent Japan or an expansionist China similarly view the Marianas and Carolines.

The economic significance of the trust territory to the United States is negligible. On the other hand the larger volcanic islands, especially Saipan and Tinian, became important sources of sugar and fish to metropolitan Japan between the two world wars. Their resources were thoroughly exploited for the benefit of the mandatory power, and the islands provided a home for thousands of Japanese agricultural colonists, all of whom have since been repatriated by the Americans. Although not interested in the trade of the many islands, or bent upon exploiting their resources for its own benefit, the United States undertook immediately after the war a painstaking and detailed scientific survey in Micronesia—a survey of the people and their culture, of their needs and problems, and of the islands' resources and their utilization. This was done in order to ensure a rapid rehabilitation of the life and economy of the islanders and with a view to the maximum efficiency and understanding in administration; and American experience in the conduct of this work would be of great benefit to other administrations whose island groups have not had their resources and problems nearly so fully investigated, even after many decades of alien occupation.

FRENCH OCEANIA AND THE SOUTHEAST PACIFIC

East of New Zealand's Pacific island neighbourhood and south of the Equator are other clusters of numerous tiny islands all but a few of them under the jurisdiction of one power. That power is France, and the island groups concerned are: (1) the Marquesas (with less than 4000 people); (2) the Society Islands (with a population, including Polynesians, French, Chinese, British and mixed bloods, of over 60,000 people, nearly 25,000 of them living in the town of Papeete on Tahiti, the centre of French Polynesia and one of the larger towns in the Pacific island territories); (3) the Tuamotus (population 8500); (4) the Austral (Tubuai) Islands (neighbours of the Southern Cook Group, with little more than 4000 people); (5) the Mangareva Group (formerly called the Gambiers, with 510 people); and (6) lonely Rapa (further south, in the latitude of Norfolk, with barely 300 people).

For some years Air New Zealand (then TEAL) operated a regular air service from New Zealand to Tahiti—first by flying boat and later by Electras. This was suspended when France withdrew permission for landings at Faa'a jet airport on Tahiti. UTA, France's overseas airline, has a DC8 service through Noumea, Tahiti and Los Angeles. It may not be long before U.S.A., French and New Zealand jet services connect Auckland and Papeete on through routes to North America. This will bring the capital of French Polynesia and centre of a colourful and developing tourist trade into much closer and speedier contact with New Zealand than has been possible with an irregular and infrequent cargo and passenger boat connection. With improved communications and growing commercial contacts, it may become necessary to extend what we have here termed New Zealand's Pacific island neighbourhood further to the east.

However, renewed metropolitan French interest resulting in part from the revival under de Gaulle of French nationalism, the choice of Mururoa in the Gambiers as the site for experimental atomic bomb explosions in 1966, and the suspension by France of Air New Zealand's rights to land passengers in Tahiti have temporarily checked the increasing contact of French Polynesia with its Pacific ocean neighbours.

Still further east are several isolated islands—stepping-stones by which intrepid Polynesian voyagers centuries ago may have reached South America. There is Pitcairn of *Bounty* fame, with its families named Christian and Adams, which (with Henderson and Ducie, both within 200 miles) is under the jurisdiction of the United Kingdom and is administered from Fiji. Beyond, but still 1500 miles from the coast of South America and the snow on the lofty Andes, is Easter Island, the easternmost outpost of Polynesia and of the Pacific World. Its counterparts at the other two corners of the Polynesian triangle are Hawaii and the Chatham Islands over 4000 miles away—a reminder both of the vast distances of the Pacific World and of the skill and endurance of 'the greatest navigators in history'.

THE INCREASING SIGNIFICANCE OF THE PACIFIC

It is now well over half a century since an American politician coined the rather glib catch-cry: 'the Mediterranean is the ocean of the past, the Atlantic the ocean of the present, and the Pacific, the ocean of the future'. Nearly sixty years later it remains as doubtful a prophecy as when it was first uttered. It is not clear, of course, in what sense it is predicted that the Pacific is to be the ocean of the future. The Pacific is certainly not yet the ocean over which the largest part of the world's trade is carried. Trans-Atlantic commerce seems destined to remain much greater for a long time to come. The Pacific is not yet the ocean on which the mass of the world's military and political power is concentrated. Nor is it the focus of military strategy. It could indeed be claimed that since World War II the Arctic has attracted more of the attention of the military planners and of the strategists of the Great Powers than has the Pacific. Since the war ended the military significance of Pearl Harbour, Singapore, Pago Pago and Manus Island has declined. Interest has been focused rather on Green-

N

land, the Canadian Arctic and Alaska, and on the rim of the
Asian continent rather than on the island stepping-stones in the
ocean.

Nevertheless the Pacific has been of increasing significance
for a number of reasons. In North America the growth of
population and industrial development on the Pacific coast has
been relatively very much greater that that in the longer-settled
and more heavily-industrialized regions further east. And the
wars in Korea, Indo-China and Vietnam, taken together with
the assumption by the United States of responsibility for the
island territories of Micronesia and with the increasing interest
in the 'underdeveloped' areas of eastern and southeastern
Asia, has attracted American attention both to the Pacific
World and to the Oriental World beyond.

The postwar political tangle in Asia, and the confused military campaigning in different parts of the Asian rimland of the
Pacific, whilst occupying the attention and increasing the apprehension of much of the world, have in fact done much to retard
the economic, social and political advancement of the Pacific.
The progress that has been made here and there has been made
in spite of the disturbed economic climate and the turbulent
political atmosphere. From Manchuria to Indonesia and West
New Guinea political and military strife have sapped energies
and resources which might otherwise have been employed to
raise living standards and promote peaceful economic and
social advancement. The future importance of both the Pacific
and the Oriental Worlds has also been advanced by the birth
of new, independent and populous, though poverty-stricken,
nations in the two decades since the war in the Pacific was
brought to an end. India, Pakistan, Singapore, Malaysia and
Burma, on the southern rim of Asia, and Indonesia and the
Philippines, physically within the Pacific but culturally part of
the Oriental World, will all have an increasing part to play as
new, but independent, political units in the affairs of both the
Pacific and the world at large.

AUSTRALIA AND NEW ZEALAND AND THE FUTURE OF
THE PACIFIC

In the southwest Pacific, both Australia and New Zealand
have in this century been rapidly growing up. Expanding popu-

lations, high living standards, industrial and agricultural tech-nologies as advanced and up-to-date as those found anywhere, together with their growing political maturity, have prompted them (sometimes in concert) to take an increasingly independent and a more clearly-proclaimed part in the conduct of world affairs in general and of those of the Pacific World in particular.

Whatever may be the future of the Pacific Ocean, it can be said with safety that an increasingly important part in determin-ing that future will be taken by the United States, Australia and New Zealand. Until the middle of the century the part played by these nations was less than that played, at different times, by a handful of European states—by Spain in the centuries before the establishment of the English-speaking nations on the margins of the Pacific; and by Britain, France, Germany and Holland during the decades in which the founda-tions of the younger nations were being laid. On the other hand the role of the youngest nations—Indonesia and the Philippines —and that of the older nations of the Asian interior and rim-land—the U.S.S.R., China and Japan—is not at the moment so clear. It depends upon the solution first of the major problems of the Far East. But with their teeming millions of people, their enormous potential demand for goods, and the possibility, with western technology, of much expanded productivity, the nations of the Pacific borderlands of Asia—young and old—could in future contribute powerfully to the economic development and commercial prosperity of the whole Pacific World. Japan es-pecially is already doing so.

At present the conduct of the affairs of the Pacific and the administration of the dependent territories of the Pacific World are in the hands of the youthful English-speaking nations on its borders and of the two nations of Europe (France and the Unit-ed Kingdom) that retain some interest and influence there— although this is often declining. In recent years all these coun-tries have gone a long way to co-operate in efforts to improve their administration and to better the lot of the dependent people for whom they are responsible. This is evident above all in the work of the South Pacific Commission, for which Britain, Australia, New Zealand, and the United States and France are jointly responsible.

THE SOUTH PACIFIC COMMISSION

The South Pacific Commission was largely an Australian conception. It was foreshadowed in the Anzac Pact of 1944, under which Australia and New Zealand agreed, amongst other things, to promote at the earliest opportunity after the war a regional advisory organization for the southwest Pacific. It was also anticipated in part by an agreement in 1946 between the Government of Fiji, the High Commission for the Western Pacific, and the Government of New Zealand to establish a

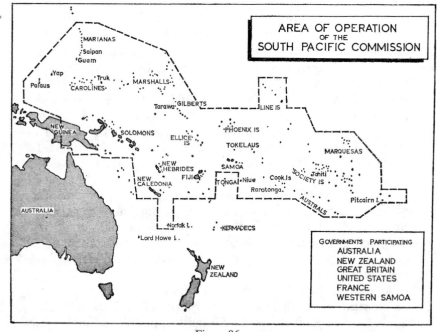

Figure 96

South Pacific Health Service for the island territories administered by the United Kingdom and New Zealand, with headquarters at a Central Medical School in Suva.

The agreement to create the South Pacific Commission was signed in 1947 by the six powers who then had responsibility for the administration of dependent territories in the area—the United Kingdom, the United States, France, the Netherlands, Australia and New Zealand. At the end of 1962, after the transfer of Netherlands New Guinea to Indonesia, the participation of the Netherlands in the Commission ceased. And in October 1964 Western Samoa, now an independent state, was admitted to the Commission as a participating government.

But in 1947 it was some time before all the partners in the establishment of the South Pacific Commission actually ratified the agreement, and it took longer still for them to agree upon the site for its headquarters. The claims of Suva—a town in which are already centred certain other administrative activities covering a large part of the Pacific Island Territories discussed in this book—Sydney and Noumea were all canvassed before a compromise decision, influenced largely by the availability of wartime military buildings, took the principal officers of the Commission to New Caledonia. Each metropolitan government is represented on the Commission by two commissioners who assemble in Noumea regularly, and all the governments contribute in differing proportions to the cost of the institution. The Commission employs a research council of full-time and part-time officials drawn from all the participating countries.

A third and very important element is the South Pacific Conference—a meeting of representatives of all the dependent territories and peoples for which the several administrations are responsible. Six meetings of the conference, which has been termed 'a kind of South Seas Parliament', have now been held—in Suva (1950), Noumea (1953), Suva again (1956), Rabaul (1959), Utulei (Pago Pago, 1962) and Lae (1965). At these meetings representatives of the native people have the opportunity of discussing their problems among themselves, of airing their worries, hopes and aspirations, and of bringing all these to the attention of the commissioners and their officials.

The Commission has also assisted in the organization of a regular series of South Pacific Games. Two such Pacific island 'Olympics' have now been held and have done much to enable athletic young islanders from scattered territories to come together and get to know each other better. They have also enabled the people of one group, following the fortunes of their games representatives, to become aware of the existence of, and the general community of interest they share with other groups, sometimes thousands of ocean miles distant from their own villages and confined island homes.

The Islanders and the Future of the Pacific World

The Commission is only an advisory body. It has the job of collecting together all available material and information about the territories in question,* and of conducting or fostering research to bring to light and ultimately to solve or remedy the many problems of the island groups. It has the task of handing on useful information to the administrations concerned, not only about the common problems of the territories but also about the much more numerous special difficulties faced by individual islands and individual groups, and of making recommendations for the improvement of administration and the betterment of native conditions. It is not concerned with political problems but with those that fall within the broad fields of economics, sociology, agriculture, education and health—problems of diet, conservation of resources, native housing, fishing methods, plant diseases, plant quarantine, systems of land use, marketing, co-operation and the like.

The South Pacific Commission has the opportunity of making a contribution to the welfare and progress of the native people of the Pacific World such as has not in the past been available to any one administrative authority. Through the activities of the South Pacific Conference the native people themselves now have, often for the first time and in advance of the attainment of self-government, the opportunity of making their own contribution to the advancement of their territories.

However, the tide of independence is rising fast for the hitherto dependent colonial territories of the Pacific. The indigenous Melanesian, Micronesian and Polynesian peoples are rapidly acquiring an increasingly important voice in the direction of their own affairs. In Western Samoa and the Cook Islands virtual independence has been achieved. Even in the largest and traditionally most inaccessible and underdeveloped territories of Australian New Guinea rapid progress is being

---

*These are defined cartographically in *Figure 96*. The territorial scope of the Commission has already been extended beyond its original limits by the inclusion in 1951 of the U.S. Trust Territory of the Pacific Islands. It was reduced, however, in 1962 when, with the transfer of the western half of New Guinea to Indonesia, Irian Barat was excluded from the territorial extent of the Commission's interests and responsibilities. Tonga, whilst not a member of the Commission, is closely associated with its work and participates in the South Pacific Conference. Western Samoa, since it attained independence in 1962, has become a participating member.

made. Independence which, a decade ago, appeared remote, if not out of the question, may now be not more than a decade away if the Papuans request it. However, the indigenous peoples of Papua and New Guinea may (like the Fijians under the Colonial Office and the Cook Islanders under New Zealand) prefer self-government under Australian sovereignty rather than complete independence and separate national existence. Neither Australia, New Zealand nor the United Kingdom will delay the granting of independence. Britain's granting of independence to a succession of new Asian, African and American states in the generation since World War II is evidence enough of that. So, too, is New Zealand's handling of the Western Samoan situation between 1946 and 1960. In any case we can be sure that the numerical dominance of the newly emergent nations at the United Nations will prod any tardy or hesitant administering power into speeding the granting of sovereign independent status to its dependent territories.

Finally, there is the possibility that as an indirect outcome of the work of the South Pacific Commission there may be some rational rearrangement or unification of Pacific island dependencies—possibly a transference of responsibility. In many cases this is clearly highly desirable. As the experience in administration of Australia and New Zealand matures, and as their economic and technological interests in the southwest Pacific expand and come to dominate larger and larger oceanic areas, it may well be that the United Kingdom, and possibly also France and the United Nations, will suggest the addition to their responsibilities of the territories for which hitherto older colonial powers have been answerable. Alternatively, as the island territories assume independent status, there will be an opportunity for them to form one or more federations of Polynesian or Melanesian States. Separately they can never count for much (the state of Western Samoa has, for example, few more people than the Dunedin metropolitan area or the city of Canberra), but in association they could well make a distinctive and notable contribution to the solution of the problems of their own and other Pacific island territories. In any event there will soon be a greater degree of co-operation, co-ordination and pooling not only of research and advisory services, as is the case already under the South Pacific Commission, but also of administrative agencies and technical services. It would be to the mutual advantage of the governments concerned, and of the territories for which they are accountable, to extend and diversify the range of co-operative administrative services which some of them already jointly provide. There is room not only for a southwest Pacific health service, but also for parallel agricultural, shipping, marketing, plant quarantine, educational (including university) and other services.

Political autonomy—even federation of newly independent small island states—will not solve the problems of the southwest Pacific island territories, though it may well be a considerable factor in their solution. Apart from its physical fragmentation and the scattering of its minute components over immense oceanic distances, the central and most fundamental problem of the island world is the accelerated rate of growth of its population. It is scarcely less than one life span since many experts were predicting the demise and disappearance of indigenous peoples in Polynesia and Melanesia. Today the threat of unprecedented fertility and growing numbers is everywhere present and increasingly urgent except only in New Guinea. The people of the islands from the Solomons to the Society Islands constitute the fastest growing population in the world.

This expansion of human numbers is occurring in physically confined and ocean-bound island areas. Limited size, isolation and oceanic environment are not their only handicaps. Much of the islands' surface is broken and elevated, consisting at times of bare rock, of deserts of basalt, or of coral sand, or of jagged pinnacles of *makatea*.

The island communities are overwhelmingly rural, and agricultural in economy. The only exceptions are Nauru and Ocean Island, and to a lesser extent New Caledonia and American Samoa. By and large there are few physical resources other than soil, climate and the waters of the abounding ocean. Tourism may bring increasing income and profit to Tahiti and Viti Levu: Japanese fishermen may continue to make possible on Tutuila the canning of the tuna they catch; Australian capital may continue to bottle beer and bake biscuits in Suva and, for a time at least, dig deeper for gold at Vatukoula; but

nine out of ten Pacific islanders must continue largely to produce from restricted and eroding soil resources.

Despite this heavy reliance on village agriculture for both
sustenance and cash income, the islander is attracted by the
bright lights of the port towns, and even the more distant and
still brighter lights of Auckland. Urbanization is becoming a
characteristic feature of all territories. What were twenty-five
years ago small ports and colonial administrative centres,
populated largely by alien administrators and businessmen,
have become fast-growing, confused, but colourful towns with
a complex multiracial population. To these towns the indigenous peoples are now being pulled by the possibility of jobs on
wages, of securing more advanced education, better health
services and the opportunity of visiting the cinema. Overcrowded and badly housed, underemployed, no longer under
the discipline or restraint of village life or tribal elders, in contact with western culture without being part of it, or able to
share it, mixed island populations, Indians, Chinese, Indo-
Chinese, French, English, part-Europeans etc. are today faced
with complex social problems in such port towns as Port
Moresby, Rabaul, Noumea, Suva and Papeete. All of these
have mixed populations growing very much faster than the
already rapidly growing population of the respective territories
in which they lie.

The transfers of political and administrative responsibility
from colonial powers to indigenous and local immigrant alien
communities, with relatively little formal education and still
less familiarity with government administration, must be viewed
in the light of the mounting pressure of population on resources,
the drift from small islands to larger ones, from village to port
town and from island port town to San Francisco, Honolulu,
Auckland and Sydney, and in the light of the increasing com-
plexity of economic and social problems.

The day of 'colonial powers' in the southwest Pacific—as
elsewhere in the world—is over. The day of enlightened,
financially generous, 'administering powers' is approaching its
end. In the Pacific, Britain, France and the Netherlands will
clearly have a diminished role in the future.

In the long term, the sooner the island communities are obliged themselves to grapple with the dilemma of fast-expanding

population and circumscribed resources, the sooner will their problems be solved, the sooner the native people will realize that the clock must be pushed forward and not back, and the sooner will it be appreciated that physical and cultural resources must be utilized to the full, institutional handicaps removed, and traditional social patterns and attitudes modified. So long as benevolent colonial administering powers are prepared to meet the budgetary deficits of territorial governments which arise largely from inadequacies in native institutions and technology, the real difficulties are being hidden and avoided.

But that the southwest Pacific will not in future be a theatre for the operation of 'administering powers' does not mean that there will be no role for Australia and New Zealand and international agencies. Australia and New Zealand have a special relationship to the southwest Pacific island territories. They are close. They are neighbours. New Zealand is in fact part of Polynesia; and Australia is virtually 'in' Melanesia. Australians and New Zealanders do not live in Europe and are not capable of playing a major role there. Much the same applies to their relations with Asia. But both countries are in and of the Pacific. Southeast Asia and the island stepping-stones of the Indonesian Mediterranean and of Melanesia constitute Australia's 'Near North.' New Zealand's 'Near North' is the expanse of the ocean and the island specks it contains. The interests of Australia and New Zealand are not identical. One is closer to Asia, the other more clearly oceanic. In the surrounding Pacific, New Zealand especially has a role to play. The Dominion is significantly—and increasingly—Polynesian. More Polynesians live there than anywhere else. The last twenty-five years have seen a larger Polynesian migration to New Zealand than occurred at any time previously. Today there are more than 200,000 Maoris, and expanding communities of 'island Polynesians' numbering more than 15,000. A considerable proportion of the 'European' population of New Zealand also has some Polynesian blood. Both Australia and New Zealand have good reason for continuing to assist the less privileged island communities of the southwest Pacific. As the island territories become autonomous and accept responsibility for the solution of their own problems, they will require and request help. Australia and New Zealand should continue to be willing to extend it. For them it is not only a humanitarian matter, but also one of self-interest.

Above all it is imperative that all people concerned—directly or indirectly—with the future of the island territories should know the nature of the islands in question and the character of their problems. Problems cannot be solved until they are recognized. Territories cannot be well administered if they are not well known.

Here lies the special value and the unique contribution to a better world of a geography conceived in simple terms as the study of 'what places are like'.

APPENDIX ONE

THE TERRITORIES OF THE 'PACIFIC WORLD'

A. THE AUSTRALIAN PACIFIC ISLAND NEIGHBOURHOOD

Territory	Designation	Area in Square Miles	Population at Dates Stipulated
THE COMMONWEALTH OF AUSTRALIA	Self-governing Dominion within the British Commonwealth of Nations	2,974,581	11,544,691 (census June 30, 1966)
New South Wales	States within the Commonwealth	309,461	4,235,030
Victoria		87,884	3,217,832
Queensland (including Torres Strait Islands)		670,500	1,661,240
South Australia		380,070	1,090,723
Western Australia		975,920	835,570
Tasmania		26,215	371,217
Northern Territory	Commonwealth Territory	523,620	37,166
Capital Territory (Canberra)	Commonwealth Territory	911	95,913
TERRITORY OF PAPUA (including the Trobriand, Woodlark, D'Entrecasteaux and Louisiade archipelagoes)	Dependent territory of the Commonwealth of Australia	90,540	559,397 natives (as at June 30, 1965) together with 7071 Europeans and 1051 half-castes, Asians, etc. (as at census June 30, 1961)
TERRITORY OF NEW GUINEA	Trust Territory of the United Nations administered by the Commonwealth of Australia	93,000	1,558,520 natives (as at June 30, 1965) together with 15,536 non-indigenes (mainly Europeans and Chinese) as at census June 30, 1961

A. THE AUSTRALIAN PACIFIC ISLAND NEIGHBOURHOOD—continued

Territory	Designation	Area in Square Miles	Population at Dates Stipulated
Northeast New Guinea (the 'Mainland') Bismarck Archipelago:		69,700	1,075,969 (1961)
New Britain		14,600	125,949
New Ireland		3,340	42,349
New Hanover (Lavongai)		460	
Admiralty Islands (Manus)		800	19,214
Solomon Islands: Bougainville		3,880	66,942
Buka		220	
IRIAN BARAT	Occupied and administered under United Nations Sanction by the Republic of Indonesia	151,789	750,000 (est. mid-year 1962) including 15,505 Europeans and 16,580 Asians
NAURU	Trust Territory of the United Nations, administered by the Commonwealth of Australia, New Zealand and the United Kingdom	8.2 (5,363 acres)	3101 (Census June 30, 1966) including 1,492 Nauruans, and 868 non-indigenes
NORFOLK ISLAND	Dependent Territory of the Commonwealth of Australia	13.3 (8,523 acres)	1,152 (Census June 30, 1966)
LORD HOWE ISLAND	Dependency of New South Wales	5.0 (3220 acres)	249 (Census June 30, 1966)
SOLOMON ISLANDS	Protectorate of the United Kingdom	12,000	140,000 (est. 1966) at the census 1959, 124,076, including 4,625 Polynesians, 781 Europeans, 366 Chinese, and 459 Micronesians

A. THE AUSTRALIAN PACIFIC ISLAND NEIGHBOURHOOD—*continued*

Territory	Designation	Area in Square Miles	Population at Dates Stipulated
Bougainville		3,880	53,130 (1959)
Guadalcanal		2500	14,500
Santa Ysabel		1802	4200
Malaita		1572	35,000
San Cristobal		981	5000
Choiseul		680	4000
New Georgia		370	12,500
Santa Cruz Group			1800
NEW HEBRIDES	Condominium administered jointly by Great Britain and France	5700	79,600 (est. 1966) at the census 1960, 60,375 including 1492 French, 485 British, 2153 Vietnamese, 600 Wallisians and Tahitians, and 216 Chinese
Espiritu Santo		1500	7010 (1960)
Malekula		450	8998
Erromanga		330	589
Efate		300	3714
Ambrym		160	3300
Tana		150	8010
Pentecost		125	5845
Aoba		105	5411
Banks Group		—	2295
Torres Group		—	228
NEW CALEDONIA	Overseas Territory of France	9435	96,900 (est. 1966) at census 1961, 80,061 including 32,334 natives, 28,454 French and Europeans, 3664 Indonesians, 4342 Vietnamese, 2402 Wallisians and 1006 Tahitians

A. THE AUSTRALIAN PACIFIC ISLAND NEIGHBOURHOOD—*continued*

Territory	Designation	Area in Square Miles	Population at Dates Stipulated
Island of New Caledonia (*La Grande Terre*)		8543	75,000 (1962)
Isle of Pines		58	
Loyalty Islands		800	15,000
WALLIS AND FUTUNA	Self-governing Territory of France Overseas (since 1959)	60.5	10,500 (est.1966)
Wallis Group		24	7500
Futuna (Hoorn)		36.5	3000

B. THE NEW ZEALAND PACIFIC ISLAND NEIGHBOURHOOD

Territory	Designation	Area in Square Miles	Population at Dates Stipulated
THE DOMINION OF NEW ZEALAND	Self-governing dominion within the British Commonwealth of Nations	103,736	2,676,919 (census March 1966) incl. 198,188 Maoris (Census March 1966)
North Island	Main Islands	44,281	1,893,592
South Island		58 093	783 327
Stewart Island		670	329
Chatham Islands		372	521
Kermadec Islands		13	9
Campbell Island		44	9
Three Kings		3	—
Solander	Minor islands	0.5	—
Bounty		0.5	—
Snares		1	—
Antipodes		24	—
Aucklands		263	—

B. THE NEW ZEALAND PACIFIC ISLAND NEIGHBOURHOOD—*continued*

Territory	Designation	Area in Square Miles	Population at Dates Stipulated
COOK ISLANDS	Self-governing Territory of the Dominion of New Zealand	199	20,120 (est. 1966) at census 1961, 18,378
Southern (Lower) Group:		84 { acres	
Rarotonga		(16,472)	8676 (1961)
Mangaia		(12,828)	1877
Atiu		(6654)	1266
Mitiaro		(2529)	307
Aitutaki		(3946)	2582
Mauke		(4552)	785
Takutea		(302)	—
Manuae		(1524)	18
Northern Group:		15 { acres	
Palmerston		(1000)	86
Penrhyn		(2432)	628
Manihiki		(1344)	1006
Rakahanga		(960)	319
Pukapuka		(1250)	718
Suwarrow		(600)	1
Nassau		(300)	119
NIUE	Separately administered Dependency of the Dominion of New Zealand	100	5120 (est. 1966) at census 1961, 4864 (incl. 82 Europeans)
TOKELAU ISLANDS	Dependency of the Dominion of New Zealand	4	2175 (est. 1966) at census Sept. 1961, 1870

B. The New Zealand Pacific Island Neighbourhood—*continued*

Territory	Designation	Area in Square Miles	Population at Dates Stipulated
Nukunono		1350 acres	513 (1961)
Fakaofo		650 acres	793
Atafu		500 acres	564
WESTERN SAMOA	Independent State (formerly a Trust Territory of the United Nations administered by the Dominion of New Zealand)	1138	131,200 (est. 1966) at census Sept. 1961, 114,427, incl. 668 Europeans, 11,813 part-Samoans, 522 other Pacific Islanders and 136 others (mainly Chinese)
Savai'i		703	31,948 (1961)
Upolu		430 }	
Manono		3 }	82,479
Apolima		2 }	
AMERICAN (EASTERN) SAMOA	Unincorporated Territory of the United States	73	20,000 (est. 1966) at census 1960, 20,051
Tutuila		54	17,250 (1960)
Tau }	Islands of American Samoa	15 }	
Ofu } Mauna		2 }	2695
Olosega }		1.5 }	
Rose		0.3 }	—
Swain's Island	Administered by American Samoa	1.25	106 (1960)

B. THE NEW ZEALAND PACIFIC ISLAND NEIGHBOURHOOD—*continued*

Territory	Designation	Area in Square Miles	Population at Dates Stipulated
TONGA	Independent Kingdom under British Protection	269	77,000 (preliminary result 1966 census) 59,627 (official estimate, Dec. 31, 1957), including 284 Europeans, 1423 people of mixed descent, including other Pacific Islanders
Niuafo'ou		19.4	
Tafahi		1.3	
Niuatoputapu		5.7	
Vava'u Group		56.1	
Ha'apai Group		50.1	
Tongatapu		99.2	
'Eua		33.7	
'Atu		0.9	
FIJI	British Crown Colony	7055	475,874 (census Sept. 1966) incl. 239,000 Indians, 198,000 Fijians and 41,000 others (Europeans, part-Europeans, Rotumans, Chinese, other Pacific Islanders etc.)
Viti Levu ⎫ The largest islands Vanua Levu ⎭ in the group		4011 2137	348,437 (1966) 85,085
Rotuma	Dependency of the Colony of Fiji	16	3367 (1966)

B. The New Zealand Pacific Island Neighbourhood—*continued*

Territory	Designation	Area in Square Miles	Population at Dates Stipulated
Viti Levu		4011	
Vanua Levu		2137	
Taveuni		168	
Kandavu		158	
Ngau	The larger islands in the group	54	
Koro		40	
Ovalau		40	
Rambi		27	
Moala		24	
Lakemba		22	

C. The Rest of the Pacific World

Territory	Designation	Area in Square Miles	Population at Dates Stipulated
GILBERT AND ELLICE ISLANDS	British Crown Colony	397	48,780 (census 1963)
Gilbert Islands		114.1	
Ellice Islands		9.6	At the Census of 1963,
Phoenix Group (Birnie, Sydney, Hull, etc.)		5.3	40,702 Micronesians (Gilbertese), 676 Polynesians
Ocean Island		2.3	(mainly Ellice Islanders),
Northern Line Islands:			346 Europeans, 105 Chinese
Fanning		12.4 } 238	(on Ocean Island) and 779
Christmas		222.7	people of mixed island blood
Washington		2.9	
Southern Line Islands:		21.9	
Malden, Starbuck, etc.			

C. The Rest of the Pacific World—*continued*

Territory	Designation	Area in Square Miles	Population at Dates Stipulated
French Oceania (Polynesia)	Overseas Territory of France	1520	82,900 (est. 1966) at census of 1956, 73,201, incl. 6748 Chinese, 2298 French and 489 other Europeans (Census, 1956)
Society Islands (Tahiti, etc.)		593	56,999
Rapa Islands		15	4029
Austral (Tubuai Islands)		53	
Tuamotus		319	8237
Gambier (Mangareva) Islands		11	
Marquesas		459	3936
Pitcairn (incl. Henderson, Dulcie, Oeno)	British Crown Colony	2.2	115 (June 1962)
Easter Island	Dependency of Chile	45	1050 (est. 1962)
United States Trust Territory of the Pacific Islands	Trust Territory of the United Nations administered by the United States of America	687 (plus Guam, 215 s.m.)	84,777 (est. 1963)
Caroline Islands		461.4	55,684
including Palay District			9965
Yap District			5931
Truk District			22,564
Ponape District			17,224
Mariana Islands (Ladrones)		399.1	9586
including Guam (U.S. Possession)			67,044 (1960. incl. natives)
Saipan District			34,762
Rota District			8532
			1054
Marshall Islands		69.8	15,710

C. THE REST OF THE PACIFIC WORLD—*continued*

Territory	Designation	Area in Square Miles	Population at Dates Stipulated
HAWAII	Fiftieth state of the United States	6,442.5	734,791 (est. 1964) at census April 1960, 632,772
Hawaii		4030	
Maui		728	61,332 (1960)
Molokai		260	35,717
Kahoolawe		45	5023
Lanai		141	—
Oahu		604	2115
Kauai		555	500,409
Niihau		72	27,922
Outlying Islands (inc. Midway)		7.5	254
			2356
OTHER UNITED STATES TERRITORIES:			
Wake Island		3	1097 (1960)
Line Islands			
Kingman			
Palmyra			
Jarvis			
Howland			
Baker			
CANTON AND ENDERBURY ISLANDS	Anglo-American Condominium	5.8	421 (incl. 191 Gilbert & Ellice islanders) All on Canton

D. AUSTRALIAN AND NEW ZEALAND ANTARCTIC TERRITORIES

Territory	Designation	Area in Square Miles	Population at Dates Stipulated
AUSTRALIAN ANTARCTIC TERRITORY	Dependency of the Commonwealth of Australia	2,472,000	—
ROSS DEPENDENCY	Dependency of the Dominion of New Zealand	175,000	—

APPENDIX TWO

TRADE STATISTICS OF SOUTHWEST PACIFIC TERRITORIES, 1963-64

EXTENT AND NATURE OF FOREIGN TRADE AND PER CAPITA VALUES

Territory	Value of Exports and Imports—Total Foreign Trade ($N.Z. millions)	Exports as Percentages of Imports (Figures of less than 100 indicate adverse trade balance)	Per capita Value of Exports ($N.Z.)	Per capita Value of Imports ($N.Z.)	Principal Destination of Exports	Principal Source of Imports	Major Export and Percentage Proportion of Total Exports by Value
Australia	4129.7	118	203	173	United Kingdom Japan U.S.A China (Mainland)	United Kingdom U.S.A. Japan	Wool 35
New Zealand	1422.5	105	286	250	United Kingdom U.S.A. E.E.C. Japan	United Kingdom Australia U.S.A. Japan	Wool 43
Australian New Guinea	83.5	44	16	36	Australia United Kingdom	Australia	Copra and coconut products 42
Papua	27.8	19	8	41	Australia	Australia	Copra and coconut products 37
Solomons	7.6	73	25	34	United Kingdom	Australia	Copra and coconut products 88

New Hebrides	11.3	133	100	74	France	Australia	Copra and coconut products 64
New Caledonia	83.8	112	540	471	France	Australia	Nickel 95
Fiji	96.0	81	89	109	United Kingdom	Australia	Sugar 77
Tonga	4.9	59	26	44	Venezuela United Kingdom	Australia	Copra and coconut products 79
Western Samoa	12.1	70	41	58	New Zealand	New Zealand	Copra and coconut products 37
American Samoa	10.8	160	318	198	U.S.A.	U.S.A.	Canned fish 99
Cook Islands	4.9	56	95	154	New Zealand	New Zealand	Fruit juice 42
Niue	.6	31	31	92	New Zealand	New Zealand	Copra and coconut products 58
Gilbert and Ellice Islands	4.5	74	39	53	Australia	Australia	Phosphates 67
Nauru	16.0	79	1440	1824	Australia	Australia	Phosphates 100
French Polynesia	59.1	16	97	631	France	France	Phosphates 42
Total of Island Territories Listed	423.2	—	48	80	Europe Australia	Australia	Copra and coconut products

KIND AND DESTINATION OF EXPORT COMMODITIES OF ISLAND TERRITORIES

Territory	Percentage Value of Categories of Exports				Major Destinations of Exports Percentage Values							
	Tropical Food Products (Cocoa, Sugar, etc.)	Raw and Crude Materials (Copra, Minerals, etc.)	Manufactured Goods	Others	Australia	New Zealand	United Kingdom	United States	France	Japan	West Germany	Netherlands
Australian New Guinea	41.1	48.1	10.8	—	44.3	0.2	32.5	3.0	0.2	4.6	4.8	6.6
Papua	3.1	96.3	0.6	—	79.9	0.1	9.0	0.4	—	4.0	0.4	0.4
Solomons	0.5	99.5	—	—	20.4	—	52.7	—	0.4	25.2	0.2	0.2
New Hebrides	12.7	87.0	—	0.3	2.7	—	—	6.4	49.7	23.6	—	—
New Caledonia	2.2	96.4	1.1	0.3	2.1	—	—	—	45.0	42.9	—	—
Fiji	80.4	13.0	6.6	—	7.6	14.3	41.2	9.1	—	1.6	2.4	1.7
Tonga	26.4	70.1	2.6	0.8	0.3	23.5	21.4	0.5	—	15.5	0.5	—
Western Samoa	62.4	37.2	0.4	—	1.0	44.8	16.1	8.4	—	0.5	20.6	3.4
American Samoa	99.2	0.7	0.1	—	—	—	—	97.9	—	1.7	—	—
Cook Islands	65.8	10.9	21.0	2.3	0.5	98.7	0.1	0.1	—	—	—	—
Gilbert & Ellice Islands	—	100.0	—	—	54.5	12.8	32.4	—	—	—	—	—
Nauru	—	100.0	—	—								
French Polynesia	11.8	81.3	2.4	4.5	1.5	23.9	—	3.3	45.0	19.2	3.0	0.1

APPENDIX THREE

EXPLANATION OF PHOTOGRAPHS

1. Forest occupied only a small part of the continent of Australia, but amongst the eucalypts were a large number of valuable hardwood timbers. Here a mill train is hauling jarrah railroad sleepers from the West Australian bush. These are exported through Fremantle. They often outlast the metal rails themselves.

2. Much of the Australian grassland in areas with more reliable precipitation has a vegetation of open, scattered savanna woodland. This mob of Hereford cattle is being driven through such country, liberally sprinkled with gum trees, between Yass and Cooma, New South Wales.

3. Even the drier areas often have a thick low-growing scrubby vegetation of eucalypt and acacia species. This photograph of the trans-Australian express heading east between the Nullarbor Plains and the head of Spencer's Gulf shows saltbush and bluebush in the foreground and the tangled thicket of mallee scrub to the left.

4. Merino sheep are the basis of Australian wealth and progress. Here is part of a flock of 2400 pure-bred merinos on a property not far from the Australian federal capital, Canberra.

5. Vast distances, poor pastures frequently stricken by drought, make it necessary for beef cattle to be driven from pastures to pastures and from inland raising areas to distant southern and eastern markets. This mob has been nine months on the trek from Northern Territory. The scraggy beasts crowd round the watering troughs at Ti-Tree Wells—just north of Alice Springs. This is a typical 'store-and-bore watering point', such as are maintained at two-day intervals along all the main stock tracks.

6. Dairying in Australia is practised under natural conditions far less favourable than those enjoyed by the New Zealand 'cow cockey'. This herd of fifty Jerseys is raised on coarse rank pastures near Taree, 160 miles north of Sydney on the coast of New South Wales.

7. This is part of the largest cattle station in Western Australia. It occupies 4000 *square miles* near the Fitzroy River in the Kimberleys. Some 8000 cattle are turned off each year. Many are shipped alive from Derby to Fremantle. The rest are driven 300 miles to the Broome meatworks. The station employs 120 native and half-caste stockmen. Here aborigines are saddling up near the homestead before a muster.

8. The large-scale extensive cultivation of wheat on former grass and savanna land is one of Australia's major primary industries. A header harvester is at work in typical rolling and still partly timbered grassland in the Victorian Wimmera. Large acreages, low yields, little labour and maximum employment of mechanical methods of cultivation and harvesting are characteristic.

9. Few parts of the vast continent of Australia are closely cultivated and intensively utilized. The moist climate of Tasmania, however, has made a mixed and intensive agriculture possible on the small lowland areas and adjacent lower slopes. Like Launceston and the Tamar estuary, the land near Hobart and the Hobart harbour has a richly-varied agriculture and a landscape of closely-divided, carefully-cultivated small farms.

10. More than a million acres of land along the Murray are under irrigation, without which the productive cultivated land in Australia would be much less than it is. Here vines are growing under irrigation on the flat terrace above the Murray at Renmark. Notice also the apricot trees on the right.

11. Vines are grown to produce grapes for sale for the table, as dried currants or raisins, or for making wine. The fruit is dried in the sun or on racks in the shade. This photograph was taken at Mildura, Victoria.

12. Queensland's principal crop is sugar cane. Well over 100,000 people owe their livelihood to it. Without it, little of the tropical coast of the state would be occupied as it is. Here a tractor drags loaded cane trucks on the first stage of their journey to the crushing mill. Behind is a field of 'plant' cane, and in the background eroded and partly deforested slopes of the hills behind Innisfail.

13. The source of the Commonwealth's longest established supply of iron ore is Iron Monarch. The ore is hauled thirty-four miles by rail to Whyalla, from where most of it is shipped to blast furnaces at Newcastle and Port Kembla, more than 1100 miles away. Today vast new deposits of iron ore are being opened up in Western Australia and the ore shipped to Japan.

14. Australia has great mineral wealth. No minerals have hitherto been more important than the combination of silver-lead-zinc, and no deposit richer than that at Broken Hill. This is the mine of Broken Hill South Ltd. Beyond is a great dump of residue and in the distance the residential portions of the town, 6000 of whose inhabitants find employment with the mining companies.

15. There are few larger and at the same time more accessible deposits of brown coal than this at Yallourn in the Latrobe valley, Victoria. Opencast workings are eating slowly into the estimated 27,000 million tons of low-grade fuel. The coal is the basis of a great thermo-electrical generating system which furnishes a large part of the electricity supply of Victoria. New and additional generating stations are under construction in the Latrobe valley. Coal is also briquetted.

16. Newcastle is 'Australia's Sheffield', the largest single centre of heavy
    metallurgical industries in the country. Broken Hill Proprietary Ltd
employs 7000 people there. Here are the steel works at the mouth of the
Hunter River. Iron ore from South Australia is unloaded by means of the
bridges on the left, and in the centre of the picture are the blast furnaces.

17. New South Wales has specially constructed trucks on the state rail-
    ways to handle bulk shipment of wheat. The trucks are loaded through
chutes directly from storage silos like that shown here. This photograph
was taken at Wallendbeen, New South Wales. Australia is exporting
increasing amounts of wheat to China and India.

18. In the absence of railways in the vast interior of the Australian
    continent, modern highways have been built during and since the war,
partly for strategic reasons. More recently, in the development of the
cattle industry and in the search for and exploitation of minerals, 'roads'
have been developed hurriedly. Here a 'prime mover' hauls three trailers,
each carrying 30 cattle, between Derby and Fitzroy Crossing.

19. Nothing has done so much to break down the isolation of the Aus-
    tralian outback and to overcome the handicap of vast, roadless
distances as the light passenger aircraft. The station owner today often
has his own plane and the doctor uses one to visit his patients. Here a
Cessna of Bush Pilots' Airways calls on request at a cattle station in
northern Queensland to take out a stockman going on leave. The homestead is partially hidden by the aircraft.

20. Australia, for all its rapidly growing population, is still an empty
    continent. Most of its people live in the few state capital cities. Much
of the inland is unoccupied and as much more is sparsely peopled. This
photograph reflects something of the loneliness and emptiness of the outback. Hall's Creek, 200 miles south of Wyndham, once a gold rush town,
is today no more than a ghost with a mere handful of houses and stores,
the centre of far-flung cattle-rearing country.

21. The inland wheat-growing and livestock-grazing areas of Australia
    are serviced by small country towns with stores, social halls, a 'pub',
garages and farm machinery repair and servicing depots. From the veranda
and the shade it provides, this stockman watches a mob of cattle in the
dusty, sun-drenched main street of such a small town in the sheep and
wheat-growing belt of New South Wales.

22. New Guinea is a mountainous and rugged tropical island three times
    the size of New Zealand. The interior is inaccessible except by aircraft.
This short landing strip lies at an elevation of 2500 feet in a deep valley
in the Owen Stanley Range in Papua. Within a short distance mountain
peaks rise to over 12,000 feet. Notice the signs of burning and cultivation
low on the right. Native agricultural practices are largely responsible for
the grassy vegetation.

23. Cleared recently from bush (background) by the menfolk of the tribe, this garden on the Tumbuda River is cared for by the women. The crop being harvested is sweet potato (*kau kau*). It is the staple article of diet throughout the highlands of both Australian and West New Guinea. Notice the net baskets suspended from the foreheads over the backs of the women.

24. High in the Buang Mountains on the northeast coast of the New Guinea mainland the village of Mapos (top left) is surrounded by a sea of kunai grass which after repeated burning and shifting cultivation has replaced the forest (right distance). Fences of matted scrub mark off and protect the yam gardens of the village families from wild animals.

25. Part of Mapos village is made up of yam houses in which yams are stored after harvesting. Raised off the ground high on the ridge the stored yams have maximum ventilation and protection.

26. In coastal and accessible lowland areas of New Guinea natives cut and dry copra. These men are spreading copra to dry in the sun. Notice the breadfruit tree to the right and the banana plants in the background. Copra production is the most securely established economic activity, and is especially important in New Britain and New Ireland.

27. This is a corner of a commercial coconut plantation in the Trobriand Islands, an idyllic group of coral islands off the tail of New Guinea. The natives, who spend part of their time diving for pearls, are here assembling nuts before they are collected by the plantation truck (left background).

28. Rabaul and Simpson Harbour, New Britain. Port Moresby is the administrative capital of the combined territories of Papua and New Guinea. Lae is the centre of air transport. But Rabaul, the former German capital occupied by the Japanese during World War II, is the chief port and the centre of the densest concentration of commercial plantations in the territories.

29. Gold mining is centred principally in the Wau and Bulolo valleys, where the gold is largely alluvial and won mainly by dredging. At the Koronga opencut near Wau native labourers are sluicing for gold under the direction of an Australian overseer.

30. For its size Nauru is economically just about the most important of the Pacific's myriad island specks. But its phosphate resources will last no more than thirty or forty years at present rates of exploitation. This photographs shows phosphate workings and the general appearance of the island's plateau surface.

31. The European and administrative buildings are grouped near the cantilever shipping point in the Aiwo district in the southwest. The crushing and drying sheds and cantilever can be seen in the left distance. Photo taken from the plateau edge overlooking the narrow belt of coastal lowland.

P

32. Some of the royalties paid by the British Phosphate Commission have
    been devoted to the construction of modern airy dwellings like this
for the housing of the Nauruan people.

33. Both before and since the first European penetration of the Pacific
    the coconut has been the most important crop. The tree is the source
of food, drink, oil and fibre. The husk provides fibre for sennit cordage;
the leaves furnish fibre for plaiting and for roofs and sides of native houses.
The trunk makes a serviceable timber. One tree may carry from sixty to
eighty nuts at any one time. The two dark nuts on the right are ripe and
will soon fall to the ground.

34. From the Pacific World there comes almost a fifth of the coconut
    products entering international trade—mainly copra, coconut oil and
coconut meal. The nut is split in two (notice the thick fibrous husk) and
the white meat is cut from the hard inner shell. This is dried by natural or
artificial means to form the blue-grey copra of commerce (right). Oil is
extracted from copra to leave a powdered meal which is a valuable livestock food.

35. In the Solomons copra production is the only significant economic
    activity. This is a healthy and well-planted commercial holding, but
weed growth is getting away, making it difficult to gather fallen nuts.
More intensive grazing by cattle is desirable to keep plantations tidy.

36. Activities on a coconut plantation are largely concentrated on or near
    the drying sheds. In fine weather trays of copra are run out into the
sun. In wet weather copra is dried inside the low, corrugated-iron sheds
by heat produced by burning the husks and shells.

37. Like the scattered large islands of the New Hebrides condominium,
    the Solomons have not been the scene of much successful large-scale
European economic penetration. Village life is often not vastly different
from what it was before the missionary and the trader came. A coastal
village on Malaita.

38. Native dwellings are still predominantly constructed of traditional
    local materials and in traditional style. Local timbers and coconut-
leaf thatching, bamboo and sennit (for lashing timbers together) are still
employed. Bachelors' quarters in Lisiala village, Malaita, Solomon
Islands.

39. Native canoes are still used for local coastal travel and coastal villagers
    depend on fishing from canoes for part of their subsistence. From Lake
Sentani near Soekanopura in Irian Barat to the reef-sheltered lagoon of
Penrhyn canoes are handled by Pacific island children at a very early age.

40. It is from Malaita (see 37) that labour is principally recruited for the
    coconut plantations on Gizo and the Russell Islands. These 'boys'
from Malaita (notice their Melanesian ethnic features) have agreed to
work on plantations. The photograph was taken on Guadalcanal on their
way to the Russell Islands.

41. A village street typical not only of the Solomons but also of the New Hebrides.

42. Noumea is one of the larger towns of the island territories of the southwest Pacific. It is the headquarters of the administration of the French territories in the southwest Pacific, the official headquarters of the South Pacific Commission, centre of the nickel smelting industry, tourist town and jet air terminal.

43. In the hilly interior of New Caledonia the native tribes practise a modified indigenous system of agriculture. Here at Col de la Pirogue, taro is cultivated on narrow irrigated terraces leeward of the main ranges. Notice also the roofs of native hutments.

44. Norfolk Island is Australian territory. It is a small hilly island of 'European' garden cultivators, their small-holdings strung along the roads amidst the remnants of a once extensive woodland of Norfolk Island pines. This is part of the island behind Kingston.

45. Most of New Zealand, especially the North Island, carried a heavy forest cover. It was rich and varied in physiognomy and composition. North of the Tauranga-Kawhia line the lordly kauri, with its massive trunk rising a hundred feet without branches, was often the dominant species. Little kauri remains today. The largest remnant is the Waipoua forest, north of Dargaville, Northland.

46. Most of the forest was wasted. After 1880 hundreds of thousands of acres of heavily timbered land were cleared by burning. Bush fires like this were burned whenever the weather and season allowed. Landscapes, raw and ugly and littered with blackened logs and stumps, were widespread, especially in the North Island. It was by means of the 'bush-burn technique' that a forested land was converted into a land of pasture grasses and livestock farms.

47. New Zealand is characterized above all by the ruggedness and high elevation of all but a small part of its surface. Its mountain terrains, however, reveal a striking variety of forms and disposition. This aerial view from above Mitre Peak at the head of the Milford Sound shows the profound glacial dissection of Fiordland, its hard and ancient rocks, faulted and fractured and deep-cut by moving ice. Inaccessible, unoccupied and partly unexplored, its deep-water fiords provided shelter for the early navigators, especially Captain James Cook.

48. Today rich, closely-cropped pastureland, divided into small enclosures and dotted with occasional clumps and lines of planted North American, Australian and European trees sweeps over hill and valley flat where no more than seventy years ago a dense subtropical forest of largely endemic species stood dark, sombre, virgin, penetrated only here and there by Maori tracks.

49. It is paradoxical that a land in which grazing and browsing animals were unknown should in so short a time have become one which,

today, is, for its size, tordden by a denser population of domestic animals than any other in the world. There are sixty million sheep in New Zealand (mostly Romneys) and sixty per cent of them on the deforested hills of the North Island interior (here the hill country inland of Wanganui) and the easier flats (see next plate).

50. Sheep on the flats, where the world's most productive pastures have often been established. 'Canterbury lambs' (the progeny of Southdown rams and Romney ewes) will be fattened on these rotational pastures of ryegrass and clover before being separated permanently from their mothers and sent on the journey to the freezing works and Smithfield. This is the northern, narrowing end of the Canterbury Plains.

51. In the more remote parts of the tussock high country merino flocks still graze the indigenous grassland, but rarely more than 20 sheep (often wethers) to each hundred acres of grass, scrub, rock and scree. Here in Canterbury high country, near Lake Coleridge (left distance) on Glenthorne Station (homestead lower right), halfbred sheep are run. To the right is the Harper River and beyond it the upper Rakaia.

52. Sheep on the mountainsides graze the tussock grassland, and the large holdings, sometimes as much as 40,000 acres in extent, are still operated much as they were when the grazing licences were taken up in the 1850s. This mob of 2500 halfbred ewes is being turned out after dipping in spring on to the more elevated blocks of the run. The danger of heavy snow is over for eight months or more. On the extreme right is a corner of Lake Wanaka.

53. The woolshed is the centrepiece of sheepfarms, both extensively operated high-country runs and lowland lamb-fattening properties. In a shed like this with stands for six or eight shearers as many as 2000 sheep a day may be shorn by electrically operated machine shears.

54. The dairy lands are found in the once-forested or swamp-filled low-land areas of the North Island. Taranaki with its mature circle of pasture and closely divided, well sheltered fields around the base of Mount Egmont is the oldest of them, although in 1880 this area was a damp and dripping wilderness of dense forest. Most cows on dairy farms are grade Jerseys. Since this photograph was taken both pastures and farm management have improved, and higher livestock densities and larger herds are found than this view of the Egmont landscape suggests.

55. The most important building on a dairy farm, the cowshed, is smaller than the shearing shed on sheep farms. The introduction of the 'herring-bone' design, electrically-operated gates, the half-circle yard and tanker collection of milk from a refrigerated stainless steel vat in the dairy (out of sight) have lessened labour requirements and shortened milking time. With better topdressed pastures, some dairy farmers have been able to increase the size of herds by 50-100 per cent without additional labour.

56. Arable farming, ploughed fields, waving crops of grain are characteristic features of only the drier eastern plains and downland of the

South Island; but even here livestock products are usually the principal source of income. Both cash (grain and seed) crops and fodder crops are grown. Wheat is the chief cash crop. Farming is mechanized. Here a header harvester delivers sacks of ripe grain. Alternatively, it can pour the wheat in bulk into an accompanying truck. Yields are high. In recent years an average of almost 50 bushels an acre has been produced.

57. Processing farm products is the Dominion's most characteristic industrial activity. There are dairy factories, some of them giants of their kind, in most rural townships in the dairying regions. In the Waikato great modern factories produce butter, dried milk, and casein. In Taranaki smaller cheese factories are characteristic.

58. New Zealand is ill-supplied with coal. It is mostly of inferior quality and occurs in small broken pockets. Most of it is in the steep and hilly coastal areas of Westland. Here an endless rope is taking trucks of coal from the Stockton opencast mine down a steep incline before shipment through Westport. With the burning of coal to generate electricity and the growth of North Island industries and towns coal production in the Waikato now exceeds that of Westland.

59. New Zealand's principal source of energy is water power. It has advantages in the regularity and abundance of rain and in the steepness of slopes. In the North Island the Waikato River and in the South Island the Waitaki River are the major drainage systems that have so far been harnessed. Latest dam and power station on the Waitaki is this at Benmore. The station came into operation in 1965 and its six generators will have an ultimate capacity of 540,000kW. Benmore power is transmitted via the Cook Strait cable to the North Island.

60. Almost half New Zealand's people live in the four main centres. In recent years the population of the Auckland, Christchurch and Wellington metropolitan areas has been growing rapidly. The capital, Wellington, however, is hemmed in by steep hills, and its recent industrial and residential expansion has overflowed into the Hutt Valley (middle distance). In the foreground of this picture are hilly residential suburbs of Wellington. The central core of the city is on the waterfront off to the right.

61. Intensive cultivation of special crops and orcharding are confined to small pockets of land with especially favourable climatic characteristics. The Waimea Plain between Nelson and Motueka has the largest acreage of orchards, but also grows practically all the hops and tobacco produced in the country. It is the sunniest spot in New Zealand and is protected by encircling mountain ranges from unusually strong winds.

62. Most rapidly growing of the four main centres is Auckland with a metropolitan population of 560,000—one in every five people in New Zealand. The city sprawls especially to the south of the isthmus. This area—Penrose, Ellerslie, Otahuhu and Papatoetoe (distance)—around the head of the Mangere Inlet (Manukau Harbour) has filled up with in-

dustry and housing in the last two decades, and the new urban motorway and old South Trunk railway line (parallel in foreground) are facilitating the further southward growth into Manukau City, and to Wiri, Manurewa and Papakura.

63. Still a third of the population, including most of the Maori population, is classed as rural. The country township with its garage, store, social hall, church and possibly a dairy factory is the centre of country life. The cream lorry carries mail, passengers and a variety of goods, news and messages. These Maori women are not perturbed by the frequent delays.

64. The Cook Islands are New Zealand's most distant outpost. Rarotonga is linked, but not as frequently as is desirable, with the outlying atolls of the Northern Cook Group by copra cutters like this. Notice the crowd of passengers and the elevated volcanic profile of Rarotonga in the background.

65. The fringing coral reef of the Pacific's myriad islands makes the loading and unloading of ships difficult. Only native canoes can usually cross the reef, and off-shore there is deep water in which larger vessels can rarely find anchorage. Here the people of Mauke unload cargo from small boats while the ship stands off in deep water.

66. A handful of Europeans on Rarotonga still operate small plantations. Copra and oranges are the chief products. Here a well-established citrus orchard lies centrally within a plantation of 150 acres of coconut trees.

67. The only significant agricultural product of the Southern Cook Group is the orange. It was formerly gathered from trees growing wild but the administration has sought to establish small plantations of improved and seedless varieties. This is a government citrus nursery near Avarua, Rarotonga. Today the juice is extracted and exported. This saves losses due to lack of shipping, provides employment in Rarotonga and saves shipping space.

68. Here is a three-year-old plot of oranges planted and cared for by the Department of Agriculture on individualized native land. Departmental employees are mulching and fertilizing the young trees. It is hoped that when they come to maturity their cultivation will be taken over by the native landholder and that the cost of establishment will be charged against the future crop.

69. These Maori girls in the village packing shed at Titikaveka are carefully packing island oranges into crates, made of *Pinus radiata* timber and imported in shooks from New Zealand.

70. Chief subsistence crop is taro. On Rarotonga, Mauke and Mangaia patches of swamp are carefully irrigated and cultivated and taro is the staple food. Coconut plays a lesser part, alongside kumaras, which are grown on light coral sand soils in coastal areas.

71. On Rarotonga in recent years tomatoes have been a popular cash crop. They are grown with little care and attention after rather laborious clearing of weeds. They are planted in the hope that a vessel will arrive as they ripen to take them to the New Zealand market. For two days before its arrival there is unaccustomed bustle and activity. But often no vessel does arrive as the tomatoes ripen and the crop is left to rot on the vine. As a result production is declining.

72. The packing depots in Rarotonga are large, airy buildings. Here village gardeners are unloading tomatoes from their one-horse drays. The tomatoes will be picked-over and carefully packed before shipment.

73. Rarotonga is a high volcanic island. Mangaia is a raised atoll. This is a view from the deck of the *Moana Roa* of Oneroa, largest village on Mangaia. The narrow coastal rim of the island is bounded by scrub-covered limestone cliffs beyond which stretches the plateau-like, rough, rocky surface of the *makatea*. Between the ship and the shore ply the small boats bringing and taking passengers and goods.

74. Typical scene along the coastal road of *makatea* on the New Zealand island territory of Niue. A party of young men is returning to Alofi after a day's work on the distant village gardens.

75. Manihiki in the Northern Cook Group is a typical atoll. Notice the coconut-clad *motus* on the reef across the lagoon. The trade winds blow steadily, ruffling the blue-green surface of the water and bending over the rustling palms.

76. Pukapuka is another atoll. Here nearly the whole population of the islet is gathered together to greet the arrival of a cutter with six months' mail and precious supplies of stores.

77. The Kingdom of Tonga is a land of small garden cultivators, most families living comfortably off the subsistence produce and occasional commercial crops from an $8\frac{1}{4}$-acre *api*. Here is a corner of an *api* on Tongatapu. This year, after clearing, yams will be cultivated. Next year the same patch of ground will support a jumbled array of various crops, including bananas, cassava, melons, kava, paper mulberry and young coconuts.

78. A few European plantations are still found in Tonga, although it is the policy of the government not to renew leases of land to plantation operators when they fall due. This plantation of 800 acres, all in coconuts, is on the island of Tongatapu and is operated by the original German landholder. The labour employed is from the New Hebrides.

79. It is when a feast is held in honour of the ruling family or of some distinguished visitor, that the profusion of native produce is apparent. Here Tongans are laying out foodstuffs on a grassy lawn beside the Mua lagoon, Tongatapu, on part of the royal estates in preparation for a feast. Pigs and poultry are saved for such occasions after which there may be a dearth of them in the villages for months.

80. The elevated island of 'Eua to the east of Tongatapu long remained
    sparsely settled, until in 1948 the people of Niuafo'ou were taken
there after continued volcanic disturbance made their former island home
no longer safe. This is a view of their new surroundings. Houses have
been built in traditional style using largely thatch and sidings of matted
coconut leaves. Around them is a wilderness of burned and blackened
forest amidst which incredibly heavy crops of food plants are already
being grown on the virgin volcanic soils.

81. This picture of a corner of the *kolo* of Kolovai, western Tongatapu,
    shows the typical short-grass lawn surrounding the houses, the varied
pattern, construction and materials from which the Tongans today build
their villages. Behind the houses are cooking sheds and sometimes small
primitive village copra driers. Each Tongan male is entitled to a village
house site together with an *api* on reaching the age of eighteen.

82. The people from Niuafo'ou are rather different in stature and culture
    from the Tongatapuans. They are shorter, darker in skin colour,
more active and vigorous, and speak a different Polynesian language. They
were not happy at being removed to 'Eua but are making the best of it
and going about the making of a new home with determination and vigour.

83. The Samoan *fale* is distinctive amongst traditional Polynesian native
    house types. Notice the basalt stones providing a raised floor, the
round shape and the hive-like roof structure. Temporary sides of coconut
matting are let down at night.

84. Samoan village scene—on the little island of Apolima between Upolu
    and Savai'i. The sea, the beach, the coastal village site and forested
hills behind are representative of all Samoa.

85. Apia, formerly the centre of German administration, is now the
    capital of the first Polynesian state to win sovereign independence.
Like other port towns in the southwest Pacific it is growing rapidly with
the recent tendency for many indigenous families to seek urban life and
employment.

86. The deep quiet waters of Pago Pago Harbour reach back far into the
    volcanic hills of Tutuila. For over half a century the harbour has
been an American naval base and the town the headquarters of American
interests in the southwest Pacific. Here tuna is canned for export to the
United States. The fish is caught and landed by Japanese.

87. The colony of Fiji is a rich and varied territory and of greater sig-
    nificance at present than any other island territory within the Pacific
island neighbourhood of New Zealand. This aerial view is of a portion
of the dry side of Viti Levu. It shows the intensive cultivation and small
cane farms along the flats of the Mba River.

88. Here the cane is being harvested. A temporary rail track is laid along-
    side the standing cane. Zebu-cross oxen drag the rake of trucks
before the cane is loaded. The harvesting gangs, like the cane farmers,

are Indians. A row of trimmed cane ready for loading lies beside the trucks. The 'trash' in the foreground will be burned.

89. The loaded trucks are taken to the permanent lines and dragged off to the mill by small steam engines. Notice the cane farm on the far bank of the river. The Indian tenant usually operates on a ten or twelve-acre holding leased from the South Pacific Sugar Mills. The one-room thatched hutments are typical of the cane lands.

90. Lautoka, western Viti Levu, is one of five mill towns in Fiji. Like the others it is both an Indian town and a company town. The crushing mill is the town's central feature. Notice the lines of cane trucks and the assemblage of ancillary buildings. Cane grows almost up to the walls of the mill. In the right foreground are labour lines for Indian mill workers. On the hill to the right are the homes of European employees, and beyond the commercial and shopping core of the Indian settlement.

91. This is a close-up view of an Indian tenant farmer's home. Notice the plough, the cane crop in the background and the reed-grass thatching of the house.

92. The rolling and hilly areas of the 'dry zone' are occupied either by Indian cultivators who barely scratch a living from the thin and eroding soils and who allow goats and cattle to roam the hills, or (as here) by the cattle ranch of the South Pacific Sugar Mills, a subsidiary of the Australian Colonial Sugar Refining Company. At Yanggara the company runs 3000 cattle on 17,000 acres of tropical grassland.

93. The Fijian *koro* is still usually built in the traditional style, inland on a terrace clearing beside the river and below the forested valley slopes, or beneath clustered palms along a reef-fringed shore. This village on the banks of the Wainimala, tributary of the Rewa, is typical of inland villages. Gardens are shifted about on the steep hill slopes around, and bananas for sale are cultivated amidst tall reeds and grasses on other river-terrace clearings.

94. The Fijian is a Melanesian. He is typically tall, dark-skinned and has a mop of frizzy hair. In the Lau Group and even in the eastern-most parts of Viti Levu Polynesian ethnic and cultural features have been added, and the chiefly families especially often carry a strong strain of Polynesian blood.

95. The houses of village and tribal chiefs are masterpieces of craftsman-ship and demonstrate a high level of skill in the use of local raw materials. This house was constructed for the *tui* of the Fijian village at Tavua. The foundation is of stone, the structure of stout timbers, the walls of plaited bamboo and the roof thatch, in places three feet thick, of reeds and coconut fibre. No nails were used in its construction, only sennit.

96. On Viti Levu the chief commercial crop of the Fijians is the banana; elsewhere copra is the principal source of cash income. Here a village family is poling its bananas down the Rewa River on a home-made raft

of bamboo. At the open-air packing station on the river bank downstream the bananas are cut into individual fingers and packed in wooden cases. The raft is abandoned, and the Fijians return to their villages by muddy forest tracks.

97. The preparations being made here in the village of Tumbau, on Lakemba, in the Lau Group, to entertain members of the provincial council provide a close-up view of some traditional Fijian foodstuffs. On the right is a heap of yams. The other pile is one of taro and the boys are carrying more. In the foreground is a row of turtles.

98. This striking picture is a view of the gold mines at Vatukoula, Viti Levu. Gold to the value of more than $2,600,000 a year is mined by companies established with Australian capital. Several hundred Fijians are employed in the mines.

99. Suva, the seat of the colonial administration of Fiji, is the chief port and largest town in the island territories of the southwest Pacific. Today it has a population of more than 50,000 people—Indians, Fijians, Chinese, Europeans, Gilbertese and other Pacific islanders. It is a cosmopolitan and colourful town, the centre of a growing tourist trade. Its factories are also of increasing number and significance.

Glossary

artifacts: a term used by ethnologists to refer to the products of the arts and crafts of primitive peoples, e.g. tools, weapons.

andesite: an igneous rock, not basic like basalt, nor acid like rhyolite, but intermediate. Associated with the continents and 'continental' islands and not with the 'volcanic' islands of the Pacific proper.

arcuate islands: a string or series of islands disposed in a line bent like a bow: bowed, arched. Such arcuate island chains mark the western rim of the structural 'basin' of the Pacific.

auriferous lodes: a *lode* is a vein of minerals occurring in a crack or fissure in certain rocks; *auriferous* means 'gold-bearing'. Gold, and other minerals, may also occur in alluvial deposits. The lodes are destroyed by erosion, the minerals washed out and later deposited in gravel and alluvium and river flats, called *placers.*

avifauna: fauna and *flora* are collective and comprehensive terms used to refer respectively to all animals and all plants. *Avifauna* refers collectively to the birds of any area.

Barringtonia: B. asiatica is a large, wide-spreading tree occurring as part of a rich mixed strand flora, on the coasts of the larger, rainier islands of the Pacific. It has a heavy nut-like fruit which can apparently travel without harm for long periods in salt water.

basalt: a dark-coloured igneous rock of volcanic origin—solidified lava found frequently in the volcanic islands of the Pacific.

bêche-de-mer: a sea slug; a marine animal found on the coral reef off the shores of the Pacific's many islands, and collected for food. Sometimes dried and exported to China for making soup. The slug is sometimes called sea cucumber, and when dried is alternatively referred to as *trepang.*

biotic resources: plant and animal resources.

bituminous: see *coal.*

'blackbirding': refers to the practice of kidnapping native peoples to sell them as labourers. Such traffic led to the depopulation of some Pacific islands. The term 'blackbird' was first applied to the negro slaves kidnapped from West Africa and sold in North America.

'Blue laws': a term used to refer to the strict moral code introduced by early missionaries to the islands of the Pacific.

bonanza: indicates prosperity or good luck. A term applied to a productive mine or to a prosperous and productive system of agriculture. Usually indicates a short-term prosperity, or a wasting or exhausting of agricultural resources.

brigalow: a shrub community dominated by an acacia (*Acacia harpophylla*) and occurring widely in savanna and savanna woodland areas of inland Queensland. When trees and shrubs are killed by being ring-barked the scrub is replaced by mixed grass pastures. The same areas were at one time also invaded at times by prickly pear.

Carboniferous: see *geological time-scale*.

cirque: a large, rocky, steep-sided basin or armchair-shaped excavation high on a mountainside, eroded by ice.

coal: a sedimentary rock of organic origin. It occurs in several forms—anthracite, bituminous, sub-bituminous, and lignite with decreasing degrees of hardness, decreasing proportions of carbon, and increasing proportions of waste (volatile matter) in them.

condominium: a territory governed jointly by two or more countries, e.g. the New Hebrides.

contour planting: planting (of crops or trees) on the contour to prevent excessive or rapid run-off of water and erosion of soil.

Cretaceous: see *geological time-scale*.

distributary: the numerous branch streams into which a river divides in its delta are called *distributaries*. The streams which come together to form the river are tributaries.

ecological balance: the balance which is established in nature between different groups of plants and/or of animals. This balance is disturbed by natural changes (of climate, for example) and especially by human interference as when grassland or forest is burned or when new species of animals or plants are introduced.

edaphic: pertaining to soil but used generally to refer to the factors (other than climate) conditioning the growth of plants, especially soil, drainage, and aspect.

endemic: a plant (or animal, or disease) endemic in New Zealand (or some other place) is one that is not only regular in its occurrence there but is native to the area specified.

entomologist: a student of the science of entomology, a branch of zoology concerned with insects.

entrepôt: a port (or city) with an entrepôt trade is one which collects export produce for transhipment and receives imports for distribution over a wide area; or a storehouse, a depot, a point of exchange.

ethnic: refers to 'race'. Ethnology is the study of the racial and cultural differences between groups of men, between the so-called 'races' of men.

exotic: alien, strange; a term applied to plants and animals introduced to an area from outside. New Zealand's introduced pine trees (mainly from North America) are thus referred to as 'exotic conifers', and the plantations of them as 'exotic forests'.

fale: the Samoan name for a native round or oval-shaped house built of native timbers and thatch.

fauna: see *avifauna*.

foliated: split into thin sheets; a term applied to metamorphic rocks (like schist) which on weathering peel into thin plates, sheets or leaves. *Exfoliation* is the process of peeling under the influence of heat, cold, frost, and rain.

geopolitical: refers to the related geographical and political aspects of the character of any place.

geological time-scale: geologists divide geological time into Archean, Primary, Secondary, Tertiary and Quaternary *eras*. The Quaternary is the latest. The Primary (Palaeozoic) era may have commenced 500 million years ago. Each era is divided into *periods*. The Carboniferous period is one of six major subdivisions of the Palaeozoic era. It was the period in which most of the best coal-bearing rocks were laid down. Triassic, Jurassic and Cretaceous are the three subdivisions of the Secondary (or Mesozoic) era. Cretaceous rocks are rocks originating in the Cretaceous period, say twenty million years ago.

geomorphology: the science which studies the origin and development of land-forms—a branch of geology.

gidgee: a shrub (*Acacia cambagei*) occurring in arid and semi-arid areas in inland Queensland.

greywacke: a strongly indurated fine-grained sandstone, characteristic of the mountainous areas of the South Island of New Zealand, grey in colour and much jointed.

heat equator: a highly generalized line—near the Equator, but not coinciding with it—which joins places having the highest temperatures. It varies with the season and trends poleward over the land masses in the summer of the hemisphere in question.

high latitudes: high latitudes are those nearer the poles, say beyond latitudes 60° north and south. *Low latitudes* are those near the Equator, say from 0° to 25° north and south. Those between are referred to as the *middle latitudes.*

hurricane: a tropical cyclone. The term is used in the Pacific south of the equator. North of the equator—off the coasts of China and Japan—tropical storms of similar nature and origin are called *typhoons.*

igneous rocks: the rocks of the earth's crust are classified into three main groups. *Igneous rocks* are molten matter from the earth's interior which has been solidified. They may solidify on the surface—as lava from a volcano—or deep down under a cover of other rocks. *Sedimentary rocks* are those which have been deposited (usually under water) in layers or beds, being made up of clays, sands, marine organisms (limestone) or decayed vegetation (coal). *Metamorphic rocks* are sedimentary or igneous rocks which have been subjected to greater heat or pressure and have so lost their original character and appearance (e.g. New Zealand's greywacke and schists).

indenture: a contract, voluntarily agreed to, binding a person to serve an apprenticeship; used here to refer to the contract system of securing labour for work in mines or on plantations. The indentured worker agrees to work on wages for a fixed period and has his fare paid from his home (island) and back.

indigenous: native. *Indigenes* are the native people of an area. The adjective *indigenous* is frequently applied to the people of an area and their economy and culture; also to the native plants and animals of an area.

Indonesian 'Mediterranean': a term applied to the sea and islands within it between Malaya and Australia (see text pages 145-8).

induced (vegetation, etc.): a vegetation cover brought about indirectly and unintentionally by human interference. Plants might be induced by burning or by grazing.

indurated: hardened. When applied to rocks it refers to partially metamorphosed or metamorphosed rocks hardened by heat or pressure.

intertropical front: a line of contact—and discontinuity—between different air masses (represented by the trade winds) which extends more or less around the globe near the equator.

ionosphere: a layer, sixty-five to 150 miles above the surface of the earth, of great interest to the physicist because of its effect on shortwave radio transmission.

isohyet: a line on a map joining places having an equal amount of precipitation in a given period of time (cf. *isotherm, isobar,* etc.).

kanaka: a term used to refer to the islanders removed by 'blackbirders', or indentured, principally from the Solomons and New Hebrides to work on the early sugar estates on the coast of Queensland.

kenaf: a commercial fibre plant, recently introduced as an experimental plantation crop in New Guinea. Botanically a hibiscus (*H. cannabinus*) which provides from its stem a soft fibre found suitable as a substitute for jute.

kurrajong: a 'fodder' tree, a non-eucalypt tree (*Sterculia diversifolia*) occurring in the drier grassland and savanna woodland areas of Southeastern Australia, cut down in time of drought to provide fodder for sheep. Also planted for shade and ornament.

kunai: a tall tropical grass widespread on the larger islands of the western Pacific, largely induced by forest burning. Found characteristically in New Guinea and the Solomons.

lalang: strictly a tall tussock-forming grass which invades forest clearings in tropical areas following fire or cultivation; a term applied in Indonesia to such clearings and the shifting 'fire-farming' which produces them.

laterite(s): a major world soil group with little organic matter, heavily leached, on deeply weathered, red parent material, developed under tropical rainforest in hot, moist, wet-dry climates with moderate to heavy rainfall. The term comes from the Latin word for 'brick'.

leached: applied to a soil from which soluble salts and organic matter have been removed by percolating rainwater.

lingua franca: a common language spoken and understood over a wide area by people with different native languages.

littoral: seashore, coast.

low latitudes: see *high latitudes.*

makatea: a term applied in Polynesia to the rough, pitted, limestone surface of the plateau-like raised atolls. Sometimes the location of phosphate deposits. (See text on Nauru, Mangaia, etc.) Also the name of an island (raised atoll with phosphates) in the Tuamotus, French Oceania.

mallee: a community of eucalypts all of which have the growth habit of producing a series of co-dominant stems from an undergrowth stock. The eucalypts sometimes have a dwarf form; they also grow to tree height. The mallee scrub was difficult to clear before the introduction of machines. Occurs widely in South Australia, western Victoria, and Western Australia.

matagouri: a shrubby plant found in the tussock grassland of New Zealand, almost leafless, sometimes called also *matagowrie*, or wild Irishman, and —by the Maori—*tumatakuru.*

matanggali: a social group amongst Fijians claiming descent from a common ancestor and officially recognized as the land-holding unit.

mbure: the Fijian word for the native village type of house built of local timber, grass, reeds, and coconut fibres.

metamorphic rocks: see *igneous rocks.*

Mitchell grass: a perennial tussock grass growing two or three feet high, especially in western Queensland. Associated with other tussock species and annual grasses which spring into life after rain; it forms good beef-cattle pasture.

monoculture: the cultivation of almost only one crop on a commercial farm or plantation to the exclusion of others—highly specialized commercial cultivation of only one crop.

mulga: an acacia (*A. aneura*), the dominant plant—a shrub 8-20 feet high—in a sparse, open shrubland which stretches around the southern margin of the Australian desert. In the shrubland annual grasses grow after rain and provide sparse grazing for short periods.

Myall: Acacia sowdenii, a shrub which occasionally and locally is the dominant plant in an arid scrub community in South Australia.

Neolithic: pertaining to the New Stone Age.

niaouli: a shrub (*Melaleuca viridiflora*), a eucalypt growing on the poorer hill soils especially on the leeward side of New Caledonia. Its stalk, bark and oil are all used locally.

nipa: a palm (*Nipa fruticans*) growing naturally only in the western Pacific.

oceanography: the science concerned with the study of the oceans, including the plant and animal life therein.

pandanus: a small, many-branched tree, not unlike the New Zealand cabbage tree in appearance, occurring widely on coral strands and on the smallest Pacific islets: sometimes called *screw pine*. The ripe fruit is eaten, or can be preserved. The leaf provides a fibre for making mats, baskets and hats. On scattered low atolls about the equator, pandanus, coconut, and fish are the basis of life.

papa: a Maori term meaning 'earth' but applied to soft Tertiary rocks, especially mudstones and sandstones.

placer: see *auriferous.*

poaching (of soils): is accomplished by the frequent treading of cattle (or sheep) when the soil is wet. It leaves lumps and hollows which when dry are difficult to negotiate and become a refuge for weeds.

podocarps: a family of shrubs and trees found in tropical and subtropical forest areas, often bearing fleshy edible fruit. Represented in New Zealand by the totara, miro, rimu, matai, and kahikatea.

podsol(s): a major world soil group developed in cool climates under a coniferous or mixed forest cover; leached and grey or grey-brown in colour.

primary industries: manufacturing industries are classed by economists into three main groups. Primary industries include agriculture, mining, quarrying, fishing, and timber getting. Secondary industries are 'true' manufacturing industries. Tertiary industries are 'service' industries—building, printing, transport, commerce, etc.

motu: an islet of sand or broken coral on a coral reef, standing rarely more than fifteen feet above high tide, and sometimes swamped by storm waves. (See text, especially pages 18 and 19.)

rain-shadow: an area to the leeward of a mountain range which cuts it off from prevailing rain-bearing winds. It tends to have a lower annual rainfall than areas to windward of the range. The Canterbury Plains form a rain-shadow area.

ratoon: a ratoon crop is a second crop from the same plants. Sugar cane is ratooned. 'Plant' cane is harvested by cutting above the ground. The stool grows a second (ratoon) crop. The second (and third) crops are lighter. New plants (seed cane) are set out usually in Fiji and Queensland after the first ratoon crop.

residual (*soil*): a soil or soil material derived by weathering from the rock upon which it rests.

Rhodes grass: a tropical grass (*Chloris gayana*), native to South Africa and named after Cecil Rhodes. Palatable to stock, and growing three feet high, it was introduced as a pasture grass to the coastal summer-rainfall areas of northern New South Wales and Queensland.

schist: a metamorphosed rock, produced by intense heat and pressure from argillaceous (clayey) rocks—clays, shales, mudstones. The schists of the South Island of New Zealand are fine-grained, foliated, metamorphic rocks containing mica.

sclerophyll(y): a term applied to plants whose leaves are few, hard and leathery; predominantly woody shrubs and trees with little foliage; evergreens; includes eucalypts and acacias.

secondary industries: see *primary industries.*

sedimentary rocks: see *igneous rocks.*

sennit (or sennet): a cord or rope made from the fibres of the husk of coconuts; used for many purposes by indigenous Pacific island communities, but especially for lashing together the timber framework of a house or canoe in the absence of nails, glue or dowelling.

sensitive plant: a low-growing leguminous plant occurring in the tropical Pacific, where it is one of the few legumes to be established in tropical pastures. It is a mimosa (*Mimosa pudica*) with frail leaves which, when touched, fold up immediately—hence its name.

skeletal (soils): soils composed of freshly or imperfectly weathered materials, largely confined to steep-sloping and mountainous land.

'*snow raking*': rescuing sheep buried in deep snow on the high-country runs of the South Island of New Zealand. The merino can survive in snow 'caves' many days, and when a track is made through the snow still have energy enough to walk to safety.

subsistence economy: refers to a self-contained, predominantly agricultural community—the opposite of commercial. Such a community produces locally its own food, clothing, tools, and shelter.

sudan grass: a tall grass growing from four to seven feet high, native to Africa as its name indicates: a summer annual forage grass providing good feed for cattle; tolerates dry conditions; introduced into Queensland, New Guinea and Fiji.

talus: fragments of rock (rough and angular) collected at the foot of cliffs or steep rocky slopes. In some cases a deep mantle of talus might occupy the lower slopes of mountains—as in New Zealand's Southern Alps.

Tertiary: see *geological time-scale.*

tertiary industries: see *primary industries.*

trace elements: mineral elements in soil in minute quantities which, if absent, may be the cause of poor plant growth or of sick or malformed animals: cobalt, copper, manganese, boron, etc.

trash (in canefields): rubbish left in canefields after the cane has been cut; leaves, stools and decayed foliage; usually burned to destroy insect pests, but better ploughed in to make humus.

Triassic: see *geological time-scale.*

trochus: a conical shell, which, together with that of the pearl oyster and the green snail, forms the pearl shell of commerce; used for knife handles, inlays, buttons and toilet articles. Trochus shell is collected in shallow water on the reefs of Pacific islands.

tsunami: a Japanese term used to refer to a broad shallow wave (or series of waves) caused by earthquake disturbances of the ocean floor. Rushing on-shore *tsunamis* pile up and cause great damage. Mis-called 'tidal waves', they have no connection with tides.

typhoon: see *hurricane.*

Wimmera ryegrass: a strain of ryegrass developed in Australia, widely sown and cultivated in the better pastures of southern New South Wales, Victoria, and Tasmania, including the irrigated pastures along the Murray and the Murrumbidgee.

Bibliography

This bibliography is intended, not as a detailed reference to the scholarly works on the many areas dealt with in *Southwest Pacific*, but as an outline guide to further reading and particularly to the more accessible of the works available. It should be of value especially to those readers of *Southwest Pacific* for whom this book is primarily an introduction to a part of the world which is crammed with interest in many fields. It should also form a valuable aid to teachers who employ *Southwest Pacific* as a text in providing for them a list of titles for their further reading and as suitable also for addition to the school library.

CHAPTERS 1-2: THE SETTING, THE PEOPLE

Australian Geographer, Sydney (irregular).
Beaglehole, J. C.: *The Exploration of the Pacific*, London, 1934.
Buck, P. H.: *Vikings of the Sunrise*, New York, 1938.
Fosberg, F. R. (Editor): *Man's Place in the Island Ecosystem: A Symposium*, Honolulu, 1963.
Freeman, O. W. (Editor): *Geography of the Pacific*, New York, 1951.
Hobbs, W. H.: *The Fortress Islands of the Pacific*, Ann Arbor, 1945.
Hogbin, H. I.: *Peoples of the Southwest Pacific*, New York, 1946.
Keesing, F. M.: *The South Seas in the Modern World*, New York, 1946.
   The Pacific Island Peoples in the Postwar World, Eugene, 1950.
New Zealand Geographer, Christchurch (half-yearly).
Oliver, D. L.: *The Pacific Islands*, Cambridge, Mass., 1962.
Pacific Islands Year Book, Sydney (annual).
Robinson, K. W.: *Australia, New Zealand and the South Pacific*, London, 1960.
South Pacific Commission: *Quarterly Bulletin*, Noumea (monthly).
Spate, O. H. K.: *Australia, New Zealand and the Pacific*, London, 1965.
Wiens, H. J.: *Atoll Environment and Ecology*, New Haven, Connecticut, 1962.

CHAPTER 3 : AUSTRALIA

Andrews, J. W.: *Australia's Resources and their Utilization*, Sydney, 1965.
Atlas of Australian Resources, Sydney, 1954 *et seq.*
Australian Environment, C.S.I.R.O., Melbourne, 1960.
Grattan, H. (Editor): *Australia*, Berkeley, 1947.
Greenwood, R. H.: 'The Challenge of Tropical Australia', *Pacific Affairs*, Vol. 29, No. 2, June 1956, pp. 126-140.
Holmes, J. M.: *The Murray Valley*, Sydney, 1948.
Lawton, G. H. (Editor): *Australian Geographies* (a series of 22 regional studies including also essays on New Guinea, New Zealand and the Pacific Islands), Adelaide, various dates.

Leeper, G. W. (Editor): *Introducing Victoria*, Melbourne, 1955.

National Development, Canberra (quarterly).

Official Year-Book for the Commonwealth of Australia, Canberra (annual).

Quarterly Survey (Australia and New Zealand Bank), Melbourne (quarterly).

Resources and Development of the Murray Valley, Canberra, 1947.

Robinson, K. W.: 'Sugar Growing in Australia', [N.Z] *Post-Primary School Bulletin*, Vol. 5, No. 4, 1951.

'Sheep Farming [in Australia]', [N.Z.] *Post-Primary School Bulletin*, Vol. 6, No. 5, 1952.

Scott, P.: 'Transhumance in Tasmania', *N.Z. Geographer*, Vol. 12, No. 2, 1955, pp. 155-172.

Taylor, G.: *Australia*, London, 1940.

Trends (Rural Bank of New South Wales), Sydney (quarterly).

Tweedie, A. D.: 'Sugar Cane in Queensland', *N.Z. Geographer*, Vol. 9, No. 2, 1953, pp. 125-143.

Wadham, S. M. and Wood, G. L.: *Land Utilization in Australia*, Melbourne, 1942 and 1950.

Wilkes, J. (Editor): *Northern Australia: Task for a Nation*, Sydney, 1954.

Wills, N. R.: 'The Growth of the Australian Iron and Steel Industry', *Geographical Journal*, Vol. 115, 1950, pp. 208-217.

Wood, G. L. (Editor): *Australia: Its Resources and Development*, New York, 1947.

CHAPTER 4 : AUSTRALIA'S PACIFIC ISLAND
NEIGHBOURHOOD

Barrau, J.: *Subsistence Agriculture in Melanesia*, Honolulu, 1958.

Subsistence Agriculture in Polynesia and Micronesia, Honolulu, 1961.

Belshaw, C. S.: *Changing Melanesia:* Social Economics of Culture Contact, Melbourne, 1954.

Bowman, R. G.: 'Land Settlement in New Guinea', *N.Z. Geographer*, Vol. 4, No. 1, 1948, pp. 29-54.

'Acclimatization in New Guinea', *Geographical Review*, Vol. 39, No. 2, 1949, pp. 311-314.

Brookfield, H. C.: 'The Highland Peoples of New Guinea', *Geographical Journal*, Vol. 127, Pt. 1, 1961, pp. 436-448.

Brookfield, H.C. and Brown, Paula: *Struggle for Land: Agriculture among the Chimbu of the New Guinea Highlands*, Melbourne, 1962.

Davis, C. M.: 'Coconuts in the Russell Islands', *Geographical Review*, Vol. 37, No. 3, 1947, pp. 400-413.

Elkin, A. P.: *Social Anthropology in Melanesia*, Melbourne, 1953.

Ellis, Sir A. R.: *Mid-Pacific Outposts*, Auckland, 1946.

Faivre, J. P., Poirier, J., and Routhier, P.: *La Nouvelle-Calédonie: Géographie et Histoire . . .*, Paris, 1955.

Huetz de Lemps, A.: 'La Nouvelle Guinée', *Les Cahiers d'Outre-Mer*, Vol. 9, No. 33, 1956, pp. 5-35.

Klein, W. C. (Editor): *Nieuw Guinea*, The Hague, Vol. 1, 1953, Vol. 2, 1954.

McAuley, J.: 'Australia's Future in New Guinea', *Pacific Affairs*, Vol. 26, No. 1, 1953, pp. 59-69.

'Island Administration in the South West Pacific', *Pacific Affairs*, Vol. 23, No. 3, 1950, pp. 323-326.

'Defence and Development in Australian New Guinea', *Pacific Affairs*, Vol. 23, No. 4, 1950, pp. 371-380.

Parsons, J.: 'Coffee and Settlement in New Caledonia', *Geographical Review*, Vol. 35, No. 1, 1945, pp. 12-21.

Reed, S. W.: *The Making of Modern New Guinea*, New York, 1943.

Report on Netherlands New Guinea . . . *Ministry of Overseas Territories*, The Hague (annual).

Report . . . on the Administration of the Territory of Nauru, Canberra (annual).

Report . . . on the Administration of the Territory of New Guinea, Canberra (annual).

South Pacific, Sydney (quarterly).

Stanner, W. E. H.: *The South Seas in Transition*, London, 1949.

Territory of Papua: Annual Report, Canberra (annual).

CHAPTER 5 : NEW ZEALAND

New Zealand Journal of Agriculture, Wellington (monthly).

Belshaw, H. (Editor): *New Zealand*, Berkeley, 1946.

Bishop, F. H.: 'Air Services in New Zealand', *N.Z. Geographer*, Vol. 9, No. 2, 1953, pp. 107-124.

Buck, P. H.: *The Coming of the Maori*, Wellington, 1949.

Clark, A. H.: *The Invasion of New Zealand by People, Plants and Animals*, New Brunswick, 1949.

Cockayne, L.: *The Vegetation of New Zealand*, Leipzig, 1928.

Condliffe, J. B.: *New Zealand in the Making*, London, 1929.

Cumberland, K. B.: 'A Century's Change: Natural to Cultural Vegetation in New Zealand', *Geographical Review*, Vol. 31, No. 4, 1941, pp. 529-554.

Soil Erosion in New Zealand, Christchurch, 1944, and Wellington, 1945.

'The Agricultural Regions of New Zealand', *Geographical Journal*, Vol. 112, Nos. 1-3, 1948, pp. 43-63.

This is New Zealand, Christchurch, 1949-1956.

'Moas and Men: New Zealand about A.D. 1250', *Geographical Review*, Vol. 52, No. 2.

New Zealand Topical Geographies
The Moahunter;
The Maori;
The European—to 1938;
Contemporary Population;
Social and Political Affairs;
Agriculture;
Structure, Lithology and Landforms;
Climate and Weather;
Soils;
Vegetation;
        Christchurch, *1965, 1966, 1967*.

Cumberland, K. B. and Fox, J. W.: *New Zealand: A Regional View*, Christchurch, 1964.

Fox, J. W.: 'Railway Transport in New Zealand', *N.Z. Geographer*, Vol. 7, No. 2, 1951, pp. 154-161.

Garnier, B. J. (Editor): *New Zealand Weather and Climate*, Christchurch, 1950.

The Climate of New Zealand, London, 1958.

Hamilton, W. M.: *The Dairy Industry in New Zealand*, Wellington, 1944.

Making New Zealand: Pictorial Surveys of a Century, Wellington, 1940-1941.

New Zealand Official Year-book, Wellington (annual).

[N.Z.] *Post-Primary School Bulletins*, Wellington (about twenty issues a year).

New Zealand Royal Commission upon the Sheep-farming Industry: Report, Wellington, 1949.

Pownall, L. L.: 'The Functions of New Zealand Towns', *Annals Association of American Geographers*, Vol. 43, No. 4, 1953, pp. 332-350.

Pownall, L. L. and Chapman, J. E.: 'The Location of Factory Industry in New Zealand', [N.Z.] *Post-Primary School Bulletin*, Vol. 8, No. 4, 1954, pp. 1-32.

Wallace, W. H.: 'New Zealand Landforms', *N.Z. Geographer*, Vol. 11, No. 1, 1955, pp. 17-27.

CHAPTER 6 : NEW ZEALAND'S PACIFIC ISLAND
NEIGHBOURHOOD

Beaglehole, E. and P.: *Pangaii: A Village in Tonga*, Wellington, 1941.

Belshaw, H. and Stace, V. D.: *A Programme for Economic Development in the Cook Islands*, Wellington, 1956.

Coulter, J. W.: *Land Utilization in American Samoa*, Honolulu, 1941.

Fiji, Little India of the Pacific, Chicago, 1942.

Cumberland, K. B.: 'Some Pacific Island Groups Important to New Zealand', [N.Z.] *Post-Primary School Bulletin*, Vol. 3, No. 6, 1949, pp. 113-144.

'The Similarity of Agricultural Problems in the Southwest Pacific', [Fiji] *Agricultural Journal*, Vol. 19, Nos. 3-4, 1948.

'New Zealand's "Pacific Island Neighbourhood"': The Postwar Agricultural Prospect', *N.Z. Geographer*, Vol. 5, No. 1, 1949, pp. 1-18.

'Man's Role in Modifying Island Environments in the Southwest Pacific', in Fosberg (Editor), see above, pp. 187-206.

'The Future of Polynesia', *Journ. Polynesian Society*, Vol. 71, No. 4, Dec. 1962, pp. 386-396.

Derrick, R. A.: *The Fiji Islands: A Geographical Handbook*, Suva, 1951.

Falla, R. A.: 'The Outlying Islands of New Zealand', *N.Z. Geographer*, Vol. 4, No. 2, 1948, pp. 127-154.

Fox, J. W. and Cumberland, K. B. (Editors): *Western Samoa: Land, Life, and Agriculture in Tropical Polynesia*, Christchurch, 1962.

Grattan, F. J. H.: *An Introduction to Samoan Custom*, Apia, 1948.

Huetz de Lemps, A.: *L'Océanie Francaise*, Paris, 1955.

'Les Isles Fidji', *Les Cahiers d'Outre-Mer*, Vol. 6, No. 23, 1953, pp.201-231.

Kennedy, T. F.: *Geography of Tonga*, Nuku'alofa, 1957.

Farmers of the Pacific Islands, Wellington, 1961.

N.Z. Department of Island Territories: *Report on the Cook, Niue and Tokelau Islands*, Wellington (annual).

N.Z. Department of Island Territories: *Western Samoa . . . Report*, Wellington (annual).

Roth, G. K.: *Fijian Way of Life*, Melbourne, 1954.

Simkin, C. F. G.: 'Modern Tonga', *N.Z. Geographer*, Vol. 1, No. 2, 1945, pp. 99-118.

Stace, V. D.: *Economic Survey of Western Samoa*, Noumea, 1955.

'Copra Production in the South Pacific', *South Pacific Bulletin*, Vol. II, No. 3, July 1961, pp. 33-38.

Whitelaw, J. S.: 'Suva, Capital of Fiji', *South Pacific Bulletin*, Vol. 14, No. 3, July 1964, pp. 33-37, p. 54.

Ward, R. G.: *Land Use and Population in Fiji: A Geographical Study*, London, 1965.

'The Banana Industry of Western Samoa', *Economic Geography*, Vol. 35, No. 2, April 1959, pp. 123-137.

'A Note on Population Movement in the Cook Islands', *Journ. Polynesian Society*, Vol. 70, No. 1, March 1961, pp. 1-10.

Ward, R. G.: *Islands of the South Pacific*, London, 1961.

CHAPTER 7 : PROSPECT AND RETROSPECT

Beaglehole, E.: 'Trusteeship and New Zealand's Political Dependencies', *Journal Polynesian Society*, Vol. 56, No. 2, 1947, pp. 128-157.

Crawford, R. M.: *Ourselves and the Pacific*, Melbourne, 1941.

Dulles, F. R.: *America in the Pacific*, Boston, 1938.

Fox, J.W.: 'New Zealand and the Pacific: Some Strategic Implications', *N.Z. Geographer*, Vol. 4, No. 1, 1948, pp. 15-28.

Greenwood, G.: 'Australian Attitudes towards Pacific Problems', *Pacific Affairs*, Vol. 23 No. 2 1950 pp. 153-168.

Lowe, W. S. and Airey, W. T. G.: 'New Zealand Dependencies and the Development of Autonomy', *Pacific Affairs*, Vol. 18, No. 3, 1945, pp. 252-272.

Monk, W. F.: 'New Zealand Faces North', *Pacific Affairs*, Vol. 26, No. 3, 1953, pp. 220-229.

Munro, L. K.: 'New Zealand and the New Pacific', *World Affairs*, Vol. 31, No. 4, 1953, pp. 634-647.

Thompson, W. S.: *Population and Peace in the Pacific*, Chicago, 1946.

Vincent, J. C. and Kennedy, R. (*et alia*): *America's Future in the Pacific*, New Brunswick, 1947.

Index

ABORIGINES (Australian), 53-4, 69, 192
Adelaide, 55, 60, 61, 129, 142
Admiralty Islands, 152, 157, 167
Aerial topdressing, 221, 222, 226
Agriculture: in Australia, 70-115; in New Guinea, 158-65; in New Caledonia, 196-9, in New Zealand, 221-44; in Fiji, 347-55
Air India, 50
Air New Zealand (formerly TEAL), 47, 50, 135, 278, 279, 324, 366
Airways: across Pacific, 46-50; in Australia, 133-5; in New Guinea, 166-9; in New Zealand, 276-81; in Fiji, 335, 349
Aitutaki, 47, 301, 302, 305, 310, 313
Alofi, 313, 334
American Samoa, 328-30
Anguar Island, 20, 44
Antarctic: Australian territory, 150; New Zealand territory (Ross Dependency), 293, 294
Anthropology, research, 25
Antipodes Islands, 293, 294, 297
Anzac Pact (Canberra Pact), 149-50, 370
ANZUS Agreement, 149-50
Aore, 187, 189
Aotearoa, 203-4, 244, 290
Apia, 46, 319, 320, 321, 324, 326
Api, 314, 316
Apolima, 320, 324
Apples, 99, 243
Archaeology, research in Pacific, 25
Artesian basins, 63, 64, 80
Atafu, 301, 330
Atherton plateau, 57, 90, 91
Atiu, 11, 301, 303, 307, 311
Atoll, 9-12, 303-4; almost atoll, 9, 10; raised atoll, 9, 11, 303-4; raised almost—atoll, 9, 11
Auckland, 46, 172, 199, 201, 209, 243, 262, 264, 265, 266, 267-72, 276, 278, 279, 280, 281, 287, 350, 354

Auckland Islands, 297
Aurora, 187
Australia: aborigines, 53-4; exploration, 54-5; early European settlement, 55-6, 67-9; surface configuration, 56-67; vegetation, 57-62, 64-7; climate, 62-8, 71; agriculture, 70-115; manufacturing, 113-5; minerals and mining, 66, 100, 114-23; transport, 131-5; trade, 135-7; population, 138-43; island territories, 144-202; and Asia, 145-6; interests in the Pacific, 40-1, 368-9
Austral Islands (Tubuai), 300, 366
Avarua, 46, 305, 307
Avatiu, 305, 307

BALIM VALLEY, 158-60, 169
Bamboo, 21, 354
Banabans, 353
Bananas, 43, 44, 98, 112, 113, 159, 161, 174, 196, 201, 299, 306, 309, 310, 312, 313, 326, 327, 334, 345, 346, 348, 350, 354-5
Banks Islands, 187, 188
Barley, 92, 96, 236
BCPA, 134
Bêche de mer, 88, 344
Bellona Island, 177
Benmore (power station), 248, 250
Biak, 166
Bismarck Archipelago, 54, 156-9, 162
Bluebush, 62, 71
BOAC, 49, 50, 135, 278
Bougainville, 152, 153, 157, 163
Bounty Islands, 293, 294, 297
Breadfruit, 310, 327, 334
Brisbane, 46, 55, 99, 142
British Phosphate Commission, 172-3, 295
Broken Hill, 61, 115, 116
Broken Hill Proprietary Co. (B.H.P.), 115, 125
Buka, 152, 153, 157, 163
Burrinjuck dam, 104, 105, 107

Ninety Mile Desert (South Australia), 74
Niuafo'ou, 8, 20, 315, 316
Niue Island, 293, 301, 303, 311-13
Nokonoko (see Casuarina)
Norfolk Island, 47, 150, 199-202, 294
Northern Territory, 87, 88, 135
Noumea, 189, 190, 192, 195, 197, 198, 200, 370, 371
Nuku'alofa, 316, 317, 318
Nukunono, 301, 330

OATS, 83, 90, 92, 96, 238
Ocean Island, 12, 20, 44, 126, 173, 232, 265
Ofu, 330
Olosega (see Swain's Island)
Ontong Java, 176
Oranges, 92, 106, 107, 108-10, 201, 243, 306, 308, 310-11, 334
Orchards, 103, 106, 107, 108, 241-4
Otago, 207, 208, 212, 216, 220, 229, 237, 238, 243, 248, 256, 257
Ovalau, 301, 335, 337, 351, 353

PACIFIC OCEAN: immensity of, 3-4; structural provinces in, 4-6; islands of, 6-12, 18-22; climates, 12-6; vegetation; 16-8; island peoples, 23-9; exploration of, 29-33; native economy and population, 33-6; trade, 38-42, 44-6; mining, 43-4
Palmerston Island, 301-2
Pandanus (screw pine), 19, 34, 66, 157, 299, 331, 332, 341
Pago Pago, 319, 320, 321, 328, 329, 367
Pan American airline, 135, 279
Papeete, 46, 366
Paper mulberry, 51, 204, 318, 334
Papua, Territory of (see New Guinea)
Pastures, 68, 71-5, 83, 87, 91, 94, 96, 113, 210-12, 214-5, 222, 224-7, 230-6
Papaw, 113, 163, 174, 327, 331
Peanuts, 98, 113
Pearl shell, 19, 88, 302, 303, 308
Peas, 83, 195, 236
Penal settlement, 55, 193
Penrhyn, 9, 293, 301, 302, 363
Pentecost, 187
Perth, 55, 140, 141, 142
Petroleum, 118-21, 166, 253-4, 266
Phalaris tuberosa, 73, 75
Phoenix Islands, 38
Phosphate, 44, 172-4, 265, 279
Pineapples, 43, 98, 112, 113, 189, 201, 309, 346, 350
Pinus radiata, 100, 245, 280
Pitcairn Islands, 47, 200, 367

Plantation agriculture: in Pacific, 42-4; in New Guinea, 161-5; in Solomons, 179-83; in Cook Islands, 304; in Tonga, 315, 317; in Samoa, 326-7; in Fiji, 342-5, 351-4
Polynesia(ns), 25-9, 35-6, 176, 192-3, 203-6, 244, 291, 292-3, 296, 299-301, 312, 314, 319-22, 330-1, 335, 342, 363, 366, 376-7
Population: in Australia, 138-43; in New Zealand, 283-90; in Fiji, 357-62; in Pacific islands, 374-5
Port Moresby, 153, 157, 161, 162, 167, 168
Potatoes, 92, 201, 236
Power resources: in Australia, 115-21; in New Zealand, 246-55
Prickly pear, 18, 82
Pukapuka, 301, 302

QANTAS, 47, 134, 135, 169, 198, 208, 278
Queensland, 54, 57, 59, 61, 62, 63, 66, 68, 72, 74, 76, 77, 78, 79, 80, 86, 87, 88, 90, 110-13, 114, 116, 129, 131, 132, 133, 138, 141

RABAUL, 154, 167, 168
Rabbits, 18, 71, 78, 82
Railways: in Australia, 131-3; in New Zealand, 272-4, 276
Rakahanga, 301, 302
Rambi, 353
Ramu River, 153, 154, 160, 164, 165
Raoul (Sunday) Island, 298, 299
Rapa, 366
Rarotonga, 9, 20, 47, 300, 301, 303, 305, 306, 307, 309, 310, 311
Refrigeration, 85, 238, 258-9
Renmark, 108-10
Rennell Island, 176, 177
Reparation Estates (see Western Samoa Trust Estates)
Rewa River, 337-8, 342, 349, 355
Rice, 106, 195, 196, 347, 350
Riverina, 96
Roads: in Australia, 131-3; in New Zealand, 275, 276; in Cook Islands, 305; in Fiji, 349
Roebourne, 67, 80
Rose Island, 320, 328
Ross Dependency, 293, 294
Rotorua, 218, 262
Rotuma, 295, 301, 335, 353
Rubber, 161, 163, 166
Russell Islands, 176, 178, 179-83
Ryukyu Islands, 5

PRINTED BY WHITCOMBE AND TOMBS LIMITED— G5200